CCCC
Bibliography of Composition and Rhetoric
1992

Gail E. Hawisher
Cynthia L. Selfe
Editors

Sibylle Gruber, Margaret F. Sweany, and William J. Williamson
Associate Editors

Conference on College Composition and Communication, A Conference of the National Council of Teachers of English

Southern Illinois University Press
Carbondale and Edwardsville

Copyright © 1994 by the National Council of Teachers of English
All right reserved
Printed in the United States of America
Production supervised by Natalia Nadraga

ISSN 1046–0675
ISBN 0-8093-1959-4
ISBN 0-8093-1960-8 pbk.

The paper used in this publication meets the minimum requirements of American National Standard for Information Sciences—Permanence of Paper for Printed Library Materials, ANSI Z39.48-1984. ∞

This volume is dedicated to the CCCC Officers—William W. Cook, Anne Ruggles Gere, Lillian Bridwell-Bowles, Jacqueline Jones Royster, Mike Anzaldúa—and CCCC administrative assistant Deborah Fox. They have been invaluable to us during the two years we have edited the *Bibliography*, and knowing that they are only a phone call or e-mail message away has contributed greatly to our confidence as editors. We thank them and look forward to another year of working with such a fine group of colleagues.

Contents

Preface   ix
Gail E. Hawisher
Cynthia L. Selfe

Guidelines for Users of the *CCCC Bibliography*   xi
Erika Lindemann

Contributing Bibliographers   xv

Journal Abbreviations   xvii

Abbreviations in Entries   xxi

1. **Bibliographies and Checklists**   1

2. **Theory and Research**   3
   Entries that discuss concepts or hypotheses, that explain how people learn, that describe fields or general methodologies, that examine historical developments, that review previous explanations of a subject, or that advance conclusions drawn from empirical evidence.
   2.1   Rhetorical Theory, Discourse Theory, and Composing   3
   2.2   Rhetorical History   24
   2.3   Political, Religious, and Judicial Rhetoric   32
   2.4   Computer and Literacy Studies   38
   2.5   Advertising, Public Relations, and Business   53
   2.6   Literature, Film, and Theater   55
   2.7   Reading   62
   2.8   Linguistics, Grammatical Theory, and Semantics   64
   2.9   Psychology   75

2.10 Education 79
2.11 Journalism, Publishing, Television, and Radio 84
2.12 Philosophy 88
2.13 Science and Medicine 91
2.14 Cross-Disciplinary Studies 93
2.15 Other 96

3. **Teacher Education, Administration, and Social Roles** 98
   Entries that discuss the education of teachers, that examine administrative or personnel policies and procedures, that describe services supporting classroom instruction, or that treat relations between educational institutions and the larger society.
   3.1 Teacher Education 98
   3.2 Administration 101
   3.3 Support Services 103
   3.4 Role in Society 108
   3.5 Other 109

4. **Curriculum** 110
   Entries that explain teaching methods, that describe courses or units of instruction, or that combine theory with practice in a specific subject area or skill.
   4.1 General Discussions 110
   4.2 Higher Education 116
       4.2.1 Developmental Writing 116
       4.2.2 First-Year College Composition 119
       4.2.3 Advanced Composition 126
       4.2.4 Business Communication 127
       4.2.5 Scientific and Technical Communication 129
       4.2.6 Writing in Literature Courses 139
       4.2.7 Communication in Other Disciplines 141
   4.3 Adult and Graduate Education 143
   4.4 English as a Second Language 145
   4.5 Research and Study Skills 152

5. **Testing, Measurement, and Evaluation** 154
   Entries that examine ways to assess students' work, that describe statistical or analytical techniques to measure or evaluate teaching and learning, or that discuss appropriate criteria for and uses of tests, scales, or other instruments.
   5.1 Evaluation of Students 154
   5.2 Evaluation of Teachers 159
   5.3 Evaluation of Programs 160
   5.4 Other 161

Subject Index 165

Name Index 171

Preface

Gail E. Hawisher
Cynthia L. Selfe

Now in our second year as editors of the *CCCC Bibliography of Composition and Rhetoric*, we are growing more confident of our ability to work on the only annual and comprehensive scholarly resource available to scholars and teachers in composition and rhetoric. For this 1992 volume, we have compiled 1656 titles that, with few exceptions, were published during the 1992 calendar year.

Last year we identified a set of priorities for our work with the *CCCC Bibliography*. These included (1) mastering the process of producing a first-rate *Bibliography* and improving its overall quality and accessibility; (2) increasing its promotion and hence sales, along with expanding member involvement. We made considerable progress toward these goals over the past two years and outline our successes below.

PRODUCING THE *BIBLIOGRAPHY* AND IMPROVING ITS QUALITY AND ACCESSIBILITY

One of the changes we implemented for the 1991 *Bibliography* and continue in 1992 has to do with the entries of the edited collections. Since all contributors who are listed in the index now appear in the bibliographical entries, readers will not have to search futilely for chapter authors. We have also tried to increase the range of texts represented within the *Bibliography*, with an eye toward annotating a greater number of entries dealing with feminism, critical theory, technology, and cultural studies as they relate to composition and rhetoric.

We are pleased with the changes we have made and see them as contributing directly to improving the quality and distribution of the *Bibliography*. But we also note that accessibility to the entries would be greatly improved with an online version. And while it is not difficult for us to create an online version per se, we need help in identifying other issues that might interfere with the sales and production of the standard print version. We also believe that the profession needs both a print and electronic version of the *Bibliography*, for without a published print version, the move to an electronic edition disenfranchises a sizable number of readers who still do not have access to technology.

We are grateful to the Executive Committee

for appointing a CCCC committee to explore in greater depth the consequences of bringing the *Bibliography* online. Next year we hope to have the publication well on its way to appearing both in print and electronic form.

PROMOTING AND SELLING THE *BIBLIOGRAPHY* AND INCREASING MEMBERSHIP INVOLVEMENT

In order to reach a greater number of *CCCC*'s members, we developed a brochure to promote the *Bibliography*. Members, in addition to being asked to purchase a *Bibliography* for their own use, were asked to forward the order form we provided to their college library. We ask you here, again, to urge college libraries to place standing orders for the *Bibliography*.

As a result of our promotional work with the brochure, we have increased sales during this past year, especially for the paperback. The increased sales argue strongly for our belief that we have not as yet tapped the full market for the *Bibliography*.

Our next step is to institutionalize the promotion of the *Bibliography* so that it becomes part of the yearly business of CCCC. Last year, in addition to sending brochures to all CCCC members, we announced and described the *Bibliography* at the preliminary "Starting Places" sessions of the conference itself. We also provided additional brochures for every person during the plenary session. By making these procedures standard for each conference, we believe that the *Bibliography* will begin to receive the kind of attention it needs and have a greater chance of becoming integral to the professional work of CCCC's members. We are grateful to the Executive Committee for providing the necessary funds to ensure better promotion of the publication.

As the 1992 edition of the *CCCC Bibliography* goes to press, we thank the many contributing bibliographers for their conscientious and valuable work. We are also grateful to our associate editors, Sibylle Gruber, Margaret Sweany, and Bill Williamson. Without their painstaking efforts to produce and improve upon the *Bibliography,* our readership would be poorly served indeed. And, finally, we appreciate the continued support Erika Lindemann provides for us and the publication that she founded. For these past two years she has chosen to remain never more than an e-mail message away, and for this we thank her.

Guidelines for Users of the *CCCC Bibliography*

Erika Lindemann

The *CCCC Bibliography of Composition and Rhetoric,* published by the Conference on College Composition and Communication, offers teachers and researchers an annual classified listing of scholarship on written English and its teaching. The *Bibliography* lists each work only once, but it descriptively annotates all citations, cross-references them when appropriate, and indexes all authors and editors. A group of contributing bibliographers, listed on pages xv–xvi, prepared the citations and annotations for all entries appearing in this volume.

SCOPE OF THE BIBLIOGRAPHY

The *CCCC Bibliography* includes works that treat written communication (whether the writing people do is in English or some other language), the processes whereby human beings compose and understand written messages, and methods of teaching people to communicate effectively in writing. The *Bibliography* lists entries in five major categories (see the Contents for a more complete description of these categories):

Section 1. Bibliographies and Checklists
Section 2. Theory and Research
Section 3. Teacher Education, Administration, and Social Roles
Section 4. Curriculum
Section 5. Testing, Measurement, and Evaluation

The *Bibliography* makes few restrictions on the format, medium, or purpose of the works it includes, so long as the subject of a given work falls into one of the five categories described in the preceding list. It lists only published works: books, articles, monographs, published collections (of essays, conference presentations, or working papers), bibliographies and other reference works, films, microforms, videotapes, and sound recordings. It includes citations for unpublished doctoral dissertations appearing in *Dissertation Abstracts International*. It also includes review articles that discuss several works, define movements or trends, or survey an individual's contribution to the discipline. It excludes masters theses, textbooks, computer software, book reviews, and works written in a language other than English.

SOURCES

The *CCCC Bibliography* cites works from four major sources.

Periodicals. Journals publishing articles on composition and its teaching are the source for approximately 1000 entries. Each journal is identified by an abbreviation; an alphabetical list of Journal Abbreviations begins on page xvii. With few exceptions, the contributing bibliographers preparing entries for journal articles examined the material firsthand.

Publishers. A second source of materials are commercial publishers and university presses. These publishers, whose participation in the bibliography project is voluntary, provided contributing bibliographers with written information for the books listed in this volume. Often, contributing bibliographers were unable to examine books firsthand and had to rely on these materials for their entries.

This volume also includes scholarly essay collections, books that bring together essays, articles, or papers by several authors. The *Bibliography* annotates these collections but does not annotate each essay. All authors contributing to the collection are included in the annotation and listed in the Name Index.

Dissertation Abstracts International (DAI). *DAI* represents a third source for citations. Not all degree-granting institutions list their unpublished doctoral dissertations in *DAI,* and as a rule, the contributing bibliographers have not examined these dissertations firsthand. The citations in this volume serve only to direct readers to abstracts in *DAI.* Users will want to consult the *DAI* abstracts for additional information, including who supervised the degree candidate's work and which institution granted the degree.

Resources in Education (RIE). A fourth source of materials in the *CCCC Bibliography* is the Educational Resources Information Center (ERIC), a federally funded document retrieval system coordinated by sixteen clearinghouses.

ERIC indexes its materials in two reference works. Journal articles appear in *Cumulative Index to Journals in Education (CIJE)*. *Resources in Education (RIE)*, on the other hand, indexes documents in the ERIC microfiche collection, available in 2600 regional libraries or directly from ERIC. These documents, frequently published elsewhere, include government documents, research and project reports, bibliographies, and conference papers. Documents indexed in *RIE* receive a six-digit "ED" number (e.g., ERIC ED 305 701) and are cross-referenced under various subject headings or "descriptors."

Some documents may be listed in *RIE* and may become available through ERIC several years after they were written. For convenience and to ensure comprehensiveness, the *CCCC Bibliography* reports ERIC documents cited in *RIE* during the years covered in the current volume; that is, this volume cites ERIC documents listed in *RIE* in 1992, even though the works themselves may have an earlier "date of publication." Also as a convenience, each ERIC entry includes the six-digit "ED" number.

Contributing bibliographers working with ERIC materials have developed the following criteria for determining what documents to include in this volume:

Substantiveness. Substantive documents of general value to college composition teachers and researchers are included. Representative publications are curriculum guides, federal government final reports, and technical reports from various publication series, such as those published, for example, by the Center for the Study of Writing and Literacy and the Center for the Study of Reading.

Relevance. Documents that seem to represent concerns of high interest to researchers are included. Topics related to first-year composition, computers and literacy, and gender studies, for example, represent concerns of greater relevance than the teaching of handwriting.

Inclusiveness. Relevant papers on composition and rhetoric available in ERIC and delivered at the annual meetings of the Conference on College Composition and Communication (CCCC) and the National Council of Teachers of English (NCTE—Fall and Spring conven-

GUIDELINES FOR USERS

tions) are included. Papers delivered at other regional and national meetings—for example, meetings of the American Educational Research Association (AERA), the International Reading Association (IRA), and the Modern Language Association (MLA)—have also been selected for inclusion on the basis of their substantiveness and relevance.

Reference value. Items for which the ERIC microfiche system might provide unique access are included. Representative of entries meeting this criterion would be books or collections of articles no longer available from their original publishers.

Alternate access. Many professional organizations regularly make copies of book and monograph publications available as ERIC microfiche. And many papers presented as reports or conference talks and available in ERIC are later published as monographs or as articles in journals. When such information is available, the entry in this volume will include ERIC ED numbers to indicate an alternate source of access to the document. However, users of this volume should keep in mind that, although a book in ERIC reflects the exact contents of the published work, an article in ERIC is a manuscript that may see substantial revision before it is published.

The following criteria determine which items cited in *RIE* are excluded from this volume:

Local interest. ERIC documents concerned with composition and rhetoric but judged to be primarily of local interest are excluded. For example, this volume omits annual evaluation reports of writing programs in local schools.

Availability. Publications of commercial publishers and other organizations that are listed in *RIE* and assigned ERIC ED numbers but are not available through the ERIC microfiche system are omitted.

Users of the *CCCC Bibliography* may wish to supplement this resource by consulting *RIE* or various computer-assisted retrieval systems that access ERIC documents. Copies of most documents indexed in *RIE* can be purchased in paper or microform from the ERIC system. ERIC clearinghouses also make available free or inexpensive guides to special topics of interest to rhetoric and composition teachers and researchers. Order forms and current addresses for these clearinghouses appear at the back of each monthly issue of *RIE*.

A few entries in this volume show publication dates earlier than 1992. By and large, these materials have two sources. They represent articles published in 1992 but appearing in journals showing earlier volume numbers, or they represent materials accessioned by ERIC clearinghouses in 1992 but originally published earlier.

The items listed in the annual bibliography are not housed in any single location or owned by any single individual. The *CCCC Bibliography* lists and describes these materials but does not provide users of the bibliography any additional means of retrieving them. However, librarians can be extremely helpful in finding copies of particular works to examine firsthand. Some materials may be available through interlibrary loan, OCLC and on-line catalogues, ERIC and other information retrieval systems, or state and university libraries. To locate materials cited in this volume, ask your librarian to help you.

CONTRIBUTING BIBLIOGRAPHERS

The reliability and usefulness of these annual volumes depend primarily on a large group of contributing bibliographers. Contributing bibliographers accept responsibility for compiling accurate entries in their areas of expertise, for preparing brief, descriptive annotations for each entry, for determining where each entry will appear within one of the five sections of the *Bibliography*, for cross-referencing entries when appropriate, and for submitting completed entries by a specified deadline.

To ensure consistency, contributing bibliographers receive a *Handbook for Contributing Bibliographers* to guide them in their work and fill out a printed form for each entry. Contributing bibliographers agree to serve a three-year term and, thereafter, may request reappointment for another two-year term. In return for their valuable service to the profession, they receive a copy of each annual volume they have had a substantial hand in preparing. Graduate students, teachers, researchers, or other individuals who wish to become contributing bibliographers may write to the editors.

ANNOTATIONS

Annotations accompany each entry in this volume. They describe the document's contents and are intended to help users determine the document's usefulness. Annotations are brief and, insofar as the English language allows, are meant to be descriptive, not evaluative. They explain what the work is about but leave readers free to judge for themselves the work's merits. Most annotations fall into one of three categories: they present the document's thesis, main argument, or major research finding; they describe the work's major organizational divisions; or they indicate the purpose or scope of the work.

CROSS-REFERENCES AND INDEXES

This volume cites and annotates each document only once, in one of the five major sections of the *Bibliography*. Every entry, however, receives an "entry number" so that cross-references to other sections are possible. Cross-references are necessary because much scholarship in composition and rhetoric is interdisciplinary. Cross-references appear as a listing of entry numbers preceded by "*See also*," found at the end of each subsection of the *Bibliography*.

The Subject Index lists most of the topics discussed in the works cited in this volume. Consulting the Subject Index may help users locate sections and subsections of the *Bibliography* that contain large numbers of entries addressing the same topic.

The Name Index lists all authors, editors, and contributors to publications cited in this volume.

Contributing Bibliographers

Valentina M. Abordonado
Elizabeth H. Addison
Jim Addison
Clara Alexander
Ken Autrey
Linda Bannister
Bonnie Mae Barnard
Carole Bencich
Pam Besser
Renee Betz
Virginia A. Book
Lady Falls Brown
Mary Louise Buley-Meissner
Dan Callahan
Guanjun Cai
Barbara Cambridge
John Centers-Zapico
Shelley Circle
Gregory Clark
Thomas Clemens
John Clifford
Joseph Rocky Colavito
Louise Rodriguez Connal
Lenora Cook
Elizabeth J. Cooper

Amanda Inskip Corcoran
Patricia Coward
Rick Cypert
Donald A. Daiker
Thomas E. Dasher
Kenneth W. Davis
Bonnie Devet
Ronda Dively
William M. Dodd
Ray Drake
Ann Duin
Elizabeth Ervin
Chuck Etheridge
Timothy J. Evans
Lahcen Elyazghi Ezzaher
Marisa Farnum
Julia K. Ferganchick
Janis Forman
Richard Fulkerson
T. Clifford Gardiner
Gregory R. Glau
Joan I. Glazer
Judith Goleman
Gwendolyn Gong
Alice A. Goodwin

Perry M. Gordon
Patricia Goubil-Gambrell
Siiri Granfelt
Jane Greer
Stephen Hahn
Leanna Hall
Liz Hamp-Lyons
Kathy Haney
James P. Hanlon
Kristine Hansen
James S. Harper
Patrick Hartwell
Malcolm Hayward
Nancy Hayward
Cozette K. Heller
Marguerite H. Helmers
John Hendricks
Alexandra R. Henry
Douglas Hesse
Dona Hickey
Dixie Elise Hickman
Betsy Hilbert
Elizabeth Hodges
Deborah H. Holdstein
Sylvia A. Holladay

CONTRIBUTING BIBLIOGRAPHERS

Alice S. Horning
Matthew Howard
Elizabeth Huettman
Rebecca Innocent
Deborah James
Jack Jobst
Patricia E. Kedzerski
Deborah Kehoe
Joyce Kinkead
Karla Kitalong
Michael J. Klein
Renee Kuperman
Janice M. Lauer
Mary M. Lay
Elizabeth Vander Lei
Cynthia Lewiecki-Wilson
Erika Lindemann
Kim Brian Lovejoy
Joyce MacAllister
Donald A. McAndrew
Robert McDonald
Dana Gulling Mead
Vincent P. Mikkelson
Emily P. Miller
Charles Moran

Max Morenberg
Michele Noel
Ed Nolte
Terence Odlin
Cliff Oldham
Suzanne C. Padgett
Barry Pegg
Michael A. Pemberton
Elizabeth F. Penfield
Virginia Perdue
Virginia G. Polanski
James Postema
John W. Presley
Teresa M. Purvis
D. R. Ransdell
Valerie Reimers
Duane Roen
Sara L. Sanders
Peter Sands
Lew Sayers, Jr.
Judy Scheffler
Cynthia Miecznikowski Sheard
Dorothy Sheldon
Deneen Shepherd
Barbara M. Sitko

Elizabeth Overman Smith
Penelope Smith
James Strickland
Patricia Sullivan
Bernard Susser
Suzanne Swiderski
Josephine Koster Tarvers
Barn Taylor
Nathaniel Teich
Patricia Terry
Laura Thomas
Charlotte Thralls
Kelly Truit
Billie J. Wahlstrom
Cynthia Walker
Molly Walter-Burnham
Keith Walters
Robert H. Weiss
Jackie Wheeler
David E. Wilson
J. Randal Woodland
George Xu
Kathleen Blake Yancey
Gretyl Young

Journal Abbreviations

Contributing bibliographers reviewed the journals listed below in preparing entries for this volume. Each for journal article cited in this volume will include an abbreviation identifying the journal or serial in which it was published.

AA	American Anthropologist	AS	American Speech
AAF	Adult Assessment Forum	ASch	The American Scholar
AAHE	AAHE Bulletin		
ACE	The ACE Newsletter	BABC	Bulletin of the Association for Business Communication
ACEN	Assembly for Computers in English Newsletter	B&L	Brain and Language
ADEB	The Association of Departments of English Bulletin	Boundary	Boundary 2: A Journal of Postmodern Literature and Culture
AdEd	Adult Education		
AdLBEd	Adult Literacy and Basic Education	CACJ	Computer-Assisted Composition Journal
A&EQ	Anthropology and Education Quarterly	CalE	California English
AERJ	American Educational Research Journal	CALS	Carleton Papers in Applied Language Studies
AJS	American Journal of Semiotics	C&C	Computers and Composition
AM	Academic Medicine	CCC	College Composition and Communication
AmE	American Ethnologist		
AmP	American Psychologist	CCR	Community College Review
Annals	Annals of the American Academy of Political and Social Sciences	CCrit	Cultural Critique
		CE	College English
		CEA	CEA Critic
ArEB	Arizona English Bulletin	CEAF	CEA Forum
Arg	Argumentation	CEd	Communication Education

xvii

CHE	Chronicle of Higher Education	ERQ	Educational Research Quarterly
CHum	Computers and Humanities	ESP	English for Specific Purposes
C&I	Cognition and Instruction	ET	English in Texas
CJL	Canadian Journal of Linguistics	ETC	ETC.: A Review of General Semantics
CLAJ	College Language Association Journal	ETS	ETS Developments
Cognition	Cognition	ExEx	Exercise Exchange
CollL	College Literature		
CollM	Collegiate Microcomputer	FLA	Foreign Language Annals
CollT	College Teaching	Focuses	Focuses
ComM	Communication Monographs	FSt	Feminist Studies
CompC	Composition Chronicle		
CompEd	Computers and Education	GaR	Georgia Review
CompQ	Composition Quarterly		
ComQ	Communication Quarterly	HCI	Human-Computer Interaction
ComR	Communication Research	HCR	Human Communication Research
ComS	Communication Studies	HD	Human Development
CPsy	Cognitive Psychology	HER	Harvard Education Review
CritI	Critical Inquiry	HT	History Teacher
CSc	Cognitive Science	Hypermedia	Hypermedia
CS/FEN	Composition Studies/Freshman English News	IDJ	Information Design Journal
CSSJ	Central States Speech Journal	IEEE	IEEE Transactions on Professional Communication
Daedalus	Daedalus: Journal of the American Academy of Arts and Sciences	IL	Informal Logic
		IlEB	Illinois English Bulletin
		IndE	Indiana English
DAI	Dissertation Abstracts International	Intelligence	Intelligence
		IPM	Information Processing and Management
DP	Developmental Psychology		
DPr	Discourse Processes	IRAL	International Review of Applied Linguistics in Language Teaching
D&S	Discourse and Society		
EdEPA	Educational Evaluation and Policy Analysis	Issues	Issues in Writing
EdM	Educational Measurement: Issues and Practice	JAC	Journal of Advanced Composition
EdPsy	Educational Psychologist	JAF	Journal of American Folklore
EdTech	Educational Technology	JBC	Journal of Business Communication
EEd	English Education		
EES	Explorations in Ethnic Studies	JBS	Journal of Black Studies
EJ	English Journal	JBTC	Iowa State Journal of Business and Technical Communication
ELTJ	English Language Teaching Journal		
		JBW	Journal of Basic Writing
ELQ	English Leadership Quarterly	JC	Journal of Communication
EnEd	Engineering Education	JCBI	Journal of Computer-Based Instruction
EngR	English Record		
EnT	English Today	JCE	Journal of Chemical Education
EQ	English Quarterly	JCS	Journal of Curriculum Studies

JCST	Journal of College Science Teaching	JTWC	Journal of Technical Writing and Communication
JDEd	Journal of Developmental Education	Lang&S	Language and Style
JEd	Journal of Education	LangS	Language Sciences
JEdM	Journal of Educational Measurement	LangT	Language Testing
		Language	Language
JEdM&H	Journal of Educational Multimedia and Hypermedia	L&E	Linguistics and Education: An International Research Journal
JEdPsy	Journal of Educational Psychology	Leaflet	The Leaflet
		Learning	Learning
JEdR	Journal of Educational Research	Linguistics	Linguistics
JEngL	Journal of English Linguistics	L&M	Literature and Medicine
JEPG	Journal of Experimental Psychology: General	L&S	Language and Speech
		LSoc	Language in Society
JEPH	Journal of Experimental Psychology: Human Perception and Performance	LT	The Language Teacher
		M&C	Memory and Cognition
JEPL	Journal of Experimental Psychology: Learning, Memory, Cognition	MCQ	Managment and Communication Quarterly
		MEd	Medical Education
JFR	Journal of Folklore Research	MissQ	Mississippi Quarterly
JGE	JGE: The Journal of General Education	MLJ	The Modern Language Journal
		MLQ	Modern Language Quarterly
JL	Journal of Linguistics	MLS	Modern Language Studies
JLD	Journal of Learning Disabilities	M&M	Media and Methods
JMEd	Journal of Medical Education	MR	Multimedia Review
JMemC	Journal of Memory and Cognition: Learning, Memory, Cognition	MSE	Massachusetts Studies in English
		MT	Mathematics Teacher
		Multimedia	Multimedia
JMemL	Journal of Memory and Language	NYRB	The New York Review of Books
JNT	Journal of Narrative Technique		
JOC	Journal of Organizational Computing	OralHR	Oral History Review
JourEd	Journalism Educator	PC	The Professional Communicator
JPsy	Journal of Psychology	Perspectives	Perspectives
JPsyR	Journal of Psycholinguistic Research	PhiDK	Phi Delta Kappan
		PhS	Philosophical Studies
JR	Journal of Reading	P&L	Philosophy and Literature
JRB	JRB: Journal of Reading Behavior: A Journal of Literacy	PMLA	Publication of the Modern Language Association
JRDEd	Journal of Research and Development in Education	PMS	Perceptual and Motor Skills
		PoT	Poetics Today
JSLW	Journal of Second Language Writing	PPR	Philosophy and Phenomenological Research
JT	Journal of Thought	PR	Partisan Review
JTEd	Journal of Teacher Education	P&R	Philosophy and Rhetoric
JTW	Journal of Teaching Writing	Pre/Text	Pre/Text

PsyR	Psychological Review	StHum	Studies in the Humanities
PsyT	Psychology Today	Style	Style
		SubStance	SubStance
QJS	Quarterly Journal of Speech		
QNWP/ CSW	The Quarterly for the National Writing Project and the Center for the Study of Writing	TC	Technical Communication
		TCQ	Technical Communication Quarterly
QRD	Quarterly Review of Doublespeak	TECFORS	TECFORS
		TESOLQ	Teachers of English of Speakers of Other Languages Quarterly
Raritan	Raritan	TETYC	Teaching English in the Two-Year College
Reader	Reader		
RER	Review of Educational Research	TEXT	TEXT: An Interdisciplinaly Journal for the Study of Discourse
RHE	Research in Higher Education		
Rhetorica	Rhetorica		
RIE	Resources in Education	TWM	Teachers and Writers Magazine
RMR	Rocky Mountain Review of Language and Literature	TWT	The Technical Writing Teacher
RR	Rhetoric Review	UEJ	Utah English Journal
RRQ	Reading Research Quarterly	VLang	Visible Language
RSQ	Rhetoric Society Quarterly	V&R	Visions and Revisions
RTDE	Research and Teaching in Developmental Education		
		WAC	Writing Across the Curriculum
RTE	Research in the Teaching of English	WC	Written Communication
		WCJ	Writing Center Journal
R&W	Reading and Writing: An Interdisciplinary Journal	WE	Writing on the Edge
		WI	The Writing Instructor
		WJSC	Western Journal of Speech Communication
SAF	Studies in American Fiction		
ScAm	Scientific American	WLN	The Writing Lab Newsletter
SCJ	Southern Communication Journal	WLWE	World Literature Written in English
SCL	Studies in Canadian Literature		
ScT	Science Teacher	WN	The Writing Notebook
SFS	Science Fiction Studies	WPA	Journal of the Council of Writing Program Administrators
Signs	Signs		
SLang	Studies in Language	Writer	The Writer
SNNTS	Studies in the Novel	WS	Women's Studies

Abbreviations in Entries

AAHE	American Association for Higher Education	EST	English for Science and Technology
ACT	American College Test	ETS	Educational Testing Service
APA	American Psychological Association	FL	Foreign Language
		GPA	Grade Point Average
ATTW	Association of Teachers of Technical Writing	IVD	Integrated Videodisc
		JTPA	Job Training Partnership Administration
CAI	Computer-Assisted Instruction		
CCCC	Conference on College Composition and Communication	L1	First Language
		L2	Second Language
CIM/GEMS	Computer-Integrated Manufacturing/General Equipment Maintenance System	LD	Learning Disability
		LSU	Louisiana State University
		MLA	Modern Language Association
EDRS	ERIC Document Reproduction Service	NAEP	National Assessment of Educational Progress
EFL	English as a Foreign Language	NCTE	National Council of Teachers of English
ERIC	Educational Resources Information Center	NEA	National Education Association
ERIC/FLL	ERIC Clearinghouse on Language and Linguistics	NNS	Nonnative Speaker
		NS	Native Speaker
ERIC/RCS	ERIC Clearinghouse on Reading and Communication Skills	NTE	National Teacher Examination
		NTID	National Technical Institute for the Deaf
ESL	English as a Second Language		
ESP	English for Specific Purposes	OCLC	Online Computer Library Center

PC	Personal Computer	TWE	Test of Written English
RP	Received Pronunciation	UNCC	University of North Carolina at Charlotte
SAT	Scholastic Aptitude Test		
TA	Teaching Assistant	WAC	Writing across the Curriculum
TESOL	Teachers of English to Speakers of Other Languages	WPA	Writing Program Administrator
		YBA	Youth Basketball Association
TOEFL	Test of English as a Foreign Language		

CCCC
Bibliography of Composition and Rhetoric
1992

1 Bibliographies and Checklists

1 BIBLIOGRAPHIES AND CHECKLISTS

1. *Bibliographic Guide to Conference Publications: 1991*. G. K. Hall Bibliographic Guides. Boston: G. K. Hall, 1992. 1031 pages

    Lists conference publications catalogued during the year by The Research Libraries of the New York Public Library, with additional entries from LC MARC tapes. Indexes some 26,000 private and government conference publications annually, including proceedings, reports of conferences, and collections of papers. Covers all disciplines, countries, and languages.

2. *Bibliographic Guide to Education: 1991*. G. K. Hall Bibliographic Guides. Boston: G. K. Hall, 1992. 600 pages

    Lists material recorded on the OCLC tapes of the Columbia University Teachers College during the year, with additional entries from the New York Public Library for selected publications. Covers all aspects of education. Provides a supplement to the 1970 Dictionary Catalog of the Teachers College Library.

3. CCCC Committee on Assessment. "A Selected Bibliography on Postsecondary Writing Assessment, 1979–1991." *CCC* 43 (May 1992): 244–55.

    Updates the 1979 bibliography on testing. Reports a shift from testing per se to a more general assessment. Points out that 26 states now require assessments.

4. "From Closed Conversation to Active Dialogue: Recent Books of Critical Theory." *EJ* 81 (November 1992): 73–76.

    Presents a 14-item annotated bibliography. Includes works on new criticism, feminism, new historicism, deconstruction, and narratology. Points out that students need to be aware of authorial intent and cultural bias to resist manipulation and to take responsibility for providing meaning to literary works.

5. *Index to Journals in Communication Studies through 1990*. Edited by Ronald J. Matlon, 2 vols. Annandale, VA: Speech Communication Association, 1992. 836 pages

   Contains combined indexes and a table of contents for 19 journals from their inception to the present.

6. "*JTW* Index: 1982–1991." *JTW* 11 (Spring/Summer 1992): 139–62.

   Lists all articles which were published in *JTW* from 1982–1991 in alphabetical order.

7. Rothschild, Joyce M., Thomas T. Barker, Laura E. Casari, Judy Fowler, Sam Geonetta, Daniel R. Jones, and Russell Rutter. "1991 ATTW Bibliography." *TCQ* 1 (Fall 1992): 85–114.

   Presents a bibliography of technical and business communication.

2 Theory and Research

2.1 RHETORICAL THEORY, DISCOURSE THEORY, AND COMPOSING

8. Ahmad, Aijaz. *In Theory: Nations, Classes, Literature*. London: Verso, 1992. 300 pages

    Ahmad, a committed socialist, disagrees with Fredric Jameson, Edward Said, and the Subaltern Studies group and challenges the accepted definitions of "Third World" and "colonial discourse theory."

9. Alcoff, Linda. "The Problem of Speaking for Others." *CCrit* 20 (Winter 1991–92): 5–32.

    Explores the impact of writers from privileged groups speaking for the oppressed. Asks whether it is valid to speak for others who are unlike oneself or less privileged than oneself.

10. Alway, Joan. "To Interpret and to Change the World: Critical Theory as Theory with Practical Intent." *DAI* 53 (November 1992): 1691A.

    Examines the works of Horkheimer, Adorno, Marcuse, and Habermas. Explores the status of critical theory and practical intent. Insists that because of the dissatisfaction with a subject-object dichotomy, a transformation in meaning of theory must take place.

11. Anderson, Kristi S. "Post-Poststructuralism: Gender, Race, Class, and Literary Theory." *DAI* 53 (November 1992): 1505A.

    A tripartite study of recent feminist, ethnic, and Marxist criticism reveals that poststructuralist critics have failed to integrate gender, race, and class. Argues for an evolution of critical language that connects and does not essentialize.

12. "Argument Evaluation Contest Results." *IL* 13 (Fall 1991): 167–85.

    Presents four evaluative analyses of an argumentative text, two each by English professors and philosophy professors, with evaluations of the analyses by editors and two experts.

13. Armstrong, Isobel, ed. *New Feminist Discourses: Critical Essays on Theories and Texts*. New York: Routledge, 1992. 350 pages

   Presents a collection of articles by young British feminists who "utilize and question the disciplines of literary criticism, art history, photography, psychoanalysis, Marxist history, and poststructuralist theory." They argue for "forging new feminist discourses."

   Essayists: Ballaster, Ros; Bowlby, Rachel; Guest, Harriet; Hutson, Lorna; Jordan, Elaine; Kanneh, Kadiatu; LaFarge, Catherine; Leighton, Angela; Marcus, Laura; McDonagh, Josephine; Moore, Jane; Nead, Lynda; Raitt, Suzanne; Smith, Lindsay; Watts, Carol; Williams, Linda R.; Wiseman, Sue.

14. Atwill, Janet Marie. "Refiguring Rhetoric as Art: Aristotle's Concept of *Techne* and the Humanist Paradigm." *DAI* 53 (November 1992): 1506A.

   Argues that the gradual suppression of the ancient concept of *techne*, or art, is important to the rise of Western humanist ideology. While Atwill focuses on Aristotle, she also looks at the origins of *techne* in Hesiod, Aeschylus, the sophists, and Plato.

15. Augustine, Catherine. "The Effects of Paraphrase Variations on the Processing of Written Prose." *DAI* 53 (November 1992): 1378A.

   Looks at the skills that paraphrasing requires and at the elements that make paraphrasing an adjunct to learning. Discusses the effects of paraphrase variations on subsequent recall of prose. Confirms the usefulness of paraphrase.

16. Auten, Janet Beghart. "How Students Read Us: Audience Awareness and Teacher Commentary on Writing." *WI* 11 (Winter 1992): 83–94.

   Based on a survey of 100 students, this article suggests that teachers and students develop a mutual context for the speech act of teachers' commentary on student writing.

17. Ayim, Maryann. "Dominance and Affiliation: Paradigms in Conflict." *IL* 13 (Spring 1991): 79–88.

   Argues that "dominant confrontational" speech styles (male) are ideologically inferior to "affiliative nurturant" styles (female).

18. Azuike, Macpherson Nkem. "Style: Theories and Practical Application." *LangS* 14 (January–April 1992): 109–27.

   Presents six perspectives on style and describes an eight-step procedure for analyzing a text.

19. Baker, James Wesley. "The Hope of Intervention: A Rhetorical Analysis of the English Translation of the Writings of Jacques Ellul." *DAI* 52 (May 1992): 3776A.

   Argues that Ellul's writings promote a rhetoric of social intervention by challenging the reader's ideological assumptions about technology.

20. Beddoes, Julie A. "A Necessary Fiction: The Textual Author and What She Can Do for Us." *DAI* 53 (July 1992): 146A.

   Uses Foucault's model of discourse universe to "propose a notion of authorship as both product and produce of specified texts."

21. Berlin, James A. "Poststructuralism, Cultural Studies, and the Composition Classroom: Postmodern Theory in Practice." *RR* 11 (Fall 1992): 16–33.

   Presents central features of postmodern rhetoric, including the status of the subject, signifying practices, and master theories. Includes a course description.

22. Biber, Douglas. "On the Complexity of Discourse Complexity: A Multidimensional Analysis." *DPr* 15 (April–June 1992): 133–63.

   Identifies five dimensions needed to represent the complexity of texts and their functions. Argues that spoken and written texts differ in their complexity profiles.

23. Biesecker, Barbara A. "Towards a Transactional View of Rhetorical and Feminist Theory: Rereading Hélène Cixous's 'The Laugh of the Medusa.'" *SCJ* 57 (Winter 1992): 86–96.

    Suggests rereading the essay as a rhetoric that posits what women can and must do to intervene effectively in the public sphere.

24. Bishop, Wendy. "I-Witnessing in Composing: Turning Ethnographic Data into Narratives." *RR* 11 (Fall 1992): 147–58.

    Explores theoretical concerns of doing ethnographic research; suggests that writers employ metadiscourse as a way to "reflect on our institutions and practices."

25. Black, Edwin. *Rhetorical Questions: Studies of Public Discourse*. Chicago: University of Chicago Press, 1992. 224 pages

    Probes incongruities between form and substance that open public discourse to significant interpretations. Focuses on the ideological component of seemingly literary texts and the use of literary devices to advance political advocacy. The subject matter ranges from nineteenth-century oratory, to *The New York Times* editorials, to the rhetoric of Richard Nixon.

26. Boser, Judith A. *Gender Differences: Let's See Them in Writing*. Lexington, KY: Mid-South Educational Research Association, November 1991. ERIC ED 341 980. 16 pages

    Bases her results on a survey of 149 women and 48 men. Finds that women tend to write longer and more formal responses than men.

27. Bowles, George. "Evaluating Arguments: The Premise Conclusion Relation." *IL* 13 (Winter 1992): 1–20.

    Examines six theories of argument validity, concluding that validity depends upon attributed and actual degrees of favorable (premise/conclusion) relevance.

28. Bridwell-Bowles, Lillian. "Discourse and Diversity: Experimental Writing within the Academy." *CCC* 43 (October 1992): 349–68.

    Argues for experimentation of form, language, and thought to develop new discourses to help overcome patriarchal ways of thinking, living, and writing.

29. Brinkman, Carolyn Ruth. "Problems of Stance in Composition Theory and Student Critical Writing: A Hermeneutic Theory for Composition Pedagogy." *DAI* 52 (May 1992): 3845A.

    Argues that problems of stance in student critical writing correspond to the current composition theory's view of stance as a social or subjective construct.

30. Brodkey, Linda. "The Somewhat Unitary World of Clifford Geertz [response to Geertz, *JAC* 11 (Fall 1991)]." *JAC* 12 (Winter 1992): 201–7.

    Motivated by an interview with Geertz, Brodkey speculates on rhetoric as a contingent value in axiological terms. Argues for ethnographies of our professional practices, especially publications.

31. Brown, Andrew. *Roland Barthes: The Figures of Writing*. New York: Oxford University Press, 1992. 320 pages

    Examines the twentieth-century French critic's aesthetic techniques as a writer, their relationship to scientific and psychoanalytic discourse, and the concept that writing is closer to visual art than to speech.

32. Brown, Stuart C. "I. A. Richards' New Rhetoric: Multiplicity, Instrument, and Metaphor." *RR* 10 (Spring 1992): 218–31.

    Views Richards' ideas as basis for a "rhetoric for the twenty-first century." Explores Richards' emphasis on multiplicity in making meaning.

33. Burleson, Brant R., Wendy Samter, and Anne E. Lucchetti. "Similarity in Communication Values as a Predictor of Friendship Choices: Studies of Friends and Best Friends." *SCJ* 57 (Summer 1992): 260–76.

Extends the general similarity-attraction hypothesis to the influence of communication activities and interaction styles on interpersonal relationships.

34. Capossela, Toni-Lee, ed. *The Critical Writing Workshop: Designing Writing Assignments to Foster Critical Thinking.* Portsmouth, NH: Boynton/Cook, 1992. 225 pages

    Twelve essays explore ways to encourage the development of critical thinking through writing and emphasize the translation of theory into practice. The editor includes a selected annotated bibliography on the subject.
    Essayists: Birken, M.; Capossela, T. L.; Coon, A. C.; Jenseth, R.; Jones, L.; Lawrence, S. M.; Nydahl, J.; Olson, C. B.; Pytlik, B.; Rubin, L.; Sandberg, K.; Zeiger, W.

35. Carlton, Susan Brown. "Poetic, Rhetoric, and Disciplinary Discourse." *DAI* 53 (July 1992): 135A.

    Addresses the relationship between literature and composition in English studies through an analysis of the deployment of the poetic/rhetoric topos in disciplinary histories and domain theories written between 1922 and 1990.

36. Cirkesena, M. Kathryn. "Access, Competence, and Gender in Political Persuading: 1964–1984." *DAI* 53 (July 1992): 8A.

    Proposes a new approach to understanding women's political persuading that is based on models previously applied to women's general political participation.

37. Clairborne, Gay Don. "Japanese and American Rhetoric: A Contrastive Study." *DAI* 52 (May 1992): 3901A.

    Describes cultural influences that have shaped Japanese rhetoric into a communication style that facilitates social harmony.

38. Coles, William E., Jr. "The Dialogues of Teaching: Learning to Listen." *CS/FEN* 20 (Fall 1992): 34–46.

    Reflects upon 35 years of teaching and how he has learned the importance of listening as part of teaching.

39. Condravy, Joan C. "Women's Talk in a Women's Studies Reading and Discussion Group: A Descriptive Study of Cooperation and Competition." *DAI* 52 (May 1992): 3767A.

    Suggests that most women will communicate cooperatively rather than competitively and build on one another's statements.

40. Crosswhite, James. "Authorship and Individuality: Heideggerian Angles." *JAC* 12 (Winter 1992): 91–109.

    Uses Heidegger as grounds for arguing that expressivism and social constructionism need not be mutually exclusive.

41. D'Angelo, Frank. "The Four Master Tropes: Analogues of Development." *RR* 11 (Fall 1992): 91–109.

    Traces the roots of several new theories of rhetoric. Chronicles the author's own theory, structured around Burke's four master tropes: metaphor, metonymy, synecdoche, and irony.

42. D'Angelo, Frank. "The Rhetoric of Sentimental Greeting Card Verse." *RR* 10 (Spring 1992): 337–45.

    Claims that the rhetoric in cards is seldom trite or sentimental. Values its language as ceremonial discourse. Suggests careful study as introduction to classic rhetoric.

43. Daniell, Beth. *Composing (as) Power.* Cincinnati, OH: CCCC, March 1992. ERIC ED 344 222. 10 pages

    Traces the spiritual journeys and "coming of voice" of six women, aged 35 to 55, through their journals, letters, poems, and stories.

44. Daughton, Suzanne Marie. "The Rhetorical Nature and Function of First-Person Narrative." *DAI* 52 (January 1992): 2322A.

Studies over 400 speeches and concludes that first-person is utilized in more than one-third of them.

45. Davis, Robert Con, and Ronald Schleifer. *Criticism and Culture: The Role of Critique in Modern Literary Theory*. White Plains, NY: Longman, 1992. 280 pages

    Defines literary criticism and discusses its origins, development, and relationship with culture; explains the importance of the philosophical concept of critique in understanding critical theory.

46. Davy, George Alan. "Argumentation in Thomas Jefferson's 'Notes on the State of Virginia.'" *DAI* 53 (November 1992): 1516A.

    Argues that social, political, economic, and other proposals in "Notes," while widely accepted today, were often impractical when they first appeared. This, according to Davy, suggests that Jefferson was addressing a universal audience.

47. DiCamilla, Frederick Joseph. "Private Speech and Private Writing; A Study of Given/New Information and Modality in Student Compositions." *DAI* 52 (March 1992): 3260A.

    Examines functions of speaking in writing processes of inexperienced writers; notes a variety of contributions to planning.

48. Dickstein, Morris. *Double Agent: The Critic and Society*. New York: Oxford University Press, 1992. 220 pages

    Examines the work of several nineteenth- and twentieth-century critics to argue for a new, more publicly accessible approach to critical writing.

49. Dixon, Kathleen Grace. "Divisions and Recollections: Gender in the Forming of Academic Community." *DAI* 52 (January 1992): 2442A.

    Investigates how the student-teacher relationship might help acculturate writers—particularly women—into an academic discourse community.

50. Dugan, Penelope Ann. "The Pedagogy of Inclusion: Narratives of Teaching and Learning." *DAI* 52 (February 1992): 2847A.

    Examines "landscapes" of teaching and learning, taking as its thesis that the pedagogical is the personal, blurring genres of cultural study, case study, and autobiography.

51. Ede, Lisa. "Clifford Geertz on Writing and Rhetoric [response to Geertz, *JAC* 11 (Fall 1991)]." *JAC* 12 (Winter 1992): 208–12.

    Praises Geertz for teaching us to look closely at what is most commonsensical. Questions his view of rhetoric and his easy acceptance of disciplinary pluralism.

52. Edelstein, Arnold, and Jeffrey Carroll. "The Annotated Space: A Dialogue on the Marriage of Composition and Literary Theories." *JAC* 12 (Fall 1992): 321–36.

    The authors examine the fictions of language which define literature and composition as separate fields; they argue for a more inclusive language which incorporates reading and writing.

53. Edlund, John R. "A Phenomenological Critique of Protocol Analysis in Composing Process Research." *DAI* 52 (April 1992): 3546A.

    Details limitations of protocol-analysis done by Emig and Flower and Hayes, based on Ricoeur's "phenomenology of the will"; suggests "reflective methodologies" to improve research.

54. Edmond, White Eugene. *The Context of Human Discourse: A Configuration Criticism of Rhetoric*. Studies in Rhetoric and Communication. Columbia, SC.: University of South Carolina Press, 1992. 307 pages

    Considers how historical and cultural contexts shape rhetorical discourse and discusses its consequences. Includes a case study of John C. Calhoun's defense of slavery in his last speech before the United States Senate on 4 March 1850.

55. Eichhorn, Jill, Sara Farris, Karen Hayes, Adriana Hernandez, Susan C. Jarratt, Karen

Powers-Stubbs, and Marian M. Sciachitano. "A Symposium on Feminist Experiences in the Composition Classroom." *CCC* 43 (October 1992): 297–322.

> The authors report on experiences with feminist composition pedagogies.

56. Enos, Theresa, and Stuart C. Brown, eds. *Defining the New Rhetorics*. Written Communication Annual, vol. 7. Newbury Park, CA: Sage, 1992. 320 pages

> Eighteen essays illustrate the history, evolution, and pluralism of twentieth-century rhetoric, especially as it applies to composition.
> *Essayists:* Bazerman, C; Berlin, J. A.; Brown, S. C.; Burnham, C. C.; Corder, J. W.; Dasenbrock, R. W.; Enos, R. L.; Enos, T.; Flower, Linda; Fulkerson, R.; Goggin, M. Daly; Halloran, S. M.; Lauer, J. M.; Miller, C. R.; Phelps, L. Wetherbee; Porter, J. E.; Scott, R. L.; Young, R.

57. Eribon, Didier. *Michel Foucault*. Translated by Betsy Wing. Cambridge: Harvard University Press, 1992. 392 pages

> Provides a biographical account of Michel Foucault's life.

58. Farmer, Frank Marion. "Dialogic Imitation: Vygotsky, Bakhtin, and the Internalization of Voice." *DAI* 53 (August 1992): 486A.

> Shows that a social conception of imitation is largely absent in the literature of the process movement.

59. Fennick, Ruth McLennan. "The Creative Processes of Prose-Fiction Writers: What They Suggest for Teaching Composition." *DAI* 52 (February 1992): 2847A.

> Surveyed invention, planning, drafting, and revising practices of 10 prose-fiction writers, using manuscript facsimiles, notebooks, journals, and revisions as primary and secondary sources.

60. Ferrara, Kathleen. "The Interactive Achievement of a Sentence: Joint Production in Therapeutic Discourse." *DPr* 15 (April–June 1992): 207–28.

> Points out that unlike interruptions, joint productions are cooperative ventures having distinct functions such as to elicit information and to insure verity. Interlocutors provide clause-by-clause contributions.

61. Ferry, Christopher Joseph. "Liberation Theology, Freire's Liberatory Pedagogy, and Composition Studies." *DAI* 52 (February 1992): 2903A.

> Questions whether Freire's educational philosophy, developed in the cultural context of Latin America, can be transplanted successfully to the United States.

62. Flynn, Thomas Richard. "Rhetorical Elements in Historical Revisionism: A Burkeian Analysis of the Neoconservative Interpretation of the American Experience in Vietnam." *DAI* 52 (April 1992): 3475A.

> Studies books by Podhoretz and Lewy and provides insight into how history is reconstructed through language.

63. Fontaine, Sheryl I. "Rendering the 'Text' of Composition." *JAC* 12 (Fall 1992): 395–406.

> Celebrates the potential and the incompleteness of composition as a means of achieving its illusive definition as a discipline.

64. Forman, Janis, ed. *New Visions of Collaborative Writing*. Portsmouth, NH: Boynton/Cook, 1992. 200 pages

> Nine essays explore definitions, politics and ethics, sites and practices, and conceptual frameworks for the study of collaborative writing.
> *Essayists:* Braun, L. A.; Clifford, J.; Gere, A. R.; Horton, M. S.; Lay, M. M.; Locker, K. O.; Rogers, P. S.; Roop, L. J.; Schilb, J.; Selfe, C. L.; Thralls, C.; Trimbur, J.

65. Foster, David. *A Primer for Writing Teachers: Theories, Theorists, Issues, Problems*. 2d ed. Portsmouth, NH: Boynton/Cook, 1992. 256 pages

> Provides an introduction to composition studies, with a revised chapter on current

issues in the field, a new theoretical chapter entitled "Writing and Reading, Writers and Readers," and an updated bibliography.

66. Fukuchi, Isamu. "Donald Davidson's Theory of Meaning." *DAI* 52 (April 1992): 3624A.

    Presents arguments for and against Davidson's position that the meaning of a sentence comes about when its "truth condition" is specified.

67. Gadamer, Hans-Georg. "The Expressive Power of Language: On the Function of Rhetoric for Knowledge." *PMLA* 107 (March 1992): 345–52.

    Describes the "mediative" function of written rhetoric as an art of "agreement" between the expert and the nonexpert. Specifically addresses scholarly writing.

68. Gannett, Cinthia. *Gender and the Journal: Diaries and Academic Discourse*. Literacy, Culture, and Learning: Theory and Practice, edited by Alan C. Purves. Albany, NY: State University of New York Press, 1992. 262 pages

    Explores the gendered history, social contexts, and discursive traditions that have characterized journals and diaries in academic discourse. Argues that "journal" has positive public and scholarly connotations, while "diary" is understood as a feminized, trivial, and confessional kind of writing inappropriate for school.

69. Gardiner, Michael Edward. "The Dialogics of Critique: M. M. Bakhtin and the Theory of Ideology." *DAI* 52 (February 1992): 3099A.

    Explores Bakhtin's concepts and insights on social and cultural theory, encompassing methodological and epistemological concerns centering around the theory and critique of ideology.

70. Geisler, Cheryl. "Exploring Academic Literacy: An Experiment in Composing." *CCC* 43 (February 1992): 39–54.

    Argues that conventions of academic literacy keep personal and multiple-voiced accounts from being heard during composing and reading, thereby restricting our understanding of literacy.

71. Gervasi, Anne. "A Rhetoric for Professional Writing: Global Writing." *DAI* 53 (November 1992): 1430A.

    Extends Walter H. Beale's *A Pragmatic Theory of Rhetoric* to create a pedagogy for professionals who write.

72. Gessey, Patricia A. "Writing the Decolonized Self: Autobiographical Narrative from the Maghreb." *DAI* 52 (February 1992): 2920A.

    Argues that the autobiographical act in the other tongue reopens old wounds suffered as a result of colonization, becoming an "auto-autopsy" instead of an autobiography.

73. Gilbert, Michael A. "The Enthymeme Buster: A Heuristic Procedure for Position Exploration in Dialogic Dispute." *IL* 13 (Fall 1991): 159–66.

    Presents a systematic procedure for clarifying enthymemes in dialectic by proposing a counterexample to the arguer and by analyzing the response.

74. Gilder, Eric. "Uniting the Alpha and Omega of Critical Discourse: A Kellean Rhetorical Analysis of Wayne C. Booth as 'Career Author.' " *DAI* 53 (August 1992): 348A.

    Uses Aristotle's rhetorical theory and George Kelly's personal construct theory to devise a rhetorical method for examining "subjectively-centered meta-criticism."

75. Gillam, Alice M. "Feminism and Composition Research: Researching as a Woman." *CS/FEN* 20 (Spring 1992): 47–54.

    Claims that feminist research methodologies are often dismissed as not sufficiently objective; suggests that the composition field needs to be receptive to self-criticism.

76. Giroux, Henry A. "Paulo Freire and the Politics of Postcolonialism." *JAC* 12 (Winter 1992): 15–26.

Argues that the West's appropriation of Freire has increasingly lost awareness of its own post-colonialism, adopting the theory without calling into question Western power relations and ideology.

77. Goodell, Elizabeth, and Jacqueline Sachs. "Direct and Indirect Speech in English-Speaking Children's Retold Narratives." *DPr* 15 (October–December 1992): 395–422.

Points out that a u-shaped pattern characterizes children's acquisition of discourse. Argues that in contrast to their older and younger counterparts, six-year-olds prefer direct speech.

78. Gordon, Barbara Elizabeth. "The Rhetoric of Community Ritual: The Blessing of the Shrimp Fleet at Chauvin, Louisiana." *DAI* 52 (March 1992): 3125A.

Analyzes the rhetoric and functions of a specialized ritual and illuminates the affirmation of culture.

79. Gray, Nancy. *Language Unbound: On Experimental Writing by Women*. Urbana, IL: University of Illinois Press, 1992. 192 pages

Uses feminist literary theory and women's experimental writing to disclose the best means of resisting the gendered silences of "woman" by radically disrupting the "law and order" of Western patriarchal systems of meaning.

80. Greenblatt, Stephen, and Giles Gunn, eds. *Redrawing the Boundaries: The Transformation of English and American Literary Studies*. New York: Modern Language Association, 1992. 650 pages

Reviews scholarship from major historical periods and surveys new directions in literary criticism and in composition studies. *Essayists:* Bender, John; Bhabha, Homi K.; Cohen, Walter; Esch, Deborah; Ferguson, Frances; Fisher, Philip; Gates, Henry Louis, Jr.; Graff, Gerald; Kerrigan, William; Levine, George; Marcus, Leah S.; Marius, Richard; McQuade, Donald; Middleton, Anne; Montrose, Louis; Perloff, Marjorie; Robbins, Bruce; Rowe, John Carlos; Sedgewick, Eve Kosofsky; Skura, Meredith; Stimpson, Catherine R.; Tichi, Cecelia.

81. Greenhalgh, Anne M. "Voices in Response: A Postmodern Reading of Teacher Response." *CCC* 43 (October 1992): 401–10.

Calls for an examination of teachers' voices in written responses to student texts in order to expand awareness of implicit authority, role, modulation, and appropriateness.

82. Haefner, Joel. *A Dialogic Approach to the Composing Process: Table Talk and the Romantic Essay*. Cincinnati, OH: CCCC, March 1992. ERIC ED 346 493. 17 pages

Claims the historical reality of the Romantic era in England supports a collaborative approach to writing and knowing that has been buried for decades.

83. Hannah, Matthew Gordon. "Foucault Deinstitutionalized: Spatial Prerequisites for Modern Social Control." *DAI* 53 (November 1992): 1528A.

Attempts to understand the maintenance of normality among the "already normal." Takes into account the differences between preconditions for control of the confined and control of the spatially free.

84. Harlin, Rebecca, Sara Lipa, and Rosemary Lonberger. *The Whole Language Journey*. Pippin Teacher's Library. Portsmouth, NH: Heinemann, 1992. 112 pages

Presents a guide to transforming traditional pedagogy into a whole language approach. Includes an annotated bibiliography.

85. Harris, Muriel. "Collaboration Is Not Collaboration Is Not Collaboration: Writing Center Tutorials Versus Peer-Response Groups." *CCC* 43 (October 1992): 369–83.

Defines the difference between collaborative writing and collaborative learning and the difference between collaborative learning in tutorials and in peer-response groups.

86. Hartford, Beverly, and Kathleen Bardovi-Harlig. "Closing the Conversation: Evidence from the Academic Advising Session." *DPr* 15 (January–March 1992): 93–116.

   The author points out that differences in the closing patterns of nonnative speakers of English show how advising conversations work by rules of institutional discourse.

87. Hatch, Gary Layne. "Reviving the Rodential Model for Composition: Robert Zoellner's Alternative to Flower and Hayes." *RR* 10 (Spring 1992): 244–49.

   Rejects the cognitive problem solving model, especially its think-write metaphor, in favor of Zoellner's emphasis on behavior.

88. Hawryluk, Paul. "The Composing Processes of Seven Saskatchewan Writers." *DAI* 52 (March 1992): 3207A.

   Illuminates the development of seven local writers, focusing on the influences of locale and community support.

89. Hayes, John R., Richard E. Young, Michele L. Matchett, Maggie McCaffrey, Cynthia Cochran, and Thomas Hajduk, eds. *Reading Empirical Research Studies: The Rhetoric of Research*. Hillsdale, NJ: Lawrence Erlbaum, 1992. 584 pages

   The contributors argue that empirical methods are not inherently alien to the humanities; they point out that methods extend the power of humanist researchers trying to solve the problems of their discipline.
   Essayists: Bauman, J. F.; Beach, R.; Bracewell, R. J.; Braddock, R.; Brezin, M. K.; Dansereau, D. F.; Floriak, M.; Freedman, S. W.; Funk, J. L.; Haas, C.; Hayes, J. R.; Heath, S. B.; Hillocks, G., Jr.; Hunt, R. A.; Hytheker, V. I.; Lambiotte, J. G.; Lampert, D. A.; Larson, C. O.; Nash, J. G.; Nelson, J.; O'Donnell, A. M.; Palmquist, M.; Rocklin, T.; Serra, J. K.; Shumacher, G.; Scott, B. T.; Smith, W. L.; Spivey, N. N.; Stein, S. E.; Thomas, C.; Wallace, D. L.; Wendler, L.; Young, R. E.

90. Heilker, Paul. "Public Products/Public Processes: Zoellner's Praxis and the Contemporary Composition Classroom." *RR* 10 (Spring 1992): 232–38.

   Wants to revive Zoellner's 1969 monography. Claims it was a mistake to ignore his emphasis on how students can be taught process-writing.

91. Henricksen, Bruce, and Thaïs E. Morgan, eds. *Reorientations: Critical Theories and Pedagogies*. Urbana, IL: University of Illinois Press, 1990. 288 pages

   Recovers the classroom as a site of cultural criticism. Discusses feminist criticism and the academy, a new essentialism, and a textshop for an experimental humanities.
   Essayists: Comley, Nancy R.; Ewell, Barbara C.; Dasenbrock, Reed Way; Davis, Robert Con; Ewell, Barbara C.; Flynn, Elizabeth A.; Henricksen, Bruce; Landow, George P.; Lefkovitz, Lori H.; Morgan, Thaïs E.; Scholes, Robert; Shoaf, R. A.; Thomas, Brook; Ulmer, Gregory L.

92. Hesse, Doug. *Strange Attractors: Chaos Theory and Composition Studies*. Seattle, WA: NCTE, November 1991. ERIC ED 342 010. 9 pages

   Argues that writing resembles chaotic systems in that it is nonlinear and complex.

93. Hoffman, Regina M. "Temporal Organization as Rhetorical Resource." *SCJ* 57 (Spring 1992): 194–204.

   Proposes a time-vocabulary model to uncover previously undetected temporal aspects of rhetorical texts.

94. Holland, Dorothy, and Margaret A. Eisenhart. *Educated in Romance: Women, Achievement, and College Culture*. Chicago: University of Chicago Press, 1990. 274 pages

   Holland and Eisenhart expose a pervasive peer system that propels women into a world where their attractiveness to men counts most. The study draws on ethnographic interviews and observations of young women studied for nearly a decade.

95. Holmes, Janet. "Women's Talk in Public Contexts." *D&S* 3 (April 1992): 131–50.

    Argues that men make more frequent contributions than females in formal, expository contexts. Shows that women are more vocal in exploratory talk. Provides suggestions for reducing the unequal distribution of public discourse.

96. Holt, Mara. "The Value of Written Peer Criticism." *CCC* 43 (October 1992): 384–92.

    Brings together the works of Belanoff, Elbow, and Bruffee to set up a model of peer-response and collaborative learning.

97. Holub, Robert C. *Crossing Borders: Reception Theory, Poststructuralism, Deconstruction*. Madison: University of Wisconsin Press, 1992. 244 pages

    Describes how theories of literature are affected by the countries they are used in; concentrates on postwar Germany and the United States; discusses the reaction of American intellectuals to continental theory.

98. Horner, Bruce. *Re-Inventing the Epistemic Approach: Continuing a Resistant Tradition*. Cincinnati, OH: CCCC, March 1992. ERIC ED 346 509. 15 pages

    Defines resistant tradition as resisting identification of itself, teaching students to resist knowledge as statically conceived, resisting the notion of resistance as a method.

99. Horner, Bruce. "Rethinking the 'Sociality' of Error: Teaching Editing as Negotiation." *RR* 11 (Fall 1992): 172–99.

    Argues that the distinction between error and its social implications is false. Urges a more "fully social" view of error.

100. Howell, Charles. *The Rhetoric of Real Experience: Case Studies and the Representation of the Human Subject*. Cincinnati, OH: CCCC, March 1992. ERIC ED 346 479. 14 pages

     Argues that designs and emphases of case studies are rhetorically constructed; points out that their true subject is the teacher-researcher whose understanding is rhetorically reconstructed.

101. Iaumsupanimit, Somchit. "The Interaction between the Writer's and the Reader's Purposes through Text." *DAI* 53 (October 1992): 1109A.

     Studies the interaction between writers and readers to set purposes and looks at the influence of language proficiency. Shows that writers' and readers' purposes should be complementary and that motivational and affective states influence the construction of a meaningful text.

102. Irving, Katrina Mary. "The Discursive Construction of the Immigrant Woman in America, 1890–1925." *DAI* 52 (July 1992): 150A.

     Argues that the European immigrant was portrayed as a racialized "other," which was articulated through the concepts and terms ordinarily pertaining to the female gender.

103. Jablonski, John Jesse. "A Rhetoric of Intermedial Argument: Implicit, Informal Features in Student Composition." *DAI* 53 (November 1992): 1431A.

     Examines patterns of informal argument that beginning writers bring with them into university composition classes and use in formal academic essays. The study is based on works by Perelman, Bartholomae and Quasthoff, and Schiffrin.

104. Jacobsen, Cheryl. "Lifting the Curse of Eve: Textual Constructions of Gender and Identity in Women's Writings of Childbirth." *DAI* 53 (July 1992): 326A.

     Presents a survey of the questions raised concerning identity and role in women's fictional discourse in the 1890s, 1930s, and 1970s.

105. Johnson, Donna M., and Duane H. Roen. "Complimenting and Involvement in Peer Re-

views: Gender Variation." *LSoc* 21 (March 1992): 27–57.

Shows that an analysis of peer reviews of academic writing in form of letters revealed a greater use of complimentary intensifiers and personal referencing by women than by men.

106. Johnson, Wendell. "You Can't Write Writing." *ETC* 50 (Winter 1992/1993): 442–54.

    Maintains that graduates in English have not been taught how to write with precision and that they do not use language to "map experience."

107. Kelb, Barbara Jeanne. "Martin Buber's Philosophy of Dialogue and Three Modern Rhetorics." *DAI* 52 (February 1992): 2903A.

    Tests the applicability of Martin Buber's concepts within his philosophy of dialogue to the rhetorics of Carl Rogers, Kenneth Bruffee, and Henry Johnstone.

108. Keyes, Cheryl. "Rappin' to the Beat: Rap Music as Street Culture among African-Americans." *DAI* 53 (September 1992): 913A.

    Explores the philosophy and aesthetic ideology of rap music and places it within a continuum of black expression.

109. Killingsworth, M. Jimmie. "Discourse Communities—Local and Global." *RR* 11 (Fall 1992): 110–23.

    Urges competing concepts of discourse communities. Suggests that most people stand between local and global communities.

110. Killingsworth, M. Jimmie. "Realism, Human Action, and Instrumental Discourse." *JAC* 12 (Winter 1992): 171–200.

    Argues that Beale's instrumental discourse plays a central role in other sorts of discourse. Killingsworth's use of Habermasian philosophy leads him to a reading of Whitman and a modern novel as significantly instrumental.

111. Killingsworth, M. Jimmie, and Michael K. Gilbertson. *Signs, Genres, and Communities*. Baywood Technical Communication Series, edited by Jay R. Gould. Amityville, NY: Baywood Publishing, 1992. 280 pages

    Offers a descriptive theory of technical communication, analyzes the components of technical communication according to a general theory of signs, and interprets genres as "crystals" of social action that serve special needs within discourse communities.

112. Killingsworth, M. Jimmie, and Jacqueline S. Palmer. *Ecospeak: Rhetoric and Environmental Politics in America*. Carbondale, IL: Southern Illinois University Press, 1992. 327 pages

    A systematic rhetorical analysis of both environmental and developmental discourses in a variety of genres calls attention to their limits. The authors propose alternatives and discuss a genealogy of environmentalism. They draw illustrations from actual discourse, including samples developed by activists, governmental agencies, and the news media.

113. Kirby, John R., and Denise Pedwell. "Students' Approaches to Summarization." *EdPsy* 12 (1992): 297–321.

    Considers the effect of students' approaches to learning on their ability to summarize a text and to learn from the summarizing process.

114. Kirby, John T. "Toward a Rhetoric of Poetics: Rhetor as Author and Narrator." *JNT* 22 (Winter 1992): 1–22.

    The article explores the rhetorical strategy that underlies the roles of author and narrator.

115. Kirsch, Gesa, and Patricia A. Sullivan, eds. *Methods and Methodology in Composition Research*. Carbondale, IL: Southern Illinois University Press, 1992. 368 pages

    Fourteen essays by established composition researchers are divided into two sec-

tions. The first, "Methods and Methodology," covers feminist, historical, textual, case study, ethnographic, cognitive, experimental, metadiscursive, and other approaches to composition research. The second, "Problems and Issues," addresses methodological pluralism, coding, collaboration, and the politics of knowledge.
Essayists: Beach, Richard; Connors, Robert J.; Ede, Lisa; Grant-Davie, Keith; Huckin, Thomas N.; Kirsch, Gesa; Miller, Susan; Mittan, Robert K.; Mortensen, Peter L.; Moss, Beverly J.; Newkirk, Thomas; Ray, Ruth; Roen, Duane H.; Schriver, Karen A.; Sullivan, Patricia A.

116. Kraemer, Don J., Jr. "Gender and the Autobiographical Essay: A Critical Extension of the Research." *CCC* 43 (October 1992): 323–39.

    Explores how language affects our perception of gender and gender markings in narratives.

117. Larson, Marion Hogan. "Writers in Transition: Undergraduate Interns Face New Demand." *DAI* 53 (December 1992): 1885A.

    Demonstrates transitional stages of communication when writers adjust to a different workplace.

118. Latchaw, Joan S. "A Pedagogical Model Designed to Help Students Develop Strategies for Critical Thinking within a Reading and Writing Context." *DAI* 52 (April 1992): 3547A.

    Argues for the interrelatedness of reading and writing; uses metaphorical reasoning as a model for teaching critical thinking.

119. Latiolais, Christopher. "Habermas's Concept of the Lifeworld." *DAI* 53 (November 1992): 1540A.

    Explores and critiques Habermas's attempt to provide the theoretical-normative underpinnings of a critical social theory. Argues that Habermas's basic conceptions are not adequately developed and that his theory is therefore not viable.

120. Lauer, Janice. "A Note to *JAC* Readers [response to Arrington, *JAC* 11 (Fall 1991)]." *JAC* 12 (Fall 1992): 421–22.

    Argues that Arrington's classification of her work is incorrect.

121. Lazere, Donald. "Teaching the Political Conflicts: A Rhetorical Schema." *CCC* 43 (May 1992): 194–213.

    Subscribes to a theory that rhetorical education improves citizenship and describes a pedagogy that empowers student decision making through awareness of ideology.

122. Levine, Linda. "The Argument on Language and the Language of Argument: Kenneth Burke and Wilbur Samuel Howell." *DAI* 52 (April 1992): 3591A.

    Explores the theoretical and rhetorical dimensions of and conflict between Burke's constructionist and Howell's realist theory of language and meaning.

123. Levy, Elena, and David McNeill. "Speech, Gesture, and Discourse." *DPr* 15 (July–September 1992): 277–301.

    The authors argue that gestures contribute to a communicative dynamism in language which can be measured in longer stretches of discourse. Points out that gestures accompanying initial parts of narratives are especially common.

124. Luke, Carmen, and Jennifer Gore, eds. *Feminism and Critical Pedagogy*. New York: Routledge, 1992. 224 pages

    The essays map the field of feminist pedagogy and outline the current status of the debate between feminist educators and critical pedagogy theorists over the concept of power, theorization of gender, and attention to educational subjects.
    Essayists: Ellsworth, Elizabeth; Gore, Jennifer; Greene, Maxine; Kenway, Jane; Lather, Patti; Lewis, Magda; Luke, Carmen; Modra, Helen; Orner, Mimi; Walkerdine, Valerie.

125. Lunsford, Andrea A. "Intellectual Property, Concepts of Selfhood, and the Teaching of Writing." *JBW* 11 (Fall 1992): 61–73.

Critiques the academy's dominant writing pedagogies. Challenges their masculinist, hierarchical assumptions and proposes constructing alternative "scenes for writing" that characterize writing in postmodern composition studies.

126. Lyon, Arabella. "Re-Presenting Communities: Teaching Turbulence." *RR* 10 (Spring 1992): 279–90.

    Seeks a more dynamic concept of discourse communities than conventional models. Emphasizes the diversity of communities and the need for invention.

127. MacDonald, Martin. "Images/Words." *EQ* 24.1 (1992): 19–21.

    Illustrates the importance of putting ideas into words quickly before their meaning is lost.

128. Makaryk, Irene. *Dictionary of Contemporary Criticism and Literary Terms*. Toronto: University of Toronto Press, 1992. 1488 pages

    Presents articles from 150 scholars across the range of current theory.

129. Matalene, Carolyn. "Experience as Evidence: Teaching Students to Write Honestly and Knowledgeably about Public Issues." *RR* 10 (Spring 1992): 252–65.

    Argues that to empower student writers, their experiences must be valued if they are to write effectively about public issues.

130. McCartney, Sarah T. "Authors, Text, and Talk: The Internalization of Dialogue from Social Interaction during Writing." *DAI* 53 (July 1992): 89A.

    Investigates what students internalize from the dialogue that occurs during the writing period in a process-oriented writing classroom.

131. McDonald, Robert L. "Interview with Gary Tate." *CS/FEN* 20 (Fall 1992): 36–50.

    Uses question and answer format to reflect on Gary Tate's role in the field of composition studies and to look at the nature of the discipline.

132. McGowan, Kate. "The Woman-in-Effect: A Textual Study of Discursive Representations of the Female Sexual Subject in Britain in the Nineteen Twenties." *DAI* 53 (August 1992): 642A.

    Examines the ways in which sexual meanings have, historically, been constructed and contested for women by a number of conflicting discourses.

133. McGregory, Jerrilyn. " 'There Are Other Ways to Get Happy': African-American Urban Folklore." *DAI* 53 (November 1992): 1626A.

    Demonstrates that African-American sacred and secular creative expressions grow out of social interaction rituals.

134. McLoughlin, Maryann. "Female Utopian Writers and the Environment." *CEAF* 22 (Winter 1992): 3–6.

    Discusses differences in female and male utopian writers.

135. McNenny, Geraldine, and Duane H. Roen. "The Case for Collaborative Scholarship in Rhetoric and Composition." *RR* 10 (Spring 1992): 291–310.

    Cites examples of successful and unsuccessful collaboration; explores institutional suspicions of collaboration; lists advantages and guidelines for success.

136. McPhail, Mark Lawrence. "Quantum Inferential Leaps: The Rhetoric of Physics." *SCJ* 57 (Spring 1992): 178–93.

    Illustrates how the discoveries of quantum physics complement contemporary conceptions of rhetoric as epistemic.

137. McQuade, Donald. "Living In—and On—the Margins." *CCC* 43 (February 1992): 11–22.

    Reflects on the marginalized, both students and teachers, and on the courage it takes to express oneself.

138. Meyers, Renée A., Dale Brashers, Candy Center, Christine Beck, and Stacia Wert-Gray. "A Citation Analysis of Organization Communication Research." *SCJ* 57 (Spring 1992): 241–46.

   Analyzes publication rates and citation patterns published in 15 communication journals between 1979 to 1989; discusses implications of the findings for the practice of organizational communication research.

139. Middleton, Timothy Andrew. "The Operating of Discourse as a Motive for Critical Practice: A Bakhtinian Perspective." *DAI* 53 (November 1992): 1527A.

   Offers a Bakhtinian perspective on the effect of discourse in critical practice. Argues that Bakhtin's explanation of individuals' relation to language is the basis for the examination of how discourse acts as a constraint on motive for acts of interpretation.

140. Miles, Suzanne Laura. "A Pentad Analysis: Jeane J. Kirkpatrick at the United Nations." *DAI* 52 (April 1992): 3476A.

   Suggests that Kirkpatrick's speeches most often utilize pragmatic lines of argument and indicate a conservative view of the world.

141. Miller, Gregory Robert. "America Run Amok: The Rhetoric of the Ku Klux Klan." *DAI* 52 (February 1992): 2757A.

   Examines the Klan and its rhetoric from an historical perspective by utilizing theories from Kenneth Burke and Walter Fisher.

142. Miller, Susan. *The Disciplinary Processing of Writing-as-Process*. Cincinnati, OH: CCCC, March 1992. ERIC ED 346 491. 16 pages

   Asserts that the dominance of the process theory has not shifted teaching or research toward the settings and assumptions inherent in "actual" acts of writing.

143. Mohan, Rajeswari. "Dodging the Crossfire: Questions for Postcolonial Pedagogy." *Mohan* 19 (October 1992): 28–44.

   Examines "the global politics of nomenclature and the micro-politics of literary study in the American academy insofar as they guide the study of postcolonial texts."

144. Moonilal-Masur, Patricia, Elena Cincik, and Claudia Mitchell. " 'Dear Diary': Exploring Gender and Genre in the 'Writing-to-Learn Classroom.' " *EQ* 24.2 (1992): 30–37.

   Presents and interprets three short case studies in which gender is related to punctuation.

145. Moran, Michael O. *Frank Aydelotte, Oxford University, and the Thought Movement in America*. Cincinnati, OH: CCCC, March 1992. ERIC ED 344 230. 16 pages

   Describes Aydelotte's theory that writing can only be taught in conjunction with reading and thinking.

146. Morse, Philip S. *The Writing Teacher as Helping Agent: Communicating Effectively in the Conferencing Process*. Seattle, WA: NCTE, November 1991. ERIC ED 342 012. 33 pages

   Finds that teachers do not generally use communication skills which are defined as effective in helping relationships while conferencing with students. Bases his results on a study of 10 teachers.

147. Moshenberg, Daniel. "The Problem with Note-Taking." *CS/FEN* 20 (Fall 1992): 3–28.

   Suggests that many classrooms are simply places where notes are taken. Reviews the literature of theorists, including Dewey, Mills, and Freire, who offer alternatives.

148. Murphy, Gregory. "Comprehension and Memory of Personal Reference: The Use of Social Information in Language Processing." *DPr* 15 (July–September 1992): 337–56.

   Argues that instead of being incidental information, choices such as first or last name affect how readers remember the attitudes implicit in references made to a person.

149. Murphy, Peter F. "Cultural Studies as Praxis: A Working Paper." *CollL* 19 (June 1992): 31–43.

Explores the development of cultural studies and presents a discussion of the blending of theory and practice in such programs.

150. Nash, Walter. *An Uncommon Tongue: The Uses and Resources of English.* New York: Routledge, 1992. 232 pages

    Reflects on the practice and status of the English language in the modern world.

151. Nelson, Carol Jean. "Eliciting Educators' Views about the Writing Process." *DAI* 52 (May 1992): 3816A.

    Examines the views of preservice teachers, in-service teachers, and teacher educators about process writing strategies in elementary school.

152. Neuleib, Janice. "The Friendly Stranger: Twenty-Five Years as Other." *CCC* 43 (May 1992): 231–43.

    Analyzes why teachers cannot reach resisting students; sets forth an approach to help teachers change their attitudes toward and their methodology for such students.

153. North, Stephen M. "On Book Reviews in Rhetoric and Composition." *RR* 10 (Spring 1992): 348–62.

    Explores practical and theoretical aspects of reviewing. Suggests guidelines for a more effective process such as a centralized journal to review texts in English Studies.

154. Obbink, Laura Apol. "Feminist Theory in the Classroom: Choices, Questions, Voices." *EJ* 81 (November 1992): 38–43.

    Analyzes the relationship between what we read and how we read it. Argues for the need to develop feminist strategies for reading women's texts.

155. Ochs, Elinor, Carolyn Taylor, Dina Rudolph, and Ruth Smith. "Storytelling as a Theory-Building Activity." *DPr* 15 (January–March 1992): 37–72.

    The authors maintain that stories and comments on them help interlocutors to structure and reinterpret world views. They point out that the familiarity of interlocutors with each other affects the theory-building.

156. Ohtsuka, Keisuke, and William Brewer. "Discourse Organization in the Comprehension of Temporal Order in Narrative Texts." *DPr* 15 (July–September 1992): 317–36.

    The authors argue that global patterns of text organization facilitate comprehension. They point out that a new event has to be immediately integrated with old information.

157. Olson, Gary A. "Fish Tales: A Conversation with 'The Contemporary Sophist.'" *JAC* 12 (Fall 1992): 253–77.

    Interviews Stanley Fish and explores various aspects of composition theory and the progress in the field.

158. O'Shea, Carol Sue. "Post-Positivism in Rhetoric and Composition: Kuhnian Epistemology and a Popperian Alternative." *DAI* 53 (September 1992): 787A.

    Traces the rise and fall of positivism; suggests that the critical radicalism of Popper is more compatible with current work done in rhetoric and composition than is Kuhn's theory of consensus.

159. Oswal, Sushi K. *The Writing Processes of a Blind Administrator: A Case Study.* Cincinnati, OH: CCCC, March 1992. ERIC ED 345 235. 14 pages

    Observes the composing techniques of a blind executive; draws conclusions for the teaching of writing to blind students.

160. Otte, George. "Why Read What? The Politics of Composition Anthologies." *JAC* 12 (Winter 1992): 137–49.

    Argues that "accessibility" was the overriding concern of twenty reviewers of a proposed anthology. Points out that since we do not read for models or aesthetic immersion, interest is more important.

161. Papin, Liliane. "This Is Not a Universe: Metaphor, Language, and Representation." *PMLA* 107 (October 1992): 1253–65.

   Defends the dominance of a "more holistic" and metaphorical view of language and the world by using contemporary language theory.

162. Peckham, Irvin Wherry. "The Necessary Illusion of Genres: An Argument for the Importance of Genres in Composition Studies." *DAI* 52 (April 1992): 3596A.

   Explores the benefits of teaching genres to composition students; outlines the benefits and flaws of Bain's, Moffett's, Britton's, Kinneavy's, and Beale's genre theories.

163. Penrose, Ann. "To Write Or Not to Write: Effects of Task Interpretation on Learning through Writing." *WC* 9 (October): 465–500.

   Compares through think-aloud protocols reading-to-study with reading-to-write; finds that factual knowledge is enhanced by the former and higher cognitive operations by the latter.

164. Popken, Randall. "A Theoretical Study of Indirect Speech Acts in Résumés." *CS/FEN* 20 (Fall 1992): 74–83.

   Reviews literature about speech acts and applies it to the way professionals read résumés. Suggests insights that can affect the teaching of résumé writing.

165. Porter, James. *Audience and Rhetoric.* Englewood Cliffs, NJ: Prentice Hall, 1992. 288 pages

   Invokes the archaeological methodology of Michel Foucault to critique selected treatments of audience in rhetoric and composition from the classical era to the present. Reconstructs a postmodern rhetorical notion of audience.

166. Pratt, Mary Louise. *Imperial Eyes: Travel Writing and Transculturation.* New York: Routledge, 1992. 304 pages

   Argues that "travel books by Europeans create the domestic subject of European imperialists"; discusses "how they engage metropolitan reading publics with expansionist enterprises whose material benefits accreed mainly to the very few." Includes analyses of travel writing on South America (1800–1840) and eighteenth-century writings by Europeans on South Africa.

167. Rains, Charleen. " 'You Die for Life': On the Use of Poetic Devices in Argumentation." *LSoc* 21 (June 1992): 253–76.

   Describes the function of poetic elements, designated as repetition of ideas, words, expressions, and structures to strengthen argumentative discourse.

168. Rolph, Daniel. " 'To Shoot, Burn, and Hang': Folk-History from a Kentucky Mountain Family and Community." *DAI* 53 (November 1992): 1627A.

   Elucidates such subjects as the genres of Southern violence, memorates, belief systems, and supernatural lore.

169. Roob, Andy. *Vehicles to Belief: Aristotle's Enthymeme and George Campbell's Vivacity Compared.* Chicago, IL: Central States Speech Communication Association, April 1991. ERIC ED 337 819. 25 pages

   Argues that the rhetorical systems of Aristotle and George Campbell suggest different but parallel paths by which reason leads to knowledge.

170. Rudinow, Joel. "Argument-Appreciation/Argument-Criticism: The 'Aesthetics' of Informal Logic." *IL* 13 (Spring 1991): 89–97.

   Maintains that evaluating real-world argumentation is analogous to art criticism, not an algorithmic procedure but one based on experts' intersubjectivity, and is thus teachable.

171. Rushing, Janice Hocker. "Introduction to 'Feminist Criticism.' " *SCJ* 57 (Winter 1992): 83–85.

   Provides an overview to a special issue on a feminist approach to the interpretation of public communicative events.

172. Schwichtenberg, Cathy. "Madonna's Postmodern Feminism: Bringing the Margins to the Center." *SCJ* 57 (Winter 1992): 120–31.

　　Illustrates gender deconstruction and sexual multiplicity.

173. Sebberson, David. *From Rhetorical Action to Compositionist Behavior: Reconsidering the Tyranny of Process*. Seattle, WA: NCTE, November 1991. ERIC ED 341 996. 15 pages

　　Surveys the work of Plato and Aristotle and questions the belief that writing can be best understood through an understanding of psychology.

174. Severino, Carol. "Rhetorically Analyzing Collaboration(s)." *WCJ* 13 (Fall 1992): 53–65.

　　Outlines 18 "features" to consider when rhetorically analyzing collaborative tutoring sessions. Suggests that this system will help researchers accurately describe many collaborative models.

175. Sills, Chip, and George H. Jensen, eds. *The Philosophy of Discourse: The Rhetorical Turn in Twentieth-Century Thought, Volume One*. Portsmouth, NH: Boynton/Cook, 1992. 276 pages

　　Nine essays offer a critical introduction to topics in discourse theory, including "Science, Realism, and Pragmatism," "The Frankfurt School," "Russian Formalism, Prague Structuralism, and the Bakhtin Circle," and "The Revival of Rhetoric."
　　Essayists: Comprone, Joseph J.; Holt, Mara; Ingram, David; Jensen, George H.; Kellner, Hans; Kleine, Michael; Shank, Michael H.; Sills, Chip; Skagestad, Peter; Trimbur, John; Vampola, David; Zuidervaart, Lambert.

176. Sills, Chip, and George H. Jensen, eds. *The Philosophy of Discourse: The Rhetorical Turn in Twentieth-Century Thought, Volume Two*. Portsmouth, NH: Boynton/Cook, 1992. 280 pages

　　Nine essays continue the discussion in discourse theory, including "Structuralism and Poststructuralism," "Hermeneutics," "Myth, History, and Discourse," and "Feminism."
　　Essayists: Bammer, Angelika; Boon, James A.; DiPiero, Thomas; Donougho, Martin; Guignon, Charles; Jensen, George H.; Johnston, John; Knoblauch, C. H.; Roth, Michael S.; Sills, Chip; Warnke, Georgia.

177. Simons, Jennifer Allen. "Mikhail Bakhtin: Man and His Penultimate Word. A Radical Humanistic Philosophy of the Unfinalizable Whole." *DAI* 53 (July 1992): 180A.

　　Differentiates Bakhtin's work from current critical thought to show that his work is more comprehensive than contemporary critical positions allow.

178. Smart, Graham. "Exploring the Social Dimension of a Workplace Genre and the Implications for Teaching." *CALS* 9 (1992): 33–46.

　　Argues that writing instructors can devise teaching strategies by developing local, genre-related expertise in the conventions of specific disciplines' discourse communities through naturalistic research.

179. Smith, Jeanne Jacoby. "The Origins of the Individual Voice in Writing from 1890 to 1990." *DAI* 52 (March 1992): 3207A.

　　Surveys the development of voice as an item of focus in the field of rhetoric and composition.

180. Smith, Ralph Handy. "Language Behavior in Old and New Comedy: Some Applications of Discourse Analysis to a Study of Aristophanes' 'Clouds' and Menander's 'Dyskolos.' " *DAI* 53 (July 1992): 142A.

　　Applies the methodology of discourse analysis to an investigation of language behavior and textual cohesion in ancient comedy.

181. Smith, Sidonie, and Julia Watson, eds. *De/colonizing the Subject: The Politics of Gender in Women's Autobiography*. Minne-

apolis: University of Minnesota Press, 1992. 484 pages

> Discusses the methods in autobiography and biographical writing from first- and third-world women through the lens of colonial/post-colonial theory.
> *Essayists:* Andrews, William L.; Badran, Margot; Beverley, John; Castillo, Debra A.; Chester, Suzanne; Davies, Carole Boyce; Gould, Janice; Gunn, Janet Varner; Kaplan, Caren; Lim, Shirley Geok-lin; Lionnet, Françoise; Longley, Kateryna Olijnyk; Paxton, Nancy L.; Quinby, Lee; Rajan, Gita; Raynaud, Claudine; Sarris, Greg; Smith, Sidonie; Watson, Julia.

182. Sommers, Nancy. "Between the Drafts." *CCC* 43 (February 1992): 23–31.

> Argues that students should be encouraged to use their personal stories as primary evidence, along with traditional sources, in academic writing.

183. Sotiriou, Peter Elias. "The Pedagogy of Reading and Writing: Pedagogical Responses to Hans-Georg Gadamer's Philosophical Hermeneutics." *DAI* 52 (April 1992): 3596A.

> Outlines Gadamer's theories in which textual understanding privileges neither text nor reader; compares Gadamer to reader-response theorists; connects Gadamer's theories to Mariolina Savatori's current pedagogical efforts.

184. Sperling, Melanie. *Discourse Patterns in One-to-One, Teacher-Student Writing Conference Conversation.* Cincinnati, OH: CCCC, March 1992. ERIC ED 347 562. 13 pages

> Discusses methods for and problems in data collection and analysis of teacher-student writing conference discourse patterns.

185. Sprott, Richard. "Children's Use of Discourse Markers in Disputes: Form-Function Relations and Discourse in Child Language." *DPr* 15 (October–December 1992): 423–39.

> Argues that not until their fourth year do children show an ability to use markers such as *because* and *but* to signal topic shifts or new arguments.

186. Stacey, David Edward. "Kenneth Burke's Comic-Tronic 'Attitudes' and the Defeat of Expectation in the Writing Program: A Redescription of the Conversation Model." *DAI* 53 (August 1992): 349A.

> Questions the appropriateness of applying the Bruffean model of "conversation in a community" to the writing classroom given the "academic disempowerment" of most writing instructors.

187. Stearney, Lynn M. "Private Expression in the Public Sphere: The Rhetoric of Contemporary Feminism and Its Implications for an Understanding of Public Discourse in Rhetorical Theory and Criticism." *DAI* 53 (November 1992): 1324A.

> Argues for a conception of discourse as capable of creating the conditions necessary for an emerging public consciousness.

188. Steckline, Timothy Jerome. "The Rhetoric of American Apocalyptic." *DAI* 52 (June 1992): 4148A.

> Studies apocalyptic mythology by utilizing Burke's theory of dramatism.

189. Stein, Edward, ed. *Forms of Desire: Sexual Orientation and the Social Constructionist Controversy.* New York: Routledge, 1992. 384 pages

> The book contains essays supporting and opposing social constructionism, a theory which supports the view that the categories of sexual orientation are cultural constructs rather than universal categories of nature.
> *Essayists:* Boswell, John; Davidson, Arnold; Dynes, Wayne R.; Epstein, Steven; Foucault, Michel; Hacking, Ian; McIntosh, Mary; Padgug, Robert; Stein, Edward; Tiefer, Leonore; Weinrich, James.

190. Stolarek, Elizabeth A. *Prose Modeling: Panacea or Poppycock?* Cincinnati, OH: CCCC, March 1992. ERIC ED 341 989. 16 pages

Examines the effectiveness of prose modeling to teach unfamiliar prose forms.

191. Strasma, Kip, and Gavin Foster. "Collaboration within Writing Classes: An Ethnographic Point of View." *WI* 11 (Spring/Summer 1992): 111–27.

    Uses ethnographic data collected from three writing classes to examine how collaborative activities can engage students at a higher level than teacher-centered activities.

192. Stratton, Marcia. "Jim Jones and the Peoples Temple: A Rhetorical Analysis Using Narrative Theory." *DAI* 53 (August 1992): 350A.

    Uses Fisher's theory of narrative to examine the power of Jones' rhetoric.

193. Sutton, Jane. "The Taming of *Polos/Polis*: Rhetoric as an Achievement without Women." *SCJ* 57 (Winter 1992): 97–119.

    Describes how rhetoric came to be written historically in relation to woman's body.

194. Taylor, Charles. *The Ethics of Authenticity*. Cambridge: Harvard University Press, 1992. 152 pages

    Discusses ideas and ideologies from Friedrich Nietzsche to Gail Sheehy, from Michel Foucault to Allan Bloom. Looks at the network of thought and morals that link the quest for self-creation with the impulse toward self-fashioning, and shows how such efforts must be conducted against an existing set of rules, or a gridwork of moral measurement.

195. Teich, Nathaniel, ed. *Rogerian Perspectives: Collaborative Rhetoric for Oral and Written Communication*. Norwood, NJ: Ablex, 1992. 304 pages

    Presents 20 essays that focus on the dynamics of Rogerian communication in classroom interactions, peer response groups, and other collaborations. Theoretically, the discussions situate Rogerian principles within persuasive and dialogical rhetoric and within psychoanalytic and philosophical intersubjectivity.
    Essayists: Bator, Paul G.; Baumlin, James S.; Baumlin, Tita French; Blau, Sheridan; Halasek, Kay; Madigan, Chris; Pounds, Wayne; Rogers, Carl R.; Ryback, David; Stephens, Rebecca; Young, Richard E.; Zappen, James P.

196. Thomas, David. *Putting Nature to the Rack: Narrative Studies as Research*. Liverpool, England: The Teachers' Stories of Life and Work Conference, April 1992. ERIC ED 346 461. 26 pages

    Explores the nature, characteristics, and usefulness of narrative study of teachers and teaching.

197. Tingle, Nick. "Self and Liberatory Pedagogy: Transforming Narcissism." *JAC* 12 (Winter 1992): 75–89.

    Argues that student resistance to challenging texts in liberatory classrooms is not a cognitive rejection but a psychological response to narcissistic wounds resulting from a critique of "selfobjects."

198. Tompkins, Gail E. "Assessing the Processes Students Use as Writers." *JR* 36 (November 1992): 244–46.

    Discusses three measures of process assessment—checklists, conferences, and self-assessment; provides sample checklists and a self-assessment questionnaire.

199. Tyler, Lisa. "Ecological Disaster and Rhetorical Response: Exxon's Communications in the Wake of the Valdez Spill." *JBTC* 6 (April 1992): 149–71.

    Argues that ineffective communication practices on the part of Exxon contributed to negative public perceptions.

200. Uchida, Aki. "When 'Difference' is 'Dominance': A Critique of the 'Anti Power-Based' Cultural Approach to Sex Differences." *LSoc* 21 (December 1992): 547–68.

    Argues that a focus on difference in the study of sex differences is less useful than a focus on dominance that acknowledges power issues.

201. Vandenberg, Peter. "Pick Up This Cross and Follow: (Ir)responsibility and the Teaching of 'Writing for Audience.' " *CS/FEN* 20 (Fall 1992): 84–97.

Suggests problems involved in "teaching audience" in the first-year composition classroom after considering relevant theoretical assumptions from James Berlin, Richard Fulkerson, Peter Elbow, and others.

202. Venuti, Laurence, ed. *Rethinking Translation: Discourse, Subjectivity, Ideology.* vol. 16 . New York: Routledge, 1992. 204 pages

The essayists present a political and philosophical discussion, animated by Marxism, psychoanalysis, feminism, and poststructuralism. They argue that every act of translation presents an appropriative and imperialist movement.

Essayists: Benjamin, Andrew; Chamberlain, Lori; Conley, Tom; Jacquemond, Richard; Johnston, John; Levine, Suzanne Jill; Mehlman, Jeffrey; Mehrez, Samia; Simon, Sherry; Venuti, Laurence; Willis, Sharon.

203. Vivian, Barbara G. *Gertrude Buck on Metaphor: Twentieth-Century Concepts in a Late Nineteenth-Century Dissertation.* Cincinnati, OH: CCCC, March 1992. ERIC ED 345 256. 19 pages

Finds an organic model of metaphor, drawn from psychology, in Buck's 1899 dissertation.

204. Wallace, M. Elizabeth. "Work with Us, James Sledd: A Response [*JAC* 11 (Fall 1991)]." *JAC* 12 (Winter 1992): 212–15.

Wallace, a member of the MLA Committee on Academic Freedom, responds to Sledd's critique of MLA for its inadequate support of the Wyoming Resolution. Includes Sledd's answer to the critique.

205. Walters, Amy R. "The Discourse of Interpersonal Communication: A Critical Perspective." *DAI* 53 (August 1992): 350A.

Explores interpersonal communication as a discipline and a power structure through Michel Foucault's conception of genealogical strategies.

206. Walters, Margaret Bennett. "Robert Zoellner's 'Talk-Write Pedagogy': Instrumental concept for Composition Today." *RR* 10 (Spring 1992): 239–43.

Examines Zoellner's idea that vocal skill increases writing skills. Compares his use of behavioral psychology with current cognitive approaches.

207. Walton, Douglas N. *The Place of Emotion in Argument.* University Park, PA: The Pennsylvania State University Press, 1992. 294 pages

Uses 56 case studies to examine how appeals to emotion function in argument.

208. Walton, Douglas N. *Slippery Slope Arguments.* New York: Oxford University Press, 1992. 312 pages

Analyzes four forms of the argument in which a first step is taken, followed by a series of consequences, down a "slippery slope," to a disastrous conclusion. The case studies illustrate correct and incorrect ways in which the arguments are used to discuss such issues as euthanasia and censorship.

209. Wang, Chaobo. "Paragraph Organization in English and Chinese Academic Prose: A Comparative Study." *DAI* 53 (September 1992): 796A.

Finds that Chinese and English academic writing is similar although English writers employ more deductive organization whereas Chinese writers are more writer-based.

210. Watson, Graham, and Robert M. Seiler, eds. *Text in Context: Contributions to Ethnomethodology.* Sage Focus Editions, vol. 132. Newbury Park, CA: Sage, 1992. 256 pages

Twelve interdisciplinary essays investigate the role of extratextual material in ethnomethodology and discourse analysis.

Essayists: Bilmes, J.; Bjelic, D.; Garfinkel, H.; Hak, T.; Heap, J. L.; Hester, S.; Lynch, M.; Moerman, M.; Psathas, G.; Watson, R.; Wieder, L.; Zimmerman, D. H.

211. Weiser, Irwin. "Ideological Implications of Social-Epistemic Pedagogy." *CS/FEN* 20 (Fall 1992): 29–35.

  Suggests that social-epistemic pedagogy is manipulative. Reviews literature and discusses the dangers of that manipulation.

212. West, James Thomas. "Discursive Practices and Relations of Power: A Qualitative Study of Intimate Violence." *DAI* 53 (November 1992): 1325A.

  Examines three groups' choices in addressing the problem of intimate violence. Defines terminology, theoretical conceptualization and methodology; uses Foucault's concepts of power/knowledge, rarity, and exteriority to examine ethnographic data. Summarizes differences in meanings among the groups.

213. White, Eugene E. *The Context of Human Discourse: A Configurational Criticism of Rhetoric*. Studies in Rhetoric/Communication, edited by Thomas W. Benson. Columbia, SC: University of South Carolina Press, 1992. 250 pages

  Develops an approach to judging the effectiveness of rhetorical statements within historical and social contexts, which the author calls "configurations." Contains major sections on the function of rhetoric, on the concept of "provoking urgency" in rhetoric, and on audience reception.

214. Whittenberger-Keith, Kari. "The Good Person Behaving Well: Rethinking the Rhetoric of Virtue." *SCJ* 58 (Fall 1992): 33–43.

  Describes the historically grounded meanings of "virtue" that appear in etiquette manuals; explores the implications for public discourse.

215. Wiley, Mark. "Reading and Writing in an American Grain." *RR* 11 (Fall 1992): 133–46.

  Uses Emerson to examine the profession's attention to process as opposed to product. Believes that process makes knowledge a commodity to be used for power.

216. Wilson, Ronald Bruce. "A Study of the Acquisition of Curriculum Knowledge and Influence on the Writing Skills of Caribbean Writers." *DAI* 53 (October 1992): 1045A.

  Studies 24 Carribean students and shows that the acquisition of curriculum knowledge influences their writing skills.

217. Winterowd, W. Ross. "I. A. Richards, Literary Theory, and Romantic Composition." *RR* 11 (Fall 1992): 59–78.

  Traces Richards' influence on literary theory; sees him as the founder of the New Rhetoric and as a Romantics scholar. Views him as the "epitome" of a modern literary humanist.

218. Witte, Stephen P., Neil Nakadate, and Roger D. Cherry, eds. *A Rhetoric of Doing: Essays on Written Discourse in Honor of James L. Kinneavy*. Carbondale, IL: Southern Illinois University Press, 1992. 384 pages

  Eighteen essays treat rhetoric as a dynamic enterprise of inquiry, exploration, and application which reflects James L. Kinneavy's belief in the vital relationship between theory and practice, and his commitment to a spirit of accommodation and assimilation.

  Essayists: Bazerman, Charles; Berlin, James A.; Brodkey, Linda; Carey, Linda; Cherry, Roger D.; Connors, Robert J.; Crusius, Timothy W.; Dillon, George L.; Doheny-Farina, Stephen; Enos, Richard Leo; Flower, Linda; Haas, Christina; Hampton, Sally; Hayes, John R.; Henry, Jim; Herrington, Anne J.; Jolliffe, David A.; Vande Kopple, William J.; Lauer, Janice M.; Miller, Carolyn; Nakadate, Neil; Odell, Lee; Schriver, Karen A.; Swearingen, C. Jan; Witte, Stephen P.

219. Wood, Elizabeth Springston. "Imitation in Writing: Studies in Traditions and Conflicts." *DAI* 52 (February 1992): 2904A.

Argues that imitation is neglected in contemporary composition studies; examines traditions and conflicts about imitation in order to explain its omission.

220. Yang, Xiao-Ming. "The Rhetoric of Propaganda: A Tagmemic Analysis of Selected Documents of the Cultural Revolution in China, 1966–1976." *DAI* 52 (May 1992): 3902A.

Uses a tagmemic analysis of propaganda discourse to find a workable model for textual analysis.

221. Young, Ida Delores. "Between the Voices of Our Ancestors: Afrocentric Strategies, Symbols, Forms of Revolution, and Philosophical Implications of the Rhetorical Discourse of Abolitionist Maria W. Stewart (1803–1879)." *DAI* 53 (November 1992): 1634A.

Argues that a study of Maria W. Stewart's discourse will deepen the understanding of African-American female experience. Argues that Stewart's public speaking career and her abolitionist contributions illustrate a diversified approach to rebellion.

2.2 RHETORICAL HISTORY

222. Bizzell, Patricia. "Opportunities for Feminist Research in the History of Rhetoric." *RR* 11 (Fall 1992): 50–57.

Proclaims the need for research on women and rhetoric in traditional and nontraditional canons. Notes the importance of being a "resisting reader" of rhetoric.

223. Boyd, Todd Edward. "It's a Black Thang: The Articulation of African-American Cultural Discourse." *DAI* 53 (July 1992): 5A.

Examines the development of Afrocentric cultural discourse.

224. Brant, Clare, and Diane Purkiss, eds. *Women, Texts and Histories, 1575–1760.* New York: Routledge, 1992. 304 pages

Presents writings by women and writings about gender from the sixteenth to the eighteenth century. The essayists argue that these texts "undermine many of the received assumptions on which readings during this time depended."

Essayists: Ballaster, Rosalind; Brant, Clare; Chalmers, Hero; Hackett, Helen; Hutson, Lorna; Orr, Bridget; Purkiss, Diane; Tomlinson, Sophie.

225. Brinton, Alan. "The Passions as Subject Matter in Early Eighteenth-Century British Sermons." *Rhetorica* 10 (Winter 1992): 51–69.

Shows the role of the passions in eighteenth-century British sermons and the relations to moral philosophy and rhetorical theory.

226. Brooks, Anne M. "The Historical Perspective: Ralph Waldo Emerson and the Process Paradigm in Composition Theory and Teaching." *DAI* 53 (August 1992): 386A.

Examines the depth of Emerson's roots in the process paradigm; suggests that Emerson influenced cognitivists and social-epistemics as well as romantic expressionists.

227. Bushman, Donald E. "Thomas De Quincey on Rhetoric, Conversation, and the Literature of Power." *DAI* 53 (September 1992): 787A.

Argues that De Quincey's dynamic prose style can be attributed to his model of conversation; analyzes his distinction between "literature of knowledge" and "literature of power."

228. Campbell, JoAnn. "Controlling Voices: The Legacy of English-A at Radcliffe College 1883–1917." *CCC* 43 (December 1992): 472–85.

Describes the experience of women students in composition at Radcliffe; argues that experience is needed to value diversity of experience in composition.

229. Casey, Kenneth Stewart. "The Quarrel between Rhetoric and Philosophy: Ethos and the

Ethics of Rhetoric." *DAI* 53 (December 1992): 1941A.

> Explores the conflicts among rhetoricians and philosophers over the formation of students' souls as part of rhetorical pedagogy.

230. Chrysostom, Dio. *Dio Chrysostom, Orations VII, XII, and XXXVI*. Cambridge Greek and Latin Classics, edited by D. A. Russell. New York: Cambridge University Press, 1992. 266 pages

> Presents and comments on *Euboicus*, *Olympicus*, and *Borystheniticus*, three speeches by the Greek sophist and orator who lived in Rome in the first and early second century A.D.

231. Cole, Thomas, and Francis M. Dunn, eds. *Beginnings in Classical Literature*. New York: Cambridge University Press, 1992. 245 pages

> Presents twelve essays on rhetorical structures and strategies used in works of classical literature.
> *Essayists:* Clay, Diskin; Cole, Thomas; Conte, Gian Biagia; Dunn, Francis M.; Gold, Barbara K.; Habinek, Thomas N.; Pedrick, Victoria; Pelliccia, Hayden; Race, William H.; Rosenmeyer, Thomas G.; Segal, Charles; Slater, Niall W.

232. Cook, Linda Anne McFerrin. "A Rhetoric of Delivery." *DAI* 52 (February 1992): 2903A.

> Defines delivery as having several features of oral discourse which extend to written discourse, tracing the development of delivery from the classical period until today.

233. Covino, William A. "Magic and/as Rhetoric: Outlines of a History of Phantasy." *JAC* 12 (Fall 1992): 439–58.

> Locates a common thread (language) in the histories of rhetoric and magic, extending Janet Emig's metaphor which identifies process pedagogy as nonmagical.

234. Culley, Margo, ed. *American Women's Autobiography: Fea(s)ts of Memory*. Wisconsin Studies in American Autobiography, edited by William L. Andrews. Madison: University of Wisconsin Press, 1992. 329 pages

> Fourteen essays cover women's autobiography from Puritan times to the present. The contributors take recent theoretical approaches into account.
> *Essayists:* Bloom, Lynn Z.; Culley, Margo; Diamond, Arlyn; Gordon, Ann D.; Greve, Janis; Hennesy, C. Margot; Geoklin Lim, Shirley; Mason, Mary G.; Sands, Kathleen Mullen; Smith, Sidonie; Stimpson, Catherine T.; Swain, Katheleen M.; Taves, Ann; Walker, Nancy

235. de Asua, Miguel J. C. "The Organization of Discourse on Animals in the Thirteenth Century, Peter of Spain, Albert the Great, and the Commentaries on 'De Animalibus.'" *DAI* 52 (April 1992): 3695A.

> Focuses on the relationships among the thirteenth-century commentaries and collections; discusses Peter of Spain's role in developing the *quaestio* genre.

236. de Romilly, Jacqueline. *The Great Sophists of Periclean Athens*. Translated by Janet Lloyd. New York: Oxford University Press, 1992. 260 pages

> Examines the "dialogue that took place between the Sophists and Athenian public opinion" to expose a pattern of philosophical and rhetorical discovery, public rejection, and "modified acceptance" of theories still used today in rhetoric.

237. Donovan, Brian R. *Eloquence as Virtue in Ancient Theory*. Cincinnati, OH: CCCC, March 1992. ERIC ED 346 515. 17 pages

> Advocates that civic virtue and specialized technical skill be combined in the teaching of rhetoric.

238. Enders, Jody. "Memory and the Psychology of the Interior Monologue in Chretien's Cligés." *Rhetorica* 10 (Winter 1992): 5–23.

> Argues that Chretien offers a "psychological" drama through mnemonic presentation of interior monologue, thereby privileging

the art of memory as an epistemological system.

239. Enders, Jody. *Rhetoric and the Origins of Medieval Drama*. Rhetoric and Society, edited by Wayne A. Rebhorn. Ithaca, NY: Cornell University Press, 1992. 304 pages

Analyzes the dynamic interplay among various medieval discourses, including rhetoric, law, theology, and literature by focusing on the rhetorical canon of *actio*, or delivery. Offers a new approach to the interrelations among orality, literacy, and the history of aesthetics.

240. Enos, Richard Leo. "Why Gorgias of Leontini Traveled to Athens: A Study of Recent Epigraphical Evidence." *RR* 11 (Fall 1992): 1–15.

Uses recent epigraphical evidence to explore the "birth" of rhetoric. Asserts that the motives for promoting rhetoric were as much political as intellectual.

241. Fink, Steven. *Prophet in the Marketplace: Thoreau's Development as a Professional Writer*. Princeton, NJ: Princeton University Press, 1992. 352 pages

Focuses on Thoreau's career before *Walden* (1854). Shows how his sensitivity to the reading public and to the literary marketplace shaped his development as a writer.

242. Fischer, Claude S. *America Calling: A Social History of the Telephone to 1940*. Berkeley, CA: University of California Press, 1992. 439 pages

Focuses on three California communities in a study of the telephone's integration into social life.

243. Gaillet, Lynee Lewis. "A Nineteenth-Century Scottish Rhetorician, George Jardine: Prefiguring Twentieth-Century Composition Theory." *DAI* 53 (August 1992): 419A.

Investigates the contributions of Jardine to modern writing theory; outlines the significance of Jardine's prefiguring of modern pedagogical theory.

244. Goodwin, David. "Imitatio and Eighteenth-Century Rhetorics of Reaffirmation." *Rhetorica* 10 (Winter 1992): 25–50.

Explains how Larson and Ward explicate persuasive theory and practice, championing *imitatio*, internalizing loci of the preferable, hierarchies of degree, and images of disciplinary perfection.

245. Greenwald, Marilyn Sue. "The Life and Career of Journalist Charlotte Curtis: A Rhetorical Biography." *DAI* 52 (January 1992): 2305A.

Traces the life of Curtis through her discourse and outlines how her life affected her rhetoric.

246. Guderian, Gregory Joseph. "The Paleography of Later Roman Cursive." *DAI* 52 (May 1992): 3980A.

Examines the origins, practice, and evolution of later Roman cursive.

247. Gugino, Vincent F. "On Ethos." *DAI* 52 (January 1992): 2542A.

Examines ethos from the revival of the question in German idealism to Heidegger's explicit confrontation with it.

248. Gustafson, Thomas. *Representative Words: Politics, Literature, and the American Language, 1776–1865*. New York: Cambridge University Press, 1992. 469 pages

Discusses theories that connect social and political disruption in early republican America to representation and misrepesentation in language.

249. Hallin, Annika. "Discourses of Separation: The Relation between Rhetoric and Poetics in the Work of Hoyt Hudson and Herbert Wichelns." *RR* 11 (Fall 1992): 124–32.

Discusses how these early twentieth-century rhetoricians legitimized rhetoric but "simultaneously subverted it by undermining the rhetor's role."

250. Harding, Wendy. "Medieval Women's Unwritten Discourse on Motherhood: A Read-

ing of Two Fifteenth-Century Texts." *WS* 21 (1992): 197–209.

> Investigates problems of feminine voice in medieval writing, especially about motherhood, in the texts of Margaret Paston and Margery Kempe.

251. Horner, Winifred Bryan. *Nineteenth-Century Scottish Rhetoric: The American Connection*. Carbondale, IL: Southern Illinois University Press, 1992. 264 pages

> Argues that an understanding of the changes that occurred in the content of nineteenth-century courses in logic, rhetoric, and *belles lettres* taught in Scottish universities provides important critical insight into the development of twentieth-century American composition courses, as well as courses in English literature and critical theory.

252. Jenkyns, Richard, ed. *The Legacy of Rome: A New Appraisal*. New York: Oxford University Press, 1992. 479 pages

> Traces the history and influence of Roman rhetoric, especially as it survived in formal education and in the practice of composition from late antiquity through the neoclassical period.
>
> *Essayists:* Braden, Gordon; Davis, Charles; Feenstra, Robert; Grafton, A. T.; Griffin, Jasper; Jenkyns, Richard; Kennedy, George A.; Martindale, Charles; Posner, Rebecca; Purcell, Nicholas; Rouse R. H.; Sullivan, J. P.; Watkin, David; Waywell, Geoffrey.

253. Johnson, M. K. " 'No Bananas, Giraffes, or Elephants': Margery Kempe's Text of Bliss." *WS* 21 (1992): 185–96.

> Critiques and explains readings of Kempe's book from traditional approaches and offers a new reading strategy.

254. Johnston, Mark D. "Parliamentary Oratory in Medieval Aragon." *Rhetorica* 10 (Spring 1992): 99–117.

> Analyzes the formats of medieval political discourse in the Kingdom of Aragon, showing civil eloquence in that period.

255. Kaplan, Andrew. "The Rhetoric of Circumstance in Autobiography." *Rhetorica* 10 (Winter 1992): 71–98.

> Using the *Apology of Socrates* and Augustine's *Confessions*, the author demonstrates how autobiography deals with issues of praise and the communication of values.

256. King, Nathalia. "The Mind's Eye and the Forms of Thought: Classical Rhetoric and the Composition of Augustine's *Confessions*." *DAI* 53 (September 1992): 802A.

> Argues that Augustine purposefully makes connections between his religious conversion and his conversion from a primarily oral to a primarily written culture.

257. Kramer, Michael P. *Imagining Language in America: From the Revolution to the Civil War*. Princeton, NJ: Princeton University Press, 1992. 241 pages

> Analyzes the rhetoric of late eighteenth- and nineteenth-century writings on language.

258. Labio, Catherine. "Enlightenment and the Epistemology of Origins." *DAI* 53 (September 1992): 802A.

> Outlines a history of genetic epistemology by studying Augustine, Le Roy, Vico, Pope, Locke, Kant, and others.

259. Larsen, Elizabeth. "The Progress of Literacy: Edward Tyreel Channing and the Separation of the Student Writer from the World." *RR* 11 (Fall 1992): 159–71.

> Claims that Channing's ideas caused a rupture with tradition and focused writing on product, aiding the rise of current-traditional rhetoric.

260. Leeman, Richard. *"Do Everything" Reform: The Reform Oratory of Frances E. Willard*. New York: Greenwood Press, 1992. 226 pages

> Presents a critical analysis of the speaking style of a late nineteenth-century suffragette, prohibitionist, and Christian leader of women. Includes texts of representative

speeches, a chronology, and a bibliography of significant primary and secondary sources.

261. Lloyd, Michael. *The Agon in Euripides.* New York: Oxford University Press, 1992. 145 pages

   Studies rhetoric and formal debating techniques in ancient Greece.

262. Lloyd-Jones, Richard. "Who We Were, Who We Should Become." *CCC* 43 (December 1992): 486–96.

   Reviews CCCC's history and its present and upcoming challenges, and calls for an expanded vision of CCCC's role and mission.

263. Lowe, Gail. "A Bio-Bibliography of American Reformers, 1865–1917, with a Case Study of Temperance-Prohibition." *DAI* 53 (July 1992): 193A.

   Uses the Rose Bibliography to assess character, motivation, and achievements of reformers and reform movements from 1865–1917.

264. Lu, Xing. "Recovering the Past: Identification of Chinese Senses of *Pien* and a Comparison of *Pien* to Greek Senses of Rhetoric in the Fifth and Third Centuries BCE." *DAI* 52 (March 1992): 3125A.

   Defines, analyzes, and traces the functions and contributions of *pien* in Eastern and Western rhetorical history.

265. McArthur, Tom. "Models of English." *EnT* 8 (October 1992): 12–21.

   Reviews the major scholarly representations of the language in the nineteenth and twentieth centuries.

266. McComiskey, Bruce. "Disassembling Plato's Critique of Rhetoric in the *Gorgias* (447a–466a)." *RR* 10 (Spring 1992): 205–16.

   Argues that the *Gorgias* had a relativistic epistemology that would not have accepted Socrates' negative claims about rhetoric. Accuses Plato of misrepresenting the *Gorgias*.

267. McVitty, John Dwight. "Erasmus and the Rhetorical Tradition." *DAI* 52 (February 1992): 2912A.

   By employing a restated classical rhetorical criticism, the writer aims to recover the theoretical intentions of Erasmus's texts.

268. Melnick, Jane. "When Women Went from Good to Bad: Gender, Narrative, and Cultural Politics in New York, 1890–1935." *DAI* 53 (September 1992): 859A.

   Traces a "transvaluation of gender"—a change in the way language tended to value the genders—in the United States between 1890 and 1935.

269. Metzger, Dwayne. "The (Im)possibility of Rhetoric: The Relation of Rhetoric and Geometry in Aristotle and Lacan." *DAI* 52 (April 1992): 3476A.

   Describes Aristotle's and Lacan's concepts of rhetoric in mathematical terms, using a vector analysis to indicate the relationship between metonymy and metaphor.

270. Monfasani, John. "Episodes of Anti-Quintilianism in the Italian Renaissance: Quarrels on the Orator as a *Vir Bonus* and Rhetoric as the *Scientia Bene Dicendi*." *Rhetorica* 10 (Spring 1992): 119–38.

   Reviews the Renaissance controversy over Quintillian's definition of rhetoric as *scientia bene dicendi* rather than as the art of persuasion.

271. Munslow, Alan. *Discourse and Culture: The Creating of American Society, 1870–1920.* New York: Routledge, 1992. 232 pages

   Uses theories of Althusser, Gramsci, and Hayden to examine the public discourse of Andrew Carnegie, Terence V. Powderly, Frederick J. Turner, Jane Addams, Booker T. Washington, and W. E. B. DuBois.

272. Nettles, Evelyn Elaine. "Literary Voices of Nineteenth-Century Reform Movement: An Examination of the Literary Works of Frances E. W. Harper." *DAI* 53 (September 1992): 811A.

Examines Harper's poetry and prose in support of anti-slavery, women's, and temperance movements by using historical-critical and materialist-feminist methodologies.

273. O'Banion, John D. *Reorienting Rhetoric: The Dialectic of List and Story*. University Park, PA: The Pennsylvania State Univeristy Press, 1992. 312 pages

Examines the role of narrative in the history of Western rhetoric.

274. O'Rourke, Sean Patrick. "The Rhetoric of Law in the Scottish Enlightenment." *DAI* 53 (September 1992): 664A.

Examines forensic oratory as it develops from legal rhetoric to school, belletristic, neoclassical, and commonsense rhetoric.

275. Peluso, Robert. "Incorporating Cultural Practice: The Origin and Meaning of a National Institute and an American Academy of Arts and Letters." *DAI* 53 (September 1992): 859A.

Outlines a distinctively American brand of cultural politics, one based on collective action carried out through organizational means.

276. Persak, Christine Anne. "Representing the Social Order: Rhetoric and Victorian Hierarchy, 1939–1952." *DAI* 53 (July 1992): 135A.

Concludes that Burke's dramatistic analysis provides a valuable resource for investigating rhetoric in the nineteenth century in its manifestation as social discourse.

277. Porth, Helen Louise. "Indian and Pioneer Oral Narratives: An Examination of Their Divergence from the Standard Written History of Western North Dakota (1905–1950)." *DAI* 53 (September 1992): 745A.

Collects sixty narratives to determine how they compare or diverge from the standard recorded history of western North Dakota and to encourage students to recover their heritage.

278. Rakow, Lana F. *Gender on the Line: Women, the Telephone, and Community Life*. Ilinois Studies in Communications. Urbana, IL: University of Illinois Press, 1992. 168 pages

Presents interviews with women from three generations in a small midwestern community. Shows how gender meanings can shift with economic and political circumstances.

279. Ramus, Peter. *Peter Ramus's Attack on Cicero: Text and Translations of Ramus's* Brutinae Quaestiones. Translated by Carole Newlands. Edited by James J. Murphy. Davis, CA: Hermagoras Press, 1992. 282 pages

Part I traces Ramus's career and discusses the context in which Ramus frames his attack on Cicero's concepts of rhetoric, style, and public virtue. Part II presents the Latin text and a facing-page translation of *Petri Rami Veromandi Brutinae Quaestiones* (1549).

280. Reed, Joel. "Academically Speaking: Language and Nationalism in Seventeenth- and Eighteenth-Century England." *DAI* 52 (June 1992): 4341A.

Considers how Camden, Carew, Bolton, Hooke, Sprat, Defoe, and Swift contributed to the formulation of English nationalistic discourse in a state-supported academy.

281. Reynolds, Nedra. "Composition's Ethos in the 1970s: Locations, Subjects, and Practices." *DAI* 52 (January 1992): 2524A.

Looks at where Kinneavy, Emig, Elbow, and Shaughnessy locate composition within the academy. Concludes that ethos is constructed on sites of conflict and struggle.

282. Rouse, Joy. "Rhetorics of Citizenship in Nineteenth-Century America." *DAI* 53 (January 1992): 2688–89A.

Finds that white women and African-Americans engaged in rhetorics of citizenship, while the universities transformed classical rhetoric into a study of form, taste, and correctness.

283. Rutter, Russell. "Review of *Writing in the Academic Disciplines, 1870–1990: A Curricular History* and *The Politics of Writing Instruction: Postsecondary*." *TCQ* 1 (Fall 1992): 58–65.

Reviews these two historical studies of writing instruction and curriculum while arguing for the need for historical studies of technical and professional writing programs, which share similar problems with writing across the curriculum programs.

284. Sanger, Kerran L. "The Rhetoric of the Freedom Songs in the American Civil Rights Movement." *DAI* 52 (February 1992): 2758A.

Concludes that freedom songs had the potential to enable activists to redefine the conceptions of blacks held by most whites.

285. Sauerbrey, Judith L. "My Letter to the World: Twentieth Century American Women and Their Diaries." *DAI* 52 (May 1992): 4118A.

Identifies major themes in eight twentieth-century American women's diaries in Part One; analyzes the diary of Anne Morrow Lindbergh in Part Two.

286. Skerpan, Elizabeth Penley. *The Rhetoric of Politics in the English Revolution, 1642–1660*. Columbia, MO: University of Missouri Press, 1992. 280 pages

Studies the relationship between discourse and ideology as revealed in petitions, speeches, and pamphlets from three stages of the English Revolution. Focuses on John Milton, John Foxe, and James Harrington.

287. Spaeth, Catherine Therese Christians. "Purgatory or Promised Land? French Emigrés in Philadelphia and Their Perception of America during the 1790s." *DAI* 53 (September 1992): 860A.

Uses diaries, memoirs, and letters to show how America was seen as a land of wonders, miracles, and social progress; shows that immigrants became quickly disenchanted.

288. Stewart, Donald C. "Cognitive Psychologists, Social Constructionists, and Three Nineteenth-Century Advocates of Authentic Voice." *JAC* 12 (Fall 1992): 279–90.

Locates three advocates (G. H. Lewes, T. H. Wright, and Fred Newton Scott) for an individual presence in writing within the very camps which promote its absence.

289. Stewart, Donald C. "Harvard's Influence on English Studies: Perceptions from Three Universities in the Early Twentieth Century." *CCC* 43 (December 1992): 455–71.

Investigates the influence of Harvard's composition program on other universities and on the MLA. Reports on the resistance to Harvard's influence.

290. Strom, Sharon Hartman. *Beyond the Typewriter: Gender, Class, and the Origins of Modern American Office Work, 1900–1930*. Urbana, IL: University of Illinois Press, 1992. 416 pages

Draws upon archival and anecdotal data to tell of the everyday lives of women officeworkers and to explore how the management and secondary vocational education affected those workplaces.

291. Tebeaux, Elizabeth, and Mary Lay. "Images of Women in Technical Books from the English Renaissance." *IEEE* 35 (December 1992): 196–207.

Points out that technical books from the English Renaissance show women as active and literate.

292. Thomas, Rosalind. *Literacy and Orality in Ancient Greece*. New York: Cambridge University Press, 1992. 201 pages

Discusses the history of rhetoric and writing in Greek language and culture in the context of recent theoretical debates about literacy and orality.

293. Tinkler, John F. "J. S. Mill as a Nineteenth-Century Humanist." *Rhetorica* 10 (Spring 1992): 165–91.

Argues that Mill's rhetorical commitments and his humanist social position help to explain his political liberalism.

294. Toth, Csaba. "The Transatlantic Dialogue: Nineteenth-Century American Utopianism and Europe." *DAI* 53 (September 1992): 860A.

Explores the extent to which nineteenth-century American utopian thought and practice influenced discourse and practices in Europe.

295. Tribby, Jay. "Body/Building: Living the Museum Life in Early Modern Europe." *Rhetorica* 10 (Spring 1992): 139–63.

Traces a cultural history of civility within the European court, with emphasis on rhetorical training and body building to develop social capacities.

296. Turbin, Carole. *Working Women of Collar City: Gender, Class and Community in Troy, 1864–86*. Urbana, IL: University of Illinois Press, 1992. 272 pages

Explores why some working women were successful at organizing in spite of obstacles to labor activity; how they were able to form alliances with male workers. Develops new perspectives on gender and demonstrates that women's family ties are not necessarily a conservative influence, but may encourage women's and men's collective actions.

297. Varnum, Robin. "The History of Composition: Reclaiming Our Lost Generations." *JAC* 12 (Winter 1992): 39–55.

Disputes the view (held by Berlin, Kitzhaber, and others) that the first five decades of the twentieth century were a rhetorical wasteland. Does not challenge current/traditional rhetoric.

298. Vonnegut, Kristin Sawin. "'If You Would Have Freedom, Strike for It': Sarah Moore Grimke's Struggle for the Rights of Woman." *DAI* 52 (March 1992): 3127A.

Presents an historical and rhetorical study of Grimke's speeches and writing.

299. Welch, Kathleen A. *Recovering the Work of Students and Teachers in Nineteenth-Century Composition Books*. Cincinnati, OH: CCCC, March 1992. ERIC ED 337 769. 12 pages

Examines two nineteenth-century composition textbook prefaces; finds that the strategies for writing are similar to those of contemporary composition teachers.

300. Wikoff, Katherine Hennessey. "The Problematics of Plagiarism." *DAI* 53 (November 1992): 1499A.

Traces the historical development of plagiarism and its current definition in the university.

301. Winkelmann, Carol L. "The Discourse of Conflict and Resistance: Elizabeth Cellier and the Seventeenth-Century Pamphlet Wars." *DAI* 53 (November 1992): 1531A.

Examines how pamphleteers exploited language to sustain social power and control over cultural text. Concludes with a treatment of the Meal-Tub Plot by commentators and historians. Proposes that a better understanding of Cellier's contributions has to be based on the text of her era.

302. Witek, Catherine A. "Samuel Johnson's Alchemy: Fusing Aristotelian Invention into Eighteenth-Century Rhetoric." *DAI* 53 (October 1992): 1169A.

Identifies Johnson's invention theory of rhetoric as an art rather than an intuitive or inspirational activity.

303. Wolin, Ross. "Kenneth Burke's Early Works: A Study in Permanence within Change." *DAI* 52 (January 1992): 2326A.

Argues that Burke suffers partial readings that miss his keen social and political interests; examines Burke's life and early works.

304. Wyatt-Brown, Anne. *From the Clinic to the Classroom: D. W. Winnecott, James Britton, and the Revolution in Writing Theory*. Cincinnati, OH: CCCC, March 1992. ERIC ED 347 567. 17 pages

Claims that Winnicott, through Britton, has influenced current thinking about collaborative classrooms.

305. Xiao, Xiaosui. "China Encounters Western Ideas (1895–1905): A Rhetorical Analysis of Yan Fu, Tan Sitong, and Liang Qichao." *DAI* 53 (November 1992): 1325A.

Uses Lloyd Bitzer's conception of the rhetorical situation to explore the ways that "foreign ideas" are introduced into culture.

See also 329

2.3 POLITICAL, RELIGIOUS, AND JUDICIAL RHETORIC

306. Aronowitz, Stanley. *The Politics of Identity: Class, Culture, Social Movements*. New York: Routledge, 1992. 288 pages

A former trade union activist, steelworker, and a current professor and academic administrator, Aronowitz argues that "economic identities are partially responsible for how, when, and where classes act in the social realm."

307. Belz, Herman. "Liberty and Equality for Whom? How to Think Inclusively about the Constitution and the Bill of Rights." *HT* 25 (May 1992): 263–77.

Examines recent criticisms and primary historical sources to defend an inclusive reading of the Constitution and the Bill of Rights.

308. Blanchard, Margaret A. *Revolutionary Sparks*. New York: Oxford University Press, 1992. 624 pages

Presents a discussion of freedom of speech ranging from questions of national security to those of public morality, from loyalty during times of national stress to the right to preach on a public street corner.

309. Bosmajian, Haig A. *Metaphor and Reason in Judicial Opinions*. Carbondale, IL: Southern Illinois University Press, 1992. 255 pages

Examines the role of metaphor, personification, and other forms of figurative language in judicial decisions.

310. Brasefield, Marleen JoAnn. "The Social Construction of Meaning: An Analysis of Women's Discourse." *DAI* 52 (April 1992): 3742A.

Investigates how everyday discourse shapes social and religious interpretations for women in positions of religious leadership.

311. Briscoe, P. Annette. "The Paths of Law and Rhetoric from Protagoras to Perelman: Case for a Jurisprudential Pedagogy of Argument." *DAI* 52 (June 1992): 4311A.

Points out that the current-traditionalist overattention to form constrains inquiry by ignoring social values and public opinion. Argues for a pedagogy that recognizes the mind's ability to create knowledge.

312. Buckrop, Jacquelyn Jo. "Homelessness in America: An Analysis of the Rhetorical Relationship between Legitimacy and Guilt." *DAI* 53 (November 1992): 1322A.

Uses a Burkean pentadic analysis to examine seven Congressional committee hearings.

313. Burgchardt, Carl R. *Robert M. La Follette, Sr.: The Voice of Conscience*. Great American Orators, no. 14. New York: Greenwood Press, 1992. 264 pages

Analyzes the major speeches of La Follette, an early twentieth-century governor of Wisconsin, United States senator, and political reformer.

314. Campbell, J. Louis III. "John Hampden Chamberlayne and the Rhetoric of Southern Histories." *SCJ* 58 (Fall 1992): 44–54.

Examines the rhetorics of monumental and critical history and their application in a post-Reconstruction South.

315. Cervetti, Nancy. "The Resurrection of Milly Barton: At the Nexus of Production,

Text, and Reproduction." *WS* 21 (1992): 339–59.

> Reads George Elliot's fiction anew through the lenses of female subjectivity and religion.

316. Courtright, Jeffrey Lee. " 'Tactics' and 'Trajectories': The Argumentative Resources of Supreme Court Dissenting Opinions." *DAI* 53 (July 1992): 17A.

> Uses a Toulminian analysis and the terminology of Michel de Certeau to examine 35 opinions from the 1980s.

317. DelFattore, Joan. *What Johnny Shouldn't Read: Textbook Censorship in America.* New Haven, CT: Yale University Press, 1992. 209 pages

> Discusses federal court cases in six states to describe how challenges to textbooks gather steam, leading publishers to practice self-censorship.

318. Earl, Elizabeth Noel. "A Comparison of Billy Graham and Jerry Falwell: Ministers and Their Presidents." *DAI* (February 1992): 2755A.

> Describes and examines examples of the religious rhetoric of Billy Graham during Nixon's presidency, and Jerry Falwell during Reagan's, to determine if politics influences religion.

319. Eisenberg, Anne. "Women and the Discourse of Science." *ScAm* 267 (July 1992): 122.

> Argues that scientific and technical journals exhibit sexual bias in their use of pronouns.

320. Elmes-Crahall, Jane Matilda. "Gender as Exigence: A Situational Analysis of the 1984 Vice-Presidential Campaign of Geraldine Ferraro." *DAI* 53 (August 1992): 347A

> Examines the relationships between gender and language abuse as well as the adequacy of Lloyd Bitzer's theory for women's campaign rhetoric.

321. Epps, Garrett. "Emperor Clothed." *QRD* 18 (July 1992): 1–2.

> Presents a reprint of an updated tale of the naked emperor that satirizes the roles of government and the press in delivering "whitewash" of truth.

322. Flexo, Scott W. "Strategies in Information Processing of Campaign Communications: The Mediation of Political Motivation and Cognitive Ability." *DAI* 52 (June 1992): 4457A.

> Studies the assumption that political experts demonstrate more complex information processing strategy than nonexperts.

323. Forbes, Ella. "African Resistance to Enslavement: The Nature and the Evidentiary Record." *JBS* 1 (September 1992): 39–59.

> Argues that narratives of enslaved and Eurocentric writers substantiate resistance to enslavement.

324. Friedman, Rachelle Elaine. "Writing the Wonders: Puritan Historians in Colonial New England." *DAI* 53 (March 1992): 3402A.

> Considers how Puritans used history-writing to define themselves, make sense of their experience, and set the terms for subsequent history-writing.

325. Gale, Frederic Gordon. "Rhetoric, Ideology, and the Possibility of Justice." *DAI* 53 (September 1992): 796A.

> Examines how the rhetoric of legal interpretive theories can disguise political or ideological purposes.

326. Gibson, Walker, and William Lutz. *Doublespeak: A Brief History, Definition, and Bibliography, with a List of Award Winners, 1974–1990.* NCTE Concept Paper Series, no. 2. Urbana, IL: NCTE, 1991. 46 pages

> The authors explain how to recognize and analyze doublespeak in public discourse; they name Doublespeak Award winners who have used language unethically, and Orwell Award winners who have used language clearly and honestly.

327. Gillmor, Donald M. *Power, Publicity, and the Abuse of Libel Law*. New York: Oxford University Press, 1992. 240 pages

>Draws on more than 600 libel suits in the 1980s to argue for reforms in United States libel law that safeguard freedom of speech and of the press while giving plaintiffs the opportunity to respond to charges through the media.

328. Helgerson, Richard. *Forms of Nationhood: The Elizabethan Writing of England*. Chicago: University of Chicago Press, 1992. 384 pages

>Explains the relation of poems, maps, law books, plays, ecclesiastical polemics, and narratives of overseas exploration to the making of the newly autonomous English state. Shows that, behind the rhetoric of national uniformity and wholeness, differences remain an element of modern English culture and have recurred in American and postcolonial nation-building.

329. Hyland, Paul, and Neil Sammells, eds. *Writing and Censorship in Britain*. New York: Routledge, 1992. 368 pages

>The contributors examine English censorship from Tudor times to the present by looking at familiar authors as well as less familiar figures, groups, and voices.
>*Essayists:* Barry, Peter; Booth, Alan; Brown, Richard; Clare, Janet; Goldstein, Robert J.; Grant, Damian; Hyland, Paul; Kerridge, Richard; Patterson, Annabel; Roberts, M. J. D.; Rolley, Katrina; Sabor, Peter; Sammells, Neil; Saunders, David; Smith, Adrian; White, Barbara; Winton, Calhoun.

330. Iltis, Robert S. "Textual Dynamics of 'The New South.'" *ComS* 43 (Spring 1992): 29–41.

>Presents a symbolic interpretation of the past based on Burke's observations of substance, tropes, and imagery.

331. Inch, Edward Spencer. "Clearer Than the Truth: NSC–68 and the Metaphoric Construction of World Visions." *DAI* 53 (September 1992): 663A.

>Explores the ways this "rhetorical blueprint for the Cold War" attempted to propagate a message of anti-communism.

332. Jamieson, Kathleen Hall. *Dirty Politics: Deception, Distraction, and Democracy*. New York: Oxford University Press, 1992. 335 pages

>Explores the history and techniques of negative campaigning in electoral politics. Topics include how campaign advertisements appropriate the language and formats of news media and how, in turn, news coverage is influenced by themes from negative campaigns.

333. Jensen, Richard J. *Clarence Darrow: The Creation of an American Myth*. Great American Orators, vol. 12. New York: Greenwood Press, 1992. 352 pages

>Traces the American lawyer's development as an orator. Provides texts of his important speeches and a complete speech chronology.

334. Jhappan, Carol Radha. "The Language of Empowerment: Symbolic Politics and Indian Political Discourse in Canada." *DAI* 52 (April 1992): 3711A.

>Argues that disadvantaged minorities seeking political voice first conduct politics at the symbolic level.

335. Jones, Kevin T. *"One More Time, Let Us Justify This War": An Analysis of President Bush's Declaration of Days of Thanksgiving*. Atlanta, GA: Speech Communication Association, November 1991. ERIC ED 344 273. 11 pages

>Analyzes President Bush's declaration of the "Days of Thanksgiving" as rhetorical justification for the Persian Gulf War.

336. Lang, Berel. *Writing and the Moral Self*. New York: Routledge, 1991. 160 pages

>Analyzes the relation between writing and ethics in politics, the university, daily so-

cial practice, and in the ethical structure of language itself.

337. La Russo, Dominic A. "The Rhetoric of Law in the Scottish Enlightenment." *DAI* 53 (September 1992): 664A.

Examines the way the new eighteenth-century rhetoric was developed and also how it was situated within the larger realm of moral philosophy.

338. Logue, Cal M. "Coping with Defeat Rhetorically: Sherman's March through Georgia." *SCJ* 58 (Fall 1992): 55–66.

Findings have implications for studying the rhetorical consequences in a variety of circumstances where people, organizations, and institutions encounter losses.

339. Lovitt, Carl R. "The Rhetoric of Murderers' Confessional Narratives: The Model of Pierre Reviere's Memoir." *JNT* 22 (Winter 1992): 23–34.

The article provides an examination of the rhetoric of criminal confessions.

340. Lowrey, Burling. " 'Deconstructionism' on Capitol Hill." *QRD* 18 (January 1992): 9–10.

Cites Clarence Thomas's confirmation hearings to argue that "deconstructionism" used in political discourse is more "insidious" than doublethink.

341. Lunengeld, Marvin. "What Shall We Tell the Children? The Press Encounters Columbus." *HT* 25 (February 1992): 137–44.

Argues that although right-wing reactions to a media reevaluation of Columbus has curtailed federal funding for academic research, teachers should present an accurate image of him.

342. Maltese, John Anthony. *Spin Control: The White House Office of Communications and the Management of Presidential News*. Chapel Hill, NC: University of North Carolina Press, 1992. 292 pages

Chronicles the development of the White House Office of Comunications and examines its role in molding people's perceptions of the modern American presidency.

343. McVicar, Ken E. "Political Communication and Verbal Foreign Policy Behavior: A Comparative Adaptation of Harold Lasswell's Concept of Values to Public Discourse in the European Economic Community, 1958–1968." *DAI* 52 (May 1992): 4087A.

Examines the semantic content of 515 public statements made by 31 Foreign Ministers, Presidents, and Heads of Government.

344. Mondak, Jeffery J. "Information Processing and Cognitive Efficiency: Source Cues and Public Opinion in American Politics." *DAI* 53 (March 1992): 3415A.

Argues for the prevalence and significance of heuristic processing of source cues in constructing well-grounded political judgments.

345. Morello, John T. "The 'Look' and Language of Clash: Visual Structuring of Argument in the 1988 Bush-Dukakis Debates." *SCJ* 57 (Spring 1992): 205–18.

Suggests that camera shots transmuted the process of argument in the debates.

346. Mountford, Roxanne Denise. "The Feminization of the *Ars Praedicandi*." *DAI* 53 (September 1992): 664A.

Presents an ethnographic study of three women ministers; argues that by defining their goal in terms of creation of the community, they break with traditional modes of preaching.

347. Mullen, Faith Elizabeth. "Ten Years of Hate: A Fantasy Theme Analysis of the White Supremacy Rhetoric of Robert E. Miles." *DAI* 52 (May 1992): 3768A.

Conducts a Fantasy Theme analysis of the white supremacy rhetoric of Aryan leader Robert E. Miles.

348. Murphy, John M. "Epideictic and Deliberative Strategies in Opposition to War: The

Paradox of Honor and Expediency." *ComS* 43 (Summer 1992): 65–78.

> Argues that like presidential discourse advocating military action, congressional dissent can be understood in terms of appeals to honor and expediency.

349. Murphy, John M. "Presidential Debates and Campaign Rhetoric: Text within Context." *SCJ* 57 (Spring 1992): 219–28.

> Argues that debates must be studied within the rhetorical context created by previous campaign discourse to fully understand their significance.

350. National Council for the Social Studies. "The Columbian Quincentenary: An Educational Opportunity." *HT* 25 (February 1992): 145–52.

> Outlines seven basic points about Columbus that teachers can use in the classroom.

351. Nicasio, Lino Evora. "The Rhetoric of Fulton J. Sheen: A Fantasy Theme Analysis of the Television Speeches on Russia and Communism." *DAI* 52 (March 1992): 3126A.

> Overviews Sheen's rhetorical training and analyzes the techniques manifested in televised speeches.

352. Nichols, M. Celeste. "The Rhetorical Structure of the Traditional Black Church." *DAI* 53 (August 1992): 483A.

> Investigates the misconceptions of the Black sermon tradition as illogical, emotional, and deviant; presents a unified structure and rhetorical models that give focus and new meaning to Black sermons.

353. Nimmo, Dan D., and James E. Combs. *The Political Pundits*. New York: Praeger Publishers, 1992. 224 pages

> Critiques the activities and influence of the small group of people who provide the bulk of political commentary for the news media. Argues that punditry produces symbolic rather than effective healing of political ills, political paternalism rather than political reflection, and in the end, public disenchantment with politics.

354. Okigbo, Charles. "Horserace and Issues in Nigerian Elections." *JBS* 3 (March 1992): 349–65.

> Uses play theory to study media coverage of Nigerian political campaigns.

355. Patton, Cynthia Kay. "Resistance without the 'Subject.' " *DAI* 53 (December 1992): 1712A.

> Looks at political resistance in the wake of critiques of the transcendental subject made by poststructuralist theorists.

356. Petersen, Debra Lynn. "President Corazon Aquino's Official Working Visit to the United States, September 15–23, 1986: A Case Study in Intercultural Rhetoric." *DAI* 52 (May 1992): 3768A.

> Presents a case study of problems faced by international cross-cultural political communicators; discusses the special concerns of female rhetors.

357. Pierce, John C. *Citizens, Political Communication, and Interest Groups: Environmental Organizations in Canada and the United States*. New York: Praeger Publishers, 1992. 256 pages

> Examines how interest groups shape the public's understanding of scientifically complex policy issues. Focuses on the problem of acid rain in Michigan and Ontario.

358. Reese, Carol McMichael. "The Politician and the City: Urban Form and City Beautiful Rhetoric in Progressive Era Denver." *DAI* 53 (October 1992): 969A.

> Examines Robert Speer's use of political and reform rhetoric to achieve environmental reform in early twentieth-century Denver.

359. Rice, Donald E. *The Rhetorical Uses of the Authorizing Figure: Fidel Castro and Jose Marti*. New York: Praeger Publishers, 1992. 163 pages

> Analyzes rhetorical uses of the authorizing figure during the Cuban revolution. Argues that this figure defines and unifies the

emerging revolutionary movement, contributes to the application of the sanctioning authority of the state, and legitimizes the revolutionary vision over time.

360. Riggs, Douglas Lee. "A Rhetorical-Critical Interpretation of the Divorce and Remarriage Passages in the Synoptic Gospels." *DAI* 52 (January 1992): 2589A.

   Concludes that a functional view of marriage was emphasized, and that the speaker's/writer's primary purpose was to deter divorce.

361. Ritter, Kurt K. W., and David Henry. *Ronald Reagan: The Great Communicator*. New York: Greenwood Press, 1992. 248 pages

   Presents a critical analysis of Ronald Reagan's style as a public speaker. Includes a chronology of his major speeches, reproduces a set of selected speeches, and provides a bibliography of primary and secondary sources.

362. Rojas, Gomez, and Claudia Fiorella. "Spiritualizing the Political: A Rhetorical Analysis of Oscar Arias' Discourse on Peace." *DAI* 53 (December 1992): 664A.

   Uses cluster criticism to explore the rhetorical structure, strategies, and philosophy that Arias uses to communicate his view of the world.

363. Ross, Susan. "A Rhetorical Analysis of the Writings of Women Prisoners: A Thematic Examination." *DAI* 53 (December 1992): 1726A.

   Studies the writings of life-sentenced prisoners to determine how this group uses discourse in response to its imprisonment.

364. Rosteck, Thomas. "Narrative in Martin Luther King's *I've Been to the Mountaintop*." *SCJ* 58 (Fall 1992): 22–32.

   Examines the rhetorical use of existing narrative as an inventional and argumentative strategy.

365. Shapiro, Michael J. *Reading the Postmodern Polity: Political Theory as Textual Practice*. American Culture, edited by Stanley Aronowitz, Nancy Fraser, and George Lipsitz. Minneapolis: University of Minnesota Press, 1992. 177 pages

   Asserts that political practices are inherently textual; reviews a variety of approaches to political theory, analysis, interpretation, and epistemological and theoretical issues.

366. Struening, Karen. "Gender and the Division between Public and Private in the Political Writings of Aristotle and Rousseau." *DAI* 52 (June 1992): 4462A.

   Argues that the distinctions male/female and public/private have been conflated.

367. Tarbox, James Jeffrey. "The Constitutive Function of Woodrow Wilson's Rhetoric, 1914 to 1917." *DAI* 53 (November 1992): 1324A.

   Analyzes 28 speeches to determine how Wilson united the public and obtained its support during his presidency.

368. Thomson, Elizabeth Lee. " 'The Woman's Bible': Heritage and Harbinger of Hope for Feminist Biblical Hermeneutics." *DAI* 52 (March 1992): 3455A.

   Describes the methods and agenda of Elizabeth Cady Stanton and her committee and applies their interpretative principles to two New Testament passages.

369. Trautman, Karl. "The Competition of Discourses and the Discourse of Competition: An Interpretation of Federal Antitrust Law; Historical Development and Selected Cases." *DAI* 53 (December 1992): 2094A.

   Shows how the concept of economic competition has changed over the last 120 years.

370. Twitchett, Denis Crispin. *The Writing of Official History under the T'ang*. New York: Cambridge University Press, 1992. 336 pages

   Describes the establishment in T'ang Dynasty China of a government organization designed to select, process, and edit material for inclusion in official histories.

371. Varg, Paul A. *Edward Everett: The Intellectual in the Turmoil of Politics*. Selinsgrove, PA: Susquehanna University Press, 1992. 256 pages

> Presents a biography of the nineteenth-century American orator and politician who served as a governor of Massachusetts, as president of Harvard Unversity, and as a United States Secretary of State.

372. Weiler, Michael, and W. Barnett Pearce, eds. *Reagan and Public Discourse in America*. Studies in Rhetoric and Communication, edited by Clark E. Culpepper, Raymie E. McKerrow, and David Zarefsky. Tuscaloosa, AL: University of Alabama Press, 1992. 320 pages

> Fifteen essays analyze Ronald Reagan's impact on public political discourse, linking his rhetorical strategies to his ability to acquire and maintain political power.
> *Essayists:* Auer, J. Jeffrey; Bass, Jeff D.; Blankenship, Jane; Branham, Robert J.; Burnier, DeLysa; Carter, Robin; Descutner, David; Goodnight, G. Thomas; Jasinski, James; Johnson, Deborah K.; Muir, Jannette Kenner; Palczewski, Catherine Hellen; Pearce, W. Barnett; Weiler, Michael; Young, Marilyn J.

373. Weitzel, Al R. "A Pedagogical Treatment of King's 'I Have a Dream' Speech: Toward Incorporating Orality in Rhetorical Criticism." San Diego State University, San Diego, CA, 1991. ERIC ED 344 248. 47 pages

> Discusses how Martin Luther King, Jr.'s speech demonstrates fundamental principles of rhetoric and how it can be used to teach rhetorical criticism.

374. Zagacki, Kenneth S. "Rhetoric, Failures, and the Presidency: The Case of Vietnam." *ComS* 43 (Spring 1992): 42–55.

> Locates the constraints upon presidential discourse about failure within the culture and within the institution of the Presidency.

2.4 COMPUTER AND LITERACY STUDIES

375. Amato, Joe. "Science-Literature Inquiry as Pedagogical Practice: Technical Writing, Hypertext, and a Few Theories, Part I." *C&C* 9 (April 1992): 41–54.

> Argues for the expressive within the scientific/technical; uses Serres' work to illustrate interconnections between literature and science.

376. Amato, Joe. "Science-Literature Inquiry as Pedagogical Practice: Technical Writing, Hypertext, and a Few Theories, Part II." *C&C* 9 (April 1992): 55–70.

> Argues that hypertexts should allow readers to alter connections; otherwise, hypertextual worlds—despite their flexibility—can be perceived as fixed bodies of knowledge.

377. Amdahl, Mark. "Aspects 1.0." *C&C* 10 (November 1992): 89–91.

> Describes *Aspects*, a program that supports collaboration over a network. Notes that the program includes a chat box as well as multiple cursors.

378. Annas, Camille, Caroline Connet, and Mary Elizabeth Staiger. "Journals." *CACJ* 6 (Summer 1992): 2–26.

> Presents a continuation of Sharon Morissey's study on the positive impact of computer technology on writing abilities of college students.

379. Arnold, Jack David. "Marshall McLuhan: Technologizing the Word." *CACJ* 6 (Summer 1991): 1–5.

> Suggests that McLuhan's thoughts on technology's effect on education should be "required reading" for all those in higher education, particularly those in computer-aided writing courses.

380. Bagley, Carole, and Barbara Hunter. "Restructuring, Constructivism and Technology:

Forging a New Relationship." *EdTech* 32 (July 1992): 22–27.

Attempts to negotiate and locate an educational agenda between all three.

381. Blattner, Meera M. "Messages, Models, and Media." *MR* 3 (Fall 1992): 15–21.

Makes the argument that multimedia is a genuine shift of paradigm ultimately changing the way we think and work.

382. Blomeyer, Robert L., Jr., and C. Dianne Martin, eds. *Case Studies of Computer Aided Learning*. Bristol, PA: Falmer Press, 1991. 270 pages

The papers examine the place of computers in school and present case studies on the introduction, diffusion, and uneven adoption of a highly popular, and costly, educational innovation.
Essayists: Beynon, John.; Blomeyer, Robert L., Jr.; Martin, C. Dianne; McLaughlin, Daniel; Pohland, Paul A.; Rist, Ray; Smith, Louis M; Stake, Bernadine Evans; Strudler, Neal.

383. Bolter, Jay David. "Locus: A Computer Program for Topographical Writing." *CACJ* 6 (Winter 1992): 15–20.

Suggests that *Locus* software will convince composition instructors and students that hypertext is appropriate for their writing needs.

384. Borgmann, Albert. *Crossing the Postmodern Divide*. Chicago: University of Chicago Press, 1992. 184 pages

Argues that people begin to reorder their social world with a flexible organization of work, with enabling technologies of the personal computer, and with a return to small-scale communities.

385. Bown, Lalage. "Preparing the Future-Women, Literacy and Development: The Impact of Female Literacy on Human Development and the Participation of Literate Women in Change (Development Report Number 4)." ActionAid, Chard, England, 1990. ERIC ED 340 881. 59 pages

Reports on 43 project case studies and a country case study (Nepal), examining the impact of adult women's literacy in developing countries.

386. Boyle, Craig, and Kelly Ratliff. "A Survey and Classification of Hypertext Documentation Systems." *IEEE* 35 (June 1992): 98–111.

Describes and classifies existing hypertext documentation systems.

387. Brockmann, John. "Review of *Computers and Writing, Perspectives on Software Documentations: Inquiries and Innovation*, and *Writing Space: The Computer, Hypertext, and the History of Writing*." *TCQ* 1 (Fall 1992): 77–82.

Asks if the research imagination is played out at the nexus of writing and computers.

388. Brown, Lady Falls. "The *Daedalus Integrated Writing Environment*." *C&C* 10 (November 1992): 77–88.

Describes ways of using various components of the *Daedalus Integrated Writing Environment*. Focuses on features that support collaborative learning.

389. Brown, R. A. "Literacy Assessments in Polyscriptal Societies: Chinese Character Literacy in Korea and Japan." *VLang* 25 (Fall 1991): 18–39.

Argues that literacy in countries such as Japan and Korea is always multiplicitous and variable. Points out that different "literacies" entail different social cognitive consequences.

390. Cazden, Courtney B. *Whole Language Plus: Essays on Literacy in the United States and New Zealand*. New York: Teachers College Press, 1992. 328 pages

Argues that people who learn to read and write need deliberate help to focus on specific features of written language. Points out that learners need to understand cultural and situational contexts of written language forms.

391. Clewell, Suzanne, ed. *Literacy: Issues and Practices*. 1991 Yearbook of the State of Maryland International Reading Association Council, Volume 8, 1991. ERIC ED 339 007. 80 pages

> Provides nine articles and two book reviews on literacy. Topics include reading assessment, computer peer mentoring, teacher as writing model, comprehension problems, and captioned video technology. *Essayists:* Afflerbach, Peter; Huagh, Jane; Dreher, Mariam Jean; Hanus, Karen; Sulentic, Margaret Mary; Koskinen, Patricia; Clark, Anne; Pirkle, James; Clewell, Suzanne; Kusterer, Faith; Almasi, Janice; Winograd, Peter.

392. Condon, William. "Selecting Computer Software for Writing Instruction: Some Considerations." *C&C* 10 (November 1992): 53–56.

> Offers criteria for the evaluation of software: purpose, versatility, and ease of use. Suggests that teachers consider using *Hypercard* to create their own software.

393. Coulliard, Ted V. "The Academic Recession: Word Processing Can Be Learned in Two Hours; Yet Many Still Want No Part of It." *CACJ* 6 (Summer 1991): 6–7.

> Discusses possible reasons why "time-pressed scholars" resist learning the time-saving skills of word processing.

394. Cox, Gary N. *Orality and Literacy—The Real Difference: A Historical Perspective*. Cincinnati, OH: CCCC, March 1992. ERIC ED 346 472. 10 pages

> Reexamines the Western views of orality and literacy, using historical evidence and reinterpretations of historical evidence.

395. Curtis, Marcia, and Charles Moran. "Userhome, Sweet Userhome: A Review of Novell's *NETWARE*." *C&C* 10 (November 1992): 63–75.

> The authors describe the components of *NETWARE* by detailing how faculty have been able to customize it for their own needs.

396. Delamaramo, Mark James. "Microcomputers and the Writing Process: A Survey and Critique." *DAI* 52 (May 1992): 3845A.

> Provides a discussion and critique of the place and practicality of the computer in the modern college classroom.

397. Dorner, Jane. "Virtual English." *EnT* 8 (October 1992): 29–34.

> Describes and evaluates aids for writers currently available as computer software packages.

398. Dorwick, Keith. "SEEN: Tutorials for Critical Reading." *C&C* 10 (November 1992): 101–7.

> Reviews the critical reading features of SEEN and praises the features which allow an instructor to carry on a written dialogue with students.

399. D'Souza, Patricia Veasey. "Electronic Mail in Academic Settings: A Multipurpose Communications Tool." *EdTech* 32 (March 1992): 22–25.

> Delineates costs and benefits of e-mail use in the academe. Argues that space and time constraints of conventional communication instruction are erased.

400. Duin, Ann Hill, and Kathleen S. Gorak. "Developing Texts for Computers and Composition: A Collaborative Process." *C&C* 9 (April 1992): 17–40.

> Describes the authors' collaboration on a textbook which integrates word processing and the teaching of writing and suggests that computer/content area documents require new publication practices.

401. Dyson, Anne Haas, and Sarah Warshauer Freedman. "Critical Challenges for Research on Writing and Literacy: 1990–1995." Center for the Study of Writing, Berkeley, CA, 1991. ERIC ED 335 676. 45 pages

Develops a research agenda for the Center for the Study of Writing; includes principles of assessment and instruction.

402. Edelsky, Carole. *With Literacy and Justice for All: Rethinking the Social in Language and Education*. Bristol, PA: Falmer Press, 1991. 200 pages

Presents research-based analyses of educational and research practices with an eye toward both criticism and alternate possibilities. Shows research on the language strengths of minority children. Focuses on whole language and emphasizes theoretical assumptions, possibilities, and limitiations.

403. Eiler, Mary Ann. "Perspectives on Software." *C&C* 10 (November 1992): 59–61.

Based on her experience in industry, Eiler suggests that "language learning rather than technology" should direct software use; notes that software should support curricular goals.

404. Enzenberger, Hans M. *Mediocrity and Delusion*. Translated by Martin Chalmers. London: Verso, 1991. 180 pages

The book is divided into two parts: the first claims that Western culture now deliberately produces a citizen who is a "secondary illiterate"; and the second argues that German civilization and culture "displays a diversity unimaginable thirty years ago."

405. Evans, Richard Allen. "Toward an Understanding of Literacy as Communicative Competence: Patterns of Literate Language Learning and Use." *DAI* 52 (March 1992): 3261A.

Describes a new model for analyzing literacy and literate activities.

406. Fagan, William T. "Literacy: The Crisis Mentality." *ELQ* 13 (October 1992): 7–9.

Examines the conception and promotion of illiteracy as a crisis in Canada, and looks at literacy within a socioeconomic, political, and cultural context.

407. Feldman, Tony. "Human Pespectives in Multimedia." *MR* 3 (Spring 1992): 56–61.

Documents that the essence of multimedia has less to do with electronic engineering and more with human values.

408. Fingeret, Hanna Arlene. *Literacy in the U.S.A.: The Present Issues*. Hamburg, Germany: Future of Literacy and the Literacy of the Future Conference, December 1991. ERIC ED 340 924. 11 pages

Identifies six issues in literacy research and practice; notes the need to develop organizing principles and to empower local efforts.

409. Fischer, Gerhard, Johntan Grudin, Andreas Lemke, Raymond McCall, Jonathan Ostwald, Brent Reeves, and Frank Shipman. "Supporting Indirect Collaborative Design with Integrated Knowledge-Based Design Environments." *HCI* 7 (Summer 1992): 281–314.

Presents a conceptual framework and a demonstration system for long-term, indirect communication needs of project teams.

410. Flammia, Madelyn. "A Desktop Publishing Course: An Alternative to Internships for Rural Universities." *TCQ* 1 (Fall 1992): 43–57.

Describes a desktop publishing program replacing internships which are not available in a rural area. Benefits included hands-on experience for students, free services, and public relations for the university.

411. Fortune, Ron. "*Toolbook*: A Hypermedia Authoring Program" *C&C* 10 (November 1992): 117–25.

Reviews *Toolbook* and notes that the designer must recognize that if readers use the run-time version of hypertext, they cannot alter the stacks.

412. Fox, Thomas. "Repositioning the Profession: Teaching Writing to African-American Students." *JAC* 12 (Fall 1992): 291–304.

Urges a reconception of African-American literacy and writing pedagogy which will reverse the exclusion of African-Americans from higher education.

413. French, Martha Stone. "A Comparison of the Effects of Word Processing on the Writing Performance and Attitudes of Adult and Traditional College Students in a Developmental Writing Program." *DAI* 52 (February 1992): 2804A.

Addresses the effects of using word processing on writing performance and attitudes of adult and traditional-age college developmental writing students.

414. Furniss, Elaine, and Pamela Green, eds. *The Literacy Agenda: Issues for the Nineties*. Portsmouth, NH: Heinemann, 1991. 175 pages

Discusses the effect of current theories of literacy development when put into practice.
Essayists: Allen, C.; Atkinson, N.; Dilena, M.; Dufficy, P.; Furniss, Elaine; Green, Pamela; Gummer, P.; Kale, J.; Leaker, J.; Lowe, K.; Luke, A.; Mooney, M.; Poulton, M.; Rhedding-Jones, J.; Toomey, D.; Walters, J.

415. Gelb, Richard G. *Literacy as Magic: The Role of Oral and Written Texts in the Santeria Religious Community*. Cincinnati, OH: CCCC, March 1992. ERIC ED 346 429. 11 pages

Presents a case study of Juanita (a senteria/businesswoman) using oral and written texts in religious activities and business transactions.

416. Gibson, Carolyn M. "A Study of the Integration of Computers into the Writing Process of First-Year College Composition Students." *DAI* 53 (August 1992): 472A.

Suggests that although students master the basics of word processing, they bring paper and pen habits to the computer lab.

417. Glushko, Robert J. "Seven Ways to Make a Hypertext Project Fail." *TC* 39 (May 1992): 226–30.

Argues that educators who use hypertext must be aware of its limitations.

418. Gordon, Sallie, and Vicki Lewis. "Enhancing Hypertext Documents to Support Learning from Text." *TC* 39 (May 1992): 305–8.

Researches Hypertext navigation problems; argues that if readers traverse an entire document, hypertext is not a good substitute for traditional text.

419. Gowen, Sheryl Greenwood. *The Politics of Workplace Literacy: A Case Study*. Language and Literacy Series, edited by Dorothy S. Strickland and Celia Genishi. New York: Teachers College Press, 1992. 149 pages

A case study of a nine-month workplace literacy program in a Southern hospital illustrates the roles classism, racism, and sexism play in the workplace environment.

420. Grandgenett, Neal, Ray Ziebarth, Jeff Koneck, Mary L. Farnham, Jodi McQuillan, and Becky Larson. "An Investigation of the Anticipated Use of Multimedia by Preservice Teachers." *JEdM&H* 1 (Winter 1992): 91–101.

The researchers find significant statistical relationships for learning style, gender, and certification category, but not for computer anxiety and equipment familiarity.

421. Griggs, Kenneth A. "Visual Agents That Model Organizations." *JOC* 2 (Spring 1992): 203–24.

Explores the extension of icons to a prototype implementation that uses object-oriented programming.

422. Gurak, Laura J. "Toward Consistency in Visual Information: Standardized Icons Based on Task." *TC* 39 (February 1992): 33–37.

Surveys research on icons (symbols appearing on computer displays to represent tasks or objects); shows that standardization does not exist.

423. Halio, Marcia Peoples. "The Student Edition of Workbench." *CHum* 26 (February 1992): 79–80.

Reviews this writing software, which helps students practice prewriting, outlining, drafting, revising, and editing.

424. Handel, Ruth D. "The Partnership for Family Reading, a Collaboration of Montclair State and Newark Public Schools: Guide to Replication." Montclair State College, Upper Montclair, NJ, 1991. ERIC ED 341 744. 57 pages

    Recounts a university/public school system partnership for literacy, designed as a guide for replication.

425. Haney, Steve, Molly Hepler, Doug Short, Kim Richardson, Hugh Burns, Dimitri Korhanis, Cynthia Selfe, Gail Hawisher, and Paul LeBlanc. "Forum: A Conversation about Software, Technology, and Composition Studies." *C&C* 10 (November 1992): 151–68.

    Includes a conversation with editors, publishers, and panelists who have developed their own academic software.

426. Harkin, Patricia, and James Sosnoski. "The Case for Hyper-Gradesheets: A Modest Proposal." *CE* 54 (January 1992): 22–30.

    Outlines in the spirit of Jonathan Swift that the grading practice can be made transparent through hypertextual gradesheet systems that reduce performance invisibility and rely on calibration.

427. Harris, Elizabeth Ann. "The Relationship of Attitudes and Writing Abilities to Computer Writing and Peer Critique Writing." *DAI* 53 (December 1992): 1828A.

    Points out that teachers conveyed a new commitment to the teaching of writing as they observed that students began to see themselves as writers.

428. Hawisher, Gail, and Paul LeBlanc, eds. *Re-Imagining Computers and Composition: Teaching and Research in the Virtual Age.* Portsmouth, NH: Boynton/Cook, 1992. 240 pages

    Twelve essays discuss the theoretical and practical implications of society's shift to electronic technology for communication, with particular focus on what this means for instruction and research in composition studies.
    Essayists: Burns, H.; Corbett, Edward P. J.; Curtis, M.; Eldred, J. Carey; Fortune, R.; Hawisher, G. E.; Kaufer, D. S.; Klem, E.; LeBlanc, P.; Neuwirth, C. M.; Moran, C.; Selfe, C. L.; Selfe, R. J.; Sommers, E.; Taylor, P.; Wright, W. W.

429. Hedden, Chet. "Hypertext and Collaboration: Observation on Edward Barrett's Philosophy." *TCQ* 1 (Fall 1992): 27–41.

    Explores some of the premises of Edward Barrett's arguments, especially in relation to the debate between "authorial imperative" in highly structured discourse and open-ended, conversational writing which allows collaboration and creation of reality.

430. Hepler, Molly. "Things to Consider When Evaluating Software." *C&C* 10 (November 1992): 57–61.

    Provides guidelines for software selection: look around, select software before hardware, and plan for support and training.

431. Hesse, Doug. "Analysis, File Sharing, and Freestanding Computers: An 'Exigential' Sequence." *C&C* 9 (April 1992): 87–94.

    Describes a set of assignments on the same topic, designed by the author to stimulate collaborative writing and critical thinking.

432. Hockey, Susan. "Some Perspectives on Teaching Computers and the Humanities." *CHum* 26 (August 1992): 261–66.

    Discusses how computers can enhance humanities instruction, including critical thinking and writing, and how faculty should be trained to use computers to improve their teaching.

433. Hollingsworth, Sarah, and Margaret A. Gallego. "Redefining School Literacy: Teachers' Evolving Perceptions (Research Series Number 210)." Michigan State University, Institute for Research on Teaching, East Lansing, MI, 1991. ERIC ED 341 691. 24 pages

Describes a middle school/university collaboration across the disciplines, exploring the "multiple literacies" of students and teachers.

434. Hon, David. "Butcher, Baker, Candlestick Maker: Skills Required for Effective Multimedia Development." *EdTech* 32 (May 1992): 14–19.

Explores business, artistic, and technical skills required to succeed in multimedia projects.

435. Hudspeth, LeLayne. "Just-in-Time Education." *EdTech* 32 (June 1992): 7–11.

Reviews requirements for effective educational computer software such as critical thinking, immediate feedback, supervision, and update possibilities.

436. Huenecke, Dorothy. "Educational Technology Research Section: An Artistic Criticism of a Computer-Based Reading Program." *EdTech* 32 (July 1992): 53–57.

Ethnography of this writing-to-read program reveals time and balance constraints; suggests broader teacher education as answer.

437. Hull, Glynda. "Hearing Other Voices: A Critical Assessment of Popular Views on Literacy and Work." National Center for Research in Vocational Educational Materials Distribution Service, Macomb, IL, November 1991. ERIC ED 338 865. 47 pages

Discusses cognitive and historical research on literacy in light of changing demographics; reassesses the effects of illiteracy, workers' perspectives on literacy, and workplace needs.

438. Hunter, John O. "Technological Literacy: Defining a New Concept for General Education." *EdTech* 32 (March 1992): 26–29.

Explores the perceived and actual relationship between science and technology in terms of community.

439. Hur, Young. "Effects of Communication Media on Human-Computer and Human-to-Human Interactions in Distant Group Decision-Making." *DAI* 53 (December 1992): 2004A.

Shows that groups in telephone communication have more centralized communication with each other and recalculated potential decisions more times than groups in written communication.

440. Irizarry, Estelle. "Courseware in the Humanities: Expanded Horizons." *CHum* 26 (August 1992): 275–84.

Presents a nontechnical overview of educational computing to encourage classroom teachers to use the technology as an instructional tool.

441. Irizarry, Estelle. "Writing Aids for Term Papers: Notebook II Plus." *CHum* 26 (February 1992): 74–76.

Reviews this writing software which helps students compile a bibliography, take notes from sources, and organize a research paper.

442. Johnson, Eric. "PowerEdit." *CHum* 26 (August 1992): 309–11.

Reviews this grammar and style checker which identifies a variety of student errors and which suggests revisions.

443. Johnson, Robert Ralph. "Rhetoric and Use: Toward a Theory of User-Centered Computer Documentation." *DAI* 53 (July 1992): 135A.

Investigates the nature of user-centered print and online documentation; draws from the disciplines of rhetoric to argue that print and online user documents are part of a situationally constrained discourse complex.

444. Johnson-Eilola, Johndan. "Structure and Text: *Writing Space* and *StorySpace*." *C&C* 9 (April 1992): 95–131.

The author includes in his review essay a critical reflection on hypertext in general as well as a review of two books on hypertext.

445. Joyce, Michael. "New Teaching: Toward a Pedagogy for a New Cosmology." *C&C* 9 (April 1992): 7–16.

   Argues that technological classrooms require that teachers reexamine and reshape their teaching; proposes that teachers view the classroom as a constantly changing network.

446. Kahn, Russell L. "Technical Communicators and the National Research and Education Network—Opportunity Knocks." *TC* 39 (February 1992): 14–21.

   Describes NREN, a government-supported computer network that will allow expanded research opportunities for technical writers.

447. Katz, Yaacov J. "Toward a Profile of a Successful Computer-Using Teacher." *EdTech* 32 (February 1992): 39–41.

   Details the necessary behavior of teachers who use computers to improve instructional techniques and student response.

448. Kemp, Fred. "Who Programmed This? Examining the Instructional Attitudes of Writing-Support Software." *C&C* 10 (November 1992): 9–24.

   Maintains that the ideology of the programmer is revealed in the software; notes that instructors need a command of writing instruction to teach effectively with software programs.

449. Kiefer, Kate. "Should Basic Writers Use Text Analysis Software?" *CollM* 10 (November 1992): 204–8.

   Finds that students' positive attitudes toward text-analysis software do not correlate with increased skills or achievement. Uses a 1982–83 study as basis for her argument.

450. Kirk, David. "Gender Issues in Information Technology as Found in Schools: Authentic/Synthetic/Fantastic?" *EdTech* 32 (April 1992): 28–31.

   Traces socialization differences between genders in terms of comfort with advanced technology; finds much speculation in research but little conclusive evidence.

451. Klonoski, Edward. "Recycled Writing: The Macro Function of Word Processing." *CollM* 10 (February 1992): 20–22.

   Describes writing prompts that cause students to "recycle" text in a variety of formats.

452. Knotts, Lester William. *Personal Literacy Experience*. Boston, MA: CCCC, March 1991. ERIC ED 336 747. 11 pages

   Argues that literacy is inextricably linked to the social context in which it is taught and used.

453. Lamazares, Ivonne Mercedes. "The Effects of Computer-Assisted Instruction on the Written Performance and Writing Anxiety of Community College Developmental Students." *DAI* 53 (September 1992): 703A.

   Argues that statistical analysis found no significant differences in written performance; points out that analytical scores favored computer-assisted writing.

454. Landow, George P. *Hypertext: The Convergence of Contemporary Critical Theory*. Baltimore, MD: Johns Hopkins University Press, 1992. 240 pages

   Discusses the effects of advanced computer technology on reading, writing, publication, and scholarship. Shows how certain forms of electronic text demonstrate major conceptual points in contemporary literary and semiological theory.

455. Latta, John N. "A New Periscope." *MR* 3 (Spring 1992): 41–47.

   Documents that visualization is a new periscope for understanding data while seeking information on the world around us.

456. Lea, Martin, and Russell Spears. "Paralanguage and Social Perception in Computer-Mediated Communication." *JOC* 2 (Fall 1992): 321–41.

   Results suggest that the meaning of paralinguistic marks is dependent on the group or individual context that is preestablished for the communication.

457. LeBlanc, Paul. "Choosing Software: What's Available and How to Evaluate It." *C&C* 10 (November 1992): 3–7.

Explains that the current issue of *Computers and Composition* focuses on software because little attention has been given to it since the publication of the NCTE software evaluator guidelines.

458. Lewis, Michael. "Situated Visualization: Building Interfaces from the Mind Up." *MR* 3 (Spring 1992): 23–40.

Documents a metamorphosis in our relation to computers, maintaining that a new paradigm will be distinguished by a shift toward a cognitive symbiosis with machinery.

459. Linton, David. "The Making of a Pariah: The Case of the Luddites." *ETC* 48 (Winter 1991/1992): 404–13.

Reviews the history of the term Luddite and clarifies its meaning. Concludes that a Luddite is a person who challenges the uncritical acceptance of new technologies.

460. Litchfield, Brenda C., and John V. Dempsey. "The IVD-Equipped Classroom: Integrating Videodisc Technology into the Curricula." *JEdM&H* 1 (Winter 1992): 39–49.

Addresses basic considerations regarding the selection of videodisc programs and provides a checklist of main activities to be completed before, during, and after integrating videodisc technology.

461. LoNano, Mari. "Computerized Collaboration in Technical/Professional Composition." *CACJ* 6 (Winter 1992): 30–32.

Discusses the importance of integrating "computerized collaboration" into composition and technical/professional composition courses in order to prepare students for the professional world.

462. Luke, Allan. *Reading and Critical Literacy: Redefining the "Great Debate."* Wellington, New Zealand: New Zealand Conference on Reading, May 1992. ERIC ED 345 211. 22 pages

Uses historical and cross-cultural examples to define a critical social literacy for postmodern culture.

463. Mabrito, Mark. "Real-Time Computer Network Collaboration: Case Studies of Business Writing Students." *JBTC* 6 (July 1992): 316–36.

Compares face-to-face and computer-mediated collaboration in the business writing classroom.

464. Macdonald, Gina. "Computer Enhancement of Grammar Study for the English as a Second Language Student." *CollM* 10 (August 1992): 183–92.

Argues that ESL students find grammar study more effective and enjoyable on-line.

465. Maddux, Clebourne D. "User Developed Computer-Assisted Instructions: Alternatives in Authoring Software." *EdTech* 32 (April 1992): 7–14.

Advises educators of pros and cons to create their own software.

466. Marquez, Candida Colon. "The Effects of Microcomputer Word Processing on the Business Writing Communication Skills of College Secretarial Students." *DAI* 52 (April 1992): 3548A.

Shows that while post-tests indicated no improvement in writing quality, there was an "increase in the students' self-esteem" when they learned to use word processing programs.

467. Marsden, James D. "Teaching Desktop Publishing at a Business College: Lessons from One Experience." *JBTC* 6 (October 1992): 467–79.

Describes a Desktop Publishing course, with guidelines on assignments as well as hardware, software, and textbooks.

468. Maule, R. William. "Online Multimedia for Education." *JEdM&H* 1 (Spring 1992): 169–77.

2.4 COMPUTER AND LITERACY STUDIES

Presents a network-based computer communications system that delivers educational information organized as reference, instructional, or communications and classified as static, dynamic, or modular.

469. Mayer, Kenneth R., and Sandra J. Nelson. "Design Options for a Desktop Publishing Course." *JBTC* 6 (October 1992): 458–66.

Describes an undergraduate course, including objectives, methodologies, assignments, evaluation techniques, and course outline.

470. McAfee, Christine O'Leary. "Cognitive Readability and Desktop Publishing." *CACJ* 6 (Winter 1992): 33–36.

Applies cognitive readability theories to decoding/encoding functions of computers and discusses these functions in terms of the presentation of visual information.

471. McGhee, W. P. T., and T. F. McLaughlin. "The Effect of a Computer Tutorial of At-Risk High School Students." *EdTech* 32 (January 1992): 50–54.

Focuses primarily on computer software skills; suggests that such skills advance computer literacy text creation skills.

472. McLaughlin, Daniel. *When Literacy Empowers: Navajo Language in Print*. Albuquerque, NM: University of New Mexico Press, 1992. 216 pages

Examines the increased acceptance of written Navajo, originally regarded as an imposition of white schools and churches. Shows how written language has been used both to maintain traditional culture and to "indigenize" Anglo institutions.

473. McLeod, Poppy L. "An Assessment of the Experimental Literature on Electronic Support of Group Work: Results of a Meta-Analysis." *HCI* 7 (Summer 1992): 257–80.

Examines electronic group support systems and finds that such systems increase decision quality, time needed to reach decisions, equality of participation, and degree of task focus.

474. McMillan, Katie, and Margaret Honey. "Laptops: Supporting the Learning Process." *M&M* 29 (September–October 1992): 72–73.

Presents a chart comparing features of six popular laptops and describes a writing project using laptop computers.

475. Meek, Margaret. *On Being Literate*. Portsmouth, NH: Heinemann, 1992. 276 pages

Points out that parents need to help their children to learn the literacies they will need in a society that considers the word processor as a symbol of modern literacy.

476. Mirel, Barbara. "Review of *Literacy as Involvement: The Acts of Writers and Readers and Texts* and *Dialogue, Dialectic, and Conversation: A Social Perspective on the Function of Writing*." *TCQ* 1 (Summer 1992): 95–99.

Argues that social constructionist writing theorists should address not only tensions between theory and practice, but also everyday realities in writing classes.

477. Mitch, David Franklin. *The Rise of Popular Literacy in Victorian England: The Influence of Private Choice and Public Policy*. Philadelphia, PA: University of Pennsylvania Press, 1992. 340 pages

Compares the relative importance of government policy and popular demand in the development of mass education in England.

478. Morissey, Sharon. "A Field Study of Computer-Assisted Composition in the North Carolina Community College System: Results." *CACJ* 6 (Spring 1992): 42–65.

Reports on the positive impact of computer technology on the writing ability of college students.

479. Morrison, James L. "The Computer Conference: Adaptive Problem-Solving within a Spontaneous Technological Framework." *EdTech* 32 (December 1992): 42–92.

Researches computer-shared problem solving between law students; concludes that computer-conferencing aids argumentation and negotiation skills.

480. Mortensen, Peter L. *Literacy and Regional Differences: Problems with the Invention of Appalachia*. Cincinnati, OH: CCCC, March 1992. ERIC ED 346 428. 19 pages

Argues that discourse on Appalachia, a creation of the urban imagination, reveals more about urban preoccupation than about social conditions in the mountains.

481. Mulvihill, Peggy. "*StorySpace*: A Deep and Welcomed Emptiness." *C&C* 10 (November 1992): 127–34.

Reviews *StorySpace* and describes her experience learning how to use the program. Suggests that it may be more useful for writing than for reading.

482. Nagarkatte, Umesh P., and Shailaja U. Nagarkatte. "Hypertext and Its Use in Developing Tutorials." *JEdM&H* 1 (Fall 1992): 481–93.

Provides step-by-step help on creating features like unlimited branching, ease of navigation, and prescriptive analysis of performance.

483. NCTE Instructional Technology Committee. "NCTE Guidelines for Review and Evaluation of English Language Art Software." *C&C* 10 (November 1992): 37–44.

Presents a set of guidelines from the early eighties to prompt readers' reactions.

484. Nelson, Wayne A., and David B. Palumbo. "Learning, Instruction, and Hypermedia." *JEdM&H* 1 (Summer 1992): 287–99.

Examines the psychological basis of hypermedia as a medium for learning, surveys characteristics of systems, and suggests ways to make hypermedia more valuable instructional environments.

485. Norton, Priscilla. "When Technology Meets the Subject-Matter Disciplines in Education, Part 1: Exploring the Computer as Metaphor." *EdTech* 32 (June 1992): 38–46.

Presents the first part of a three part series that begins by examining how computers change relationships between the humanities, hard sciences, and social sciences in terms of metaphor for literacy definitions.

486. Norton, Priscilla. "When Technology Meets the Subject-Matter Disciplines in Education, Part 2: Understanding the Computer as Discourse." *EdTech* 32 (July 1992): 36–46.

Explores discourse (the computer) as social reality by using McLuhan's theory that "the medium is the message."

487. Norton, Priscilla. "When Technology Meets the Subject-Matter Disciplines in Education, Part 3: Incorporating the Computer as Method." *EdTech* 32 (August 1992): 35–44.

The final installment brings metaphor and discourse to practice in a "nuts-and-bolts" implementation of computer writing and learning.

488. Novek, Eleanor M. "Read It and Weep: How Metaphor Limits Views of Literacy." *D&S* 3 (April 1992): 219–33.

Argues that literacy is identified as a personal attribute rather than a social construction. Points out that literacy metaphors commonly used in public and scholarly discourse obscure the economic, social, and political factors that constrain people from learning how to read and write.

489. O'Donoghue, Rosemary. "Entering Electronic Reality." *WLN* 17 (October 1992): 6.

After being "tutored" by a computer guru, the author realizes that "hearing" how to do something doesn't insure the ability to do it.

490. O'Neal, Betty. "Technological Solutions for Individuals with Disabilities." *M&M* 29 (September–October 1992): 34–35.

Describes computer hardware and software that enable individuals with disabilities to compose independently.

491. Oram, Andrew. "Do We Dare to Free Our Computer Users?" *TC* 39 (February 1992): 60–68.

Looks at users, the developing organization, and the role of the writer to discover what kinds of manuals should accompany today's computer systems.

492. Patthey, Ghislaine G. "The Language of Problem-Solving in a Computer Lab." *DAI* 52 (February 1992): 2909A.

 This ethnographic study of problem-solving consultations in a student computer lab reveals formative relationships between setting, action language, and cognition.

493. Payette, Julie, and Graeme Hirst. "An Intelligent Computer-Assistant for Stylistic Instruction." *CHum* 26 (April 1992): 87–102.

 Reports on STASEL, a newly developed instructional software that analyzes syntax in student writing and helps teach students to revise style for specific rhetorical contexts.

494. Pennington, Martha C., and Vance Stevens, eds. *Computers in Applied Linguistics: An International Perspective*. Bristol, PA: Taylor and Francis Group, 1991. 336 pages

 Provides a theoretical background and conceptual frameworks for designing and evaluating computer-assisted language learning in the 1990s. Reports on research into applications of computer-based tools for enhancing writing skills and grammatical competence. Describes some computer-based tools which are of value for research and software development.
 Essayists: Brock, Mark N.; Cheung, Anthony; Doughty, Catherine; Dunkel, Patricia; Esling, John H.; Harrison, Colin; Hubbard, Philip; Jansen, Louise; Lian, Andrew; Mohan, Bernard; Pienemann, Manfred; Pennington, Martha C.; Sampson, Geoffrey; Stevens, Vance; Witton, Nic.

495. Petrovic, Otto. "Empirical Research in Electronic Meeting Systems: A Demand Side Approach." *JOC* 2 (Fall 1992): 263–75.

 Studies the time spent by managers in meetings and identifies the requirements of an information technology system for supporting meetings.

496. Phillippakis, Andrew, and Michael Goul. "Concepts and Models of Group Membership in Computer-Supported Knowledge and Decision Tasks." *JOC* 2 (Fall 1992): 243–62.

 Defines group properties of synthesis, redundance, and synergy and relates these properties to concepts for selecting group members.

497. Phillips, Theodore Hart. "Impact of a Computer-Based, Process Writing Curriculum upon the Written Language and Self-Esteem of Residentially-Placed At-Risk Students." *DAI* 53 (December 1992): 1782A.

 Shows significant positive impact upon the written language of the subjects, especially with the younger students.

498. Posey, Evelyn. "*Writer's Helper for Windows*: A Comprehensive Prewriting and Revision Program." *C&C* 10 (November 1992): 93–98.

 Presents research results on the use of *Writer's Helper for Windows* that note its effectivenss with basic rather than advanced writers.

499. Powell-Hart, Betty Leona. "The Improvement of Writing Skills of College Freshman through Computer-Based Instruction." *DAI* 53 (July 1992): 90A.

 Concludes that computer-based instruction has a significant influence on the improvement of the participating students' writing in terms of reducing their writing anxieties and increasing their levels of revision activity.

500. Proudfoot, Gail. "Pssst! There Is Literacy at the Laundromat." *EQ* 24.1 (1992): 10–11.

 Pleads for recognition of the literacy which children already have in their homes and communities.

501. Rabin, Karen M. "Making Company Information Accessible: How to Develop an On-

line Information System." *IEEE* 34 (March 1992): 2–6.

> Describes a five-step process for creating an online information system for a company.

502. Ramanathan, Srinivas, P. Venkat Rangan, and Harrick M. Vin. "Designing Communication Architectures for Interorganizational Multimedia Collaboration." *JOC* 2 (Fall 1992): 277–302.

> Proposes a multilevel conferencing paradigm called super conference for supporting interactions between geographically separated groups of users, each belonging to a different organization.

503. Ransdell, Sarah, and Michael McCloskey. "Automated Feedback on Psychology Assignments Using a Comments Checklist." *CollM* 10 (February 1992): 33–37.

> Describes a method for automating feedback on students' writing.

504. Reigeluth, Charles M., and Robert J. Garfinkle. "Envisioning a New System of Education." *EdTech* 32 (November 1992): 17–23.

> Outlines a cooperative, multimedia educational system in Indiana that promotes student-created programs as text.

505. Reinking, David. "Differences between Electronic and Printed Texts: An Agenda for Research." *JEdM&H* 1 (Winter 1992): 11–24.

> Argues that the critical differences emerging from a review of electronic versus printed texts are conceptual rather than visual.

506. Roper, Donna G. "Desktop Publishing, Professional Writing, and Classical Rhetoric." *CACJ* 6 (Summer 1991): 8–14.

> Argues that desktop publishing requires the recursiveness and "full power of all five canons" of classical rhetoric.

507. Roush, Rick. "Taking the Error Out of Explaining Error Messages." *TC* 39 (February 1992): 56–59.

> Offers a method for making computer error messages easier to understand.

508. Roy, Emil. "Evaluating Placement Exams with a Structured Decision System." *C&C* 9 (April 1992): 71–86.

> Maintains that style-analysis software can predict the ratings of experienced readers accurately.

509. Rude, Carolyn, and Elizabeth Smith. "Use of Computers in Technical Editing." *TC* 39 (August 1992): 334–42.

> Shows that of 94 surveyed editors, 62.8 percent use computers for editing and "visual aspects"; points out that everyone still uses a hard copy. Argues that the computer is not a replacement for an editor.

510. Schenkenber, Mary Martin. "A Rationale for Teaching Writing as Process in an Electronic Environment." *DAI* 53 (July 1992): 90A.

> Claims that teaching writing with a word processor can enhance the teaching of writing as a process provided the class meets in an electronic environment.

511. Schmeltzer, Dennis K. "Computer-Mediated Communication: An Analysis of Message Structure and Message Intention." *EdTech* 32 (June 1992): 51–54.

> Studies an educationally oriented bulletin board and CMC systems; finds that when the intent is to give information, message length, complexity, and readability increase.

512. Schrum, Lynne. "Educational Technology Research Section: Professional Development in the Information Age—An Online Experience." *EdTech* 32 (December 1992): 49–53.

> Points out that a teacher-as-learner online experience with electronic mail and computer conferencing shows positive results.

513. Shannon, Patrick, ed. *Becoming Political: Readings and Writings in the Politics of Literacy Education.* Portsmouth, NH: Heinemann, 1992. 304 pages

Twenty-five essays affirm the need to acknowledge the political nature of the pedagogy and administrative practices related to the teaching of reading and writing.
Essayists: Begelow, W.; Bietila, S.; Bishop, J. L.; Bloome, D.; Brodkey, L.; Cameron, S. M.; Church, S. M.; Cook, L.; Gee, J. P.; Gilmore, L.; Giroux, H. A.; Hartling-Clarck, J.; Hammett, R. F.; Heath, S. Brice; Levine, D.; Moody, L.; Nieto, S.; Paterson, K.; Pierce, B. N.; Shannon, P.; Simon, R. I.; Sturk, A.; Tenorio, R.; Tolan, S. S.; Townsend-Fuller, C.; Trimbur, J.

514. Shapiro, Arthur, Jim Heck, and Philip Freedenberg. "The Planning, Design and Implementation of a Statewide Distance Learning System." *EdTech* 32 (July 1992): 28–32.

   The study outlines needs for a successful statewide distance learning network on local, state, and national levels.

515. Shilling, Wynne A. "Kindergarten Learners Constructing Knowledge about Literacy Using Conventional Materials and Computers." *DAI* 52 (May 1992): 3876A.

   Investigates the written language developmental processes of kindergarten children using conventional materials and computers.

516. Silverman, Barry G. "Human-Computer Collaboration." *HCI* 7 (Spring 1992): 165–96.

   Offers a model and research on six factors important in collaboration: cognitive orientation, deep knowledge, intention sharing, control plasticity, adaptivity, and experience or memory.

517. Slatin, John M. "*Hypercard* and the Extension of Writing." *C&C* 10 (November 1992): 109–16.

   Suggests that the authors of *Hypercard* have to grapple with concerns that authors of print text did not have to deal with. Notes that the document itself is the interface.

518. Sloane, Sarah Jane. "Interactive Fiction, Virtual Realities, and the Reading-Writing Relationship." *DAI* 52 (February 1992): 2937A.

   Explores the experience of reading and writing interactive fiction, proposing a rhetorical theory that encompasses computer-supported fictions and suggests directions for development.

519. Small, Ruth V., and Barbara L. Grabowski. "An Exploratory Study of Information-Seeking Behaviors and Learning with Hypermedia Information Systems." *JEdM&H* 1 (Fall 1992): 445–64.

   Results indicate that changes in motivation occurred the greatest with males, but that gender did not appear to affect the amount or type of learning.

520. Smith, Eric E., and Guy M. Westhoff. "The Taliesin Project: Multidisciplinary Education and Multimedia" *EdTech* 32 (January 1992): 15–23.

   Discusses the implementation of computer-assisted integration of various classes to underscore processes and connections.

521. Stanton, Neville, and Chris Baber. "An Investigation of Styles and Strategies in Self-Directed Learning." *JEdM&H* 1 (Spring 1992): 147–67.

   The authors propose that learner styles and strategies may be artifacts of the design of the courseware rather than a true representation of fundamental individual differences.

522. Stanton, N. A., R. G. Taylor, and L. A. Tweedie. "Maps as Navigational Aids in Hypertext Environments: An Empirical Evaluation." *JEdM&H* 1 (Fall 1992): 431–44.

   Suggests that navigational maps result in poorer performance, less use of the system, lower perceived control, and poorer development of cognitive mapping in users.

523. Stopford, Charles. "Desk Top Type: Tradition and Technology." *TC* 39 (February 1992): 74–79.

Discusses desktop publishing skills such as type size, line length, spacing, and white space.

524. Street, Brian, ed. *Literacy in Development: People, Language and Power (Papers from the International Seminar at the Commonwealth Institute for International Literacy Year, London, April 1990)*. London, England, and King's Lynn, England: Commonwealth Insititute and Education for Development, 1991. ERIC ED 340 871. 88 pages

Gathers nine papers and other materials from an international seminar on literacy programs.
Essayists: Alexander, David; Bown, Lalage; Didacus, Jules; Manzoor, Ahmed; McCaffrey, Juliet; Mukhapadyaya, Moitraye; Porter, James; Rogers, Alan; Saraswathi, L. S.; Stephens, David; Street, Brian; Coles, E. K. Townsend.

525. Strickland, James. "An Annotated Bibliography of Representative Software for Writers." *C&C* 10 (November 1992): 25–35.

Looks at software within the following areas: for collaboration over a network, invention, commenting, writing research papers, style analysis, usage handbooks, multimedia, and writing assessment.

526. Sullivan, Patricia. "Computer-Aided Publishing: Focusing on Documents." *C&C* 10 (November 1992): 135.

Classifies types of publishing software, describes their use in the classroom, and stresses the need to improve current networking standards.

527. Taylor, Angela L. "The Literacy Behavior Patterns of Single Parents/Homemakers in a Job-Training Program: Women's Attainment of Self-Esteem and Employment." *DAI* 53 (March 1992): 3455A.

Examines literacy behaviors used by eight informants enrolled in a development class in a job skills training program.

528. Taylor, Paul. "Evaluating Software: What Thoreau Said to the Designer." *C&C* 10 (November 1992): 45–52.

Argues that software should be theoretically focused, encourage action, manage complexity, have a consistent user interface, connect with other programs, provide feedback, and allow alteration.

529. Taylor, P. V. "Retexturing the Word and the World; Literacy and Contradiction in the Texts of Paulo Freire." *DAI* 53 (September 1992): 750A.

Analyzes the structure of Freire's pedagogy and concludes that Freire's attempts to restructure literacy have been helpful for problem-posing techniques.

530. Tharp, Marty. "Using Desktop Publishing in an Editing Class—The Lessons Learned and Students' Assessments." *TCQ* 1 (Spring 1992): 77–92.

Studies students' perceptions of learning desktop publishing systems using personal observations, a survey, and modified Nominal Group Techniques.

531. Thompsen, Philip A., and Dong-Keun Ahn. "To Be or Not to Be: An Exploration of E-Prime, Copula Deletion and Flaming in Electronic Mail." *ETC* 50 (Summer 1992): 146–63.

Presents a research study designed to determine whether "flaming" in e-mail results from an overuse of "to be" verbs.

532. Trachsel, Mary. *Institutionalizing Literacy: The Historical Role of College Entrance Exams in English*. Carbondale, IL: Southern Illinois University Press, 1992. 224 pages

Analyzes college entrance exams to understand constructions of literacy in academia. Views the split in English departments between composition and literary studies as a reflection of philosophical conflicts related to the mission of American education, the professional stature of English studies, and corporate influences. Calls for reunifying the discipline around literacy.

533. Tuman, Myron C. *Word Perfect: Literacy in the Computer Age*. Pittsburgh Series in Composition, Literacy, and Culture. Pitts-

burgh, PA: University of Pittsburgh Press, 1992. 150 pages

> Examines the relationship between technology and literacy, specifically considering how new versions of print literacy—hypertext and computer networking, the new models of reading and writing—affect language practices and policies; discusses what it means to be literate.

534. Tuman, Myron C., ed. *Literacy Online: The Promise (and Peril) of Reading and Writing with Computers*. Pittsburgh Series in Composition, Literacy, and Culture. Pittsburgh: University of Pittsburgh Press, 1992. 272 pages

> Addresses five issues concerning literacy as it is affected by computer-related reading and writing activities: hypertext and hyperspace, teaching in a computer environment, critical thinking, political issues, and epistemology.
> *Essayists:* Aronowitz, Stanley; Bolter, Jay David; Landow, George; Lanham, Richard; McCorduck, Pamela; Nelson, Ted; Provenzo, Eugene; Raskin, Victor; Schwartz, Helen; Ulmer, Greg.

535. U.S. Congress, House Committee on Education and Labor. "National Literacy Act of 1991 (Report to Accompany H.R. 751)." U.S. Congress, House Committee on Education and Labor, House Document R-102-23, Washington, DC, 1991. ERIC ED 340 889. 43 pages

> Provides the text of the proposed legislation to coordinate national adult literacy efforts, supplemented by supporting documents; includes cost estimates.

536. Vyborney, Wende Michelle. "Computer Reasons and Human Power: Epideictic Strategies in Popularized Scientific Discourse on the Nature and Potential of Computer Technology." *DAI* 43 (December 1992): 1728A.

> Uses an Aristotelian model to examine whether popular discourse is supportive of or oppositional to computers.

537. Webb, Christopher Lee. "An Observational Study of Reading during Composing at the Word Processor." *DAI* 53 (October 1992): 1111–2.

> Used keystroke-capture methodology to study 28 undergraduates composing final exams on computers; focuses on reading, rereading, and rewriting during the composing process.

538. Weston, Joan Ellard. "How the Word Processor Influences Interactions between Collaborating Grade Four Students." *DAI* 52 (March 1992): 3173A.

> Results indicate that students prefer collaboration and are more proficient at writing when doing so.

539. Williams, William F. "To Be Literate." *ELQ* 13 (October 1992): 5–7.

> Examines the rhetoric of the literacy crisis and the underlying assumptions used to define literacy.

540. Wresch, William. "Teachers Like Teaching with Computers." *ACE* 7 (Winter 1992): 2–5.

> Gives six reasons why computers are attractive to high school writing teachers, including their pedagogical, affective, and political value.

See also 564, 798, 865, 902, 917, 1019, 1030, 1058, 1059, 1060, 1093, 1181, 1371, 1495

2.5 ADVERTISING, PUBLIC RELATIONS, AND BUSINESS

541. Agmon, Ora. "The Myth of Creation: A Construct in Organizational Reading." *DAI* 52 (April 1992): 3653A.

> Uses a case study to explore organizations' myths of creation and their significance.

542. Anderson, Claire, and Giovanna Imperia. "The Corporate Annual Report: A Photo Analysis of Male and Female Portrayals." *JBC* 29 (Spring 1992): 113–28.

The authors discuss the implications of sex-role depictions in business media, following a study on how women are represented subserviently in corporate reports.

543. Beale, Marjorie. "Advertising and the Politics of Public Persuasion in France, 1900–1939." *DAI* 53 (December 1992): 2064A.

Places the social, commercial, and cultural projects of the French advertising industry within the larger history of debate over the effects of mass literacy.

544. Chakraborty, Goutam. "The Joint Effect of Advertising and Product Experience: An Empirical Investigation at the Product Attribute Level." *DAI* 53 (July 1992): 224A.

Demonstrates the utility of the attribute level analysis and the theoretical framework by offering an explanation for contradictory results obtained in past studies.

545. Crawford, Emily. "The Impact of Chum Relationships among Preadolescent Females in the Printed Media." *DAI* 53 (December 1992): 2011A.

Explores how peer influences relate to preadolescent consumer behavior.

546. Cronin, John Joseph. "The Effect of Communication Competence on Outcomes of the Buyer-Seller Dyad: An Application of the Social Relational Model." *DAI* 52 (June 1992): 4406A.

Finds that communication competence is not related to the performance of the salesperson.

547. Deetz, Stanley A. *Democracy in an Age of Corporate Colonization: Developments in Communication and the Politics of Everyday Life*. Albany, NY: State University of New York Press, 1992. 399 pages

Argues that an obsolete understanding of communication processes and power relations has prevented people from perceiving the corporate domination of public decision making.

548. Demarest, Jack, and Jeanette Garner. "The Representation of Women's Roles in Women's Magazines over the Past 30 Years." *JPsy* 126 (July 1992): 357–70.

The study explores women's magazines from 1954–1982; finds that while women were increasingly depicted in nontraditional sex roles, most depictions still reinforced traditional roles.

549. Fine, Leslie Marie. "Understanding the Relationship in the Buyer/Seller Dyad." *DAI* 52 (June 1992): 4406–4407A.

Examines early stages of the buyer/seller relationship, including communication, inference generation, and self-monitoring.

550. "Hugh Rank Recants Rent-A-Rhetorician Statement." *QRD* 18 (January 1992): 8.

Reports Rank's return from "temporary insanity," his resumption of the campaign to analyze advertising and political persuasion, and his publisher's offer of free teaching aids.

551. Hunt, James M., Jerome B. Kernan, and E. H. Bonfield. "Memory Structure in the Processing of Advertising Messages: How Is Unusual Information Represented?" *JPsy* 126 (July 1992): 343–56.

The study tests two models of memory structure and finds that, from advertisements, subjects remember unusual information (atypical arguments) more than expected statements (typical arguments).

552. Jowett, Garth S., and Victoria O'Donnell. *Propaganda and Persuasion*. 2d ed. Newbury Park: Sage, 1992. 296 pages

Provides historical insight and presents methods for discerning disinformation campaigns and for developing awareness for confronting such open communications as unethical advertising with half-truths.

553. Kaid, Lynda Lee, Chris M. Leland, and Susan Whitney. "The Impact of Televised Political Ads: Evoking Viewer Responses in the 1988 Presidential Campaign." *SCJ* 57 (Summer 1992): 285–95.

The results of the study indicate that image improvement seems directly related to the generation of specific emotions through campaign ads.

554. Karseno, Arief. "Advertising, Marketing Share and Profitability: An Experimental Study with Application to Indonesian Manufacturing." *DAI* 53 (August 1992): 563A.

    Studies the role of advertising on market share and profitability using a multimethod approach.

555. Kellner, Douglas. *The Persian Gulf TV War*. Boulder, CO: Westview Press, 1992. 460 pages

    Argues that the Bush administration manipulated the news media's coverage of the 1991 Gulf War.

556. Lee, Louise Leyi. "English as a Commercial Language: Oral Communication between American and Chinese Professionals." *DAI* 52 (May 1992): 3989A.

    Discovers that common short expressions may be a major source of error in communication, since native speakers of English and English-speaking Chinese attach different meanings to the words.

557. Orescovich, Robert. "Cigarette Industry: Analysis of Broadcast Advertising Ban on Allocative Performance." *DAI* 53 (September 1992): 903A.

    Presents an alternative explanation of the effect of the cigarette broadcast advertising ban on industry performance.

558. Perry, Devern J. "Writing for the Media." *TC* 39 (November 1992): 638–41.

    Describes the physical and written characteristics of an effective press release.

559. Rakow, Lana F. " 'Don't Hate Me Because I'm Beautiful': Feminist Resistance to Advertising's Irresistible Meanings." *SCJ* 57 (Winter 1992): 132–42.

    Cites ways in which advertising generates sexist meanings and creates sexual and racial differences through target marketing.

560. Sides, Charles H. "Should You Know How to Do Marketing, Advertising, and Public Relations Writing?" *TC* 39 (August 1992): 367–75.

    Argues that technical writers with these skills are more valuable to their companies and thus may be less likely laid off.

561. Stephens, Charlotte Stringer. "A Structured Observation of Five Chief Information Officers: The Nature of Information Technology Managerial Work." *DAI* 53 (January 1992): 2631A.

    Observes chief information officers in five industries—manufacturing, insurance, university, government agency, and utilities—to describe the new executive role.

562. Welforce, Win. "Supermarket Semantics: The Rhetoric of Food Labeling and Advertising." *ETC* 48 (Winter 1991/1992): 3–17.

    Notes that rhetorical strategies used by product copywriters will have to shift when the Nutrition Labeling and Education Act of 1990 is implemented in 1993.

563. Williams, David E., and Glenda Treadaway. "Exxon and the Valdez Accident: A Failure in Crisis Communication." *ComS* 43 (Spring 1992): 56–64.

    Argues that a slow initial response and ineffective use of burden sharing and scapegoating strategies caused communication efforts to fail.

564. Zack, Michael H. "The Role of Computer-Mediated Communication Technology in Ongoing Management Groups." *DAI* 52 (April 1992): 3662A.

    Studies the choice to use computer-mediated communications technologies by senior editorial staffs at two daily newspapers and makes recommendations to guide such choices.

2.6 LITERATURE, FILM, AND THEATER

565. Alasti, Ahmad. "The American Documentary Films of the Vietnam War." *DAI* 53 (September 1992): 649A.

Analyzes the politics of representation in the American documentary films of the Vietnam War.

566. Baker, Anna Belle. "Images of Transformation in Film: The Collective Dream." *DAI* 52 (May 1992): 3754A.

Explores film as a vehicle for contemporary Jungian style myth and as an effective agent for change.

567. Bennett, Tony, ed. *Popular Fiction: Technology, Ideology, Production, Reading*. New York: Routledge, 1990. 400 pages

The contributing authors analyze "popular fiction in its literary, filmic, and televisual forms: science fiction, soap opera, detective fiction, spy thriller, western, film noir, and comedy."
Essayists: Alvarado, Manuel; Anderson, Benedict; Belsey, Catherine; Bennett, Tony; Brand, Dana; Ellis, John; Ginzberg, Carlo; Harris, Neil; Heath, Stephen; Kerr, Paul; Kuhn, Annette; McArthur, Colin; Modleski, Tania; Moretti, Franco; Morley, David; Mulvey, Laura; Place, Janey; Porter, Dennis; Rose, Jacqueline; Tulloch, John; Turner, Graeme; Williams, Raymond; Woollacott, Janet.

568. Best, Felton. "Crossing the Color Line: A Biography of Paul Laurence Dunbar, 1872–1906." *DAI* 53 (November 1992): 1633A.

Explores the opposing perceptions of Dunbar developed by scholars of African-American history and literature.

569. Bogdan, Deanne. *Re-Educating the Imagination: Towards a Poetics, Politics and Pedagogy of Literacy Engagement*. Portsmouth, NH: Boynton/Cook, 1992. 408 pages

Analyzes why, what, and how literature is taught from the perspective that reading literature is a real and social experience.

570. Bristow, Joseph, ed. *Sexual Sameness: Textual Differences in Lesbian and Gay Writing*. New York: Routledge, 1992. 272 pages

The essayists argue that for 2000 years persistent homophobia has until recently inhibited our understanding of lesbian and gay textuality. Some of the writers analyzed are Walt Whitman, James Baldwin, Sylvia Townsend Warner, and Audre Lorde.
Essayists: Bergman, David; Bristow, Joseph; Castle, Terry; Collecott, Diana; Dollimore, Jonathan; Fletcher, John; Knopp, Sherron E.; Sinfield, Alan; Whatling, Clare; White, Chris; Yorke, Liz.

571. Bryant, Coralie, and Linda Lee. "Group Oral Response to Literature: An Experiment in Large-Scale Assessment." *EQ* 23.3–4 (1992): 15–22.

Presents procedures for discovering how well students perform in a group, respond to literature, and articulate their ideas.

572. Burns, Teresa. "Teaching the Postmodern: The Clash of Rhetorics between the Classroom and Donald Barthelme's 'The Indian Uprising.'" *CS/FEN* 20 (Fall 1992): 73–84.

Suggests teaching Barthelme's postmodern story as a way of helping students see a "metanarrative" about the way humans create meaning.

573. Carter, Nancy Carson. "Spider Woman Weaves Enchantment." *CEAF* 22 (Winter 1992): 7–9.

Considers the function of chant, sound, and resonance in Native American and Anglo-American literature.

574. Chetin, Sara. "Rereading and Rewriting African Women: Ama Ata Aidoo and Bessie Head." *DAI* 53 (September 1992): 808A.

Explores female subjectivity by examining thematic concerns and narrative strategies, audience concerns, and departures from the strategies of male writers.

575. Chi, Wei–Jan. "The Role of Language in the Plays of Mamet, Wilson, and Rabe." *DAI* 52 (January 1992): 2327A.

Analyzes the primacy of language in the works of three contemporary American playwrights.

576. Cixous, Hélène. *"Coming to Writing" and Other Essays*. Translated by Sarah Cornell, Deborah Jenson, Ann Liddle, and Susan Sellers. Edited by Deborah Jenson. Cambridge, MA: Harvard University Press, 1992. 240 pages

> Presents six essays by Cixous in which she explores how the problematics of the sexes manifest themselves and write themselves in texts.

577. Cook, William W. *Writing in the Spaces Left: Opening General Session, CCCC*. [Videotape, VHS]. Urbana, IL: NCTE, 1992.

> Discusses texts by African-Americans such as Frederick Douglass, Maya Angelou, and others, that "have served as 'talking books,'" providing openings for African-American writers, readers, and speakers to "find their own voice and inscribe their own realities."

578. Crane, Gwen Ellen. "Inquisitors, Wizards and Writers: Literary Portraits of Authority." *DAI* 53 (July 1992): 140A.

> Examines literary techniques for portraying figures of intellectual, religious, and political authority.

579. Dean, Sharon L. "Literature and Composition Theory: Joyce Carol Oates' Journal Stories." *RR* 10 (Spring 1992): 311–20.

> Uses Oates' journals to explore contradictions in literary and composition theory. Like Oates, Dean recommends uniting both literature and composition.

580. Deshpande, Shekhar A. "Historical Representations in the Cinematic *Apparatus* and the Narratives of Popular Memory." *DAI* 53 (August 1992): 332A.

> Examines the relevance of the Foucauldian concept of "popular memory" to discourse and cinematic theory.

581. Dienst, Richard Welton. "The Worlds of Television: Theories of Culture and Technology." *DAI* 52 (February 1992): 2912A.

> Develops a critical theory of television by examining various perspectives within contemporary thought, specifically examining textuality and its world.

582. Dorczah, Anita. "Signs of Crisis: A Semiotic Approach to the Theater of the Absurd." *DAI* 52 (May 1992): 3770A.

> Presents a semiotic interpretation of selected plays and traces the common themes of the Theater of the Absurd and existentialism.

583. Faust, Mark A. "Ways of Reading and 'The Use of Force.'" *EJ* 81 (November 1992): 44–49.

> Analyzes responsive, resistant, and dialogical literary theories. Proposes that the latter allows readers to "hear" the "multivoicedness of situation" in texts otherwise silenced.

584. Fischel, Anne Beth. "The Politics of Inscription in Documentary Film and Photography." *DAI* 53 (August 1992): 332A.

> Explores the politics of cultural production in documentary film and photography.

585. Gamber, Cayo. *The Translator and the Translated: Bakhtin's Intralinguistic Dialogue and Minne Bruce Pratt's "Crime against Nature."* Cincinnati, OH: CCCC, March 1992. ERIC ED 346 506. 12 pages

> Introduces two exercises demonstrating how Bakhtin's conception of novelistic language and creative interpretation are instrumental in teaching students to read creatively.

586. Ghosh, Sanjukta Tultul. "Celluloid Nationalism: Cultural Politics in Popular Indian Cinema." *DAI* 53 (September 1992): 650A.

> Explores the use of film as a harmonizing and hegemonizing tool in ethnically plural societies.

587. Glaim, Marilyn. "Failure of Androgyny in Edith Wharton's Fiction." *DAI* 53 (October 1992): 1199A.

> Emphasizes Wharton's focus on gender issues, particularly on the need to challenge

social definitions of masculine and feminine roles.

588. Graham, Robert Joe. "Adopting Adaptations: Reading the Novel, Reading the Film." *EQ* 23.3–4 (1992): 23–27.

Argues that film offers distinctive possibilities for study in regular English classrooms.

589. Graves, Darlene Richards. "Creative Drama as an Instructional Strategy in Adult Christian Education." *DAI* 53 (July 1992): 22A.

Shows that the use of creative drama benefits students with different learning styles.

590. Haefner, Joel. *Fictions of the Writer: A Critical Articulation of Collaborative Writing and Literary Studies*. Cincinnati, OH: CCCC, March 1992. ERIC ED 346 495. 14 pages

Claims that women of the Romantic period present an image of the writer vastly different from the High Romantic concept of the solitary author.

591. Hawcroft, Michael. *Word as Action: Racine, Rhetoric, and Theatrical Language*. New York: Oxford University Press, 1992. 275 pages

Examines verbal action and rhetorical theory, formal and informal oratory, monologues, persuasion, and the rhetorical categories of *inventio* and *dispositio* in Racine's drama.

592. Hays, Michael, ed. *Critical Conditions: Regarding the Historical Moment*. Minneapolis: University of Minnesota Press, 1992. 152 pages

Focuses on contemporary issues in critical theory; includes the roles of scholars and the institutions in which they work and live, as well as postcolonial theory, historical issues, and epistemology.
Essayists: Arac, Jonathan; Bové, Paul; Gearhart, Suzanne; Kay, Carol; Mohanty, Satya P.; O'Hara, Daniel T.; Pease, Donald.

593. Hegler, Barbara Finley. "Artistic Collaboration: Director/Designer Communication." *DAI* 52 (May 1992): 3771A.

Examines the use of established communication models to enhance the effectiveness of collaboration of theatrical director/designer teams.

594. Hess, John David. "Form and Ideology: History, Realism and Genre Expectations." *DAI* 52 (February 1992): 2737A.

Acknowledges that all film criticism is ideological; seeks to tie criticism to particular historical concepts.

595. Iddings, James Henry. "A Study of Rhetorical Systems in the Documentary Mode." *DAI* 52 (February 1992): 2737A.

Applies an historical-rhetorical approach to the study of documentary drama and documentary film in the 1930s and 1960s, focusing on background, rhetorical, and narrative structures.

596. Kadar, Marlene, ed. *Essays on Life Writing: From Genre to Critical Practice*. Toronto: University of Toronto Press, 1992. 234 pages

Presents 14 essays on autobiography and women's writing and on the self in literature.
Essayists: Anderson, Ellen; Buss, Helen M.; Cohen, Elizabeth; Cohen, Thomas V.; Cole, Sally; Cooke, Nathalie; Hinz, Evelyn J.; Kadar, Marlene; Neuman, Shirley; Ty, Eleanor; Van Wart, Alice; Verdun, Christl; Williamson, Janice.

597. Karolides, Nicholas J. *Reader Response in the Classroom: Evoking and Interpreting Meaning in Literature*. White Plains, NY: Longman, 1992. 251 pages

Explains how to use reader response processes to teach literature; includes specific literary works and suggests ways of using this approach to teach them; gives accounts of actual classes in which this approach was used.

598. Kingston, Maxine Hong. *Invisible Gifts: Thinglessness and Creation.* [Audiocassette]. Urbana, IL: NCTE, 1991.

> Describes how losing the manuscript to her book *The Book of Peace* in a house fire affected her writing process, by helping her focusing on spiritual gifts and creativity rather than material possessions. The recording is taken from a talk at the 1991 NCTE Annual Convention.

599. Krauss, Kenneth Gohfried. "Private Readings/Public Texts: Playreaders' Constructs of Theatre Audiences." *DAI* 53 (December 1992): 1729A.

> Proposes four ways playreaders may construct a sense of theatre audience based on a reception-oriented approach.

600. Krome, Frederic. " 'A Weapon of War Second to None': Anglo-American Film Propaganda during World War II." *DAI* 53 (December 1992): 2066A.

> Examines the use of film as a tool of British international propaganda and its evolution into joint Anglo-American film projects.

601. Langer, Judith A. "Critical Thinking and English Language Arts Instruction (Report Series 6.5)." Center for the Learning and Teaching of Literature, Albany, NY, 1992. ERIC ED 345 254. 17 pages

> Argues that the current discussion of critical thinking is too narrow. Offers suggestions for the teaching of literature.

602. Lennard, John. *But I Digress: The Exploitation of Parentheses in English Printed Verse.* New York: Oxford University Press, 1991. 344 pages

> Argues that writers can use parentheses to control tone, add humor, intensify satire, and clarify argument. Traces the history of parentheses in poetics since its first appearance in 1494.

603. Mannix, Patrick. *The Rhetoric of Antinuclear Fiction: Persuasive Strategies in Novels and Films.* Lewisburg, PA: Bucknell University Press, 1992. 192 pages

> Discusses the ethical, rational, and emotional strategies used in antinuclear books and films such as *On the Beach*, *A Canticle for Leibowitz*, and *Dr. Strangelove*.

604. McClure, Laura Kathleen. "Rhetoric and Gender in Euripides: A Study of Sacrifice Actions." *DAI* 52 (January 1992): 2541A.

> Examines the language and rhetoric of speakers in parallel tragic roles in Euripides to determine differences between men and women.

605. McCormick, Kathleen. "Teaching, Studying, and Theorizing the Production and Reception of Literary Texts." *CollL* 19 (June 1992): 4–18.

> Argues that students need to study texts from "the standpoint of their production and reception" creating a "balance between autonomy and determination."

606. Montgomery, Michael Vincent. "Bakhtin's Chronotope and the Rhetoric of Hollywood Film." *DAI* 53 (August 1992): 333A.

> Considers Hollywood film locales rhetorically using a chronotopological framework.

607. Moore, James Duff. "An Introductory Course in Dramatic Literature Adapted to the Nontraditional Needs of the Community College Student." *DAI* 52 (June 1992): 4150A.

> Presents a methodology of historical survey incorporating supplementary material, heuristic aids, and detailed lesson plans.

608. Nathanson, Tenney. *Whitman's Presence: Body, Voice, and Writing in "Leaves of Grass."* New York: New York University Press, 1992. 532 pages

> Discusses the American poet's addresses to the reader and other "performative declarations."

609. Nuttall, A. D. *Openings: Narrative Beginnings from the Epic to the Novel.* New York: Oxford University Press, 1992. 255 pages

> Examines rhetorical strategies in the beginnings of the *Aeneid*, the *Commedia*, *Para-*

dise Lost*, the *Prelude*, *Tristram Shandy*, *David Copperfield*, and *Great Expectations*.

610. O'Neill, John. *Critical Conventions: Interpretations in the Literary Arts and Sciences*. Norman, OK: University of Oklahoma Press, 1992. 335 pages

Studies literary and scientific writing in the wake of Thomas Kuhn's theory of scientific change.

611. O'Regan, Daphne Elizabeth. *Rhetoric, Comedy, and the Violence of Language in Aristophanes' "Clouds."* New York: Oxford University Press, 1992. 216 pages

Examines sophistic rhetoric in *Clouds*. Shows that *logos*—the power of argument—meets defeat when confronted with human nature.

612. Pace, Barbara G. "The Textbook Canon: Genre, Gender, and Race in U. S. Literature Anthologies." *EJ* 81 (September 1992): 33–38.

Analyzes five textbooks and concludes that the canon "exhibits an exceedingly narrow spectrum of the intellectual and emotional story of life in our country."

613. Payne, David. "Political Vertigo in *Dead Poets' Society*." *SCJ* 58 (Fall 1992): 13–21.

Explores relations among socialization, aesthetic involvement, and political expression in the film's text.

614. Petrie, Duncan. "Making Movies: The Structuring of Creativity in Contemporary British Cinema." *DAI* 53 (August 1992): 333A.

Examines the creative process during film composition.

615. Phillips, Betty Jean. "African-American Folk Archetypes and Language in the African-American Oral Tradition and Their Influence on Selected Contemporary African-American Poets." *DAI* 53 (December 1992): 1731A.

Examines poetry of the late 1960s and early 1970s through the cultural matrix of the African-American tradition for its oral interpretive performance.

616. Pinchen, Jennifer E. "The Audience Critic: A Study of Audience Response to Popular Theatre." *DAI* 52 (January 1992): 2328A.

Reassesses possibilities for positive and dynamic relations between audience and theater.

617. Powell, Johnathan, and Tony Woodman, eds. *Author and Audience in Latin Literature*. New York: Cambridge University Press, 1992. 276 pages

Analyzes how major Roman authors interacted with their audiences by using reader-response theory.
Essayists: Cairns, Francis; Feeney, D. C.; Goold, G. P.; Hill, D. E.; Le M. Duquesnay, Ian M.; Nisbet, R. G. M.; Powell, J. G. F.; Rudd, Niall; Walsh, P. G.; Williams, Gordon; Wiseman, T. P.; Woodman, Tony.

618. Robinson, Lou, and Camille Norton, eds. *Resurgent: New Writings by Women*. Urbana, IL: University of Illinois Press, 1992. 320 pages

The anthology reflects a resurgence of the literary energy of the 1920s and 30s, when Gertrude Stein, Djuna Barnes, and Virginia Woolf invented expansive forms for the female imagination.
Essayists: Adnan, Etel; Archer, Nuala; Brossard, Nicole; Broumas, Olga; Child, Abigail; Harryman, Carla; Hejinian, Lyn; Holzer, Jenny; Marlatt, Daphne; Miller, Jane; Minh-ha, Trinh T.; Scott, Gail; Shange, Ntozake; Silvers, Sally; Waldman, Anne; Warland, Betsy.

619. Scheie, Timothy Jon. "Body Trouble: Roland Barthes, Theater, and the Corporeal Sign." *DAI* 52 (December 1992): 1731A.

Traces the resistance of the performing body to semiotic theory.

620. Shalaby, Nadia Abdelgalil. "Assertion of Power: A Sociolinguistic Analysis of *'Death of a Salesman,' 'The Caretaker'* and *'Look*

Back in Anger.' " *DAI* 52 (June 1992): 4147A.

> Analyzes the linguistic strategies by which speakers attain power in conflict situations in plays by Miller, Osborne, and Pinter.

621. Short, Bryan Collier. *Cast by Means of Figures: Herman Melville's Rhetorical Development*. Amherst, MA: University of Massachusetts Press, 1992. 248 pages

> Describes Melville as a self-consciously experimental writer whose work was influenced more by rhetorical concerns than by philosophical, psychological, or social influences.

622. Shull, Ellen. "Valuing Multiple Critical Approaches: Penelope, Again . . . and Again." *EJ* 81 (November 1992): 32–37.

> Demonstrates how applying a variety of critical approaches to text encourages students to become "creative investigators" who see new ways of making meaning.

623. Silverman, Kaja. *Male Subjectivity at the Margins*. New York: Routledge, 1992. 368 pages

> Analyzes "male filmmakers, novelists, and literary and cinematic characters who position themselves more as 'women' than as 'men' and in so doing surrender male power and privilege." Focuses on R. W. Fassbinder, Henry James, T. S. Lawrence, and Proust.

624. Suleiman, Susan Rubin. *Subversive Intent: Gender Politics and the Avant-Garde*. Cambridge, MA: Harvard University Press, 1992. 272 pages

> Shows how the figure of Woman, as fantasy, myth, or metaphor, has functioned in the works of male avant-garde writers and artists. Examines the work of contemporary women artists and theorists to show the political power of feminist critiques of patriarchal ideology.

625. Templeton, Alice. "Sociology and Literature: Theories for Cultural Criticism." *CollL* 19 (June 1992): 19–30.

> Establishes definitions for cultural criticism and discusses ways of incorporating it into reading in the classroom.

626. Thomas, Anne Cameron. " 'The Honey of Poison-Flowers': Women and the Feminine in Tennyson's Poetry." *DAI* 53 (November 1992): 1530A.

> Argues that Tennyson derived great poetic power by using female voices but that he also felt a need to control them. Points out that Tennyson overtly upholds gender conventions while his verse subtly undermines them.

627. Travis, Molly Abel. "Reading the Middle Passages." *Reader* 27 (Spring 1992): 12–20.

> Describes the narrative technique of *Middle Passage*, a contemporary slave narrative which compels the reader to take an active role in constructing meaning.

628. Trimmer, Joseph. "Reading and Writing Culture: A Group Memoir." *Reader* 27 (Spring 1992): 21–28.

> Describes a course in which students' negative response to *An American Childhood*—after reading *Black Boy*—formed a kind of group memoir.

629. Udall, Ida Hunt. *Mormon Odyssey: The Story of Ida Hunt Udall, Plural Wife*. Edited by Maria S. Ellsworth. Urbana, IL: University of Illinois Press, 1992. 296 pages

> Ellsworth preserves and edits her grandmother's journal and birthday book.

630. Valdes, Mario J. *World-Making: The Literary Truth-Claim and the Interpretation of Texts*. Toronto: University of Toronto Press, 1992. 268 pages

> Suggests ways of reading claims of truth embedded in fictions.

631. Webb, Kenneth. "Quest for an American Spirituality: An Analysis of the Sacred Thematic Content in the American Science Fiction Novel, 1980–1989." *DAI* 53 (November 1992): 1563A.

Substantiates that there is an increase in the use of sacred thematic material in the research group of novels from the 1980s.

632. Wilson, Anna Marslen. "The Fiction of Change: Strategies of Resistance in Feminist Narrative." *DAI* 53 (September 1992): 812A.

Argues that feminist fiction rarely produces social change and that successful resistance is a local phenomenon.

633. Wintersole, Margaret Marian. "Film Noir, Image, and Argument: The Creation of Film Noir Style through the Visual Image and Its Persuasive Discourse." *DAI* 53 (July 1992): 5A.

Argues that film is a linguistic phenomenon, constructing arguments for the reality it represents through a figurative linguistic process.

634. Yorke, Liz. *Impertinent Voices: Subversive Strategies in Contemporary Women's Poetry*. New York: Routledge, 1991. 238 pages

Uses theories of Irigaray, Cixous, and Kristeva to analyze Sylvia Plath, Adrienne Rich, H. D., and Audre Lorde.

635. Zizek, Slavoj. *Everything You Always Wanted to Know about Lacan (without Ever Daring to Ask Hitchcock)*. London: Verso, 1992. 250 pages

Analyzes Hitchcock's films using the political and philosophical maxims of Marx and Lacan.

See also 80

2.7 READING

636. Albano, Theresa Ann. "The Effect of Interest on Reading Comprehension and Written Discourse." *DAI* 53 (July 1992): 111A.

Indicates a significant effect of interest on the writing clarity variable, the writing accuracy variable, and the reading comprehension variable. Finds, however, that interest did not have a significant effect on the gender variable.

637. Bartine, David. *Reading, Criticism, and Culture: Theory and Teaching in the United States and England, 1820–1950*. Columbia, SC: University of South Carolina Press, 1992. 168 pages

Describes how Americans departed from English traditions of reading theory and pedagogy.

638. Brent, Doug. *Reading as Rhetorical Invention: Knowledge, Persuasion, and the Teaching of Research-Based Writing*. Urbana, IL: NCTE, 1992. 135 pages

Beginning with the premise that reading is an on-going interactive process to create meaning shared between reader and writer, Brent "seeks to build a model of how we rhetorical beings accomplish this task." He connects rhetorical approaches to reading, literary theory, rhetorical theory, and the teaching of first-year college composition. Includes a bibliography.

639. Crowder, Robert G., and Richard K. Wagner. *The Psychology of Reading: An Introduction*. New York: Oxford University Press, 1992. 266 pages

Presents a nonspecialist's introduction to research conducted by cognitive psychologists into reading since the 1960s.

640. Goetz, Ernest T., Mark Sadoski, Arturo Olivarez, Jr., and Ayxa Calero-Breckeimer. "The Structure of Emotional Response in Reading a Literary Text: Quantitative and Qualitative Analyses." *RRQ* 27 (Fourth Quarter 1992): 361–72.

The authors investigate undergraduates' reactions to a story by using categorization methodology.

641. Green, Stuart. "Mining Texts in Reading to Write." *JAC* 12 (Winter 1992): 151–70.

Argues that students can learn to mine a text for future writing by attending to context, structure, and language and not to

2.7 READING

immersion, modelling, or "critical thinking."

642. Harris, Joseph. "Reading the Right Thing." *Reader* 27 (Spring 1992): 29–47.

Explores ways to teach critical reading using the movie *Do the Right Thing* as an example.

643. Harste, Jerome C. *Literature Circles.* [Videotape]. Portsmouth, NH: Heinemann, 1992.

Part of the series on whole language classrooms, this tape gives examples of ways to run a literature-based, process reading program.

644. Hughes, Jannese. "Reading in L1 and L2: Reading Is Understanding Meaning." *The Language Teacher* 16 (June 1992): 17–19.

Discusses issues in L2 reading comprehension such as cognitive processing, language competence, and background knowledge.

645. Hunter, Susan. *Reading Practices of Reviewers and Editors.* Cincinnati, OH: CCCC, March 1992. ERIC ED 344 199. 20 pages

Examines the reading practices of reviewers and editors of scholarly journals and their attitudes about their roles in the editorial process.

646. McGinley, William. "The Role of Reading and Writing while Composing from Sources." *RRQ* 27 (Third Quarter 1992): 227–48.

Presents a report of results from a study of college students composing from sources; presents a model to demonstrate how students use sources.

647. McKoon, Gail, and Roger Ratcliff. "Inference during Reading." *PsyR* 99 (July 1992): 440–66.

Proposes a minimalist theory of inference making; argues that only inferences based on easily available information are encoded automatically during reading. Argues against a constructivist account.

648. Nagasaka, Akemi. "Top-Level Text Structure in Reading L1 and FL Expository Prose." *JALT Journal* 14 (November 1992): 127–42.

Finds that 79 out of 100 Japanese college students used the top-level text structure strategy when reading Japanese, but only 26 used it when reading English.

649. Rack, John P., Margaret J. Snowling, and Richard K. Olson. "The Nonword Reading Deficit in Developmental Dyslexia: A Review." *RRQ* 27 (First Quarter 1992): 29–53.

Evaluates the hypothesis that dyslexic children have a specific deficit in phonological reading processes.

650. Rennie, John. "Defining Dyslexia: Is It a Distinct Disorder or a Problem of Degree." *ScAm* 267 (July 1992): 31–32.

Examines the current debate on whether dyslexia is a specific reading disorder or merely a variation of traits found in traditionally poor readers.

651. Ritchie, Joy S. "Resistance to Reading: Another View of the Minefield." *JAC* 12 (Winter 1992): 117–36.

Interprets a participant observer study of four male students and the socially constructed identities that lead them to resist reading in English classes.

652. Smith, Edward, and David Swinney. "The Role of Schemas in Reading Text: A Real-Time Examination." *DPr* 15 (July–September 1992): 303–16.

The authors maintain that reading times increase when readers have insufficient background knowledge. They point out that knowledge is crucial to on-line processing as well as to memory of discourse.

653. Thomas, Margaret, Gloria Jaffe, J. Peter Kincaid, and Yvette Stees. "Learning to Use Simplified English: A Preliminary Study." *TC* 39 (February 1992): 69–73.

Argues that rewriting in simplified English for non-English readers is quite difficult without extensive practice but that training tools are helpful.

654. Vine, Harold A., Jr., and Mark A. Faust. "Situating Readers: Introduction and Invitation." *EJ* 81 (November 1992): 62–67.

Discusses difficulties encountered in developing reader-based curriculum. Shares research methodology and invites others to conduct their own classroom research.

2.8 LINGUISTICS, GRAMMATICAL THEORY, AND SEMANTICS

655. Aitchison, Jean. *Language Change: Progress or Decay?* 2d ed. New York: Cambridge University Press, 1991. 269 pages

Discusses evidence for language change, how and why languages change, and how and why languages begin and end. Considers changes that occurred many years ago as well as those currently in progress.

656. Allsopp, Jeannette. "French and Spanish Loan Words in Carribbean English." *EnT* 8 (January 1992): 12–20.

Reviews some of the multilingual intricacies of West Indian language usage.

657. Andresen, Julie Tetel. *Linguistics in America, 1769–1924: A Critical History.* Routledge History of Linguistic Thought. New York: Routledge, 1990. 320 pages

Proposes that three developments capture a significant portion of American linguistic activity: the study of Native American languages, the emergence of a distinctive Anglo-American "thought" accompanied by a defense of American English, and the influence of European linguistic theories on American scholarship.

658. Aristar-Dry, Helen. "Timeline, Event Line, and Deixis." *Lang&S* 21 (Fall 1988): 399–410.

Analyzes rhetorical effects of present-deictic adverbs in past-tense narration in Dickens' *Great Expectations* and LeGuin's *A Wizard of Earthsea.*

659. Bailey, Richard W. *Images of English: A Cultural History of Language.* Ann Arbor, MI: University of Michigan Press, 1991. 344 pages

Traces changes in attitudes of English speakers toward their language.

660. Bartter, Martha. "Science, Science Fiction and Women: A Language of (Tacit) Exclusion." *ETC* 50 (Winter 1992/1993): 407–19.

Argues that language used to refer to women in science and science fiction can affect human behavior.

661. Bochard, Terrance H. "Discourse Level Functional Equivalence Translation." *DAI* 52 (March 1992): 3259A.

Uses theory, information processing, and discourse level linguistics to develop a method for analyzing the discourse structure and central message of whole discourse.

662. Britain, David. "Dialect and Space: A Geolinguistic Study of Speech Variables in the Fens." *DAI* 52 (April 1992): 3728A.

Investigates a number of sociolinguistic contact phenomena and the effect upon these phenomena of the socio-geography on everyday life.

663. Burchfield, Robert. *Points of View: An Entertaining Look at Words and Meanings.* New York: Oxford University Press, 1992. 192 pages

Comments and reflects on amusing ways in which the English language is used.

664. Bynum, Joyce. "Bigfoot—A Contemporary Belief Legend." *ETC* 49 (Fall 1992): 352–57.

Analyzes the variety of language used in personal accounts of Bigfoot. Concludes that folklorists should not attempt to prove or disprove this legend.

665. Cameron, Deborah. *Feminism and Linguistic Theory*. 2d ed. New York: St. Martin's Press, 1992. 257 pages

>Presents an introduction to the evolving body of work on feminism which encompasses linguistics, anthropology, literacy and cultural theory, psychoanalysis, and postmodern philosophy.

666. Cameron, Deborah, Elizabeth Frazer, Penelope Harvey, M. B. H. Rampton, and Kay Richardson. *Researching Language: Issues of Power and Method*. The Politics of Language, edited by Tony Crowley and Talbot J. Taylor. New York: Routledge, 1992. 148 pages

>Discusses ethical issues concerning the relationship between research and informants in linguistic and social research.

667. Cheshire, Jenny, and Viv Edwards. "Schoolchildren as Sociolinguistic Researchers." *L&E* 3 (Spring 1992): 225–49.

>Cheshire and Edwards' study demonstrates the feasibility and gains of incorporating sociolinguistic research into the classroom in ways which position students as research collaborators.

668. Chisholm, William. "Lexical Cohesion as Semantic Structure: The Case of Thoreau's 'The Battle of the Ants.' " *Lang&S* 22 (Winter 1989): 37–49.

>Analyzes the lexical patterns which create the semantic structure in Thoreau's classic, belletristic essay on nature and war.

669. Christy, Daniel Merton. "A Syntactic Language Computer Analysis of Depressed Versus Nondepressed Females." *DAI* 53 (September 1992): 1603B.

>Points out that depressed subjects use more intransitive verbs, passive voice, *being* verbs, negated nouns, and abstract nouns whereas nondepressed persons used more qualifiers, especially nonnegated ones.

670. Crawford, James, ed. *Language Loyalties: A Source Book on the Official English Controversy*. Chicago: University of Chicago Press, 1992. 536 pages

>The contributors examine topics such as the historic role of language in American identity, central arguments used in Congress and state campaigns, the social, political, and economic impact of language conflicts in American communities, legal precedents and constitutional issues regarding language and civil liberties, and implications of linguistic diversity for American schools.
>*Essayists:* Adams, John; Atkins, J.D.C.; Baron, Dennis; Bennett, William J.; Bloo, David E.; Bretzer, Joanne; Bunge, Robert; Calderón, José; Cárdenas, José A.; Castellanos, Diego; Castro, Max; Chen, Edward M.; Combs, Mary Carol; Corrada, Baltasar; Crawford, James; Draper, Jamie B.; Epstein, Noel; Fillmore, Lily Wong; Fishman, Joshua; Franklin, Benjamin; Gaarder, A. Bruce; Grenier, Gilles; Guy, Gregory; Hakuta, Kenji; Haugen, Einar; Hayakawa, S.I.; Heath, Shirley Brice; Higham, John; Horton, John; Huddleston, Walter; Inglehart, Ronald F.; Isaacs, Harold R.; Jiménez, Martha; Krashen, Stephen D.; Leibowicz, Joseph; Lemco, Jonathan; Lucas, Ceil; Lyons, James J.; McCormick, Washington J.; Montaner, Carlos Alberto; Nicolau, Siobhan; Nunberg, Geoffrey; Peréz-Bustillo, Camilo; Piatt, Bill; Reyhner, Jon; Rodríguez, Richard; Roosevelt, Theodore; Salazar, Rubén; Schmid, Carol; Shumway, Norman; Shuy, Roger; Snow, Catherine E.; Solarz, Stephen J.; Trasvina, John; Valdivieso, Rafael; Webster, Noah; Woodward, Margaret; Wright, Guy; Yarborough, Ralph.

671. Crowley, Tony. *Proper English? Readings in Language, History, and Cultural Identity*. New York: Routledge, 1991. 272 pages

>Focuses on Locke, Swift, Marebon, Webster, Pickering, and Henry James to deal with "questions of language, change and decay, correct and incorrect usage, and what to prescribe and proscribe."

672. D'Ammassa, Algernon. "A Race by Any Other Name." *QRD* 18 (July 1992): 12–13.

Discusses various terms Americans use to denote race, finds them inappropriate "evasions," and proposes "brown."

673. Davis, Alan J. "Graphs and Doublespeak." *QRD* 18 (July 1992): 11–12.

Provides illustrations and explanations to show how doublespeak functions in graphs, showing both accurate and doublespeak versions.

674. Dawkins, John. "Punctuation: Less Is More? (ERIC Digest)." ERIC/RCS, Bloomington, IN, 1992. ERIC ED 347 553. 4 pages

Suggests that punctuation should be viewed as a process—as a matter of the writer's intent—rather than a product.

675. "Doublespeak Here and There." *QRD* 18 (April 1992): 1–10.

Notes examples of doublespeak in business, education, foreign countries, government and politics, law, medicine, the military, and miscellaneous categories.

676. "Doublespeak Here and There." *QRD* 18 (October 1992): 1–8.

Notes examples of doublespeak in business, education, foreign countries, government and politics, law, the military, and miscellaneous categories.

677. "1991 Doublespeak Quiz." *QRD* 18 (January 1992): 8.

Lists 23 items in two columns, one for doublespeak term, the other for meaning, and asks readers to match the two. Answers appear in July 1992 issue.

678. Ehrlich, Susan, and Ruth King. "Gender-Based Language Reform and the Social Construction of Meaning." *D&S* 3 (April 1992): 151–66.

The authors identify factors which promote language change. However, they argue that gender-based language reform is not always successful because the dominant culture which influences meaning is sexist.

679. Fairclough, Norman. "Discourse and Text: Linguistic and Intertextual Analysis within Discourse Analysis." *D&S* 3 (April 1992): 193–217.

Argues that diverse approaches to discourse analysis can be enhanced through systematic use of linguistic and intertextual analysis. Suggests that textual analysis should be used more widely as a method in social research.

680. Firbas, Jan. *Functional Sentence Perspective in Written and Spoken Communication*. New York: Cambridge University Press, 1992. 240 pages

Focuses on the concept of "communicative dynamism" in a study of the Prague School theory of functional sentence perspective.

681. Fishman, Joshua A. *Reversing Language Shift: Theoretical and Empirical Foundations of Assistance to Threatened Languages*. Bristol, PA: Taylor and Francis Group, 1991. 448 pages

Argues that native languages of speech communities are threatened because of insufficient intergenerational continuity, with fewer and fewer speakers, readers, and writers every generation. Reviews sociolinguistic research and theory, examines attempted reversals of language shift on several continents, and suggests a more rational, systematic approach to the problem of language shift.

682. Foto, Sandra Sims. "Grammar Consciousness Raising Tasks: Negotiating Interaction while Focusing on Form." *DAI* 53 (November 1992): 1430A.

Indicates that the grammar consciousness-raising tasks successfully promoted proficiency gains and negotiated intersections in the task participants.

683. Frances, Christie. "Pedagogical and Content Registers in a Writing Lesson." *L&E* 2 (Spring 1992): 203–24.

Demonstrates genre analysis for examining the construction of classroom talk; argues that any teaching event represents some curriculum genre and that two registers make up curriculum genres.

684. Fries, Peter. "Lexico-Grammatical Patterns and the Interpretation of Texts." *DPr* 15 (January–March 1992): 73–91.

Analyzes paragraphs in terms of chains of equivalent semantic structures constrained by linkages involving both syntactic and intonational patterns.

685. Furrow, Melissa. "Listening Reader and Impotent Speaker: The Role of Deixis in Literature." *Lang&S* 21 (Fall 1988): 365–78.

Argues that the more deictics in a narrative passage, the stronger the connection between narrator and reader-as-listener.

686. George-Castagna, Susan. "Getting Things Done in Naples: A Description of Neapolitan Directives in Discourse." *DAI* 53 (September 1992): 789A.

Applies speech-act analysis to descriptions of discourse; finds that English and Italian speakers have quite different views on how to use language in different contexts.

687. Gilbert, Ron. "Text and Context in Qualitative Educational Research: Discourse Analysis and the Problem of Contextual Explanation." *L&E* 4 (Fall 1992): 37–57.

Critiques various contextual explanations in common ethnographic research models and argues that Fairclough's "critical language study" offers a superior analytical framework.

688. Givon, Talmy. "Markedness in Grammar: Distributional, Communicative and Cognitive Correlates of Syntactic Structure." *SLang* 15 (1991): 335–70.

Explores markedness through discussion of structural complexity, frequency distribution, and cognitive complexity in discourse, clause types, noun phrases, and verb phrases.

689. Gonzales, Félix Rodriguez. "Abbreviations and American Slang." *EnT* 8 (July 1992): 39–44.

Discusses acronyms and other types of abbreviations used by American students, soldiers, and nurses.

690. Gonzalez, Norma. "Child Language Socialization in Tucson: U.S. Mexican Households." *DAI* 53 (October 1992): 1202A.

Finds that the complexities of the Borderland's structural and hegemonic relationships cannot be addressed within a theoretical assumption of homeostatic and monosemic communities.

691. Gozzi, Raymond, Jr. " 'Hot' and 'Cool' Media." *ETC* 50 (Summer 1992): 227–30.

Maintains that McLuhan's use of "hot" and "cool" never caught on, nor were the two terms convincing.

692. Gozzi, Raymond, Jr. "Is the Computer a Valid Metaphor for the Human Mind?" *ETC* 48 (Winter 1991/1992): 445–51.

Sounds a caution about the use of the computer as a metaphor for mind but also notes that there are some areas where the metaphor is useful.

693. Gozzi, Raymond, Jr. "Stalking the Wild Metaphor." *ETC* 49 (Spring 1992): 82–85.

Talks about the difficulty of finding root metaphors; suggests that we explore historical accounts of nature as garden.

694. Greenberg, Joseph H., and Merritt Ruhlen. "Linguistic Origins of Native Americans." *ScAm* 267 (November 1992): 94–99.

Uses linguistic similarities to trace Asian tribes' migration to North America.

695. Greig, Flora Estella Ramírez. "Would You Talk to a Stranger? A Multicultural Study of Self-Report on Initiating and Maintaining Conversations in a Hypothetical Travel Encounter." *DAI* 52 (March 1992): 3262A.

Enquires into attitudes toward social talk with strangers in four countries: Costa Rica, Finland, Hong Kong, and the United States.

696. Herwitt, Richard M. "A New Language: Relativism in Ordinary Speech." *ETC* 50 (Winter 1992–1993): 387–97.

Discusses what Alan Bloom calls the "language of moral relativism"; examines the extent to which speakers consciously avoid definitive expressions.

697. Hicks, Deborah, and Rhoda Kanevsky. "Ninja Turtles and Other Superheroes: A Case Study of One Literacy Learner." *L&E* 4 (Fall 1992): 59–105.

Hicks and Kanevsky's case study of discourse style and literacy learning describes one child's journal use and documents his individual styles of language use in this domain.

698. Hitchens, Christopher. "Minority Report." *QRD* 18 (July 1992): 4–5.

Cites numerous examples of "politically correct language" in politics and journalism and argues that it represents "lying and jargon."

699. Hoffman, Gregg. "Conference Report." *ETC* 49 (Fall 1992): 360–62.

Describes an exercise which demonstrates the principles of general semantics and how those principles can help people to understand cultural diversity.

700. Hoffman, Gregg. "General Semantics and Cultural Diversity." *ETC* 49 (Fall 1992): 302–4.

Presents principles of general semantics that make people more aware of how they use language; recommends nonidentification and "non-allness."

701. Hoffman, Gregg. "The Semantics of a Sanity Trial." *ETC* 50 (Summer 1992): 231–33.

Points out the large number of abstractions employed by psychiatrists in the Jeffrey Daumer trial.

702. Hogg, Richard M., ed. *The Cambridge History of the English Language, Volume I: The Beginnings to 1066.* New York: Cambridge University Press, 1992. 609 pages

Presents the first volume of a chronologically oriented multivolume history of the English language; covers the history of the English language to the Norman Conquest of 1066; surveys scholarship and linguistic theory.
Essayists: Bammesberger, Alfred; Clark, Cecily; Godden, Malcolm R.; Hogg, Richard M.; Kastovsky, Dieter; Toon, Thomas E.; Traugott, Elizabeth Closs.

703. Hogg, Richard M., ed. *The Cambridge History of the English Language, Volume II: 1066–1476.* New York: Cambridge University Press, 1992. 692 pages

Presents the second volume of a chronologically oriented multivolume history of the English language; covers the Middle English period; surveys scholarship and linguistic theory.
Essayists: Blake, N. F.; Burnley, David; Clark, Cecily; Fischer, Olga; Lass, Roger; Milroy, James.

704. Hoh, Pau-san. "Writing as the Second Phase of Language Acquisition: Emergent Grammar in Basic Writing." *DAI* 53 (December 1992): 1889A.

Identifies the roots of writing problems in pregrammatical oral structure and proposes an "emergent grammar" to overcome processing constraints of syntactic/textual language.

705. Holt, Elizabeth Jane. "Figures of Speech: An Exploration of the Use of Idiomatic Phrases in Conversation." *DAI* 53 (February 1992): 3079A.

Explores the use of figures of speech, idioms, commonly used metaphors, and clichéd or formulaic language in naturally occurring conversation.

706. Hopper, Robert. *Telephone Conversation.* Bloomington, IN: Indiana University Press, 1992. 272 pages

Analyzes the rhythms, stresses, and "interactional organization" of everyday telephone conversations.

707. Jolliffe, Lee. "What's in a Name? On the Naming of Men and Sex Discrimination." *ETC* 50 (Winter 1992/1993): 490–92.

Reports research designed to learn whether men experience less prejudice than women on the basis of their names.

708. Kenkel, James M. "Argumentation Pragmatics, Text Analysis, and Contrastive Rhetoric." *DAI* 52 (May 1992): 3906A.

Finds no evidence to support Kaplan's hypothesis that language users across cultures vary in the means they use to construct coherent discourse.

709. Lazaraton, Anne. "Linking Ideas with *and* in Spoken and Written Discourse." *IRAL* 30 (August 1992): 191–206.

Presents a contrastive analysis of spoken and written texts for elements conjoined with *and*; looks at the type of connection and the semantic relations expressed by *and* in clausal connection.

710. Lea, Luanne C. "Words and Things—The Naming Game." *ETC* 49 (Fall 1992): 297–301.

Describes the negative effect of being overly concerned about specificity and precision in language; suggests that ambiguous language is often quite valuable.

711. Levine, Robert, ed. *Formal Grammar: Theory and Implementation*. New York: Oxford University Press, 1992. 439 pages

Thirteen writers, originally from a series of conferences at the Cognitive Science Programme of Simon Fraser University, discuss issues of cognition and mental representation.
Essayists: Carpenter, Bob; Church, Kenneth; Crain, Stephen; Dahl, Veronica; Dresher, B. Elan; Fodor, Janet Dean; Gawron, Mark; Hamburger, Henry; Jacobsen, Pauline; Kean, Mary-Louise; Oerhle, Richard T.; Shapiro, Lewis P.; Stabler, Edward P., Jr.; Zwicky, Arnold M.

712. Lippert, Paul. "The Semantics of Multiculturalism." *ETC* 49 (Spring 1992): 363–74.

Distinguishes between multiculturalism and cultural pluralism and maintains that multiculturalism is a rejection of intellectual excellence as a guiding idea in designing a curriculum.

713. Lovejoy, Kim Brian. "Cohesion and Information Strategies in Academic Writing: Analysis of Passages in Three Disciplines." *L&E* 3 (Summer 1992): 315–43.

Analyzes cohesion and information structuring strategies in texts from three disciplines, demonstrating differences in how various discourse communities create and share knowledge.

714. Lovejoy, Kim Brian, and Donald M. Lance. "Information Management and Cohesion in the Study of Written Discourse." *L&E* 3 (Spring 1992): 251–73.

The authors describe a system of discourse analysis which can yield detailed descriptions of how writers manage information and cohesion. They analyze scholarly texts from across disciplines.

715. Lucy, John Arthur. *Language Diversity and Thought: A Reformulation of the Linguistic Relativity Hypothesis*. New York: Cambridge University Press, 1992. 300 pages

Examines Edward Sapir and Benjamin Whorf's hypothesis that the grammar of a person's language affects her or his thinking about reality.

716. Luke, Allan. "The Body Literate: Discourse and Inscription in Early Literacy Training." *L&E* 4 (Fall 1992): 107–29.

Applying Foucault's discourse theory and Bordieu's critical sociology, Luke reframes literacy instruction as a "technology of self" which constructs and positions the literate through pedagogical discourses.

717. Lutz, William. "Bits of Information." *QRD* 18 (April 1992): 12–14.

Presents short reports on 11 items related to publications that are resources about advertising, the media, public relations, and politically correct and postmodern language.

718. Lutz, William. "Keeping Up with Your Reading." *QRD* 18 (April 1992): 14–16.

Provides an annotated bibliography of 10 recent books relevant to doublespeak.

719. Lutz, William. "News and Notes." *QRD* 18 (April 1992): 10–13.

Presents short reports on 16 items related to doublespeak in government, politics, advertising, and television, and on the QRD logo as "visual emblem of doublespeak."

720. Machan, Tim William, and Charles T. Scott, eds. *English in Its Social Contexts: Essays in Historical Sociolinguistics*. Oxford Studies in Sociolinguistics, edited by Edward Finegan. New York: Oxford University Press, 1992. 268 pages

Eleven essays address the traditional periods of English, acknowledging the effect of external social context on determining the direction of changes within the language's syntax, phonology, and lexicon. *Essayists:* Algeo, John; Carver, Craig M.; Finegan, Edward; Gunn, John; Kachru, Braj B.; Machan, Tim Williams; Rodby, Judith; Romaine, Suzanne; Scott, Charles T.; Smith, Jeremy J.; Toon, Thomas E.; Williams, Joseph M.

721. Mao, LuMing. "Pragmatic Universals and Their Implications." *DAI* 52 (February 1992): 2908A.

Studies oriental concepts of face and proposes to refine Grice's theory of conversation in light of pragmatic universals.

722. Martin, James E. *Towards a Theory of Text for Contrastive Rhetoric*. American University Studies: Linguistics, vol. 19. New York: Peter Lang, 1992. 221 pages

Addresses the issue of textuality as it relates to contrastive rhetoric, the study of culturally based differences in written discourse. Offers a theory of text with direct application to crosscultural and crossgenre research, and suggests implications for teaching ESL writing.

723. McLeod-Porter, Delma. "Gender, Ethnicity, and Narrative: A Linguistic and Rhetorical Analysis of Adolescents' Personal Experience Stories." *DAI* 52 (March 1992): 3265A.

Examines discourse and syntax to determine how adolescents "depict themselves and their worlds."

724. McNeill, David. *Hand and Mind: What Gestures Reveal about Thought*. Chicago: University of Chicago Press, 1992. 424 pages

Argues that gestures are not simply part of what is said and meant, but that they have impact on thought itself. Points out that gestures are global, synthetic, idiosyncratic, and imagistic. Manifests that the unity of gestures and language includes surface level of speech previously noted as well as semantic and pragmatic levels.

725. Meyer, Charles F. *Apposition in Contemporary English*. New York: Cambridge University Press, 1992. 152 pages

Studies the linguistic characteristics of appositon in speech and writing by analyzing the language of press reportage, fiction, learned writing, and spontaneous conversation.

726. Moore, Michael. "Double Negation." *ETC* 49 (Fall 1992): 305–9.

Presents a philosophical discussion of the effect of double negatives in different languages.

727. Murphy, John W., and Jung Min Choi. "Imagocentrism and the Rodney King Affair." *ETC* 50 (Winter 1992/1993): 478–84.

Discusses the difficulty of separating visual image from reality.

728. Nash, Walter. *An Uncommon Tongue: The Uses and Resources of English.* New York: Routledge, 1992. 232 pages

    Discusses how academic disciplines prescribe, describe, and analyze usage.

729. Nelson, Linda. "Cultural Context and Cultural Code in the Oral Life Narrative of African-American Women: An Ethnography of Speaking." *DAI* 53 (August 1992): 544A.

    Explores the influence of cultural context on the linguistic form and thematic content of life narrative discourse.

730. Nida, Eugene N. "Sociolinguistic Implications of Academic Writing." *LSoc* 21 (September 1992): 477–85.

    Argues that the language of academic journals tends to a level of technicality that unnecessarily limits its accessiblity.

731. Nietzsche, Friedrich. "Truth and Falsity in an Extra-Moral Sense [Translated by M. A. Mügge]." *ETC* 49 (Spring 1992): 58–72.

    Mügge translates Nietzsche's 1893 essay which explains truth as "a sum of human relations which become poetically and rhetorically intensified."

732. Nunan, David. *Research Methods in Language Learning.* New York: Cambridge University Press, 1992. 304 pages

    Presents an introduction to research methods in language learning aimed at teaching readers to critique language research.

733. Payne, Doris. "Narrative Discontinuity Versus Continuity in Yagua." *DPr* 15 (July–September 1992): 375–94.

    Points out that Yagua, a language spoken in Peru, has a morpheme that indicates that the information it is attached to is not completely continuous with preceding information.

734. Philipsen, Gerry. *Speaking Culturally: Exploitations in Social Communication.* Albany, NY: State University of New York Press, 1992. 154 pages

    Includes new and previously published essays on the speech of middle-class individuals living on the west coast and residents of a working-class, multiethnic neighborhood in Chicago.

735. Pocheptsov, Oleg G. "Mind Your Mind: Or Some Ways of Distorting Facts while Telling the Truth." *ETC* 50 (Winter 1992/1993): 398–405.

    Discusses how speakers can influence listeners by manipulating quantitative data.

736. Pringle, Ian. "Modality and Ethos in Academic Writing: A Comparison of Novices and Professionals." *CALS* 9 (1992): 67–88.

    Presents a comparison of student and professional choices of modals; reveals that students' struggle toward academic competence is hindered by writing for experts in their discipline.

737. *Proceedings of the 10th West Coast Conference on Formal Linguistics.* Edited by Dawn Bates. Chicago: University of Chicago Press, 1992. 536 pages

    Presents papers from traditional linguistic fields of phonology, morphology, syntax, semantics, and from developing areas of cognitive and discourse linguistics.

738. "Project Censored." *QRD* 18 (July 1992): 1.

    States the history and purpose of "Project Censored" and announces the top ten "censored" stories of 1991.

739. Pula, Robert P. "*Alfred Korzybski: Collected Writings 1920–1950*: An Appreciation and a Review." *ETC* 48 (Winter 1991/1992): 424–33.

    Discusses his work, *Alfred Korzybski: Collected Writings 1920–1950*, a book which includes letters and forewords to books as well as essays, and which takes a reader through the formation of Korzybski's thoughts and ideas.

740. Pula, Robert P. "A General Semantics Glossary." *ETC* 48 (Winter 1991/1992): 462–64.

Presents a brief glossary of semantic terms, designed to help students of general semantics to master the field's vocabulary.

741. Pula, Robert P. "A General Semantics Glossary (Part II)." *ETC* 50 (Summer 1992): 234–38.

Defines "process" and "time-bonding."

742. *QRD* 18 (January 1992): 1–8.

Announces 1991 Orwell and Doublespeak awards together with nominations for each category, resources on doublespeak, and the text of William Lutz's speech announcing awards.

743. Rank, Hugh. "Channel One/Misconceptions Three." *QRD* 18 (July 1992): 8–9.

Argues that the public's belief in advertising as "insignificant, ineffective, and not harmful" obscures the effects of Channel One's ads—significant, effective, and possibly harmful "units of persuasion."

744. "Resources." *QRD* 18 (July 1992): 2–3.

Lists without annotation, 40 articles and books from a variety of fields as resources for doublespeak.

745. "Resources." *QRD* 18 (October 1992): 9–10.

Lists, without annotation, 72 articles and books from a variety of fields as resources for doublespeak.

746. Reuter, Dennis. "Silent Knight: Protecting Yourself with Silence." *ETC* 48 (Winter 1991/1992): 434–39.

Explains that silence can protect people from pain and discomfort. Maintains that silence can lead to a decision not to translate the reality of experience into words.

747. Richardson, Ingrid. "The Production of Meaning." *QRD* 18 (July 1992): 10–11.

Cites examples to argue that evening news shows are based more on "official sources" than on in-depth reporting, resulting in superficiality and distortion.

748. Ross, Philip E. "New Whoof in Whorf: An Old Language Theory Regains Its Authority." *ScAm* 266 (February 1992): 24, 26.

Points out that the previously discredited Whorf Hypothesis, that language determines a person's perception of reality, is receiving new support.

749. Rowan, David. "Cloaking Cruelty in Kind Words." *QRD* 18 (July 1992): 16.

Cites numerous examples of euphemisms and jargon related to animal experimentation to illustrate how language separates emotion from action.

750. Rubal-Lopez, Alma. "English-Language Spread: Predicting Three Criteria." *DAI* 53 (September 1992): 964A.

Examines the spread of English in 121 non-English mother-tongue countries.

751. Saleemi, Anjum P. *Universal Grammar and Language Learnability*. New York: Cambridge University Press, 1992. 168 pages

Attempts to integrate Chomsky's theories with formal learning theory to explore the "acquisition of language as a cognitive system."

752. Sanders, Ted, Wilbert Spooren, and Leo Nordman. "Toward a Taxonomy of Coherence Relations." *DPr* 15 (January–March 1992): 1–35.

The authors argue that taxonomies of coherence must account not only for the descriptive facts but also for the psychological conditions underlying all successful inferences of coherence relations.

753. Sassoon, John. "Who on Earth Invented the Alphabet?" *VLang* 24 (Spring 1990): 144–63.

Poses possibilities for the invention, acceptance, and distribution of the alphabet.

754. Sawin, Gregory. "Chess, Science and General Semantics." *ETC* 49 (Spring 1992): 104–7.

Presents an exercise to help students articulate their cultural maps and to determine the correlation between map and territory.

755. Sawin, Gregory. "Mood, Memory, Thought, and Immunity." *ETC* 49 (Fall 1992): 349–51.

This exploration into the dynamics of human thought and behavior looks at the interrelationships between mood, thought, and language use.

756. Schleppergrell, Mary. "Subordination and Linguistic Complexity." *DPr* 15 (January–March 1992): 117–31.

Argues that responses to questions indicate that clauses beginning with *because* are not subordinate in the usual sense. Points out that definitions of complexity depending on subordination are thus problematic.

757. Schmandt-Besserat, Denise. *Before Writing Volume I: From Counting to Cuneiform*. Austin, TX: University of Texas Press, 1992. 304 pages

Argues that writing was an outgrowth of thousands of years' work of experiences at manipulating symbols. Asserts that the cuneiform script, the first written language in Western world, arose from a system of clay counters.

758. Schmandt-Besserat, Denise. *Before Writing Volume II: A Catalog of Near Eastern Tokens*. Austin: University of Texas Press, 1992. 544 pages

Presents primary data for supporting her theory that cuneiform script, the first written language in the Western World, was based on a system of clay counters.

759. Scott, Robert Ian. "Combating Doublespeak." *QRD* 18 (July 1992): 7–8.

Defines "numbspeak" and "nospeak" as related to doublespeak, describes six categories of questions aimed at getting at the truth of language, and provides a brief bibliography.

760. Semin, Gün R., and Klaus Fiedler, eds. *Language, Interaction, and Social Cognition*. Newbury Park: Sage, 1992. 262 pages

Explores the interrelationships between language, interaction, and social cognition. Addresses social categorization, stereotyping, attribution, patterns of communication, and sociocognitive syntactical rules.
Essayists: Arcuri, Luciano; Au, Terry Kitfong; Fiedler, Klaus; Gibbons, Pamela A.; Graumann, Carl F.; Hamilton, David L.; Maass, Anne; McGuire, Claire V.; McGuire, William J.; Pryor, John B.; Reeder, Glenn D.; Rothbart, Myron; Schwarz, Norbert; Semin, Gün R.; Sherman, Jeffrey; Strack, Fritz; Stroessner, Steven J.; Taylor, Marjorie; Wojciszke, Bogdan.

761. Shannon-Morla, Crystal Elaine. "Effect of Emotion on African-American Black English and Standard English Code-Shifting Bilinguals." *DAI* 53 (October 1992): 2075B.

Points out that subjects used Black English more when in emotive conditions.

762. Shapiro, Joseph P. "In Search of a Word for Disabled." *QRD* 18 (July 1992): 14–15.

Discusses various euphemisms and the way in which they are an attempt for groups to redefine themselves.

763. Sheridan, Paraic, and Alan F. Smeaton. "The Application of Morpho-Syntactic Language Processing to Effective Phrase Matching." *IPM* 28 (1992): 349–69.

Argues that a morpho-syntactic analysis of user queries is used "to generate a structured representation of text," which will become "part of an overall document retrieval strategy."

764. Siefert, Diana. "I Wish He or She Would Please Substitute His or Her Nongender-Specific Pronoun." *ETC* 49 (Spring 1992): 34–35.

Argues that it is time for grammar to change and to recognize the sense of using "they" as a nongender-specific pronoun.

765. Smith, Michael. "Soviet Language Frontiers: The Structural Method in Early Language Reforms, 1917–1937." *DAI* 53 (August 1992): 592A.

Studies how Soviet linguists applied their rudimentary structural perspectives to the tasks of language planning in the former Soviet Union.

766. Sommers, Elizabeth, and Sandra Lawrence. "Women's Ways of Talking in Teacher-Directed and Student-Directed Peer Response Groups." *L&E* 4 (Fall 1992): 1–35.

Analyzes women's talk in different peer group situations; finds that women participate more equally in teacher-directed groups than in student-directed groups.

767. Steward, Joseph L. "Comments on *To Be or Not*." *ETC* 49 (Summer 1992): 131–33.

Presents an analysis of articles in the collection of essays titled *To Be or Not*.

768. Strohner, Hans, and Roselore Brose. "A Cognitive Systems Approach to Linguistic Knowledge." *LangS* 14 (January–April 1992): 55–76.

Identifies four distinct yet interactive components of a cognitive grammar: sensorimotor, syntactic, semantic, and pragmatic.

769. Sure, Kembo. "Falling Standards in Kenya?" *EnT* 8 (October 1992): 23–28.

Discusses the state of English in Kenya and local attitudes toward the language.

770. Sutcliffe, David, and John Figueroa. *System in Black Language*. Bristol, PA: Taylor and Francis Group, 1992. 192 pages

Charts the systematic similarities between three groups of languages currently being spoken by people of African descent: United States Black English, Caribbean Creole, and the African Kwa Languages. Studies how the underlying divergences of Creole and Black English are masked by their surface resemblances to mainstream English.

771. Thomas, Andrew Lambert. "The Grammar and Pragmatics of Context-Dependence in Discourse." *DAI* 52 (April 1992): 3594A.

Explores the "interplay of grammar and pragmatics in the production of interpretation of utterances" in terms of the importance of context.

772. Toolan, Michael, ed. *Language, Text, and Context: Essays in Stylistics*. The Interface Series, edited by Ronald Carter. New York: Routledge, 1992. 335 pages

Argues that text is not separate from context, nor linguistic description from descriptive interpretation, nor language from situation.
Essayists: Clark, Kate; Dillon, George; Francis, Gill; Hastert, Marie Paule; Kintgen, Eugene R.; Kramer-Dahl, Anneliese; Leech, Geoffrey; Macleod, Norman; McHale, Brian; Mills, Sara; Nair, Rukmini Bhaya; Neumann, Anne Waldron; Simpson, Paule; Weber, Jean Jacques.

773. Traugott, Elizabeth Closs. "Semantics—Pragmatics and Textual Analysis." *Lang&S* 22 (Winter 1989): 51–65.

Argues that the study of pragmatics, because it is concerned with the nature of the interaction between text and reader, can contribute to literary theory.

774. Tyndall, Belle. "What Influences Rater's Judgment of Student Writing." *L&E* 3 (Spring 1992): 191–202.

Tyndall contrasts a linguistic analysis and a holistic evaluation of 30 student essays to see which linguistic measures of "maturity of expression" count most to individual evaluators.

775. Wajnryb, Ruth, and David Cervi. "Coping with Aussie English." *EnT* 8 (April 1992): 18–21.

Discusses some distinctive features of English in Australia.

776. Weshsler, Stephen Mark. "Argument Structure and Linking." *DAI* 52 (March 1992): 3268A.

Presents a linguistic analysis of argument structure, complement structure of verbs, and the role of lexical content.

777. Wierzbicka, Anna. *Semantics, Culture, and Cognition: Universal Human Concepts in Culture-Specific Configuration.* New York: Oxford University Press, 1992. 512 pages

Investigates ethno-philosophy and ethno-psychology; emotions; moral concepts; titles, names, and expressive forms of address; and kinship. Links the idea of universal human concepts with that of universal semantic primitives and presents culture-specific meanings as unique configuration of universal human concepts.

778. Wolf, George, ed. *New Departures in Linguistics.* New York: Garland, 1992. 266 pages

Publishes 14 essays that resulted from work in general linguistics, phonetics, and social anthropology at Oxford University. Covers such topics as feminism and linguistic theory, irony and theories of meaning, and the study of pidgin and creole languages. *Essayists:* Cameron, Deborah; Crowley, Tony; Davis, Hayley G.; Farrow, Steve; Harris, Roy; Henton, Caroline; Hutton, Christopher; Love, Nigel; Morris, Marshall; Muhlhausler, Peter; Taylor, Talbot J.; Toolan, Michael.

779. Xu, George Q. "The Major Concerns of Textlinguistics and Their Relevance to the Teaching of Writing." Clarion University, Clarion, PA, 1991. ERIC ED 338 060. 14 pages

Discusses the use of textlinguistics in writing instruction to investigate textuality rather than grammar; examines texts as acts of communication rather than individual static sentences.

2.9 PSYCHOLOGY

780. Aitken, Avril. " 'When the Woman Came Crying': Social Issues through Children's Writing." *EQ* 24.2 (1992): 20–24.

Shows how students can create characters in a discussion of gender issues that might help them face their own motives and beliefs.

781. Baily, Mary. "A Realistic Model of Writing: The Interaction between Writing Competence and Domain Knowledge." *DAI* 52 (May 1992): 6111B.

Proposes a new writing process model to incorporate the wide range of processes involved in writing in a new domain.

782. Begg, Ian Maynard, Ann Andas, and Suzanne Farinacci. "Dissociation of Processes in Belief: Some Recollection, Statement Familiarity, and the Illusion of Truth." *JEPG* 121 (December 1992): 446–58.

Presents the results of four experiments concerning the effect of repetition on determining "truth." Argues that familiarity and source recognition proved to be independent influences.

783. Bird, Gloria Frances. "Programmed Writing as a Method for Increasing Self-Esteem, Self-Disclosure and Coping Skills." *DAI* 53 (November 1992): 2536B.

Argues that writing is effective as therapy; shows that confronting experiences previously avoided can lead to positive change.

784. Bonge, Dennis R., W. John Schuldt, and Yolanda Y. Harper. "The Experimenter-as-Fixed-Effect Fallacy." *JPsy* 126 (September 1992): 477–86.

Using a model research design, this study suggests research techniques that avoid the experiment-as-fixed-effect fallacy.

785. Boninger, David Samuel. "The Effects of Cognitive Tuning and Personal Relevance on Cognitive Organization in Persuasion." *DAI* 52 (June 1992): 6697B.

Argues that people who expect to transmit persuasive information organize their responses to it more than others; points out that personal relevance also aids organization.

786. Brown, JoAnne. *The Definition of a Profession: The Authority of Metaphor in the History of Intelligence Testing, 1890–1930.* Princeton, NJ: Princeton University Press, 1992. 216 pages

> Explores the role of language in the establishment of intelligence testing as a subfield of psychology.

787. Brynes, Deborah A., and Gary Kiger. "Social Factors and Responses to Racial Discrimination." *JPsy* 126 (November 1992): 631–38.

> Explores the effects of gender and religious affiliation on college students' behavior toward authority figures, strangers, and peers who demonstrate racial discrimination.

788. Busemeyer, Jerome R., and In Jae Myung. "An Adaptive Approach to Human Decision Making: Learning Theory, Decision Theory, and Human Performance." *JEPG* 121 (June 1992): 177–94.

> Describes the "rule competition model" of decision-making, composed of two parts: how individuals predict payoff and how they fine-tune rules for predictions.

789. Castillo-Velez, Clara Maria. "Cross-Cultural Analysis of Narrative Comprehension." *DAI* 53 (September 1992): 1628B.

> Found that human memory is reconstructive and that culture affects processing; suggests that the closer the story to one's own culture, the deeper the processing.

790. Chan, Carol K. K., P. J. Burtis, Marlene Scardamalia, and Carl Bereiter. "Constructive Activity in Learning from Text." *AERJ* 29 (Spring 1992): 97–118.

> Investigates the effects of five levels of constructive activity on children's responses to short narrations.

791. Damasio, Antonio R., and Hanna Damasio. "Brain and Language." *ScAm* 267 (September 1992): 89–95.

> Examines how the brain processes language.

792. Edwards, Derek, and Jonathan Potter. *Discursive Psychology.* Inquiries in Social Construction, vol. 10. Newbury Park: Sage, 1992. 208 pages

> The authors present an integrated discursive action model which leads to a radical reworking of language, cognition, truth, knowledge, and reality. They also examine the communicative and interactional work performed when individuals describe and explain past events, construct factual reports, and attribute mental states.

793. Eidelberg, Paul. "The Malaise of Modern Psychology." *JPsy* 126 (March 1992): 109–20.

> Examines the consequences of psychological reductionism and, based on empirical evidence, concludes that the intellect has primacy over the emotions in human psychology.

794. Estes, W. K., and C. J. Burke. "Application of a Statistical Model to Simple Discrimination Learning in Human Subjects." *JEPG* 121 (December 1992): 422–26.

> Reprints a scientific study of discrimination learning as a result of reinforcement and nonreinforcement.

795. Forston, Maureen Tyson. "Disclosure of Traumatic Events Utilizing a Writing Task: Immunological, Physiological, and Psychological Consequences in a Psychiatric Population." *DAI* 52 (January 1992): 3904B.

> Points out that patients who wrote about traumatic events rather than trivia benefited in all three areas of study.

796. Fritsch, Kilian Joseph. " 'Zat Make Any Sense?' A Thick Description Discourse Analysis of Three Psychotherapy Consultations." *DAI* 52 (May 1992): 6083B.

> Argues that linguistic frames for the psychotherapeutic relationship have to be constructed on the spot, through interaction, and precisely enough to express the patient's distinctive "idioverse."

797. Gurman, Ernest B., and Keith Long. "Emergent Leadership and Female Sex Role Identity." *JPsy* 126 (May 1992): 309–16.

This study compares women's evaluations of their emergent leadership behavior with raters' evaluations to discover the effects of sex role identity on the evaluations.

798. Hartley, James. "Psychology, Writing and Computers: A Review of Research." *VLang* 25 (Fall 1991): 339–75.

Reviews and documents recent research on the nature of writing, learning to write, writing with computers, and evaluating writing.

799. Joseph, R. *The Right Brain and the Unconscious: Discovering the Stranger within.* New York: Plenum, 1992. 405 pages

Surveys developments in right brain/left brain theory as it applies to the unconscious. Contains major sections on neurodynamics, psychodynamics, defense mechanisms, and applications.

800. Junge, Maxine Borowshy. "Creative Realities: The Search for Meanings." *DAI* 53 (October 1992): 972A.

Examines the creativity process in artists and writers using McWhinney's Alternative Realities model.

801. Kellogg, Ronald T. *The Relative Ease of Writing Narrative Text.* San Francisco, CA: Annual Meeting of the Psychonomic Society, November 1991. ERIC ED 341 995. 43 pages

Presents a study of 16 college students; finds that narrative writing requires least effort and that persuasive writing exhibits the least cohesion and fluency.

802. Kounios, John, and Phillip J. Holcomb. "Structure and Process in Semantic Memory: Evidence from Event-Related Brain Potentials and Reaction Times." *JEPG* 121 (December 1992): 459–79.

This scientific study measured electrical activity of scalps of human subjects who were asked to verify the truth of statements relating categories and specific examples.

803. Leader, Zachary. *Writer's Block.* Baltimore, MD: Johns Hopkins University Press, 1992. 336 pages

Examines writer's block by discussing objections that psychoanalysts and philosophers have raised to overly simple distinctions between external and internal worlds. Finds helpful insights in poststructuralists' theory, including Derrida's view of the privileging of speech over writing and Lacan's correlations between linguistic and developmental repressions.

804. Miller, Alan. "Personality Types, Learning Styles, and Educational Goals." *EdPsy* 12 (1992): 217–37.

Argues that the conception of learning styles should be broadened and that a new typology of personality provides a system which supports such broadening.

805. Mineo, Paul James. "Argumentative Subsumption: A Test of a Cognitive Scheme for Argumentative Discourse." *DAI* 52 (April 1992): 3476A.

Provides a methodology to describe and explain the production and comprehension of argumentative discourse.

806. Mirtz, Ruth Marie. "Putting Meaning into Words: Nondiscursive Meaning-Making Processes in Students' Writing about Personal Experience." *DAI* 53 (October 1992): 1142A.

Reviews literature on the meaning-making processes of writing students and studies student cognitive processes when writing personal narratives.

807. Moore, Kathleen. "An Application of Linguistic Narrative Analysis to Psychoanalytic Process Research." *DAI* 53 (August 1992): 1070B.

Argues that the narrative of personal experience can provide a discrete discourse form to use as data in debates on the hermeneutic or scientific nature of psychoanalysis.

808. Moran, Aidan. "What Can Learning Styles Research Learn from Cognitive Psychology?" *EdPsy* 12 (1992): 239–45.

Explores how cognitive psychology can aid research on learning strategies by providing insight into the influence of prior knowledge and the value of metacognitive awareness.

809. Morgan, Oliver John. "In a Sober Voice: A Psychological Study of Long-Term Alcoholic Recovery with Attention to Spiritual Dimensions." *DAI* 52 (May 1992): 6069B.

Argues that despite diversity in the sample, the stories of long-sober alcoholics revealed common metaphors, themes, and ways of understanding recovery.

810. Riding, Richard, and Indra Cheema. "Cognitive Styles—An Overview and Integration." *EdPsy* 12 (1992): 193–215.

Reviews previous work on cognitive styles regarding methodology and definitions of cognitive styles; concludes that there are two principle cognitive styles.

811. Russ, David Allen. "The Use of Programmed Writing as a Treatment for Anxiety." *DAI* 53 (December 1992): 3165B.

Suggests that therapeutic writing, whether programmed or open-ended, reduces anxiety for both men and women.

812. Scanlon, Matthew, and James Mauro. "The Lowdown on Handwriting Analysis: Is It for Real?" *PsyT* 25 (November–December 1992): 46–58, 80.

Presents an interview with handwriting expert Andrea McNichol which lends credence to the science of graphology.

813. Schmeck, Ronald R., Elke Geisler-Brenstein, and Steven P. Cercy. "Self-Concept and Learning: The Revised Inventory of Learning Processes." *EdPsy* 12 (1992): 343–62.

Describes a learning style model which is comprised of two routes to academic achievement: reflective processing and agentic processing. Argues that the concept of self-as-student influences the success of these strategies.

814. "Sex Fetish: Dear Diary." *PsyT* 25 (May–June 1992): 18.

Presents findings by social historian Joan Jacobs Brumberg who studied women's diaries written over the past 150 years and who found a shift from the internal to the external.

815. Smagorinsky, Peter, and Michael W. Smith. "The Nature of Knowledge in Composition and Literary Understanding: The Question of Specificity." *RER* 62 (Fall 1992): 279–305.

Argues that to establish a coherent relationship between theory and practice, researchers and teachers need to articulate their assumptions about knowledge and the transfer of knowledge.

816. Sohn, David. "Knowledge in Psychological Science: That of Process or of Population?" *JPsy* 126 (January 1992): 5–16.

Discusses the benefits of researchers employing the process model rather than the population model to guide scientific studies on relationships.

817. Stroop, J. Ridley. "Studies of Interference in Serial Verbal Reactions." *JEPG* 121 (March 1992): 15–23.

Presents a reprint of a scientific study of the effects of interference on memory.

818. Vipond, Douglas. *The Write Stuff: On the Relation between Composition Studies and Psychology.* Quebec City, Quebec: The Canadian Psychological Association, June 1992. ERIC ED 347 547. 9 pages

Critiques the writing practices of psychologists.

819. Waldmann, Michael R., and Keith J. Holyoak. "Predictive and Diagnostic Learning within Causal Models: Asymmetries in Cue Composition." *JEPG* 121 (June 1992): 222–36.

The authors use the results of three experiments to prove that higher order types of learning cannot be reduced to lower order associative learning.

820. Weber, Robert J. *Forks, Phonographs, and Hot-Air Balloons: A Field Guide to Inventive Thinking.* New York: Oxford University Press, 1992. 277 pages

Argues that inventing in any discipline follows a basic set of heuristics that can be learned.

See also 640

2.10 EDUCATION

821. Aber, John. *Labels We Use to Describe Ourselves: What Do They Mean in Terms of Classroom Practice?* Cincinnati, OH: CCCC, March 1992. ERIC ED 344 235. 13 pages

Argues that theoretical labels teachers use to describe themselves may be at odds with their classroom practices. Analyzes theories and practices of three writing teachers.

822. Agnew, Eleanor. "Remedial English Ten Years after: Former Basic Writers in the Workplace." *DAI* 52 (March 1992): 3268A.

Results reveal significant development of esteem and ability in former basic writers.

823. Anderson, Warwick. " 'Where Every Prospect Pleases and Only Man Is Vile': Laboratory Medicine as Colonial Discourse." *CritI* 18 (Spring 1992): 506–29.

Emphasizes the ideological construction of texts that characterize the people and landscape of the Philipines as "dangerous."

824. Berger, Eva. "Metaphor, Mind, and Machine: An Assessment of the Sources of Metaphors of Mind in the Works of Selected Educational Theorists." *DAI* 52 (June 1992): 4311A.

Studies the metaphors of mind and knowledge in the works of selected leading theorists of education; points out the technological/social/natural conditions that characterized the time at which each educator was writing.

825. Berlin, James. "Freirean Pedagogy in the U. S.: A Response [to Olson, *JAC* 12 (Winter 1992)]." *JAC* 12 (Fall 1992): 414–21.

Supports the relevance and success of Freire's pedagogy in the United States.

826. Border, Laura L. B., and Nancy Van Note Chism, eds. *Teaching for Diversity.* New Directions for Teaching and Learning, no. 49. San Francisco: Jossey-Bass, 1992. 120 pages

Contains eight essays on diverse learning styles, ensuring equitable participation of all students in a class, and programs for helping faculty members and teaching assistants meet the needs of a changing student population.

Essayists: Anderson, James A; Adams, Maurianne; Collett, Jonathan; Greenberg, James D.; Jefferson, Debrah J.; Maher, Frances; Morrison, Minion KC; Paul, S. Pamela; Sadker, David; Sadker, Myra; Schmitz, Betty; Serrano, Basilio; Tetreault, Mary Kay Thompson; vom Saal, Diane R.

827. Bromwich, David. *Politics by Other Means: Higher Education and Group Thinking.* New Haven, CT: Yale University Press, 1992. 296 pages

Argues that the rivals in the debate over education all believe in the importance of culture. By contrast, the author contends that genuine education is concerned less with culture than critical thinking and independence of mind.

828. Buckley, William K., ed. *Beyond Cheering and Bashing: New Perspectives on* The Closing of the American Mind. Bowling Green, OH: Bowling Green State University Popular Press, 1992. 166 pages

Presents 18 essays on the 1987 book by Allan Bloom and on the debate it aroused concerning American culture and education.

Essayists: Bourgeois, Susan; Caucci, Frank; Clark, Lorraine; Graff, Gerald; Hain, Bonnie A.; Hovey, Kenneth Alan; Jones, Margaret C.; Lasch, Christopher; Lundberg, Patricia Lorimer; Peacock, John; Roche, Mark W.; Roth, John K.; Siedlecki, Peter; Stern, Milton R.; Thickstun, William; Zins, Daniel.

829. Campoy, Renee. "The Role of Technology in the School Reform Movement." *EdTech* 32 (July 1992): 17–21.

> Through discussing technology's efficacy, Campoy models its use and role as public relations tool, then places it at the top of the reform movement's priorities.

830. Chow, Mayling, Lee Dobson, Marietta Hurst, and Joy Nucich. *Whole Language: Practical Ideas*. Pippin Teacher's Library. Portsmouth, NH: Heinemann, 1992. 114 pages

> Explains classroom strategies for the whole language approach with special attention to evaluation.

831. Civikly, Jean M. "Clarity: Teachers and Students Making Sense of Instruction." *CEd* 41 (April 1992): 138–52.

> Reviews literature on instructional clarity, beginning with Rosenshine and Furst's 1971 research that identified this area as a key variable to the study.

832. Clancy, Patricia. "Referential Strategies in the Narratives of Japanese Children." *DPr* 15 (October–December 1992): 441–67.

> Argues that children under seven years can take account of a listener's needs, but their experience in successful reference may only be learned context-by-context.

833. Constas, Mark A. "Qualitative Analysis as a Public Event: The Documentation of Category Development Procedures." *AERJ* 29 (Summer 1992): 253–66.

> Argues for publicizing the process of doing qualitative research as a way to bolster the method's credibility.

834. Covington, Martin V. *Making the Grade: A Self-Worth Perspective on Motivation and School Reform*. New York: Cambridge University Press, 1992. 351 pages

> Argues that students try to maintain a positive self-image by trying to avoid failure. They try to achieve this, he suggests, by either cheating or setting goals that are so easily achieved that no risk is involved. Covington uses self-worth theory and other contemporary views to extract educational implications useful for educators and parents.

835. Delgado-Gaitan, Concha. "School Matters in the Mexican-American Home: Socializing Children to Education." *AERJ* 29 (Summer 1992): 495–513.

> Points out that parents care about education, but physical resources, emotional climate, and interpersonal interactions have an impact on how the parents act, especially toward homework.

836. Eisner, Eliot W., and Alan Peshkin, eds. *Qualitative Inquiry in Education: The Continuing Debate*. New York: Teachers College Press, 1990. 400 pages

> Points out the major issues in the qualitative versus quantitative debate in education. Discusses subjectivity and objectivity, validity, generalizability, ethics, and the uses of qualitative inquiry.
> *Essayists:* Apple, Michael; Barone, Thomas E.; Becker, Howard S.; Clark, Christopher M.; Donmoyer, Robert; Grumet, Madeline R.; Guba, Egon; Huberman, A. Michael; Jackson, Philip W.; Lincoln, Yvonna S.; Miles, Matthew B.; Phillips, D.C.; Roman, Leslie; Schofield, Janet Ward; Smith, Louis M.; Soltis, Jonas F.; Wolcott, Harry F.

837. Gallegos, Bernardo P. *Literacy, Education, and Society in New Mexico, 1693–1821*. Albuquerque, NM: University of New Mexico Press, 1992. 128 pages

> Describes the ways in which the spread of literacy both maintained and challenged the colonial social order.

838. Giroux, Henry A. *Border Crossings: Cultural Workers and the Politics of Education*. New York: Routledge, 1991. 256 pages

> Reexamines the academic disciplines by illuminating their shared intellectual and political concerns. Uses "border crossing" as a way to formulate the role cultural workers might play in the development of

a critical pedagogical practice that works across the disciplines.

839. Giroux, Henry A. "Literacy, Pedagogy, and the Politics of Difference." *CollL* 19 (February 1992): 1–11.

Argues that literacy must be defined in terms of postmodern/postcultural discourse which embraces difference and gives voice to more students.

840. Giroux, Henry A. "Post-Colonial Ruptures and Democratic Possibilities: Multiculturalism as Antiracist Pedagogy." *CCrit* 21 (Spring 1992): 5–39.

Giroux outlines plans for a "border pedagogy" of antiracist teaching within the context of a debate between liberal culture and cultural conservatism.

841. Haas, Lynda. "In Search of Dignity: Liberatory Literacy in the Two-Year College." *TETYC* 19 (December 1992): 258–65.

A writing teacher uses Freirean pedagogy to counter the idea that the sole purpose of attending college is to get a good job.

842. Halsey, A. H. *Decline of Donnish Dominion: The British Academic Profession*. New York: Oxford University Press, 1992. 344 pages

Presents a history of higher education and teaching in the twentieth century in Great Britain.

843. Harry, Beth. "An Ethnographic Study of Cross-Cultural Communication with Puerto Rican-American Families in the Special Education System." *AERJ* 29 (Summer 1992): 471–94.

Describes how professionals' inadequate explanation of events and reliance on written communication led to family mistrust in a cross-cultural special education setting.

844. Harste, Jerome C. *Children at Risk*. [Videotape]. Portsmouth, NH: Heinemann, 1992.

Part of the series on whole language classrooms, this tape shows how whole language instruction is particularly helpful for students at risk.

845. Harste, Jerome C. *Early Childhood*. [Videotape]. Portsmouth, NH: Heinemann, 1992.

Part of the series on whole language classrooms, this tape demonstrates how preschool, kindergarten, and first grade teachers can begin using whole language instruction.

846. Harste, Jerome C. *Multicultural Education*. [Videotape]. Portsmouth, NH: Heinemann, 1992.

Part of the series on whole language classrooms, this tape shows how teachers in multicultural and biblingual classes can use their students' culture and experience to create an effective curriculum.

847. Hertz-Lazarowitz, Rachel, and Norman Miller, eds. *Interaction in Cooperative Groups: The Theoretical Anatomy of Group Learning*. New York: Cambridge University Press, 1992. 294 pages

Presents recent research from education, developmental psychology, and social psychology to examine the development and social foundations of knowledge, social skills, and classroom factors in peer interaction, task and reward structures' effects on academic achievement, and positive intergroup relations.
Essayists: Dansereau, Donald F.; Gall, Sharon Nelson-Le; Harrington, Hugh J.; Hertz-Lazarowitz, Rachel; Johnson, David W.; Johnson, Roger T.; Kirkus, Valerie Benveniste; Knechel, Sharon; Maruyama, Geoffrey M.; McCarthey, Sarah J.; McMahon, Susan; Miller, Norman; O'Donnell, Angela M.; Petersen, Renee; Slavin, Robert E.; Webb, Noreen M.

848. Howe, Kenneth R. "Liberal Democracy, Equal Educational Opportunity, and the Challenge of Multiculturalism." *AERJ* 29 (Fall 1992): 455–70.

Argues that progressive liberal education theory can successfully respond to multicultural challenges if it refuses to conflate the cultural and the political.

849. Ihle, Elizabeth L., ed. *Black Women in Higher Education: An Anthology of Essays, Studies, and Documents*. Educated Women: Higher Education, Culture, and Professionalism, 1850–1950, edited by Barbara Solomon. New York: Garland, 1992. 341 pages

Presents a collection of 54 articles, essays, and other documents that illustrate the experience of African-American women pursuing higher education from the nineteenth century to the present. Individual authors are not indexed in this volume.

850. Kliebard, Herbert M. *Forging the American Curriculum: Essays in Curriculum History and Theory*. New York: Routledge, 1992. 256 pages

Argues that the decline of the humanities dates from the advent of Darwinism. Voices his concern for the acceptance of a bureaucratic model for education.

851. Knoblauch, C. H. "A Response to Gary Olson's Interview with Paulo Freire [*JAC* 12 (Winter 1992)]." *JAC* 12 (Fall 1992): 407–13.

Argues that looking to Freire for an educational philosophy may not be feasible for American educators.

852. Mahiri, Jabari. "Discourse in Sport: Language and Literacy Features of Preadolescent African-American Males." *DAI* 52 (June 1992): 4248A.

Presents an ethnographic study that details how language and literacy acquisition by young African-American males in a Youth Basketball Association was affected by the YBA program.

853. McLaren, Peter. "Critical Literacy and Postcolonial Praxis: A Freirian Perspective." *CollL* 19 (October 1992): 7–27.

Believes that "Freire's work can enable teachers to acquire forms of critical practice that can interrogate, destabilize, and disorganize dominant strategies of power/ knowledge relations and that in doing so teachers may envisage a means of enlisting pedagogy in the construction of a radical and plural democracy."

854. Noble, Douglas D. *The Classroom Arsenal*. Bristol, PA: Falmer Press, 1991. 238 pages

Examines the origins and implications of recent technological paradigms in education. Traces the influence of postwar military research on educational technology and current conceptions of learning, problem solving, and intelligence.

855. Nummikoski, Ritva M. "The Effects of Interactive Writing Assignments on the Written Language Proficiency of First Year Students of Russia." *DAI* 52 (January 1992): 2538A.

Finds that writing to the teacher did not improve the discourse fluency or discourse quality of Russian students more than did other methods.

856. Nunan, David. *Collaborative Language Learning and Teaching*. New York: Cambridge University Press, 1992. 224 pages

Presents the current theory on collaborative research, learning, and teaching.

857. Oakley, Francis. *Community of Learning: The American College and the Liberal Arts Tradition*. New York: Oxford University Press, 1992. 230 pages

Presents a history of humanistic education in the United States and asserts the continued relevance of liberal arts education.

858. Office of Educational Research and Improvement. "Abstracts of the Educational Research and Development Centers." Department of Education, Office of Educational Research and Improvement, Washington, DC, 1991. ERIC ED 341 372. 56 pages

Provides information on the 25 federally sponsored national centers for education.

859. Olson, Gary A. "History, Praxis and Change: Paulo Freire and the Politics of Literacy." *JAC* 12 (Winter 1992): 1–14.

Presents on interview in which Freire discusses liberatory pedagogy, the teacher's necessary authority, the need for "patient impatience," and the existence of a knowable, objective reality.

860. Peterson, Ralph. *Life in a Crowded Place: Making a Learning Community*. Portsmouth, NH: Heinemann, 1992. 160 pages

    Argues that a "community" atmosphere facilitates learning and provides advice for establishing a supportive classroom environment.

861. Rice, William Craig. "Toward Renewal of Audience: College Writing, Academic Culture, and Public Intellectual Discourse." *DAI* 52 (January 1992): 2524A.

    Examines the consequences of a fuller integration of public intellectual culture into higher education, specifically writing classes.

862. Richardson, John T., and Estelle King. "Gender Differences in the Experience of Higher Education: Quantitative and Qualitative Approaches." *EdPsy* 12 (1992): 363–82.

    Reviews previous research on the learning styles of men and women and concludes that parallel but distinct developmental schemes exist between genders.

863. Roth, Jeffrey. "Of What Help Is He? A Review of *Foucault and Education*." *AERJ* 29 (Winter 1992): 683–94.

    Reviews the first anthology to apply Foucault's work to education. Finds the essays intriguing but exclusively focused on the negative—domination, silencing, and categorization.

864. Rury, John L. *Education and Women's Work: Female Schooling and the Division of Labor in Urban America, 1870–1930*. SUNY Series on Women and Work, edited by Joan Smith. Albany, NY: State University of New York Press, 1991. 277 pages

    Examines the development of secondary education for urban women. Offers statistical evidence for the changing relationships between women's formal schooling and expanded opportunities for women entering the labor force.

865. Salisbury, David F. "Toward a New Generation of Schools: The Florida School Year 2000 Initiative." *EdTech* 32 (July 1992): 7–12.

    Outlines George Bush's 2000 plan for revamping one school system, its background requirements, technology, and curriculum.

866. Shor, Ira. *Empowering Education: Critical Teaching and Social Change*. Chicago: University of Chicago Press, 1992. 264 pages

    Analyzes obstacles to and resources for empowering education in a democratic society since the work of John Dewey. Addresses the economic, political, and personal needs of students.

867. Smyth, John. "Teachers' Work and the Politics of Reflection." *AERJ* 29 (Summer 1992): 267–300.

    Argues that reflective approaches to teaching, when based on practitioner forms of knowledge, do not emancipate but entrap. Offers alternative views on teaching.

868. Spanos, William. *The End of Education: Toward Posthumanism*. Pedagogy and Cultural Practice, edited by Henry Giroux and Roger Simon. Minneapolis: University of Minnesota Press, 1992. 352 pages

    Deconstructs the traditional liberal humanist pedagogy through Foucault and Heidegger and proposes a "posthumanist" dialogic model as replacement.

869. Spellmeyer, Kurt. *Common Ground: Dialogue, Understanding, and the Teaching of Composition*. Englewood Cliffs, NJ: Prentice Hall, 1992. 313 pages

    Presents a framework for postrhetorical, postconstructionist composition studies; encourages the transformation of the field by breaking with classical rhetoric and modern composition studies.

870. Stratman, John. *Reflections on Robert Brooke's "Underlife and Writing Instruction": Implications for Pre-Student Teachers in an English Methods Class.* Seattle, WA: NCTE, November 1991. ERIC ED 342 009. 13 pages

> Discusses the concept of "underlife" and how it becomes critical in achieving individual and social autonomy.

871. Tchudi, Stephen, Elaine Karls, and David Schaafsma. "Roger's City on the Moskva: A Writing Program in Moscow." *EJ* 81 (February 1992): 16–23.

> Narrates the experiences of American university professors and high school students participating in a two-week cross-cultural program; describes collaborative activities with Russian counterparts.

872. Thernstrom, Abigail. "The Drive for Racially Inclusive Schools." *Annals* 523 (September 1992): 131–43.

> Points out that "strategies to improve American education . . . frequently target inner-city schools"; argues that these unrecognized affirmative-action programs are unlikely to "close the racial gap in school performance."

873. Weaver, Constance, and Linda Henke, eds. *Supporting the Whole Language Movement: Stories of Teachers and Institutional Change.* Portsmouth, NH: Heinemann, 1992. 256 pages

> Twelve essays support whole language education over traditional education models. *Essayists:* Batten, M. A.; Clyde, J. A.; Condon, M. W. F.; Diederich, P.; Doe, J.; Files, J.; Fulwiler, L.; Hale, S.; Henke, L.; Krause, P.; Mack, N.; Mills, H.; Monson, R. J.; Moore, E.; Pahl, M. M.; Phinney, M. Y.; Siu-Runyan, Y.; Weaver, C.; Wills, P.

874. West, Richard Lee. "Exploring Student Questions in College Classrooms: The Effects of Teacher Immediacy and Biological Sex." *DAI* 53 (December 1992): 1728A.

> Examines the impact of immediacy and gender on the type of questions asked by students.

875. White House Conference on Library Information Services. "Information 2000: Library and Information Services for the 21st Century (Summary Conference Report)." U. S. Government Printing Office, Washington, DC, 1991. ERIC ED 341 399. 83 pages

> Presents a summary report of a White House conference; includes recommendations for literacy education. For related documents, see ERIC ED 337 188–202.

876. Yu, Xiao-Ming. "The Encounter between John Dewey and the Modern Chinese Intellectuals: The Case of the 1922 Education Reform." *DAI* 53 (September 1992): 751A.

> Examines Dewey's influence on reform. Argues that Dewey's pragmatism was compatible with Chinese tradition; points out that Chinese intellectuals used his ideas to establish a new culture in China.

2.11 JOURNALISM, PUBLISHING, TELEVISION, AND RADIO

877. Altschuler, Glenn C., and David I. Grossvogel. *Changing Channels: America in TV Guide.* Urbana, IL: University of Illinois Press, 1992. 232 pages

> Traces the nearly 40-year history of the weekly television magazine and describes its forays into social and political issues.

878. Audoin-Rouzeau, Stephane. *Men at War, 1914–1918: National Sentiment and Trench Journalism in France during the First World War.* Translated by Helen McPhail. Providence, RI: Berg Publishers, 1992. 223 pages

> Provides a translation of *14–18, Les Combattants des Tranchées.* Discusses broadsheets and other publications produced by and for French front-line soldiers during World War I.

879. Baldasty, Gerald J. *The Commercialization of News in the Nineteenth Century.* Madi-

son, WI: University of Wisconsin Press, 1992. 227 pages

Traces changes in newspapers' content during a period in which advertisers replaced political parties as the medium's chief financial backers.

880. Benedict, Helen. *Virgin or Vamp: How the Press Covers Sex Crimes*. New York: Oxford University Press, 1992. 309 pages

Examines the printed media's language in reporting on sex crimes to argue that slanted coverage perpetuates traditionalist, myth-ridden thinking about women.

881. Berkman, Dave. "The Promise of Early Radio and TV for Education—As Seen by Nation's Periodical Press." *EdTech* 32 (December 1992): 26–31.

Presents a history of radio and TV's relationship with education practices from the 1920s to the 1940s; finds that both had a great impact early on.

882. Chiaro, Delia. *The Language of Jokes: Analyzing Verbal Play*. New York: Routledge, 1992. 144 pages

Argues that "jokes have been neglected as rich sources of patterned creativity in language use."

883. Chin, Elaine. "Learning to Write the News." *DAI* 52 (March 1992): 3207A.

Presents an ethnographic study that describes how graduate students learn to prepare news stories.

884. Czapla, Pamela. "Analysis of Agency Appeal #88–1514 as a Decision-Making Process: A Case Study of Argument." *DAI* 53 (November 1992): 1323A.

Studies a cable television industry's appeal of the Federal Communication Commission's ruling on syndication by examining argument as causal, authoritative, analogical, and personal.

885. Dayan, Daniel, and Elihu Katz. *Media Events: The Live Broadcasting of History*. Cambridge: Harvard University Press, 1992. 320 pages

Explores the larger cultural significance of live broadcasts of public spectacles such as the Olympic games and Anwar Sadat's journey to Jerusalem.

886. Dow, Bonnie J. "Femininity and Feminism in *Murphy Brown*." *SCJ* 57 (Winter 1992): 143–55.

Demonstrates the need for greater critical attention to the range of feminist theories available for evaluation of rhetorical artifacts.

887. Ewen, Stuart. *Channels of Desire: Mass Images and the Shaping of American Consciousness*. 2d ed. Minneapolis: University of Minnesota Press, 1992. 247 pages

Studies American fashion, advertising, consumers, and popular culture.

888. Fehlman, Richard E. "Making Meanings Visible: Critically Reading T.V." *EJ* 81 (November 1992): 19–24.

Describes four modes of analysis that help make media texts visible. Discusses how teachers can use these to help students in meaning-making process.

889. Gerbner, George. "Life according to TV." *QRD* 18 (January 1992): 12.

Emphasizes the "symbolic environment" of television and argues for a new symbolic environmental movement designed to liberate the public from "manufactured daydreams."

890. Gerbner, George. "TV Versus Reality." *QRD* 18 (July 1992): 9–10.

Argues that those who watch more than four hours daily accept television's "distorted" portrayal of gender, jobs, age, health, race, and violence over reality.

891. Gilles, Roger Wayne. "Social Elite Constructionism: The Rhetoric of Commercial News." *DAI* 53 (October 1992): 1083A.

Argues that contemporary journalists require a subjectivist epistemology to comply with the standards of objectivity; discusses the institutional rhetoric of journalism.

892. Goozé, Marjanne E. "The Definitions of Self and Form in Feminist Autobiography Theory." *WS* 21 (1992): 411–29.

Surveys recent scholarship and argues that even poststructuralist readings of the genre are male-dominated and therefore marginalizing.

893. Hachten, William A., and Harva Hachten. *The World News Prism: Changing Media of International Communication*. 3rd ed. Ames, IA: Iowa State University Press, 1992. 210 pages

Describes the political, technological, and sociological environment in which journalists work. Includes two new chapters and revisions.

894. Hellweg, Susan A., Michael Pfau, and Steven R. Brydon. *Televised Presidential Debates: Advocacy in Contemporary America*. New York: Praeger Publishers, 1992. 200 pages

Discusses the sponsorship, format, character, and impact of presidential candidates' debates; focuses on the elections of 1960, 1976, 1984, and 1988.

895. Hindman, Sandra, ed. *Printing the Written Word: The Social History of Books, Circa 1450–1520*. Ithaca, NY: Cornell University Press, 1991. 332 pages

Essays discuss how early printers went about their work, what factors accounted for their economic success or failure, how artists collaborated with printers, and who made up the audience for new books.
Essayists: Armstrong, Lilian; Brown, Cynthia; Camille, Michael; Edmunds, Sheila; Heinlen, Michael; Hellinga, Lotte; Konig, Eberhard; Nellhaus, Tobin; Saenger, Paul; Tedeschi, Martha.

896. Johnson, Victoria Rae. "Utilizing Prolific Writers and Their Interconnections when Expanding on the Histories of a Discipline: American Geography as a Case Study." *DAI* 53 (September 1992): 732A.

Shows that only six percent of all geographers publishing in the two leading geographic journals wrote approximately 25 percent of the articles.

897. Korzenny, Felipe, and Stella Ting-Toomey, eds. *Mass Media Effects across Cultures*. Troy, NY: Sage, 1992. 269 pages

Attempts to navigate between polarized notions of how individuals and societies are affected in texts without being reductionist or overgeneral. Uses a three-part format: research review, approaches to research, and media's future.
Essayists: Berger, Arthur Asa; Casmir, Fred L.; Chaffee, Steven H.; Cohen, Akiba A.; Cooper, Thomas W.; Ferreira, Leonardo; Frost, Richard; Gozzi, Raymond, Jr.; Greenberg, Bradley S.; Heeter, Carrie; Hobbes, Renne; Korzenny, Felipe; Ku, Linlin; Lau, Tuen-yu; Li, Hairong; Madden, Kate; Morgan, Michael; Roeh, Itzhak; Schiff, Elizabeth; Shanahan, James; Smith, Ripley L.; Straubhaar, Joseph D.; Wicks, Robert H.; Witte, Kim.

898. LaFollette, Marcel Chotkowski. *Stealing in Print: Fraud, Plagiarism, and Misconduct in Scientific Publishing*. Los Angeles, CA: University of California Press, 1992. 298 pages

Focuses on the peer-review process in scientific journals.

899. Mann, Mary. "An Ethnographic Investigation of the Media as a Possible Antecedent of Suicidal Behavior in Hospitalized Adolescents." *DAI* 53 (July 1992): 201A.

Focuses on whether media presentation of actual or fictional suicide causes young people to imitate the behavior.

900. Mattelart, Armand. *Rethinking Media Theory: Signposts and New Directions*. Translated by James A. Cohen and Marina Urquidi. Media and Society, edited by Richard Bolton. Minneapolis: University of Minnesota Press, 1992. 219 pages

Presents an overview of theoretical developments in communications theory from the last twenty years.

901. McEnteer, James. *Fighting Words: Independent Journalists in Texas*. Austin, TX: University of Texas Press, 1992. 222 pages

Examines the lives and work of five controversial Texas journalists: William Brann, Don Biggers, John Granberry, Jr., Archer Fullingham, and Stoney Burns.

902. Neumann, W. Russell. *The Future of Mass Media*. New York: Cambridge University Press, 1991. 208 pages

Challenges the notion that new electronic media and the use of personal computers will lead to a significant fragmentation of the mass audience. Draws on a five-year study conducted in cooperation with senior corporate planners in the television, publishing, and newspaper industry.

903. Neumann, W. Russell, Marion R. Just, and Ann N. Crigler. *Common Knowledge: News and the Construction of Political Meaning*. Chicago, IL: University of Chicago Press, 1992. 172 pages

Describes how people actively reinterpret information from the news media. Draws on a survey of public perceptions of apartheid, AIDS, drug abuse, the Strategic Defense Initiative, and the 1987 stock-market crash.

904. Palen, John. "Dioxin in the News: From Ecologism to 'Enduring Values' in Press Coverage of a Science/Technology Controversy." *DAI* 53 (July 1992): 193A.

Examines *The New York Times* coverage of the emergence of the dioxin controversy from 1960 to 1988.

905. Puette, William J. *Through Jaundiced Eyes: How the Media View Organized Labor*. Ithaca, NY: ILR Press, 1992. 228 pages

Discusses how films, newspapers, television news, and entertainment programs depict unions. Includes case studies of the 1989–1990 United Mine Workers' strike against the Pittson Coal Group and of a dispute in Hawaii's construction industry.

906. Read, Donald. *The Power of News: The History of Reuters, 1849–1989*. New York: Oxford University Press, 1992. 480 pages

Traces the news agency's history from its beginnings in London in 1851 to its decision to go public in 1984.

907. Resis, Humphrey A., and Leroy L. Lashley. "The Editorial Dimensions of the Connection of Caribbean Immigrants to Their Referents." *JBS* 3 (March 1992): 380–91.

Studies communication factors that develop and reflect community among Caribbean immigrants.

908. Riffe, Daniel, and Don W. Stacks. "Student Characteristics and Writing Apprehension." *JourEd* 46 (Summer 1992): 39–49.

Describes the development of an instrument to identify dysfunctional writing attitudes exhibited by undergraduate students enrolled in mass communications courses.

909. Rose, Mark. "The Author in Court: Pope v. Curll (1741)." *CCrit* (21 Spring 1992): 197–217.

Explores copyright, author's rights, ownership of writing, and concepts of literary value by using Pope's suit against bookseller Curll for publication of Pope's correspondence with Swift.

910. Rosteck, Thomas. "Synecdoche and Audience in *See It Now's* 'The Case of Milo Radulovich.'" *SCJ* 57 (Spring 1992): 229–40.

Suggests one way in which a documentary text finds persuasive appeal via the particular case.

911. Sanders, Wayne. *Anti-Publication Rights and Fair Use: Free Speech, Copyright and the Four Factors*. Atlanta, GA: Speech Communication Association, November 1991. ERIC ED 341 081. 46 pages

Explores the implications of four recent court decisions regarding copyright; notes that they favor the rights of authors over the rights of users.

912. Schneirov, Mathew. "Popular Magazines and the Dreams of a New Social Order, 1893–1914." *DAI* 53 (December 1992): 1981A.

Explores the forerunner of modern American mass communications, the popular magazine, between 1893 and 1914.

913. Spigel, Lynn, and Denise Mann, eds. *Private Screenings: Television and the Female Consumer*. Minneapolis: University of Minnesota Press, 1992. 293 pages

The editors present ten essays about women as viewers of, and participants in, television in the United States. The collection is an expanded version of a 1988 issue of *Camera Obscura* that tries to "integrate feminist theories of representation and methods of cultural history and interpretation."
Essayists: Berry, Sarah; Bodroghkozy, Aniko; D'Acci, Julie; Deming, Robert H.; Enstein, Dan; Flitterman-Lewis, Sandy; Haralovich, Mary Beth; Joyrich, Lynne; Lafferty, William; Leibman, Nina; Lipsitz, George; Mann, Denise; Spigel, Lynn; Steinberger, Jillian; Vogt, Randall.

914. Springer, Craig Michael. "Society's Soundtrack: Musical Persuasion in Television Advertising." *DAI* 53 (December 1992): 1727A.

Develops and demonstrates a specialized methodology for the rhetorical criticism of television advertising music.

915. Taylor, Philip M. *War and the Media: Propaganda and Persuasion in the Gulf War*. New York: Manchester University Press, 1992. 352 pages

Includes a discussion of Allied and Iraqi attempts to manage the news.

916. Tulloch, John, and Simon Chapman. "Experts in Crisis: The Framing of Radio Debate about the Risk of AIDS to Heterosexuals." *D&S* 3 (October 1992): 437–67.

Explores how interviewers' procedures display of neutrality interact with intertextual authenticating devices to position each person as "expert" when interviewed singly.

917. Watkins, Patsy Guenzel. "An Analysis of the Impact of 'Desktop Publishing' on the Production and Design of Magazines." *DAI* 52 (June 1992): 4380A.

Contends that desktop publishing has not redefined the prepress operations of the magazine publishing industry.

918. Whalen, Elizabeth. "The Editing Equation: A Reply to Authors Who Ask, 'How Come You Changed My Stuff?' " *TC* 39 (August 1992): 329–33.

Describes the work of a professional editor, with an emphasis on the relationship between the editor and the writer.

919. Zaller, John R. *The Nature and Origins of Mass Opinion*. New York: Cambridge University Press, 1992. 367 pages

Explores how people form political opinions from information in the mass media.

920. Zawilinski, Kenneth. "The Affective Measurement of a Semiotic Manipulation of TV Advertising Visual Imagery." *DAI* 53 (July 1992): 226A.

Studies the applicability of semiotics to the study of visuals in the context of TV advertising.

2.12 PHILOSOPHY

921. Anderson, Amanda. "Cryptonormativism and Double Gestures: The Politics of Poststructuralism." *CCrit* 21 (Spring 1992): 63–95.

Examines "essentialism" in relation to persons and to concepts such as consciousness and will. Departs from theories of Habermas and subaltern studies of Gayatri Spivak.

922. Angus, Ian, and Lenore Langsdorf, eds. *The Critical Turn: Rhetoric and Philosophy in Postmodern Discourse*. Carbondale, IL:

Southern Illinois University Press, 1992. 240 pages

> The essays address the convergence of rhetoric and philosophy as it presents itself to a variety of interests that transcend the traditional boundaries of these fields.
> *Essayists:* Angus, Ian; Hikins, James W.; Hyde, Michael J.; Langsdorf, Lenore; Lanigan, Richard L.; McKerrow, Raymie E.; Miller, David James; Schrag, Calvin O.; Smith, Craig R.; Zagacki, Kenneth S.

923. Carruthers, Peter H. *Human Knowledge and Human Nature: A New Introduction to an Ancient Debate.* New York: Oxford University Press, 1992. 199 pages

> Focuses on tensions between empiricism and rationalism to examine the problems of skepticism in its historical context, and to rehabilitate empiricism as a mode of thinking.

924. Clark, Timothy. *Derrida, Heidegger, Blanchot: Sources of Derrida's Notion and Practice of Literature.* New York: Cambridge University Press, 1992. 219 pages

> Traces the sources of Derrida's thought; discusses his impact on deconstruction, philosophy, and literature.

925. Cohen, L. Jonathan. *An Essay on Belief and Acceptance.* New York: Oxford University Press, 1992. 163 pages

> Examines tensions between belief and acceptance in epistemology, philosophy of mind, and cognitive science.

926. Crusius, Timothy W. *A Teacher's Introduction to Philosophical Hermeneutics.* NCTE Teacher's Introduction Series. Urbana, IL: NCTE, 1991. 105 pages

> Explains in plain language the "hermeneutics of tradition" of Gadamer, Ricoeur, and Heidegger, contrasting it favorably with the "hermeneutics of suspicion" of Derrida and Nietzsche; discusses the advantages of using "positive" hermeneutics as the basis for a philosophy of composition, in particular a process approach to composition. Includes a bibliography.

927. Ducey, Mary K. "Aristotle on Pleasure: Reconciling Three Different Accounts." *DAI* 53 (September 1992): 831A.

> Asserts that Aristotle's three accounts of pleasure are distinctive yet consistent.

928. Eco, Umberto, ed. *Interpretation and Overinterpretation.* New York: Cambridge University Press, 1992. 151 pages

> Eco works out his theories of interpretation, with specific reference to his own novels; contains three response essays from Johnathan Culler, Richard Rorty, and Christine Brooke-Rose.
> *Essayists:* Brooke-Rose, Christine; Culler, Johnathan; Eco, Umberto; Rorty, Richard.

929. Gillett, Grant. *Representation, Meaning, and Thought.* New York: Oxford University Press, 1992. 213 pages

> Uses Wittgenstein's later philosophy to present a workable theory of mental content. Links topics in philosophy of mind, epistemology, philosophy of language, and philosophical psychology.

930. Golding, Sue. *Gramsci's Democratic Theory: Contributions to a Post-Liberal Democracy.* Toronto: University of Toronto Press, 1992. 221 pages

> Studies Gramscian radical democratic theory through a reading of the prison notebooks.

931. Graham, Keith. *Karl Marx, Our Contemporary: Social Theory for a Post-Leninist World.* Toronto: University of Toronto Press, 1992. 182 pages

> Identifies basic ideas and philosophical assumptions in Marx's work to place Marxist philosophy in a contemporary context.

932. Gunn, Giles. *Thinking across the American Grain: Ideology, Intellect, and the New Pragmatism.* Chicago: University of Chicago Press, 1992. 240 pages

Shows how the revival of pragmatism provides the most critically resilient and constructive response to intellectual challenges of postmodernism. Points out that pragmatism recognizes multiple truths, unstable interpretations, and competing interests.

933. Kent, Thomas. "Externalism and the Production of Discourses." *JAC* 12 (Winter 1992): 57–74.

Points out that the three dominant composition philosophies are all internalist views presupposing a Cartesian duality. Proposes instead the externalist views of Donald Davidson.

934. Kim, Tong-Sik. "The Limits of Ungrounded Rhetoric: A Criticism of Rorty's View of Language, Truth and Philosophy." *DAI* 52 (March 1992): 3311A.

Argues that Rorty's challenge to foundationalist epistemology and philosophy is flawed, partly because his rhetoric is ungrounded, and thus unsuccessful.

935. Matz, Louie John. "Freedom and Character in Plato's *Republic* and Hegel's *Philosophy of Right*." *DAI* 53 (September 1992): 834A.

Argues that Plato ignores the importance of educating experiences which enable citizens to understand the rationality of the political order. Points out that Hegel argues for subjective freedom and defines the individual in political and social terms.

936. Nealon, Jeffrey T. "Exteriority and Appropriation: Foucault, Derrida, and the Discipline of Literary Criticism." *CCrit* (21 Spring 1992): 97–119.

Determines whether theories of Derrida and Foucault are related or antagonistic. Contends that works of both writers are continuously misread.

937. Olalquiaga, Celeste. *Megalopolis: Contemporary Cultural Sensibilities*. Minneapolis: University of Minnesota Press, 1992. 112 pages

Discusses the social aspects of postmodern life and culture, city and town life, technology, and popular culture.

938. Sadoski, Mark. "Imagination, Cognition, and Persona." *RR* 10 (Spring 1992): 266–78.

Explores imagery in modern philosophy and cognitive psychology to support the contention that mental imagery and imagination are basic to composing.

939. Sartre, Jean-Paul. *Notebooks for an Ethics*. Translated by David Pellauer. Chicago: University of Chicago Press, 1992. 640 pages

Explores fundamental modes of relating to the Other. Articulates the necessary transition from individualism to historical consciousness.

940. Tankha, Vijay. "The Analogy between Virtue and Crafts in Plato's Early Dialogues." *DAI* 53 (September 1992): 835A.

Explains how philosophy is revealed as a craft of virtue.

941. Thomas, Douglas Edward. "Toward a Nietzschean Theory of Rhetoric: The Valuative Interpretation of Discourse and the Reversal of Platonism." *DAI* 53 (December 1992): 1727A.

Explores the relationship between community and language found throughout Nietzsche's oeuvre.

942. Thomassen, Niels. *Communicative Ethics in Theory and Practice*. Translated by John Irons. New York: St. Martin's Press, 1992. 232 pages

Translates *Samvaer og solidaritet*. Examines the work of Gadamer, Habermas, Kierkegaard, and other philosophers to study conflict, communication, and power.

943. Waugh, Patricia. *Practising Postmodernism/Reading Modernism*. New York: Routledge, 1992. 192 pages

Argues that postmodernism began with philosophers such as Kant, who included ideas "embodied in Romantic and modernist art."

2.13 SCIENCE AND MEDICINE

944. Ashworth, Thomas Edward. "Using Writing-to-Learn Strategies in Community College Associate Degree Nursing Programs." *DAI* 53 (September 1992): 696A.

Finds that writing-to-learn strategies improved the students' performance on critical thinking tests.

945. Burris, James F. "Review of *Research Proposals: A Guide for Success* by Thomas E. Ogden (NY: Raven, 1990)." *AM* 67 (September 1992): 574–75.

Praises the book for its advice on writing NIH grants, but points out several major inaccuracies and places where updating is needed.

946. Charon, Rita. "To Build a Case: Medical Histories as Traditions in Conflict." *L&M* 11 (Spring 1992): 115–32.

Shows that medical encounters and their resultant documents (case histories) are instances of opposition between the writer and her subject. Argues that exploring this opposition through writing can improve medical care.

947. Child, Paul William. "Discourse and Practice in Eighteenth-Century Medical Literature: The Case of George Cheye." *DAI* 53 (September 1992): 815A.

Discusses Cheyne's treatises which were published over a forty-year period and examines how he sought legitimacy through publications.

948. Cohn, Victor. "A Madison Avenue Spin on Medical Terms." *AM* 67 (February 1992): 102–3.

Reflects on the changing medical terminology that further dehumanizes and depersonalizes the patient-caregiver relationship.

949. Eisenberg, Anne. "Imperial English: The Language of Science?" *ScAm* 267 (December 1992): 162.

Argues that linguistic incompetence in science can be attributed to the neglect of foreign language study.

950. Flood, David H., and Rhonda L. Soricelli. "Development of the Physician's Narrative Voice in the Medical Case History." *L&M* 11 (Spring 1992): 64–83.

Maintains that the formulaic, depersonalized nature of the case history diminishes the patient as a cultural text; emphasizes that the physician's role as narrator can be a corrective measure.

951. Hartman, Sandee L., and Marc S. Nelson. "What We Say and What We Do: Self-Reported Teaching Behavior Versus Performance in Written Simulations among Medical School Faculty." *AM* 67 (August 1992): 522–27.

The authors argue that teachers who report admirable teaching behaviors on voluntary evaluations are less likely to incorporate those behaviors into written exercises in curricular design and performance. They point out that researchers should observe teachers and not just rely on questionnaires.

952. Hensel, William A., and Teresa L. Rasco. "Storytelling as a Method for Teaching Values and Attitudes." *AM* 67 (August 1992): 500–504.

Argues in favor of using written and oral narratives to help students see how theoretical concepts apply in medical practice.

953. Hunter, Kathryn Montgomery. "Remaking the Case." *L&M* 11 (Spring 1992): 163–79.

Argues that the written narrative of the individual case embodies the physician's fundamental way of knowing. Points out that this can yield productive knowledge.

954. Juhasz, Alexandra Jeanne. "Re-Mediating AIDS: The Politics of Community Produced Video." *DAI* 53 (September 1992): 650A.

Concludes that media representations of AIDS reinforce negative stereotypes of the disease's victims.

955. King, Nancy M. P., and Ann Folwell Stanford. "Patient Stories, Doctor Stories, and True Stories: A Cautionary Reading." *L&M* 11 (Fall 1992): 185–99.

The authors argue that an analysis of medical narratives must take into account both physicians' and patients' interpretative readings of events. Suggests avenues for such readings for the audience.

956. Krause, Katherine C. "Review of *The Medical Interview: A Primer for Students of the Art*, 2d ed., by John L. Coulehan and Marion R. Block (Philadelphia: Davis, 1991)." *AM* 67 (September 1992): 573–74.

Commends the book's treatment of writing style and writer/reader dynamics, particularly in cases where the interviewer/interviewee relationship is complicated.

957. Locke, David Millard. *Science as Writing*. New Haven, CT: Yale University Press, 1992. 237 pages

Examines scientific texts by drawing on six critical theories used in literary interpretation.

958. Morowitz, Harold J., and James S. Trefil. *The Facts of Life: Science and the Abortion Controversy*. New York: Oxford University Press, 1992. 179 pages

Provides information from several disciplines about the scientific background of the abortion debate.

959. Moyer, Albert E. *A Scientist's Voice in American Culture: Simon Newcomb and the Rhetoric of Scientific Method*. Berkeley, CA: University of California Press, 1992. 319 pages

Traces the career of American astronomer Newcomb (1835–1909) and describes his efforts to extend the scientific method to politics, economics, and other areas of society.

960. Parks, Leland H., Garold O. Minns, and Robert T. Manning. "A Computer-Based Information Access and Management System for Students." *AM* 67 (August 1992): 505–6.

The study shows that third-year medical students using notebook PCs wrote more notes on patients more accurately, accessed more data, and improved in clinical performance.

961. Poirier, Suzanne, Lorie Rosenblum, Lioness Ayres, Daniel J. Brauner, Barbara F. Sharf, and Ann Folwell Stanford. "Charting the Chart—An Exercise in Interpretation(s)." *L&M* 11 (Spring 1992): 1–22.

Presents the multidisciplinary discussion of the interpretive issues involved in a typical medical record. Discusses the nature of this kind of written text.

962. Reeves, Carol. "Owning a Virus: The Rhetoric of Scientific Discovery Accounts." *RR* 10 (Spring 1992): 321–36.

Explores the rhetoric of Robert Gallo's discovery account of AIDS. Suggests studying such accounts for insight into debates within scientific communities.

963. Stewart, Larry R. *The Rise of Public Science: Rhetoric, Technology, and Natural Philosophy in Newtonian Britain, 1660–1750*. New York: Cambridge University Press, 1992. 400 pages

Analyzes public attitudes toward science and technology before the Industrial Revolution and discusses the scientific and entrepreneurial activities of Newton's disciples.

964. Wright, Will. *Wild Knowledge: Science, Language, and Social Life in a Fragile Environment*. Minneapolis: University of Minnesota Press, 1992. 236 pages

Critiques notions of objectivity in scientific knowledge and discusses relevant critical social theory.

2.14 CROSS-DISCIPLINARY STUDIES

965. Alpern, Sara, Joyce Antler, Elisabeth Israels Perry, and Ingrid Winther Scobie, eds. *The Challenge of Feminist Biography: Writing the Lives of Modern American Women*. Urbana, IL: University of Illinois Press, 1992. 208 pages

>Looks at the lives of 10 influential twentieth-century American women and the challenges experienced by the women who have written about them. Each essay begins with a two-page profile of the biographer's subject, followed by the story of writing that woman's life.
>*Essayists:* Alpern, Sara; Antler, Joyce; Garrison, Dee; Hall, Jacquelyn Dowd; Perry, Elisabeth Israels; Rudnick, Lois; Scobie, Ingrid Winther; Sklar, Kathryn Kish; Ware, Susan; Wexler, Alice.

966. Athanases, Steven Z., David Christiano, and Susan Drexler. "Family Gumbo: Urban Students Respond to Contemporary Poets of Color." *EJ* 81 (September 1992): 45–54.

>Describes the collaborative efforts of a university professor and two high school teachers who arranged a literature and history course around social issues.

967. Axtell, James. *Beyond 1492: Encounters in Colonial North America*. New York: Oxford University Press, 1992. 376 pages

>Explores the role of imagination and perspective in the Colonial/Native American encounter; includes an analysis of the treatment of college textbooks during this early period.

968. Beach, Richard, Judith L. Green, Michael L. Kamil, and Timothy Shanahan, eds. *Multidisciplinary Perspectives on Literacy Research*. Urbana, IL: National Conference on Research in English (NCRE) and NCTE, 1992. 417 pages

>Writers "from a variety of disciplines present their approach to language research, demonstrate what data from this perspective look like, and explicate the assumptions upon which it is based." Topics include specific disciplinary approaches, difficulties involved in multidisciplinary research, and connections between disciplinary perspectives and teaching.
>*Essayists:* Bailey, Francis W.; Bloome, David; Brodkey, Linda; Cook-Gumperz, Jenny; Feldman, Ann Matsuhashi; Golden, Joanne M.; Graesser, Arthur C.; Gumperz, John J.; Gundlach, Robert; Hayes, John R.; Heap, James L.; Hillocks, George, Jr.; Hunt, Russell; Hynds, Susan; Magliano, Joseph P.; McLaren, Peter; Moll, Luis C.; Pearson, P. David; Siegel, Marjorie; Stephens, Diane; Tidwell, Paula M.; Vipond, Douglas.

969. Boulding, Elise. *The Underside of History: A View of Women through Time*. 2 vols. Newbury Park: Sage, 1992. 800 pages

>Offers an alternative to the traditional courtesans/queens/mothers/mistresses view of women in history. Provides an account of women's creativity in every age from prehistory to the present, and attempts to view women's roles in the context of the time span of human experience.

970. Claggett, Fran, and Joan Brown. *Drawing Your Own Conclusions: Mapping Metaphors in the English Classroom*. Portsmouth, NH: Boynton/Cook, 1992. 225 pages

>Offers theories and strategies linking graphics and the making of meaning in reading, writing, and thinking.

971. Constantino, Roselyn. "Resistant Creativity: Interpretative Strategies and Gender Representation in Contemporary Women's Writings in Mexico." *DAI* 53 (September 1992): 824A.

>Argues that the discursive strategies of Rosario Castellano, Sabina Berman, and Carmen Boullosa are tools for rewriting Mexican sociocultural context and history.

972. Cortazzi, Martin. *Narrative Analysis*. Bristol, PA: Falmer Press, 1992. 224 pages

> Shows how narratives can be analyzed from a variety of perspectives, drawing on several models within each of the disciplines of sociology, psychology, literary analysis, and anthropology.

973. Crow, Gary M., Linda Levine, and Nancy Nager. "Are Three Heads Better than One? Reflections on Doing Collaborative Interdisciplinary Research." *AERJ* 29 (Winter 1992): 737–53.

> Presents reflections on cross-disciplinary collaboration in a study of students who learn to teach. Four dimensions of the study are explained and critiqued.

974. Delamont, Sara. *Fieldwork in Educational Settings: Methods, Pitfalls and Perspectives*. Bristol, PA: Falmer Press, 1992. 224 pages

> Presents a guide to doing qualitative research in educational settings by using sociological and anthropological perspectives.

975. Denzin, Norman K. *Symbolic Interactionism and Cultural Studies: The Politics of Interpretation*. Oxford: Blackwell, 1992. 217 pages

> Shows how approaches to interpretation in cultural studies reenergize some of its methodological debates.

976. Draper, Virginia. *Can Writing Programs Change the University? Change from the Margins*. Cincinnati, OH: CCCC, March 1992. ERIC ED 336 439. 7 pages

> Offers reflections of a writing-across-the-curriculum coordinator about helping faculty to assist students to write better.

977. Hadaway, Nancy L., and JaNae Mundy. "Crossing Curricular and Cultural Boundaries: A Study of Family Folklore." *EJ* 81 (October 1992): 60–64.

> Describes the collaboration of a university professor and a high school ESL teacher in a reading/writing project that takes students' backgrounds into consideration.

978. Hammersley, Martyn. *What's Wrong with Ethnography?* London: Routledge, 1992. 240 pages

> Finds a number of inconsistencies in ethnography that lead to a questioning of its assumptions. Distinguishes between ethnography, case study, survey, and experiment.

979. Harrison, Viola May. "Audience Relationships from a Connected Perspective: A Feminine Approach to Writer/Reader Relations." *DAI* 53 (September 1992): 798A.

> Uses feminist literature to develop an expanded view of audience relationships by reviewing gender in its psychological, cognitive, and epistemological aspects.

980. Harste, Jerome C. *Education as Inquiry*. [Videotape]. Portsmouth, NH: Heinemann, 1992.

> Part of the series on whole language classrooms, this tape explains how reading and writing can be taught with the process approach across the curriculum.

981. Hesford, Wendy S. "Women Reading the Self, the Word, the World: A Descriptive Study of the Metaphorical Constructs of Self and Composing in the Autobiographical Writings and Meta-Texts of Eight College Women." *DAI* 53 (September 1992): 745A.

> Suggests ways to reform the use of autobiography in composition and to broaden its definition.

982. Johnson, Yvonne. "The Voices of African-American Women: The Use of Narrative and Authorial Voice in the Works of Harriet Jacobs, Zora Neale Hurston, and Alice Walker." *DAI* 53 (September 1992): 810A.

> Examines the development of the female African-American tradition by taking an interdisciplinary approach to texts of different genres.

983. Kern, Richard G., and Jean Marie Schultz. "The Effects of Composition Instruction on Intermediate Level French Students' Writing

Performance: Some Preliminary Findings." *Language Journal* 76 (Spring 1992): 1–13.

Provides evidence that instruction in the writing process and the development of higher-order skills can improve students' writing performance in the foreign language curriculum.

984. Kerns, Virginia, and Judith K. Brown, eds. *In Her Prime: New Views of Middle-Aged Women.* 2d ed. Urbana, IL: University of Illinois Press, 1992. 288 pages

Presents a collection of articles about middle-aged women in different cultures around the world.
Essayists: Antonovsky, Aaron; Boddy, Janice; Brown, Judith K; Counts, Dorothy Ayers; Datan, Nancy; Gutmann, David; Kaufert, Patricia A.; Kerns, Virginia; King, Barbara J.; Lambek, Michael; Lancaster, Jane B.; Lee, Richard B.; Lock, Margaret; Maoz, Benjamin; Raybeck, Douglas; Sacks, Karen Brodkin; Sinclair, Karen P.; Solway, Jacqueline S.; Vatuk, Sylvia; Whiting, Beatrice Blyth.

985. Klein, Joan Larsen, ed. *Daughters, Wives, and Widows: Writings by Men about Women and Marriage in England, 1500–1640.* Urbana, IL: University of Illinois Press, 1992. 320 pages

Collects 14 texts on the subject of women and marriage in Renaissance England, and provides introductions, glosses, and an up-to-date bibliography.
Essayists: Brathwaite, Richard; Du Bosc, Jacques; Leigh, Dorothy; Perkins, William; Roselin, Eucharius; Stubbes, Philip; Tusser, Thomas; Vives, Juan Luis.

986. Maddalena, Nicholas Charles. "Linking Writing to Reading: The Effect of Thematic Instruction in Geography on Retention and Writing Quality." *DAI* 52 (March 1992): 3233A.

Results indicate that writing enhances coherence, content, and retention of facts.

987. McCarthy, Lucille. *Intertextuality in Psychiatry: Revising the DSM-III Charter.* Cincinnati, OH: CCCC, March 1992. ERIC ED 345 243. 15 pages

Analyzes the rhetorical task of revising a diagnostic manual of mental disorders.

988. Pao, Miranda Lee. "Global and Local Collaborators: A Study of Scientific Collaboration." *IPM* 28 (1992): 99–109.

Maintains that collaboration in scientific fields not only advances research (shared resources) but increases productivity (authorship) and visibility and is positively linked to funding.

989. Peterson, Nancy Jean. "The Politics of Language: Feminist Theory and Contemporary Works by Women of Color." *DAI* 53 (September 1992): 812A.

Examines feminist theories and demonstrates how women of color interact in an exclusive discursive world by calling upon the power of language.

990. Raynaud, Claudine. "Rites of Coherence: Autobiographical Writings by Hurston, Brooks, Angelou and Lorde." *DAI* 53 (September 1992): 812A.

Looks at the sexual and racial dynamics at work under the surface of these women's writings.

991. Reiff, John, and Judith Kirscht. "Inquiry as a Human Process: Interviews with Researchers across the Disciplines." *JAC* 12 (Fall 1992): 359–72.

A phenomenological investigation of the research process in several disciplines yields common features and a general model for designing student research projects.

992. Reinharz, Shulamit. *Feminist Methods in Social Research.* New York: Oxford University Press, 1992. 384 pages

Presents feminist research methods as distinctive from other research methods; covers interviews, ethnography, surveys, experiments, cross-cultural work, content analysis, cases, action research, multiple methods, and original methods.

993. Rosenthal, Anne Marie. "Transforming the Cultural Politics of Writing across the Curriculum: Cross-Disciplinarity, Advanced Literacy, and Democracy." *DAI* 53 (November 1992): 1505A.

Reexamines the general/special binary in writing across the curriculum by investigating its cultural politics including representations of social, constitutions of the subject(s) of advanced literacy, perspectives on democracy, and meanings of the cross-disciplinary.

994. Schilb, John. " 'Traveling Theory' and the Defining of New Rhetorics." *RR* 11 (Fall 1992): 34–48.

Demonstrates how theory is altered as it moves from one discipline to another, using an essay by Elaine Maimon. Claims that Maimon reverses Fish's ideas about communities.

995. Schultz, Kara L. "Breaking the Sound Barrier: The Rhetoric of the 'Deaf Power' Movement." *DAI* 52 (January 1992): 2325A.

Examines the form, function, nature, and motivations of the movement's rhetoric using Burke's dramatistic method.

996. Snarrenberg, Robert. "Writing Music." *DAI* 52 (January 1992): 2317A.

Argues that readers and writers alike confront a connection between rhetoric and value whose expression can be traced in the figures of speech used by writers to present theories and analyses of music.

997. Spivak, Gayatri Chakravorty. *Outside the Teaching Machine*. New York: Routledge, 1992. 350 pages

Focuses on multicultural thinking in the university and on ideas such as postcolonialism and international feminism. The 14 chapters cover topics such as *Satanic Verses*, *Sammy and Rosie Got Laid*, the fiction of Mahasweta Devi, and Foucault's concept of "power/knowledge."

998. Stocking, George W., Jr. *The Ethnographer's Magic: And Other Essays in the History of Anthropology*. Madison: University of Wisconsin Press, 1992. 440 pages

Discusses the history of anthropology from the nineteenth century to today; focuses on the major themes of academic anthropology and ethnography.

999. Valdés, Guadalupe, Paz Haro, and Maria Paz Echevarriarza. "The Development of Writing Abilities in a Foreign Language: Contributions toward a General Theory of L2 Writing." *Language Journal* 76 (Autumn 1992): 332–52.

Examines the relationship between the foreign language profession's assumptions about the development of writing skills in the second language and the actual growth of those skills.

1000. Yahya, Zawiah. "Resisting Colonialist Discourse: Three Strategies." *DAI* 53 (September 1992): 808A.

Aims at destabilizing colonialist discourse by resisting institutionalized reading conventions. Uses the work of Foucault, Althusser, Said, Bakhtin, and Macherey to show that text does not have a universal meaning.

1001. Zumwalt, Rosemary Lévy. *Wealth and Rebellion: Elsie Clews Parsons, Anthropologist and Folklorist*. Urbana, IL: University of Illinois Press, 1992. 384 pages

Points out that Parsons was a central figure in the professionalization of anthropology, the first woman elected president of the American Anthropological Association, and a president of the American Folklore Society. Uses her papers, letters, and books to produce Parsons's autobiography.

See also 1152

2.15 OTHER

1002. Weisman, Leslie Kanes. *Discrimination by Design: A Feminist Critique of the Man-*

Made Environment. Urbana, IL: University of Illinois Press, 1992. 208 pages

Discusses why women feel unsafe in cities and why the current housing crisis poses a greater threat to women than to men. Shows how dwellings, communities, and public buildings would look if they were designed to foster relationships of equality and environmental wholeness.

1003. Whitehead, Tony L., and Barbara V. Reid, eds. *Gender Constructs and Social Issues*. Urbana, IL: University of Illinois Press, 1992. 320 pages

Addresses the theoretical work on gender, applying it to contemporary gender-related issues such as transsexuality and sex-change surgery, gender identity and mental retardation, father-daughter incest, men and family planning, career choices, tubal litigations and hysterectomies, postpartum depression, spouse battering, marital rape, and pornography.

Essayists: Angrosino, Michael V.; Bolin, Anne; Davis, Dona Lee; Eisenhart, Margaret A.; Giovanini, Maureen J.; Hoff, Lee Ann; Holland, Dorothy C.; McKinnon, Catharine A.; Reid, Barbara V.; Storer, John H.; Whitehead, Tony L.; Zagnoli, Lucinda J.

3
Teacher Education, Administration, and Social Roles

3.1 TEACHER EDUCATION

1004. Arnold, Rick, Bev Burke, Carl James, D'Arcy Martin, and Barb Thomas. "Education for Change." Doris Marshall Institute for Education and Action, Toronto, Canada, 1991. ERIC ED 336 628. 217 pages

Offers a guide to build both skills and confidence in teachers as they educate for social change.

1005. Baker, Melinda E. *The Rhetoric and Politics of Teaching Assistants*. Cincinnati, OH: CCCC, March 1992. ERIC ED 346 456. 9 pages

Reports on a survey study of communication among teaching assistants; indicates that power relationships influence the rhetoric used when they talk about being either students, teachers, or professionals.

1006. Baldwin, Dolly Langela Serreno. "Using Journal Writing to Evoke Critical Thinking Skills of Students in Teacher Education." *DAI* 53 (July 1992): 111A.

Finds that the four participating students used more inferring and analyzing skills in their journal writing than the clarifying and evaluating skills.

1007. Belanger, Joe. "Teacher Research as a Lifelong Experiment." *EJ* 81 (December 1992): 16–23.

Examines "potential contributions" of research to the individual and the profession; explains "projects which can be carried out by inquiring teachers in average classrooms."

1008. Bird, Tom. "Making Conversations about Teaching and Learning in an Introductory Teaching Education Course." Michigan State University, National Center for Research on Teacher Learning, East Lansing, MI, 1991. ERIC ED 337 454. 22 pages

Offers observational research on first-year students expecting to major in teacher education.

3.1 TEACHER EDUCATION

1009. Bishop, Wendy. "At That Spot in Our Lives: Stories of Teachers Returning to School." *CS/FEN* 20 (Fall 1992): 5–16.

Tells the stories of experienced teachers of composition and literature who returned to school for doctoral study.

1010. Boardman, Kathleen A. *Educational Autobiographies of Feminist Teachers*. Cincinnati, OH: CCCC, March 1992. ERIC ED 337 767. 11 pages

Discusses the teaching practices of three feminist writing teachers; compares their own college learning with their current classroom practices.

1011. Bullough, Robert V., Nedra A. Crow, and J. Gary Knowles. *Emerging as a Teacher*. New York: Routledge, 1991. 235 pages

Traces the professional development of teachers through the case histories of six people during their first year in the classroom.

1012. Dahl, Karin L., ed. *Teacher as Writer: Entering the Professional Conversation*. Urbana, IL: NCTE, 1992. 296 pages

The contributors argue that "teacher writers tell the educational community information it simply does not hear from other sources." The essays relate teachers' experiences in becoming published writers, explore the professional importance of writing, advise writers on writing well for publication, and give information on various "support systems" for teachers who write.
Essayists: Anson, Chris M.; Austing, Patricia J.; Casbergue, Reneé; Cochran-Smith, Marilyn; Crowe, Chris; Dahl, Karin L.; Deitrich, Margaret A.; Dillard, Jill; Donelson, Ken; Durst, Russel K.; Feathers, Karen M.; Five, Cora Lee; Frager, Alan M.; Gorrell, Nancy; Healy, Mary K.; Kibler, Thelma; Lytle, Susan L.; Maylath, Bruce; McGee, Lea M.; Milz, Vera E.; Monroe, Rick; Nelms, Ben F.; Newkirk, Thomas; Prater, Doris L.; Romano, Thom; Simmons, Jay; Swinger, Alice K.; Teale, William H.; Tompkins, Gail E.; Tway, Eileen; Van Ryder, Betty; Winters, Rod.

1013. Dilworth, Mary E., ed. *Diversity in Teacher Education: New Expectations*. The Jossey-Bass Education Series and the Jossey-Bass Higher and Adult Education Series. San Francisco: Jossey-Bass, 1992. 278 pages

Presents 12 essays on recruiting minority students and faculty members for teacher education programs. The contributors discuss ways to prepare prospective teachers of all backgrounds for culturally diverse student populations.
Essayists: Arends, Richard I.; Ashburn, Elizabeth A.; Beckum, Leonard C.; Brown, Carlton E.; Buckley, Cozetta W.; Chin, Philip C.; Clemson, Shelley; Garibaldi, Antoine M.; Gollnick, Donna M.; Henkelman, James; Irvine, Jacqueline Jordan; Manning, JoAnn B.; Mills, Johnnie Ruth; Mitchell, Jean; Nelson-Barber, Sharon S.; Schuhmann, Ana Marie; Winfield, Linda F.; Wong, Gay Yuen; Zimpher, Nancy L.

1014. Fishman, Steve. *Exploring Water-Tight Compartments*. Cincinnati, OH: CCCC, March 1992. ERIC ED 346 473. 11 pages

Claims that Dewey's ideas about integrating the compartments within an individual's personality can help composition teachers understand the struggle for integration.

1015. Freidus, Helen. *Critical Issues in the Curriculum of Teacher Education Programs*. Chicago, IL: American Educational Research Association, April 1991. ERIC ED 336 348. 28 pages

Sketches writing assignments in a teacher-training program, including journal writings, personal narratives, and reflective teaching.

1016. Gordon, Christie Marie. "The Effect of Teacher Response on Student Dialogue Journals." *DAI* 52 (March 1992): 3247A.

Investigates the effects of three different types of responses on journals prepared by preservice teachers.

1017. Harrington, Helen L., and James W. Garrison. "Cases as Shared Inquiry: A Dialogical Model of Teacher Preparation." *AERJ* 29 (Winter 1992): 715–35.

The authors argue that case-based approaches to teacher education should combine theory and practice by having cases inititate shared inquiry. They critique cases as application of theory.

1018. Hollis, Karyn L. "Feminism in Writing Workshops: A New Pedagogy." *CCC* 43 (October 1992): 340–48.

Outlines points of feminist composition theory and pedagogy that can be presented during faculty, TA, or WAC workshops to improve composition instruction.

1019. Hult, Christine. *Computers in Support of Teacher Training*. Cincinnati, OH: CCCC, March 1992. ERIC ED 345 248. 7 pages

Reports on a computer classroom used for teacher training.

1020. Hunsaker, Linda, and Marilyn Johnston. "Teacher under Construction: A Collaborative Case Study of Teacher Change." *AERJ* 29 (Summer 1992): 350–72.

Describes how an elementary teacher changes reading and writing instruction as she learns more about reflective thinking and collaboration in a four-year study.

1021. Hutchings, Pat. "Using Cases to Talk about Teaching." *AAHE* 44 (April 1992): 6–10.

Describes a method of training teachers by presenting situations that pose realistic classroom problems. Includes a sample case developed by the AAHE Teaching Initiative.

1022. Kemp, Leroy. *Relationship among Afro-American Preservice Teachers' Competence in Writing, Critical Thinking, and Learning to Teach Effectively: Pedagogical Implications*. Lexington, KY: Mid-South Educational Research Association, November 13–15, 1991. ERIC ED 340 704. 50 pages

Examines writing process as instructional strategy for enhancing writing and reflective competence. Supports the idea that focused free writings help formalize students' cognitive structures.

1023. Livdahl, Barbara Smith. "A Response-Centered Approach in the Secondary Language Arts Classroom: The Teachers' Perspective." *DAI* 52 (March 1992): 3168A.

Describes positive consequences of written and spoken response in the development of teacher-researchers.

1024. McBroom, Geraldine L. "A New Crop of Teaching Assistants and How They Grew." *WPA* 15 (Spring 1992): 62–68.

Summarizes the findings of a self-examination process conducted by teaching assistants during their first term of teaching.

1025. McClelland, Susan Mary. "The Use of Dialogue Journals and Support Groups for the Professional Development of Mentors and Interns during the Teaching Internship." *DAI* 52 (March 1992): 3249A.

Illuminates the effectiveness of keeping journals, emphasizing the development of sharing techniques and experiences.

1026. McDermott, Peter, and Julia Rothenberg. *The Role of Literature and Writing in Social Studies Methods Texts: A Case for Change in Teacher Education*. Portsmouth, NH: New England Educational Research Organization, April 1991. ERIC ED 337 339. 26 pages

Examines current Social Studies methods texts to determine how writing and literature are presented.

1027. Nussbaum, Jon F. "Effective Teacher Behaviors." *CEd* 41 (April 1992): 167–80.

Reviews literature from 1983 to 1990 and offers ideas for future studies.

1028. Parsons, Priscilla Kay. "Effects of the Wisconsin Writing Project on Teacher and Student Perceptions of the Teacher's Role in Writing." *DAI* 53 (December 1992): 1782A.

Investigates the effects of the Wisconsin Writing Project as a viable method of development by looking at the impact upon teachers' processes of teaching writing.

1029. Recchio, Thomas E. "Parallel Academic Lives: Affinities of Teaching Assistants and Freshmen Writers." *WPA* 15 (Spring 1992): 57–61.

Argues for the appropriateness of graduate students as writing teachers of first-year students because of a shared "transitional status."

1030. Rude-Parkins, Carolyn. "Computer-Based Curriculum Development Tools for Teachers." *JEdM&H* 1 (Spring 1992): 179–86.

Reports on a district's experience with initial and follow-up training on Hypercard authoring for 240 high school teachers.

1031. Russell, Tom, and Hugh Munby, eds. *Teachers and Teaching: From Classroom to Reflection*. Bristol, PA: Falmer Press, 1992. 230 pages

Twelve chapters represent recent developments in teacher education in the United States, Canada, United Kingdom, and Australia. Develops important new meanings for "reflection" in the context of teaching and teacher education.
Essayists: Artz, Sibylle; Baird, John R.; Barnes, Douglas; Bellamy, Mary Louise; Horko, Hilda; Carter, Kathy; Clandinin, D. Jean; Erickson, G.; Kilbourn, Brent; Russell, Tom; Sanders, Linda.

1032. Shulman, Judith H. "Revealing the Mysteries of Teacher-Written Cases: Opening the Black Box." Far West Laboratory for Educational Research and Development, San Francisco, CA, August 1991. ERIC ED 339 693. 301 pages

Examines processes and skills involved in helping teachers write narratives about cases rich enough to be useful in teacher education programs.

1033. Sprague, Jo. "Critical Perspectives on Teacher Empowerment." *CEd* 41 (April 1992): 181–203.

Presents a bibliographic essay that also contains recommendations for ways in which teachers can gain "organizational power."

1034. Storia, Steven R. *Peer Observation for Instructor Training and Program Observation*. Cincinnati, OH: CCCC, March 1992. ERIC ED 337 798. 13 pages

Describes benefits of peer observation for first-year composition instructors. Includes observation forms and guidelines.

1035. Strenski, Ellen. "Helping TAs across the Curriculum Teach Writing: An Additional Use for the *TA Handbook*." *WPA* 15 (Spring 1992): 69–75.

Suggests that WPAs can help teaching assistants become effective writing teachers by publishing information about student writing in a campus *TA Handbook*.

1036. Swilky, Jody. "Reconsidering Faculty Resistance to Writing Reform." *WPA* 16 (Fall/Winter 1992): 50–60.

Claims that a close look at the sources and nature of resistance to writing across the curriculum can illuminate possible resolutions for oppositional attitudes.

1037. U.S. Congress. "America 2000 Excellence in Education Act: Proposed Legislation and a Message from the President of the United States." House of Representatives Document 102–91, Washington, DC, 1991. ERIC ED 341 115. 118 pages

Presents proposed legislation, with provisions for teacher training and for regional literacy centers, accompanied by a letter from President Bush.

3.2 ADMINISTRATION

1038. Bishop, Wendy. *Writing as Therapy, Writing Teachers as Therapists, WPAs as ?—*

Underexplored Analogies for Composition. Saratoga Springs, NY: WPA Conference, June 1991. ERIC ED 337 775. 19 pages

> Argues that writing teachers and WPAs should be trained to deal with the psychoanalytic aspects of student writing and to provide support and counseling.

1039. Corbett, Edward P. J. "The Shame of the Current Standards for Promotion and Tenure." *JAC* 12 (Winter 1992): 111–16.

> Deplores the excessive stress on publication for promotion and tenure in English as unbalanced and harmful.

1040. Elman, Sandra E., and Sue Marx Smock. "A Continuing Conversation about Professional Service." *AAHE* 44 (May 1992): 10–13.

> Examines the service required of faculty by institutions and disciplinary associations and recommends that professional associations should have more influence on faculty reward decisions.

1041. Hickson, Mark, and Don W. Stacks, eds. *Effective Communication for Academic Chairs.* SUNY Series in Speech Communication, edited by Dudley D. Cahn. Albany, NY: State University of New York Press, 1992. 231 pages

> Presents 12 essays on such topics as managing grievances, departmental assessment, motivating faculty members, external public relations, and communicating with administrative peers.
> *Essayists:* Applbaum, Ronald L.; Bennett, Carla; Deetz, Stanley A.; Gillespie, Patti Peete; Jandt, Fred E.; Kable, June; Kaufman, John A.; Kovar, Susan K.; McCroskey, James C.; McGlone, Edward L.; Richmond, Virginia P.; Scott, Randall K.; Smith, Robert M.; Spicer, Christopher H.; Stano, Michael; Staton, Ann Q.; Taylor, Anita.

1042. Laurence, David. "From the Editor." *ADE Bulletin* 102 (Fall 1992): 1–5.

> Outlines five steps that help prevent factionalization and identifies first-year writing as one of the four crucial topics, posing specific questions departments and universities face.

1043. McLeod, Susan H. "Responding to Plagiarism: The Role of the WPA." *WPA* 15 (Spring 1992): 7–16.

> Looks at different definitions of plagiarism and offers practical advice for WPAs in handling the problem.

1044. O'Neal, Barbara Jean. "Sex Discrimination in Higher Education." *DAI* 53 (October 1992): 1014A.

> Discusses the increase of sexual discrimination litigations filed against institutions of higher education. Reviews the laws and history of state employment discrimination laws.

1045. Orlans, Harold. "Affirmative Action in Higher Education." *Annals* 523 (September 1992): 144–58.

> Argues that affirmative action programs have benefited women and Asians more than blacks, mainly because of "the consequences of slum life and schools."

1046. Phelps, Louise Wetherbee. "A Constrained Vision of the Writing Classroom." *ADE Bulletin* 103 (Winter 1992): 13–20.

> Defines an ethic of politics for teachers and administrators based on a theory of care tempered by the concept of legitimate power and practical contextual considerations.

1047. Rankin, Elizabeth. "In the Spirit of Wyoming: Using Local Action Research to Create a Context for Change." *WPA* 16 (Fall/Winter 1992): 62–70.

> Tells a story from her home institution and calls for an enactment of the "principles of the Wyoming Resolution within institutional contexts."

1048. Whichard, Nancy Wingardner, Cayo Gamber, Valerie Lester, Gordon Leighton, Judith Carlberg, and William Whitaker. "Life in the Margin: The Hidden Agenda in Commenting on Student Writing." *JTW* 11 (Spring/Summer 1992): 51–64.

> The six part-time writing teachers conclude that unless writing teachers are employed full-time, the status quo of writing instruction will not be challenged.

1049. Yerkes, Diane, and Sharon Morgan. "Strategies for Success: An Administrator's Guide to Writing." National Association of Secondary School Principals, Reston, VA, 1991. ERIC ED 335 683. 32 pages

> Offers solutions to the most common writing problems that administrators face.

3.3 SUPPORT SERVICES

1050. Amato, Katya. "Pluralism and Its Discontents: Tutor Training in a Multicultural University." *WLN* 17 (December 1992): 1–6.

> Argues that language theories used in ESL can be applied to all writers.

1051. Bartonsenki, Mary. "Color, Re-Vision, and Painting a Paper." *WCJ* 12 (Spring 1992): 159–73.

> Describes the collaboration between a female tutor and a female art student. Shows that revising in several "layered" ink colors helps the student to resee and transform her writing process.

1052. Brodersen, Lynn, Karen Kassebaum, Diane Pregler, and Robert Marrs. "A Database Invades the Writing Center." *WLN* 16 (February 1992): 11–14.

> Concludes that forms and databases are only supplements to one-on-one conferences that organize information about students, tutors, assignments, and tutorials.

1053. Cain, Mary Ann. "What Can a Writing Program Be When the Director Doesn't Believe in Freshman Composition?" *CS/FEN* 20 (Fall 1992): 63–72.

> Offers insights as director of writing at a campus with rapidly expanding numbers in composition classes. Suggests that writing programs should be re-imagined without first-year composition.

1054. Carino, Peter. "What Do We Talk about When We Talk about Our Metaphors: A Cultural Critique of Clinic, Lab, and Center." *WCJ* 13 (Fall 1992): 31–42.

> Examines the cultural implications of, and historical reasons for, labeling university and college writing tutoring services as "clinics," "labs," or "centers."

1055. Cavazza, Marc, and Pierre Zweigenbaum. "Extracting Implicit Information from Free Text Technical Reports." *IPM* 28 (1992): 609–18.

> The study presents a prototype information processing system that extracts pertinent information, both explicit and implicit, from a text. Uses physicians' patient discharge summaries in test situations.

1056. Crisp, Sally, Ruby Bayani, Earnest Cox, Donna Crossland, Chad Fitz, Darryl Haley, Paige James, Briget Laskowski, Ferrol Lattin, Kerri Lowry, Leroy Mayfield, Lisa Mongnobove, Cheryl Patterson, and Charlesena Walker. "Assertive Collaboration in the Writing Center: Discovering Autonomy through Community." *WLN* 16 (March 1992): 11–16.

> Distinguishes between tutoring and collaborating. Argues for assertive collaboration. Offers two definitions of the term and describes six benefits the concept/practice can promote.

1057. Croft, Mary. "Not about Heroes Is about Tutors." *WLN* 16 (April 1992): 10.

> Argues that performances should be used for tutor training because they can show one-on-one interaction.

1058. Crump, Eric. "On-Line Community: Writing Centers Join the Network World." *WLN* 17 (October 1992): 1–5.

> Explains electronic forums. Describes the writing center as a nonthreatening environment where people can discuss issues of interest online.

1059. Crump, Eric. "Voices from the Net: Grappling with Institutional Contexts." *WLN* 17 (November 1992): 10–12.

> Discusses Valerie Balester's article concerning the status of writing centers. Argues that writing centers should make themselves central to the institution's (not a department's) mission.

1060. Crump, Eric. "Voices from the Net: Lifting the Veil from Writing Anxiety." *WLN* 17 (December 1992): 10–12.

> Attributes writing anxiety to hyper-critical teachers and "higher standards," lack of self-confidence due to negative experiences, and their inability to consider themselves writers.

1061. Cullen, Roxanne. "Writing Centers as Centers of Connected Learning." *WLN* 16 (February 1992): 1–4.

> Compares tutoring to midwifery. Shows how tutors parallel the "connected teacher" described by Mary Belenky, et al. in *Women's Ways of Knowing*.

1062. Davis, Kevin. "Evaluating Writing Center Tutors." *WLN* 16 (March 1992): 1–6.

> Cites four reasons for evaluating tutors. Argues against direct observation and client evaluation in favor of an "impressionistic method." Includes two forms and explains their use.

1063. Devet, Bonnie. "National Certification of a Writing Lab." *WLN* 17 (October 1992): 12–13.

> Argues that a lab's being certified by College Reading and Learning Association (CRLA) validates a training program and the qualifications of tutors as "trained professionals."

1064. Di Pardo, Anne. " 'Whispers of Coming and Going': Lessons from Fannie." *WCJ* 12 (Spring 1992): 125–44.

> Presents a case study of a Navajo girl and her peer tutor. Concludes that tutors of linguistic minorities must look beyond an ethnocentric bias to be more reflective.

1065. Endicott, Phyllis Stevens, and Carol Peterson Haviland. "Empowering Writing Center Staff: Martyrs or Models?" *WLN* 16 (April 1992): 1–6.

> The authors show that two centers improved their campus image by incorporating computers into tutoring, writing grant proposals for new hardware, and engaging in writing across the curriculum projects.

1066. Faerm, Elizabeth. "Tutors' Column: Tutoring Anne: A Case Study." *WLN* 16 (March 1992): 9–10.

> Explains how she helped a deaf student understand poetry even though she cannot hear pitch, tone, and rhythm, devices which contribute to the meaning of the words.

1067. Farrell, Pam. "College/High School Connection." *WLN* 16 (May–June 1992): 1–2, 8.

> Cites five problems public school teachers face when working with college people. Also points out five advantages of the two groups working together.

1068. Frick, Jane. "Gathering Resources for Your Department: Using Undergraduates to Deliver Instructional Programs and to Foster Community Relations." *ADE Bulletin* 101 (Spring 1992): 31–33.

> Describes how student workers assist in a CAI lab and a developmental writing course, and how they produce publications, resulting in a bigger budget and more internships and majors.

1069. Gadbow, Kate. "Foreign Students in the Writing Lab: Some Ethical and Practical Considerations." *WLN* 17 (November 1992): 1–5.

> Discusses five works (Harris, M.; Kaplan, R.; Matalene, C.; Raimes, L. A.; and Rose, M.) that can help tutors understand and respond to ESL students' problems.

1070. Garbowsky, Maryanne. "The 'Cutting' Edge: Working in the Writing Center." *WLN* 16 (May–June 1992): 19–20.

Argues that students' use of metaphors of violence to describe teacher comments on their papers indicates how personally they take such criticism. Shows that tutors can help rebuild students' self-esteem.

1071. Gaskins, Jake. "How We've Grown as a Writing (across the Curriculum) Center." *WLN* 16 (April 1992): 6–8.

Argues that strong administrative support, an attractive, convenient facility, well-trained and experienced staff, committed faculty support, writing proficiency requirement, and cooperative program directors have contributed to the writing center's growth.

1072. Grimm, Nancy. "Contesting 'the Idea of a Writing Center': The Politics of Writing Center Research." *WLN* 17 (September 1992): 5–7.

Argues that research should include a dialogue with different departments and institutions. Points out that the definition of literacy has to be expanded to include marginalized voices.

1073. Haynes-Burton, Cynthia. "Constructing Our Ethos: Making Writing Centers 'Convenient.' " *CS/FEN* 20 (Fall 1992): 51–59.

Suggests that students, faculty, and tutors regularly convene in small response groups in writing centers as a way of creating a more productive writing environment.

1074. Hobson, Eric H. "Maintaining Our Balance: Walking the Tightrope of Competing Epistemologies." *WCJ* 13 (Fall 1992): 65–75.

Illustrates that writing centers do not fit expressivist, social, or positivist epistemologies; considers this an advantage because it allows them to maintain an equilibrium among the different views.

1075. Hobson, Eric H. "Tutors' Column: Warning: Tutoring May Make You a Researcher." *WLN* 16 (May–June 1992): 9.

Argues that examining tutoring activities, processes, and styles creates "a theoretical base upon which to build a tutoring philosophy" necessary for improving the effectiveness of staffs and directors.

1076. Horn, Susanna. "Tutoring Two Students at the Same Time." *WLN* 17 (October 1992): 14–15.

Points out three "social/psychological effects" of two students working with one tutor during hour-long tutorials. Describes five advantages for the " 'waiting' student."

1077. Keane, Ellen. "Perceptions of Tutors and Students Differ." *WLN* 16 (May–June 1992): 10.

Questionnaire reveals that students and tutors have different opinions about the effectiveness of specific tutoring strategies. Argues that tutors should try different strategies to meet different learning styles.

1078. Konstant, Shoshana Beth. "Multi-Sensory Tutoring for Multi-Sensory Learners." *WLN* 16 (May–June 1992): 6–8.

Defines a learning disability as "a perceptual or processing problem." Suggests visual, auditory, kinesthetic, and multi-sensory techniques for tutoring LD students.

1079. Kulkarni, Diane. "If I Could Only Burn My Bra Now." *WLN* 17 (October 1992): 15.

Prompted by the essay topic, a tutor attempts to share past incidents that would provide a different, deeper perspective. Shows how the young student rejects the ideas.

1080. Larking, Mamie. "Tutors' Column." *WLN* 17 (November 1992): 9.

Encourages tutors to be creative and to have fun with students during tutorials to help students improve their self-esteem and their writing ability.

1081. Leahy, Richard. "Of Writing Centers, Centeredness, and Centrism." *WCJ* 13 (Fall 1992): 43–53.

Argues that writing centers remain "centered" by building staff community. Suggests that centers avoid "centrism," which is the idea that they are the sole writing authorities within institutions.

1082. Leahy, Richard. "Writing Assistants in Writing Emphasis Courses: Toward Some Working Guidelines." *WLN* 16 (May–June 1992): 11–14.

Defines the responsibilities of writing assistants and discusses how they are often misused.

1083. Lidh, Todd. "Tutors' Column: Nothing to Fear but Fear Itself." *WLN* 17 (December 1992): 9.

Lidh describes the fear of failure he continues to experience as a tutor. Suggests ways to channel fear into productive energy that will benefit a client.

1084. Lyons, Greg. "Validating Cultural Differences in the Writing Center." *WCJ* 12 (Spring 1992): 145–58.

Suggests that validating cultural differences by encouraging all viewpoints when tutoring and teaching can be liberatory for minorities.

1085. Masiello, Lea. "Qualitative and Quantitative Strategies for Assessing Writing Center Effectiveness." *WLN* 16 (February 1992): 4–6.

Describes a three-part response sheet completed by students and tutors. Describes five tests for evaluating progress of basic writers. Reviews tutors' comments on reports.

1086. Mayher, John S. "Uncommon Sense in the Writing Center." *JBW* 11 (Spring 1992): 47–57.

Critiques "commonsense" metaphors of "skills" and "remediation" used by writing centers. Suggests "uncommon sense" alternatives based on holistic, constructivist, and transactional views of learning.

1087. McDonald, James C. "Tutoring Literature Students in Dr. Frankenstein's Laboratory." *WCJ* 12 (Spring 1992): 180–89.

Uses the Frankenstein myth as metaphor for examining the tutoring process. Suggests that tutors "befriend" "monstrous" interpretations and help students learn to interpret academic culture.

1088. McKaegue, Patricia M., and Elizabeth Reis. "Development of a Writing Center: A Bright Idea." Moraine Valley Community College, Palos Hills, IL, 1991. ERIC ED 336 154. 7 pages

Explains the planning process used to establish a Writing Center; offers an evaluation of the center's impact on composition students.

1089. Medress, Tammy. "Tutors' Column: Patience and Persistence Please." *WLN* 16 (February 1992): 9–10.

Urges tutors not to give up on students when tutorials seem futile but to continue probing, asking, and challenging.

1090. Morreale, Susan E. "Let's Talk." *WLN* 17 (December 1992): 16.

Realizes that "talk" is a valuable part of writing because "talking" enables people to generate, organize and develop their knowledge about a subject more freely.

1091. Pemberton, Michael A. "The Prison, the Hospital and the Madhouse: Redefining Metaphors for the Writing Center." *WLN* 17 (September 1992): 11–16.

Explains how each of these dominant metaphors "misrepresents writing centers and subverts their entire approach to the learning and writing process." Encourages the use of positive metaphors.

1092. Pfeifer, Mark P., and Gwendolyn L. Snodgrass. "Medical School Libraries' Handling of Articles That Report Invalid Science." *AM* 67 (February 1992): 109–13.

Points out that the nation's medical libraries do not commonly identify or have policies to handle articles on "invalid" science; cautions students and researchers against believing everything they read.

1093. Ridpath, Sandra. "The Use of Computers in the Tutoring Process: Overcoming Communication Obstacles between the Tutor and the ESL Student." *WLN* 17 (November 1992): 7–8.

> Using Evelyn Posey's concept of the "cooperating audience" Ridpath helps a student compose and revise on-line to overcome language barriers.

1094. Roberts, Ian F. "Writing Centers as Centers of Controlled Learning, Too." *WLN* 17 (December 1992): 12–13.

> Considers the "mid-wife metaphor for lab teaching . . . naive" because tutors, through their questioning, impart knowledge to students as well as facilitate the birth of their ideas.

1095. Saling, Joseph, and Kelly Cook-McEachern. "Building a Community of Writers in a Required Lab: A Paradox and a Dilemma." *WLN* 17 (November 1992): 13–15.

> Describes strategies that enable directors, tutors, and clients to "see" themselves and one another as collaborative equals.

1096. Sherwood, Steve. "Fear and Loathing in the Writing Center: How to Deal Fairly with Problem Students." *WLN* 16 (April, 1992): 12–15.

> Describes physiological/psychological manifestations of fear in students and tutors. Suggests four ways tutors may reduce their fears and five ways to reduce students' fears.

1097. Simonian, Margaret Ann. "A Tutor Needs to Know the Subject Matter to Help a Student with a Paper: Agree—Disagree—Not Sure—." *WLN* 17 (September 1992): 9–10.

> Argues that although tutors may not know a subject, they know the characteristics of good writing. By reading, questioning, and responding, they help students create strong documents.

1098. Stay, Byron L. "Writing Centers on the Margins: Conversing from the Edge" *WLN* 17 (September 1992): 1–4.

> Argues that professionals need full faculty status and institutional support, NCTE recognition of marginalization, and publications in the major composition/teaching journals to improve the status of writing centers.

1099. Trimbur, John. "Literary Networks: Towards Cultural Studies of Writing and Tutoring." *WCJ* 12 (Spring 1992): 174–79.

> Recommends researching the tutor to tutee relationship to understand how students use popular literacy gained from television to represent themselves as writers.

1100. Upton, James. " 'Talking to Myself . . .': A Writing Self-Help Worksheet." *WLN* 16 (March 1992): 7–8.

> Believes that students fail to complete assignments successfully because they have not "had practice in objectively analyzing writing assignments." Includes a worksheet.

1101. Vasile, Kathy, and Nick Chizzone. "Computer-Integrated Tutoring." *WLN* 16 (May–June 1992): 17–19.

> Describes nine computer techniques for developing, revising, and editing a paper. Shows how a student improved his paper through multiple drafts by using these strategies.

1102. Weller, Rebecca. "Tutors' Column: Authorizing Voice: Pedagogy, Didacticism and the Student-Teacher-Tutor Triangle." *WLN* 17 (October 1992): 9–11.

> Realizes she should have paid less attention to "didactic methods of education" and more to her client's distress signals. Recognizes that students have different needs.

1103. Woolbright, Meg. "The Politics of Tutoring: Feminism within the Patriarchy." *WCJ* 13 (Fall 1992): 16–29.

> Contends that patriarchal goals subvert feminist practice within writing centers. Argues that democratic collaboration is undermined by tutors' emphasis on helping students succeed academically.

1104. Young, Art. "College Culture and the Challenge of Collaboration" *WCJ* 13 (Fall 1992): 3–15.

> Calls for active campaigning for support of collaboration through WAC workshops. Reviews the evolution of collaboration and concludes by looking at several modes of collaboration useful to educators.

3.4 ROLE IN SOCIETY

1105. Caldwell, Larry W. "Readin', Rightin' and ReaganBush." *EQ* 24.3–4 (1992): 5–9.

> Argues that professional associations of educators and other concerned groups and individuals must assume a leading role in restructuring public discourse about literacy.

1106. Carroll, Jeffrey. "FreshMen: Confronting Sexual Harassment in the Classroom." *CS/FEN* 20 (Fall 1992): 60–73.

> Discusses social and legal issues related to sexual harassment in the classroom.

1107. Drain, Susan. *The Backlash against Political Correctness—A Perspective from a Canadian Composition Class*. Cincinnati, OH: CCCC, March 1992. ERIC ED 344 217. 13 pages

> Maintains that composition teachers should point out the limitations of and alternatives to the existing orthodoxy.

1108. Hurlbert, C. Mark, and Samuel Totten, eds. *Social Issues in the English Classroom*. Urbana, IL: NCTE, 1992. 356 pages

> Essays advocate teaching issues like racism, homophobia, and the environment in English classes "for a more democratic and ethical society and for a safer and healthier world"; they discuss productive approaches to difficult issues in writing and literature classrooms, involving students' own social contexts; and they examine political implications of teaching social issues.
> *Essayists:* Bell, Debbie; Blitz, Michael; Davenport, Doris; Giroux, Henry A.; Hart, Ellen Louise; Holubec, Edythe Johnson; Hurlbert, C. Mark; Johnson, David W.; Johnson, Roger T.; Kutzer, M. Daphne; Lankewish, Vincent A.; Mack, Nancy; Mason, Jimmie; Milanés, Cecilia Rodríguez; Parmeter, Sarah-Hope; Shapiro, Alan; Stotsky, Sandra; Stumbo, Carol; Tassoni, John; Tayko, Gail; Weiler, Kathleen; Wright, William; Zebroski, James Thomas; Zins, Daniel.

1109. Knoblauch, C. H., and Lil Brannon. *Critical Teaching and the Idea of Literacy*. Portsmouth, NH: Heinemann, 1992. 224 pages

> Examines the debate over how "literacy" is defined and shows how the discourses of politicians and administrators shape reading and writing instruction in schools and colleges; urges parents, teachers, and students to understand how they can affect American educational policy.

1110. Lieberman, Ann, ed. *The Changing Contexts of Teaching*. Ninety-First Yearbook of the National Society for the Study of Education, edited by Kenneth J. Rehage. Chicago: University of Chicago Press, 1992. 275 pages

> Addresses problems such as accountability in education, new routes to becoming a teacher, changes in teachers' perceptions of the profession, and teachers' privacy and colleagueship in school. Reveals possibilities and problems that arise when teachers take on new leadership roles and accept broadened responsibilities of "teacher-run" schools.
> *Essayists:* Astuto, Terry; Clark, David; Cohn, Marilyn; Darling-Hammond, Linda; Grossman, Pamela; Knudsen, Jennifer; Lichtenstein, Gary; Lieberman, Ann; Little, Warren; McClure, Robert M.; McLaughlin, Milbrey W.; Miller, Lynne; Natriello, Gary; O'Shea, Cynthia; Seashore, Louis; Snyder, Jon; Wasley, Patricia; Zumwalt, Karen K.

1111. McCracken, Nancy Mellin, and Bruce C. Appleby, eds. *Gender Issues in the Teach-*

ing of English. Portsmouth, NH: Boynton/Cook, 1992. 228 pages

Thirteen essays explore the necessity of "gender-balancing" the classroom so that all students, men and women, may develop "the potential to hear the voices of others clearly, and to use their own voices to understand, shape, and share their worlds, and imagine other worlds." Concludes with a bibliography.

Essayists: Appleby, B. C.; Blakesley, D.; Bowman, C.; Comley, N. R.; Greenwood, C. M.; McClure, L. J.; McCracken, N. M.; Miller, J. L.; Roen, D. H.; Sanborn, J.; Stover, L.

1112. Pollington, Mary. *A Tale of Two Campuses: The Part-Time English Teacher at Brigham Young University and Utah Valley Community College*. Cincinnati, OH: CCCC, March 1992. ERIC ED 345 255. 15 pages

Surveys the working conditions for part-time composition faculty at a university and at a two-year college.

1113. Schell, Eileen E. "The Feminization of Composition: Questioning the Metaphors that Bind Women Teachers." *CS/FEN* 20 (Fall 1992): 55–61.

Claims that the "feminization" metaphor in composition studies is pejorative and does not indicate a move toward feminist positions. Suggests further examination of metaphors.

1114. Shapiro, Nancy. *Rereading Multicultural Readers: What Definition of Multicultural Are We Buying?* Cincinnati, OH: CCCC, March 1992. ERIC ED 346 472. 12 pages

Characterizes the content, organization and underlying pedagogical theories of current multicultural textbooks.

1115. Wilsox, Earl J. "A New Age Document for the '90s: John Updike's *The Centaur*" *CEAF* 22 (Summer 1992): 1–4.

Suggests that *The Centaur*'s portrayal of a high school teacher offers insights regarding the teacher's role in society.

3.5 OTHER

1116. *The Almanac of Higher Education, 1992*. Edited by The Chronicle of Higher Education Staff. Chicago: University of Chicago Press, 1992. 336 pages

Presents state-by-state reports on demographics, political leadership, and key statistics about faculty, students, costs, and spending.

1117. Getman, Julius. *In the Company of Scholars: The Struggle for the Soul of Higher Education*. Austin, TX: University of Texas Press, 1992. 304 pages

Demonstrates how higher education creates a shared intellectual community among people of varied classes and races, while simultaneously dividing people on the basis of education and status. Other topics include the conflict between teaching and research, academic freedom, and multiculturalism.

1118. Laliker, William B. *Making the Wyoming Resolution a Reality: A 1992 Progress Report from Kentucky*. Cincinnati, OH: CCCC, March 1992. ERIC ED 343 129. 11 pages

Surveys writing program administrators at 40 public and private institutions to explore issues of equity and quality for graduate teaching assistants and part-time faculty.

1119. Warner, Sterling. *Teaching Communities and Two-Year Colleges: Establishing Dialogue among Composition Instructors*. Cincinnati, OH: CCCC, March 1992. ERIC ED 347 550. 15 pages

Presents a case study that examines the positive and negative implications of forming a teaching community.

4 Curriculum

4.1 GENERAL DISCUSSIONS

1120. Abbott, Susan. "Talk, Talk, Talk: Prewriting with Remedial Writers." *V&R* 2 (Spring 1990): 15–21.

Argues that the writing of students who used storytelling as a form of prewriting improved.

1121. Adler, Jonathan E. "Critical Thinking: A Deflated Defense." *IL* 13 (Spring 1991): 61–78.

Argues against McPeck's prior assertion that since there is no unitary "reasoning skill," there should be no course in "critical thinking."

1122. Agatucci, Cora. *Writing Women in(to) the Curriculum*. Seattle, WA: NCTE, November 1991. ERIC ED 343 122. 17 pages

Advocates a feminist pedagogy; discusses the unstated assumptions that define good writing.

1123. Andrews, Deborah Brunson. "An Examination of the Communicator Style of Older Instructors in the University Classroom." *DAI* 52 (June 1992): 4144A.

Studies instructors aged 64–75 and suggests more congruity than incongruity between style ratings of teachers and their students' assessments of them.

1124. Anthony, Mary Anne. "RSC Classroom Research Consortium Project: 1990–91/Year Two Report." Rancho Santiago Community College, Santa Ana, CA, 1991. ERIC ED 341 423. 214 pages

Offers an interim report on a Title III innovative teaching grant by three California community colleges, including computers and writing across the curriculum.

1125. Ball, Arnetha Fay. "Organizational Patterns in the Oral and Written Expository Language of African-American Adolescents." *DAI* 52 (March 1992): 3163A.

Results illuminate a variety of organizational strategies, a multitude of preferences

4.1 GENERAL DISCUSSIONS

in patterns of discourse, and effects on teacher evaluation.

1126. Barnes, Douglas. *From Communication to Curriculum*. 2d ed. Portsmouth, NH: Boynton/Cook, 1992. 210 pages

Urges a pedagogy based on "exploratory talk," an approach more in line with students' natural patterns of inquiry than one based on rigidly formalized modes of instruction.

1127. Bell, Jean. " 'I Think You're Going to Like This One!': A Writer-Friendly Environment Creates Pride and Self-Esteem." *V&R* 2 (Spring 1990): 22–31.

For a year, Bell had unlikely writers keep single-audience journals to create a "writer-friendly" environment and found that students began to value their writing.

1128. Bizzell, Patricia. "The Politics of Teaching Virtue." *ADE Bulletin* 103 (Winter 1992): 4–7.

Critiques teachers who disavow subjectivity and argues for negotiated egalitarian world view as solution to postmodern skepticism.

1129. Branscombe, N. Amanda, Dixie Goswami, and Jeffrey Schwartz. eds. *Students Teaching, Teachers Learning*. Portsmouth, NH: Boynton/Cook, 1992. 343 pages

Fifteen essays—detailing "projects" from a range of settings and academic levels—suggest that collaborative authority between teacher and student invigorates the learning process for both. Each contribution is followed by a response essay which encourages further speculation on the topic.
Essayists: Allen, S.; Atwell, N.; Bowen, B. A.; Branscombe, N. A.; Britton, James; Cazden, C.; Cockran-Smith, M.; Coleman, I.; Diamondstone, J.; Engel, B. S.; Fecho, R.; Garfield, E.; Greenberger, R.; Healy, M. K.; Heath, S. B.; Johnston, P.; Kazmierczak, J.; Keyes, D. E.; Lockett, H.; Lytle, S. L.; Macrorie, K.; Martin, A.; Martin, Nancy J.; McIntyre, G. G.; Merriman, N.; Meyers, C.; Moffett, J.; Murphy, R. J.; Pradl, G. M.; Scarbrough, V.; Schaafsma, D.; Schwartz, E.; Schwartz, J.; Strachan, W.; Stuckey, J. E.; Stumbo, C.; Taylor, J. B.; Thomas, C.; White, E.; Wilson, D.; Zoukis, E.

1130. Burnham, Christopher C. "Crumbling Metaphors: Integrating Heart and Brain through Structured Journals." *CCC* 43 (December 1992): 508–15.

Describes the possibility of students integrating feeling and thought through developing and deconstructing metaphors in structured journal assignments.

1131. Campbell, JoAnn. *Writing to Heal: Using Meditation in the Writing Process*. Cincinnati, OH: CCCC, March 1992. ERIC ED 343 137. 10 pages

Discusses using writing as a form of meditation rather than as an academic task.

1132. Capossela, Toni-Lee. *Writing and Critical Thinking: Points of Convergence, Points of Divergence*. Cincinnati, OH: CCCC, March 1992. ERIC ED 345 242. 7 pages

Traces the estrangement of critical thinking and writing from the 1940s; notes that cognitive approaches restore Dewey's holistic view.

1133. Chapman, David W. *Writing a Core Curriculum: Classic Books and Student Compositions*. Cincinnati, OH: CCCC, March 1992. ERIC ED 346 480. 13 pages

Argues that attention should be focused on the rhetorical power of students, the so-called "critical literacy," assigning rhetoric a central role in the core curriculum.

1134. Collins, James L., ed. *Vital Signs 3: Restructuring the English Curriculum*. Vital Signs. Portsmouth, NH: Boynton/Cook, 1992. 216 pages

Fourteen essays explore currents of change in secondary and college-level English classrooms. Sections include "Motives," "Methods," "Restructuring College Com-

position," and "Restructuring Teacher Education."
Essayists: Beichner, R. J.; Brunner, D. D.; Collins, J. L.; David, D. L.; Handa, C.; Hudson-Ross, S.; Malinowitz, H.; Mutnick, D.; Ohanian, S.; Schaafsma, D.; Smagorinsky, P.; Smith, M.; Szymaniski, S.; Thomas, S.; Vinz, R.; West, M.

1135. Collins, Marian, and Scott Baird. *Too Bad the Teachers Are Reading This*! Seattle, WA: NCTE, November 1991. ERIC ED 342 007. 31 pages

Discusses the exchange of student journals by a secondary level English teacher and a college composition instructor.

1136. Devitt, Amy J. *Reconsidering Genre in Composition*. Cincinnati, OH: CCCC, March 1992. ERIC ED 346 468. 12 pages

Expounds on the importance of genre with regard to composition pedagogy and theory, claiming that it is a powerful concept essential to any understanding of writing.

1137. Dias, Patrick. "Cultural Literacy, National Curriculum: What (and How) Does Every Canadian Student Really Need to Know?" *EQ* 24.3–4 (1992): 10–19.

Argues that collaborative group work helps students to become confident users of language.

1138. Ediger, Marlow. "Philosophy of Writing Instruction." ERIC/RCS, Bloomington, IN, 1991. ERIC ED 336 755. 10 pages

Discusses diverse philosophies of writing instruction and offers suggestions for course objectives.

1139. Ediger, Marlow. "Writing in the University Curriculum." ERIC/RCS, Bloomington, IN, 1991. ERIC ED 337 806. 12 pages

Appraises diverse philosophies of teaching writing, including existentialism, problem solving and the use of behavioral objectives.

1140. Farnan, Nancy, Diane Lapp, and James Flood. "Changing Perspectives in Writing Instruction." *JR* 35 (April 1992): 550–56.

Discusses why traditional writing instruction has to be changed; argues that writing workshops, portfolios, and think alouds can improve instruction.

1141. Finders, Margaret. "With Jix." *CCC* 43 (December 1992): 497–507.

Interweaves descriptions of a few scenes from classes taught by Richard Lloyd-Jones with his reflections on teaching made during interviews.

1142. Fletcher, Ralph. *What a Writer Needs*. Portsmouth, NH: Heinemann, 1992. 176 pages

Offers strategies for helping students see specific sites for improving their creative writing.

1143. Fraser, Rebecca Jean. "Theory and Pedagogy in Freewriting Acts: Exploring the Spaces between." *DAI* 52 (June 1992): 4248A.

Explores the interaction of teachers' pedagogies and rhetoric with their expressed use of freewriting in writing classes.

1144. Fulwiler, Toby. *Writing to Reform the English Major*. Cincinnati, OH: CCCC, March 1992. ERIC ED 345 261. 26 pages

Outlines the impact of the University of Vermont's writing across the curriculum program on the English major; describes new course developments.

1145. Gibaldi, Joseph, ed. *Introduction to Scholarship in Modern Languages and Literatures*. 2d ed. New York: Modern Language Association, 1992. 377 pages

Fifteen new essays examine the significance, underlying assumptions, and limits of an important field in linguistics, composition, and literary studies, trace the historical development of the subject, introduce key terms, outline modes of inquiry now being pursued, and postulate likely future developments.
Essayists: Allen, Paula Gunn; Baron, Dennis; Bathrick, David; Culler, Johnathan; Finegan, Edward; Gates, Henry Louis, Jr.;

Graff, Gerald; Greetham, D. C.; Gunn, Giles; Kramsch, Claire J.; Lunsford, Andrea A.; Marshall, Donald G.; Patterson, Annabel; Scholes, Robert; Schor, Naomi.

1146. Goodman, Marcia Renee. "Innocent Impostors: Gender, Genre, and the Teaching of Writing." *V&R* 2 (Spring 1990): 37–51.

Goodman discusses differences she has observed in gendered ways of engaging in writing and literature; advises teachers to be aware of these differences and their implications.

1147. Graves, Roger Charles W. "Writing Instruction in Canadian Universities." *DAI* 52 (May 1992): 3846A.

Investigates writing instruction in Canadian universities using a combination of historical analysis, survey, and case study research methods.

1148. Hamalainen, Matti, Safaa Hashim, Clyde W. Holsapple, Yongmoo Suh, and Andrew B. Whinston. "Structured Discourse for Scientific Collaboration: A Framework for Scientific Collaboration Based on Structured Discourse Analysis." *JOC* 2 (Winter 1992): 1–26.

Discusses the general requirements of a collaborative system for scientific researchers and outlines the technical design of such a prototype system.

1149. Hansen, Edmund, Nancy Totten, Siat–May Chong, and Jeannie Little. *Collaborative Learning in Higher Education*. Bloomongon, IN: Proceedings of the Teaching Conference, Indiana University, October 1991. ERIC ED 335 984. 202 pages

The participants present a panel discussion concerning the experiences of faculty and students with learning-oriented approaches to college teaching.

1150. Healy, Dave. "The Deprofessionalization of the Writing Instructor." *WPA* 16 (Fall/Winter 1992): 38–49.

Defines the problem of deprofessionalization; claims that this otherwise negative process may actually mean more effective teaching in writing classes.

1151. Heath, Christian, and Paul Luff. "Media Space and Communicative Asymmetries: Preliminary Observations of Video-Mediated Interaction." *HCI* 7 (Summer 1992): 315–46.

Notes the extent to which media space provides a means for interpersonal communication and sociability, describing the asymmetries that audiovisual technology introduces into conduct.

1152. Herrington, Anne, and Charles Moran, eds. *Writing, Teaching, and Learning in the Disciplines*. New York: Modern Language Association, 1992. 265 pages

A collection of fourteen essays outlines the social, intellectual, and political forces that have shaped writing-in-the-disciplines programs; they present perspectives from disciplines outside English studies, describe the relations among writing, teaching, and learning, and consider the future of the movement.
Essayists: Abbott, Michael M.; Bartelt, Pearl W.; Bazerman, Charles; Britton, James; Cooper, Charles R.; Dunlap, Louise; Fishman, Stephen M.; Fulwiler, Toby; Herrington, Anne; Hilgers, Thomas L.; Honda, Charlotte; Langer, Judith A.; MacDonald, Susan Peck; Marsella, Joy; Martin, Nancy; McLaren, Clemence; Moran, Charles; Odell, Lee; Royster, Jacqueline Jones; Russell, David R.; Spanier, Bonnie B.

1153. Hyland, Ken, and Fiona Hyland. "Go for Gold: Integrating Process and Product in ESP." *ESP* 11 (1992): 225–42.

Presents the course design of a process syllabus being used in Papua New Guinea to test the concept of a process-focused classroom.

1154. Kelly, Kathleen Ann. *'Languages and Not Language': The Writer, the Text, and the Quotation*. Boston, MA: CCCC, March 1991. ERIC ED 335 686. 13 pages

Examines the importance of the quotation or the paraphrase of a writer's work, stressing the need for greater student awareness.

1155. Keroes, Jo. *Things Better Shared over Coffee: Tales of Teaching to Learn.* Boston, MA: CCCC, March 1991. ERIC ED 335 674. 28 pages

Examines how novice instructors become professional writing teachers.

1156. Kline, Nancy, ed. *How Writers Teach Writing.* Englewood Cliffs, NJ: Prentice Hall, 1992. 288 pages

The contributors present their approaches to teaching expository writing at Harvard. *Essayists:* Birkerts, Sven; Cohen, Judith Beth; Farrell, Eileen; Gold, Alex; Hoy, Pat C., II.; Johnson, Alex; Kantor, Victor; Kline, Nancy; Lowry, Pei; Marchant, Fred; Marius, Richard; Rodburg, Maxine; Simon, Linda.

1157. Kynell, Teresa. "Wives, Mothers, and Scholars: What Women Write about." *TETYC* 19 (February 1992): 55–60.

Analyzes reading anthologies for composition courses and finds that the female-to-male ratio is still low. Also notes that most selections by women reflect traditional "women's" themes.

1158. Lemon, Hallie S. *Classroom Stories: Teachers' Use of Collaborative Learning.* Cincinnati, OH: CCCC, March 1992. ERIC ED 343 161. 20 pages

Finds increases in collaborative drafting strategies, focusing, prewriting, and editing in a survey of 61 composition teachers. Includes five suggestions for improving a pedagogy of collaborative learning.

1159. Lloyd-Jones, Richard. *A Goodly Fellowship of Writers and Readers.* NCTE Concept Paper Series, no. 4. Urbana, IL: NCTE, 1992. 46 pages

Discusses how English teachers can help students mature into membership in the "goodly fellowship" of language-users and how they can help students learn their own place in cultural and social relationships. Includes part of the 1987 address to the English Coalition Conference.

1160. Marius, Richard. "Politics in the Classroom." *ADE Bulletin* 103 (Winter 1992): 8–12.

Argues for teaching the right tools instead of the right attitudes; argues against a politicized classroom.

1161. Mitchell, Felicia. "Balancing Individual Projects and Collaborative Learning in an Advanced Writing Class." *CCC* 43 (October 1992): 393–400.

Describes a model of collaborative learning in which an individual course-long project is combined with periodic response from other students and the teacher.

1162. Moffett, James. *Active Voice: A Writing Program across the Curriculum.* 2d ed. Portsmouth, NH: Boynton/Cook, 1992. 216 pages

Offers advice for instituting a writing program; provides specific writing activities and sample student work.

1163. Nyberg, Adells M. "I've Read This before." *V&R* 3 (Fall 1991): 33–36.

Nyberg's story of a student's plagiarism highlights the need for teachers to serve as coaches, not critics, and to let students generate their own topics.

1164. Offen-Brown, Gail, and Jean Marie Schultz. "Of Success Stories, Tales of Failure, and Teacher Research." *V&R* 3 (Fall 1991): 19–26.

Offen-Brown and Schultz's study looks at transference between writing courses in different languages; they highlight some difficulties of research plans and realities.

1165. Piazza, Stephen, and Charles Suhor. "Trends and Issues in English Instruction." NCTE, Urbana, IL, 1991. ERIC ED 335 699. 25 pages

Compiled by the directors of six NCTE commissions, Piazza and Suhor provide in-

4.1 GENERAL DISCUSSIONS

formation on current trends and issues in English instruction.

1166. Picciotto, Madeleine. "Educational Literacy and Empowerment: An Experiment in Critical Pedagogy." *WI* 11 (Winter 1992): 59–69.

Points out that a sequence of composition courses attempting to foster students' awareness of power dynamics of academic situations was both rewarding and frustrating for teachers and students.

1167. Ranieri, Paul W. *The Dialectics of Gender: A Move beyond Dichotomies Constraining Growth*. Cincinnati, OH: CCCC, March 1992. ERIC ED 345 239. 12 pages

Uses gender studies to argue for pedagogies that integrate holistic and analytic modes of thought.

1168. Rule, Rebecca, and Susan Wheeler. *Creating the Story: Guides for New Writers*. Portsmouth, NH: Heinemann, 1992. 280 pages

The authors present a practical handbook and guide to creative writing, with an emphasis on learning through critical readings of published works.

1169. Shafer, Gregory Robert. "Creating a Context for Learning: Democracy in the Language Arts." *DAI* 52 (April 1992): 3548A.

Drawing on the works of Frank Smith, Jean Piaget, and Paulo Freire, Shafer argues that English instructors posit their methods to "create a context for democratic learning."

1170. Shearer, Brenda A. "The Long-Term Effects of Whole Language Instruction on Children's Written Composition." *DAI* 53 (December 1992): 1855A.

Argues that her findings do not support the notion that either skill-based language arts instruction or whole language instruction resulted in higher proficiency in children's written composition.

1171. Smith, Philip E., II. *Institutional and Disciplinary History in a Cultural Studies Curriculum*. Cincinnati, OH: CCCC, March 1992. ERIC ED 344 236. 12 pages

Describes the University of Pittsburgh's graduate program for composition teachers which connects theory and pratice within a cultural studies curriculum.

1172. Speer, Tom. "Part-Time Instructors: Strategies to Thrive in the 90s." *TETYC* 19 (December 1992): 266–73.

Shows how part-time writing instructors can connect to other instructors and form associations with them.

1173. Unrau, Norman J. "The Task of Reading (and Writing) Arguments: A Guide to Building Critical Literacy." *JR* 35 (March 1992): 436–42.

Describes how thesis analysis and synthesis key help students to develop critical thinking skills in their reading and writing activities.

1174. Wagner, Julia. *Glamour and Spelling: Reclaiming Magical Thinking in the Composition Classroom*. Cincinnati, OH: CCCC, March 1992. ERIC ED 346 485. 8 pages

Claims that writing instructors should attempt to bring about the wonder, inspiration, and trance that all writers experience.

1175. Walsh, Steve. *Breakthroughs in Composition Instruction Methods without Evidence of Tangible Improvements in Students' Composition: When Will Change Come?* Indianapolis, IN: NCTE, March 1991. ERIC ED 336 744. 14 pages

Reports on the teaching of writing, indicating that grammar instruction is still a focus and still doesn't improve students' writing.

1176. Washington, Gene. "Writing, Pedagogy, Modality." ERIC/RCS, Bloomington, IN, 1991. ERIC ED 337 799. 32 pages

Addresses modality in terms of college writing instruction; includes identification of markers, use of models, and pedagogical usefulness.

4.2 HIGHER EDUCATION

4.2.1 DEVELOPMENTAL WRITING

1177. Abt-Perkins, Dawn. "From Alienation to Authorship: Creating a Writing Community for High School Basic Writers." *JTW* 11 (Spring/Summer 1992): 35–50.

   Presents five students' experience with writing workshops based on writing practice, student models, peer audiences, constant support, editing conferences, and sharing written products.

1178. Agnew, Eleanor. "Basic Writers in the Workplace: Writing Adequately for Careers after College." *JBW* 11 (Fall 1992): 28–46.

   Reports that workplace environments foster better writing in basic writers. Recommends writing across the curriculum as one means of duplicating workplace writing in the classroom.

1179. Agnew, Eleanor. "Remedial English Ten Years after: Former Basic Writers in the Workplace." *DAI* 52 (March 1992): 3268A.

   Results reveal significant development of esteem and ability in former basic writers.

1180. Baker, Isabel MacDonald. "Expressive Writing Experiences of Poor College Readers: Their Effects upon Abstract Thinking and Reading Comprehension." *DAI* 53 (December 1992): 1853A.

   Demonstrates that informal writing in responses to expository texts enhances reading comprehension and abstract thinking of poor college readers.

1181. Batschelet, Margaret, and Linda Woodson. *The Effects of an Electronic Classroom on the Attitudes of Basic Writers.* Seattle, WA: NCTE, November 1991. ERIC ED 344 206. 11 pages

   Batschelet and Woodson's study found that basic writers' attitudes toward writing did not improve when taught in an electronic classroom.

1182. Bauernschmidt, Mary Catherine. "Repeated Writing to Improve Writing Fluency for Students with Mild Handicaps." *DAI* 52 (May 1992): 3887A.

   Finds that a repeated writing procedure improved writing fluency for elementary-age boys with emotional and learning handicaps.

1183. Benson, Beverly, Mary Deming, Debra Denzer, and Maria Valeri-Gold. "A Combined Basic Writing/English as a Second Language Class: Melting Pot or Mishmash." *JBW* 11 (Spring 1992): 58–74.

   Compares writings by both groups of students. Suggests that courses should not be combined and that students should be taught by teachers trained in each area.

1184. Berkowitz, Leonard J. "A Source-Spot for Arguments." *IL* 13 (Winter 1991): 41–44.

   Recommends an exercise in which students generate arguments and argument topics to replace those provided by textbooks, editorials, and letters to the editor.

1185. Butler, Sydney J., and Roy Bentley. "Literacy through Lifewriting." *EQ* 24.3–4 (1992): 33–41.

   Suggests that writing personal narratives can provide the motivation and driving force toward literacy. Reports success in programs with seniors, adult education students, adults with disabilities, and ESL students.

1186. Carpenter, Thomas W. "Three Basic Writing Classrooms: An Observational Study of the Interaction of Teachers and Students." *DAI* 53 (September 1992): 743A.

   Argues that teachers' backgrounds help explain the writing models they develop. Points out that students who were not used to process writing sometimes had trouble adjusting to it.

1187. Chapman, Iris Thompson. "A Qualitative Analysis of Selected Black Male Students Interfacing with Writing Literacy." *DAI* 52 (January 1992): 4286A.

Suggests that academic socialization, academic monitors, and self-regulatory strategies are critical to selected young black males' success in writing literacy and academic success generally.

1188. Coppinger, Stanley K. *Grammatical Transitions: A Study of One Basic Writer*. San Antonio, TX: College English Association, April 1991. ERIC ED 337 808. 13 pages

Traces the development of a college writer from basic writing through the junior year. Recommends workshop instruction and holistic evaluation as opposed to grammar instruction.

1189. DiPardo, Anne Louise. "Acquiring a Kind of Passport: The Teaching and Learning of Academic Discourse in Basic Writing Tutorials." *DAI* 52 (February 1992): 2931A.

Explores academic and political tensions in tutorials resulting from "educational equity" (more minority students) on campus; discusses the actions of the English department, two tutors, and four students.

1190. Dunn, Patricia Ann. "The 'Learning Disability' Controversy and Composition Studies." *DAI* 52 (February 1992): 2832A.

Explores learning disabilities (differences in how individuals process linguistic symbols) and shows how the controversy surrounding this subject is relevant to composition instructors.

1191. Englert, Carol Sue. "Writing Instruction from a Sociocultural Perspective: The Holistic, Dialogic, and Social Enterprise of Writing." *JLD* 25 (March 1992): 153–72.

Details specific components of a cognitive process-based instruction program as a means of promoting the empowerment of writers with learning disabilities.

1192. Greene, Brenda. "Empowerment and the Problem Identification and Resolution Strategies of Basic Writers." *JBW* 11 (Fall 1992): 4–27.

Presents a case study of three basic writers. Suggests that students are capable of evaluating surface level and rhetorical problems in their own and in peers' texts.

1193. Hamant, Sharon. "The Reading-Writing Journal as a Means to Teach Summary and Analysis to Basic and Not-So-Basic Writers." *IndE* 15 (Spring 1992): 4–8.

Discusses a course in which students use journal entries to practice summary writing, expressive writing, critique and analysis, and vocabulary building.

1194. Hull, Glynda, Mike Rose, Kay Losey Fraser, and Mariso Castellano. "Remediation as Social Construct: Perspectives from and Analysis of Classroom Discourse." Center for the Study of Writing and Literacy, Berkeley, CA, 1991. ERIC ED 335 677. 35 pages

Uses classroom studies to explore ways in which teachers inadvertently construct inaccurate and limiting notions of student learning as being cognitively defective and in need of a "remedy."

1195. Jacobson, Karen Hallinan. "Constructing Basic Writing: Institutional, Instructional, and Individual Perspectives." *DAI* 52 (January 1992): 2443A.

Seeks to understand basic writers' responses to various instructional practices, the ways in which they develop as writers, and the factors which facilitate and hinder their maturation.

1196. Keithley, Zoe. "My Own Voice: Students Say It Unlocks the Writing Process." *JBW* 11 (Fall 1992): 82–102.

Presents the results and implications of a questionnaire supporting students' claims.

1197. Lee, Christopher M., and Rosemary F. Jackson. *Faking It: A Look at the Mind of a Creative Learner*. Portsmouth, NH: Boynton/Cook, 1992. 200 pages

Christopher Lee tells how he faked his way through school until he ended up in the University of Georgia Learning Disabilities Adult Clinic, where he met Rosemary Jackson, who helped him to understand and to overcome his learning disabilities.

1198. Leonard, Marcellus J. "The Classroom Writer's Forum: Teaching Basic Writing in the Cultural Context." *DAI* 52 (January 1992): 2847A.

Examines the assumption that the classroom writer's forum in the cultural context motivates African-American basic writers and provides them with valuable writing experience.

1199. Mangelsdorf, Kate. "Rosa's Story: Learning Her Own Language." *TETYC* 19 (February 1992): 18–23.

Looks at a Chicana student who finds her voice through expressionistic writing in a basic writing class.

1200. Martin, Judy L. "Comparison of the Use of Logical Frameworks in Written Discourse by Learning-Disabled, Basic, and Normally Achieving College Writers." *DAI* 53 (August 1992): 479A.

Suggests that students need to become aware of composing processes and that teachers need to respond according to the writer's intentions.

1201. McAlexander, Patricia J., Ann B. Dobie, and Noel Gregg. *Beyond the "Sp" Label: Improving the Spelling of Learning Disabled and Basic Writers*. Theory and Research into Practice (TRIP). Urbana, IL: NCTE, 1992. 90 pages

Surveys the ways that spelling can cause problems for basic writers beyond grade school, including the complex English spelling system, learning disabilities, lack of student interest, and conflicting teacher attitudes toward spelling. Offers a wide variety of practical methods for effectively helping students improve spelling. Includes a bibliography.

1202. McDonald, James C. "Student Metaphors for Themselves as Writers." *EJ* 81 (April 1992): 60–64.

Explores sources, forms, and implications of images developed by the author's students in basic writing and other composition courses.

1203. Middendorf, Marilyn. "Bakhtin and the Dialogic Writing Class." *JBW* 11 (Spring 1992): 34–46.

Proposes and describes a process by which teachers of basic writing can initiate their students into the world of meaning and text.

1204. Newsome, Alice. *Emotional Transitions: The Studio/Peer Instructor Approach to Basic Writing*. San Antonio, TX: College English Association, April 1991. ERIC ED 337 809. 8 pages

Advocates a program of writing workshops and peer tutoring to alleviate the anxiety that basic writers face in adjusting to academic discourse.

1205. Norton, Terry, and Betty Lou Land. "A Multisensory Approach to Teaching Spelling in Remedial English." *TETYC* 19 (October 1992): 192–95.

Combines visual, auditory, and kinetic methods to teach spelling.

1206. Rubin, Lois. "Combining the Personal and Analytical: Assignments for Basic Writing." *TETYC* 19 (May 1992): 141–47.

Suggests moving beyond personal writing into analytic writing; includes suggestions for assignments.

1207. Severino, Carol. "Where the Cultures of Basic Writers and Academia Intersect: Cultivating the Common Ground." *JBW* 11 (Spring 1992): 4–15.

Presents literacy profiles of 45 basic writers which suggest that leisure reading and writing and positive high school experiences with both create common ground in the classroom.

1208. Sitko, Barbara M. *"If They're Confused You Have to Help Them": Respond to Feedback*. Chicago, IL: American Educational Research Association, April 1991. ERIC ED 336 406. 35 pages

Presents a protocol study of 24 basic writers revising with and without feedback.

1209. Sloat, Elizabeth. "Developmental Patterns in Personal Story Narrative." *EQ* 23.3–4 (1992): 28–34.

Explores one way in which teachers can provide feedback, assess growth, and monitor personal narrative writing from a positive, supportive, and holistic perspective.

1210. Wiener, Harvey S. "Inference: Perspectives on Literacy for Basic Skills Students." *JBW* 11 (Spring 1992): 16–33.

Offers a methodology for helping students build inference skills. Suggests that making students' everyday acts of inference evident will increase the successful use in other contexts.

1211. Zellermayer, Michal, Elite Olshtain, and Judith Cohen. "The Development of Elaborative Skills: Teaching Basic Writing Students to Make the Commitment to Audience and Topic." *L&E* 3 (Summer 1992): 359–83.

Reports on the development and application of an audience-response device which enabled students who used it for revision to develop their writing more significantly than students who did not.

4.2.2 FIRST-YEAR COLLEGE COMPOSITION

1212. Ademan, Deborah. "Teacher Approaches to Student Literacy in Two College Programs: Attitudes, Presuppositions, and Assessment." *DAI* 52 (June 1992): 4246A.

Describes the relationship between college composition teachers' attitudes and presuppositions about literacy and their assessment of student writing.

1213. Allister, Jan. "Building on Self-Centeredness: Structuring a Composition Course around 'Family.'" *WI* 11 (Winter 1992): 70–82.

Describes a composition course organized around issues of family which allows students to use both personal experience and formal reasoning in their writing.

1214. Ballenger, Bruce. *Rethinking the Research Paper*. Cincinnati, OH: CCCC, March 1992. ERIC ED 347 532. 25 pages

Suggests an approach that allows the use of personal experiences and observations in research papers, expands students' notion of audience, and accepts topics outside the teacher's domain of expertise.

1215. Bamberg, Betty. "Autonomy and Accommodation—Striking a Balance: Freshman Writing and English at USC." *ADE Bulletin* 101 (Spring 1992): 19–22.

Discusses the evolution of an interdisciplinary writing program, describes its present status, and assesses the program's strengths and weaknesses as a separate unit from the English Department.

1216. Brown, Julia. "The Research Paper as Exploration of Community." *CEAF* 22 (Summer 1992): 6–7.

Suggests that first-year students should do research papers only on topics related to their communities.

1217. Brown, Juliet, and Robert Brown. *The Father Speaks, the Mother Talks Back: Revisionist, Rebellious Models for the Creative Classroom*. San Antonio, TX: College English Association, April 1991. ERIC ED 337 788. 17 pages

Presents two approaches to overhauling the traditional "workshop approach" to teaching creative writing, one advocates using literary models and the other a feminist pedagogy.

1218. Campbell, Elizabeth Humphreys. "Composition Teachers Talk about Essays: A Qualitative Approach Study of a Placement Rating Session." *DAI* 52 (June 1992): 4313A.

Presents an ethnographic study of 15 part-time composition instructors and their interactions as they discussed placement essays.

1219. Chadwick, Carol Susan. "Prescriptions of Pattern: Narrative and Expository Text Perceptions and Its Implications for Inner-City Community College Freshmen." *DAI* 53 (November 1992): 1484A.

Indicates that four categories of reader-response theorists are of interest to teachers working in inner-city community colleges. Analyzes the comprehension of expository and narrative reading materials.

1220. Chase, Dorothy Rhea. "Writing Topics and Resultant Texts: A Descriptive Study Focused on the Relationship between Topic Directives and Textual Characteristics." *DAI* 52 (June 1992): 4247A.

Conducts a textual analysis to answer the question "What should students be asked to write about if teachers want to evaluate their real ability?"

1221. Comprone, Joseph J. *Managing Freshman English: Are We Really on the Right Track?* Cincinnati, OH: CCCC, March 1992. ERIC ED 344 209. 18 pages

Discusses an experimental class in first-year English which uses a combined large group/small discussion group format with graduate assistants and senior faculty sharing instructional responsibilities.

1222. Corson, Gail Shanley. "How to 'Let Them Write-Together': The Effects of Social Styles on Written Products of College Entry-Level Collaborative Writers." *DAI* 52 (May 1992): 3912A.

Suggests that the mixtures of social styles within small group interactions of entry-level college writers affects individually written products.

1223. Darling, George J. *"What Is My Audience!": Speech-Act Theory and the Composition Classroom.* Cincinnati, OH: CCCC, March 1992. ERIC ED 344 213. 13 pages

Foregrounds speech-act theory as a technique for teaching audience awareness to writing students.

1224. Davis, Judith Rae. "Voices of Authority" *TETYC* 19 (May 1992): 113–22.

Argues that analyzing their own classroom discussion helps students confront issues of gender and authority.

1225. Dinkler, Pamela Diane. "Recursive Composing in Freshman Composition: Case Studies of Four Student Writers in Search of the Self-Made Writer." *DAI* 52 (February 1992): 2846A.

In an ethnographic study of student drafting processes, the writer describes in-depth recursive strategies and evaluates the hidden agenda of the composing classroom.

1226. Dolinsky, Kaaren. "The Extended Definition: Structured Creativity." *TETYC* 19 (May 1992): 139–40.

Looks at the usefulness of teaching students to write extended definitions.

1227. Dornsife, Robert Stewart, Jr. "Invention as Process: Aristotle, Burke, and Political Correctness." *DAI* 53 (November 1992): 1381A.

Argues that the process of invention needs to be given its proper primary place in the first-year composition classroom. Uses the work of Emig, Shaughnessey, Burke, and Aristotle to propose and apply an audience-centered invention process model to the first-year composition classroom.

1228. Enright, Louisa. "Assigning Student Journals: Yes Or No?" *TETYC* 19 (December 1992): 292–95.

A graduate teaching assistant describes her first experience with assigning journals.

1229. Figg, Kristen. "Handbook Use in College English I: Classroom Practices and Student Response." *TETYC* 19 (October 1992): 185–91.

Results from a small sample indicate that while students regard handbooks as useful they need direction in using them; finds that assigning readings and grammar was least productive.

1230. Gergits, Julia M. "No, It's Not a Research Paper." *CEAF* 22 (Summer 1992): 4–6.

> Discusses how first-year students have internalized the "wrong" way to research; suggests how to alleviate the problem by renaming the assignment.

1231. Gilbert, David. "Reconsidering the Writing Workshop." *EngR* 42 (1992): 1–5.

> Describes successful writing workshops with gifted high school students. Argues that techniques relevant to college writing classes build community, provide structure, and facilitate workshop discussion.

1232. Graham, Kathryn. *Connection, Trust, and Social Responsibility: A Feminist Pedagogy*. Cincinnati, OH: CCCC, March 1992. ERIC ED 347 542. 17 pages

> Describes characteristics of the feminist/midwife model of teaching, based on trust, cooperation, and social responsibility.

1233. Griffith, Kevin. "Metalanguage about Writing and the Transition form K–12 to College: The Written Responding Processes of Six First-Year Students Entering the University." *DAI* 53 (November 1992): 1431A.

> Conducts case studies to describe and analyze the behaviors that occurred during the written response processes of six students who had not yet been trained to respond in a college writing course.

1234. Guista, Michael. "Siskel and Ebert, Move Over: Using Film to Teach Critical Thinking." *TETYC* 19 (October 1992): 206–9.

> Argues for teaching film as film rather than as literature; includes a list of film techniques.

1235. Hairston, Maxine. "Diversity, Ideology, and Teaching Writing." *CCC* 43 (May 1992): 179–93.

> Argues for a student-centered composition course where students learn about diversity through interaction and against a model of political and ideological analysis.

1236. Hamilton-Wieler, Sharon. "If I Missed the Day You Taught Me How to Write, I'm Sorry." *EQ* 23.3–4 (1992): 11–14.

> Demonstrates the positive effects of letters of transmittal and letters of response that students include in their writings.

1237. Harris, Joseph. "The Other Reader." *JAC* 12 (Winter 1992): 27–37.

> Argues that students should write about cultural "texts," such as ads and soaps, but without constructing themselves as separate and unaffected by the texts they interpret.

1238. Henderson, Sarah A. *Why Do I Have to Be Here? The Advanced Placement Student in First-Year Composition: Problems and Issues in Cognitive Development*. Cincinnati, OH: CCCC, March 1992. ERIC ED 346 474. 22 pages

> Analyzes the problems of students in first-year composition courses who have taken Advanced Placement English; recommends solutions based on cognitive-developmental theories.

1239. Hill, Charles. *The Effect of Writing on Students' Argument-Evaluation Processes*. Cincinnati, OH: CCCC, March 1992. ERIC ED 347 540. 11 pages

> Explores the influence of two different writing tasks (short answers versus essays) on the ways in which students evaluate arguments on a controversial issue.

1240. Hindman, Jane E. *Gestures? We Don't Need Your Stinking Gestures!: Empowerment through Radical Teachers and Cultural Action for Freedom*. Cincinnati, OH: CCCC, March 1992. ERIC ED 343 151. 9 pages

> Advocates the use of discourse as subject material in basic writing courses.

1241. Hoffman, Amy. *Multi-Cultural Literacy in the Composition Classroom: Report on a Pilot Program*. Cincinnati, OH: CCCC, March 1992. ERIC ED 337 778. 10 pages

Describes and evaluates a writing course which promotes "multi-cultural literacy" and humanitarian values.

1242. Holian, Gail C., and Connie Chismar. *A Difference Dynamic: The Changing Role of the Teacher in the Writing Classroom*. Old Westbury, NY: Conference on Computers and English, April 1991. ERIC ED 337 782. 10 pages

Discusses the positive changes in classroom dynamics when writing instruction shifts from the classroom to the computer lab.

1243. Ide, Richard S. "Issues of Authority and Responsibility: Freshman Writing and English at USC—An Amicable Separation." *ADE Bulletin* 101 (Spring 1992): 23–25.

Assesses results of separating first-year writing from English and argues not for recombining but for reengaging English with first-year students and writing.

1244. Inkster, Robert P. *Should We Outgrow Personal Writing? Polanyi and Perry on Reality, Truth, and Intellectual Development*. Cincinnati, OH: CCCC, March 1992. ERIC ED 345 247. 12 pages

Argues that personal writing is a valuable commitment to finding and communicating meaningful knowledge.

1245. Jackson, Alan. "Audience, Argument, and Collaboration: Ingredients for a Group Project." *ExEx* 38 (Fall 1992): 3–7.

Describes an extended group project which draws on Rogerian argument: in pairs, students develop compromise proposals in response to selected issues.

1246. Jensen, Marilyn D. "Strategy for a Cross-Disciplinary Research Paper." *TETYC* 19 (May 1992): 136–38.

Looks at a group of students who pursue research by interviewing experts in various fields.

1247. Kerr, Nancy H., and Madeleine Picciotto. "Linked Composition Courses: Effects on Student Performance." *JTW* 11 (Spring/Summer 1992): 105–18.

Shows that students who participated in linked courses in composition and another discipline received higher paper and course grades in the basic course than the students who made no connections.

1248. Kirch, Ann. *Strategies for Success: Cooperative Learning Groups in Writing Classes*. Dallas, TX: Conference of the North Texas Community/Junior College Consortium, November 1991. ERIC ED 342 441. 21 pages

Outlines cooperative learning techniques in writing classes.

1249. Kuehner, Alison. "Getting Students to Wage the Battle in Freshman Composition." *TETYC* 19 (February 1992): 45–48.

Sees the discussion of gender issues as a way of encouraging critical thinking.

1250. Lane, Barry. *After "The End": Teaching and Learning Creative Revision*. Portsmouth, NH: Heinemann, 1992. 216 pages

Offers ideas for encouraging students to take responsibility for revision and to see the process as exciting, not simply as the act of "redoing."

1251. Leigh, David. "Writing for a Live Audience" *IndE* 15 (Spring 1992): 10–13.

Describes a course in which the final product of seven assignments is sent to actual audiences. Argues that student writers overcome their "alienation, lack of care for final product, and sense of powerlessness."

1252. Lenig, Stuart. "Using Drama to Teach Composition." *TETYC* 19 (December 1992): 305–12.

Shows the benefits and techniques of having students perform scenes.

1253. Linkon, Sherry Lee. "Collaboration in the Library: Research and the Social Production of Knowledge." *CEAF* 22 (Winter 1992): 8–10.

Discusses the advantages of student collaboration in first-year composition.

1254. Long, Elenore. *From the Classroom to the Dorm: Facing the Impasse of Demanding Discourse Constraints*. Boston, MA: CCCC, March 1991. ERIC ED 336 675. 14 pages

Observes the composing processes of four first-year writers of varying proficiency who had been taught problem solving strategies for one semester.

1255. Lovas, John C. *Challenging the Freshman Writer: Integrating the Process and Product in a Course-Long Assignment*. Cincinnati, OH: CCCC, March 1992. ERIC ED 346 476. 23 pages

Introduces an assignment for composing a personal intellectual history, incorporating invention, planning, drafting, and publishing.

1256. Lu, Min-Zhan. "A Pedagogy of Struggle: The Use of Cultural Dissonance." *JTW* 11 (Spring/Summer 1992): 1–18.

Analyzes students' revision process through autobiography; encourages a formation of oppositional discourse in the academy.

1257. Luboff, Gerald F. *Searching for Objectivity and Prejudice in Writing about AIDS*. Cincinnati, OH: CCCC, March 1992. ERIC ED 336 756. 10 pages

Sketches writing assignments that give students practice in various rhetorical approaches and provides them with an opportunity to explore their own attitudes towards the AIDS crisis.

1258. MacKenzie, Nancy, and Anne O'Meara. "Teaching Collaborative Critical Thinking." *ExEx* 37 (Spring 1992): 12–14.

Describes an activity in which students brainstorm in small groups, separately analyze group processes in double-entry logs, and then assess outcomes in large group.

1259. Marbeck, Richard. *The Writing Process and the Distribution of Power*. Cincinnati, OH: CCCC, March 1992. ERIC ED 337 772. 12 pages

Argues that writing instruction focused on language as a tool for creating rather than reproducing ideas and effects enables students to grasp the rhetorical nature of authority.

1260. McClure, Michael F. *Valuing Student Texts/Students Valuing Texts*. Cincinnati, OH: CCCC, March 1992. ERIC ED 345 250. 10 pages

Contrasts "discourse convention" approaches to the writing classroom with "discussion of difference" approaches and finds the latter more productive.

1261. Miller, Richard E. *Not Just Story Collecting: Towards a Critical Ethnography*. Cincinnati, OH: CCCC, March 1992. ERIC ED 345 244. 13 pages

Discusses an ethnographically based composition course, moving from personal narrative to critical analysis.

1262. Mirtz, Ruth M. "Classroom Learning: Narratives of Emergent Occasions." *ADE Bulletin* 102 (Fall 1992): 24–26.

Uses examples to define insightful classroom experience, the "emergent occasion"; points out what teachers can learn from it.

1263. Murphy, Kathleen V. *Feminist Pedagogy and Student Constructions of Knowledge and Female Authority*. Cincinnati, OH: CCCC, March 1992. ERIC ED 345 234. 12 pages

Describes a feminist approach to an adult evening writing course; uses ethnography to focus on intellectual and moral assumptions.

1264. Ng, Joseph S. "The *Sister Carrie* Manuscript and Authorial Intentions: Reinforcing Students' Rights to Their Own Texts." *ExEx* 38 (Fall 1992): 18–23.

Describes how to improve peer editing through manuscript analysis and writing of intentions in margins for peers and for the instructor.

1265. Olendzenski, Michael Felix. "A Comparison of the Effects of Self-Evaluation and Peer Evaluation on the Revising Behaviors and Overall Composing Processes of College Freshmen." *DAI* 52 (February 1992): 2810A.

Suggests significant differences on first and final drafts in terms of large-scale revising. Interviews suggest that students showed a greater concern with pleasing their teachers than with learning how to write well.

1266. Ostrom, Hans. *Surviving to Write and Writing to Survive: The Complex Case of Langston Hughes.* Cincinnati, OH: CCCC, March 1992. ERIC ED 344 215. 9 pages

Argues that a study of the struggles of Langston Hughes can provide encouragement for first-year writers.

1267. Pacheco, Anne-Louise, and Bette Brickman. "Using Print and Electronic Ads in the Writing Classroom." *TETYC* 19 (December 1992): 289–91.

Points out that ads demonstrate writing strategies and can be used for exercises in critical thinking.

1268. Paddison, John. "Autobiographical Writing and the Building of a Freshman Composition Research Community." *EngR* 43 (1992): 26–29.

Describes a first-year writing sequence that uses autobiography to create a critical self-examination on a community issue; uses autobiographies to form a research base for an exploration of individual roles in society.

1269. Paddison, John. *Autobiographical Writing and the Building of a Freshman Composition Research Community.* Seattle, WA: NCTE, November 1991. ERIC ED 343 130. 12 pages

Finds students' personal experiences useful in both first-year composition and research writing courses.

1270. Paré, Anthony. "Review of *Balancing Acts: Essays on the Teaching of Writing in Honor of William F. Irmscher* and *Reclaiming Pedagogy: The Rhetoric of the Classroom*." *TCQ* 1 (Spring 1992): 105–7.

Examines postmodern views of writing classrooms that celebrate diversity.

1271. Perdue, Virginia. "Authority and the Freshman Writer: The Ideology of the Thesis Statement." *WI* 11 (Spring/Summer 1992): 135–42.

Argues that the advice offered by first-year composition textbooks about thesis statements can undermine students' attempts to develop authority.

1272. Purvis, Teresa M. "And Now a Few Words in Support of Media." *TETYC* 19 (May 1992): 123–27.

Shows how students can imitate advertising devices to learn argument and persuasion.

1273. Savas, Diana Natalie. "Orality, Literacy, and the Academic Writing of University Freshmen." *DAI* 53 (July 1992): 138A.

Investigates the extent to which the descriptive language of the reification version of orality/literacy theory is applicable to the thinking and academic writing of first-year college students.

1274. Segall, Mary T. "Prejudice to Prose: Composition in Context." *Leaflet* 91 (Spring 1992): 23–26.

Describes a thematic approach to writing in a first-year English class.

1275. Smit, David W. "Improving Student Writing. Idea Paper Number 25." Center for Faculty Evaluation and Development in Higher Education, Kansas State University, Manhattan, NY, September 1991. ERIC ED 339 037. 7 pages

Argues that students do not write well because they do not receive much practice or instruction in writing. Offers ways of teaching formal writing in college classes.

1276. Smith, Maggy. *Contexts for Writing on the Border: The Community and the Constraints for Hispanic Freshmen Writers.* Cincinnati, OH: CCCC, March 1992. ERIC ED 347 552. 14 pages

Uses two case studies to demonstrate cultural interference in writing classrooms, including linguistic and social differences that lead to mixed signals and unshared expectations.

1277. Smith, Mark Edward. "From Expressive to Transactional: A Case Study." *EJ* 81 (December 1992): 42–46.

Draws on Britton's research to show what did not help students write transactional essays.

1278. Stolarek, Elizabeth Ann. "Prose Modeling: Role of Model, Description and Explication in Learning Form by Expert and Novice Writers." *DAI* 52 (February 1992): 2911A.

Determines the effect on novice and expert writers incorporating sets of instructions using description, a prose model, and an explication in learning an unfamiliar prose form.

1279. Strenski, Ellen, and Madge Manfred. *The Research Paper Workbook*. 3rd ed. White Plains, NY: Longman, 1992. 340 pages

The authors provide information on developing topics, locating sources, reading critically, taking notes, synthesizing information, revising drafts, and documenting; they include examples of MLA, APA, and Chicago methods of documentation and explain number systems of the sciences. The study includes sample research papers.

1280. Swope, John Wilson. "Using Reading and Writing-to-Learn to Promote Revision." *ELQ* 13 (May 1992): 11–12.

Details a teaching strategy encouraging students to view revising from the perspective of adjusting text to fit their intentions rather than addressing conventions.

1281. Tebo, Mike. "Writing: Therapy without the Therapist." *ELQ* 13 (December 1992): 6–9.

Advocates the therapeutic benefits of asking students to write about emotionally charged topics such as suicide.

1282. Thelin, William. *Balancing Politically Charged Social Issues in Freshman Composition: The Ethical Epistemic Approach*. Cincinnati, OH: CCCC, March 1992. ERIC ED 344 221. 16 pages

Describes an approach to first-year composition which achieves a balance between indoctrination and depoliticization while still promoting writing skills.

1283. Tingley, Stephanie A. "Proposal and Problem-Solving: Strategies for Teaching the Freshman Research Paper." *CEAF* 22 (Winter 1992): 10–12.

Advocates sequencing assignments in first-year composition as a way of preparing students for a major research paper.

1284. Vatalaro, Paul. "Writing Response Groups and the Role of Adversity." *WI* 11 (Spring/Summer 1992): 128–34.

Maintains that tension and frustration during group responding activities creates opportunities for learning rather than signalling the failure of the collaborative process.

1285. Walker, Carolyn. "Teacher Dominance in the Writing Conference." *JTW* 11 (Spring/Summer 1992): 65–87.

Concludes that dominance of teacher talk is important only if the student has not set her agenda.

1286. Weinstein, Edith K. "Questions and Answers to Guide the Teaching of Critical Thinking." *TETYC* 19 (December 1992): 284–88.

Defines critical thinking; offers practical suggestions for exercises and writing assignments.

1287. White, Fred D. *'Thought across My Corpus Callosum': What Lewis Thomas's Essays Can Teach Students about Writing Well*. Cincinnati, OH: CCCC, March 1992. ERIC ED 347 564. 12 pages

Discusses how reading Lewis Thomas helps students engage in interactions with the world, become engaged holistically with a subject, and eliminate rigid notions of form.

1288. Wilhoit, Stephen, and Christine Shearer. "Critical Thinking, Reflective Skepticism, and the Introductory Composition Course." *Leaflet* 91 (Fall 1992): 19–25.

Discusses the implications of the work of theorists in critical thinking for structuring composition courses.

1289. Willey, R. J. "Fostering Audience Awareness through Interpretive Communities." *TETYC* 19 (May 1992): 148–55.

Argues that teaching first-year composition by a reader-response method encourages interactive reading and fosters an awareness of audience.

1290. Wright, William W. "Progressive Practice in Group Presentations." *ExEx* 38 (Fall 1992): 10–12.

Explains an increasingly challenging sequence of group assignments which teach students how to collaborate.

1291. Ybarra, Raul. *"Western Essayist Literacy"—A Way of Teaching*. Cincinnati, OH: CCCC, March 1992. ERIC ED 346 489. 11 pages

Reports on a case study in which discourse patterns of the essayist literary style dominated the class's written and oral communication.

See also 499

4.2.3 ADVANCED COMPOSITION

1292. Couch, Lezlie Laws. "Story ≠ Essay." *JTW* 11 (Spring/Summer 1992): 89–104.

Presents a close study of a student's drafts, reflective writing, and teacher responses; indicates that the student's awareness of her own writing is important for her improvement as an essay writer.

1293. Fleckenstein, Kristie S. "Criss-Crossing Perspectives: Writing Events within Writing Assignments." *EJ* 81 (December 1992): 37–41.

Draws on Britton's and Moffett's research to explain how students create and complete their own writing assignments through five "spiraled" activities.

1294. Fulwiler, Toby. "Provocative Revision." *WCJ* 12 (Spring 1992): 190–204.

The author offers limiting, adding, switching, and transforming as four categories of revision strategies. Provides detailed description of these categories and techniques to teach them.

1295. Griffith, Kevin. *A Community of Composition Theorists and Researchers: Collaborative Research and Theory Building in an Advanced Composition Course*. Cincinnati, OH: CCCC, March 1992. ERIC ED 345 233. 11 pages

Sketches an advanced course focusing on composition theory and collaborative writing.

1296. Laughlin, James S. "When Students Confront the Experts: Toward Critical Thinking." *EJ* 81 (February 1992): 72–75.

Presents a four-essay assignment sequence that initiates students into a "lifelong engagement with a complex, expert-dominated society."

1297. Pemberton, Michael. "Threshold of Desperation: Winning the Fight against Term Paper Mills." *WI* 11 (Spring/Summer 1992): 143–52.

Examines how one writer produces the texts that students can purchase from "paper mills." Points out that a process-oriented curriculum can discourage the use of such services.

1298. Pippen, Carol Lawson. "A Social Scene of Writing: The Peer Group Talk of Three Women English Education Majors Enrolled in an Advanced Composition Class." *DAI* 52 (May 1992): 3848A.

Conducts a naturalistic study of a peer group that attempts to understand how these women represent writing and what they value in writing and in writers.

1299. Sills, Caryl Klein. "Arguing from First-Hand Evidence." *JBW* 11 (Fall 1992): 103–10.

Describes a collaborative writing assignment that requires students to gather evidence from personal observation to form an argument and a proposal based on their conclusions.

1300. Vandenberg, Peter. "Excuse Me, Is This Thing On? Audiotape Commentary in Dialogic Classrooms." *WI* 11 (Winter 1992): 95–103.

Maintains that teachers who transfer students' papers on cassette tapes and offer audiotaped feedback can encourage revision and allow students to escape their traditionally passive role.

4.2.4 BUSINESS COMMUNICATION

1301. Barbour, Dennis H. "The Best of Both Worlds: Instructor/Group Evaluation of Business Writing Assignments." *JBTC* 6 (October 1992): 480–87.

Describes the procedure for teacher and peer evaluations; outlines advantages of dual feedback.

1302. Barker, Randolph T., C. Glenn Pearce, and Iris W. Johnson. "An Investigation of Perceived Managerial Listening Ability." *JBTC* 6 (October 1992): 438–57.

The study examines training, gender, and age in connection with listening effectiveness among managers.

1303. Belanger, Kelly, and Jane Greer. "Beyond the Group Project: A Blueprint for a Collaborative Writing Course." *JBTC* 6 (January 1992): 99–115.

Course description includes assignments as well as guidelines on establishing groups, analyzing group dynamics and writing processes, and determining instructors' roles.

1304. Charney, Davida H., Jack Rayman, and Linda Ferreira-Buckley. "How Writing Quality Influences Readers' Judgments of Résumés in Business Engineering." *JBTC* 6 (January 1992): 38–74.

A study of recruiters' responses to student résumés concludes that perceptions of effectiveness are linked to community/disciplinary communication practices.

1305. Dulek, Ronald E. "Could You Be Clearer? An Examination of the Multiple Perspectives of Clarity." *IEEE* 35 (June 1992): 84–87.

Examines the effect of precision, document accessibility, and corporate language context on readers' perceptions of "clarity."

1306. Fisk, Mary Lou. "People, Proxemics, and Possibilities for Technical Writing." *IEEE* 35 (September 1992): 176–82.

Finds that conventions of format vary across cultures. Points out that articles written in different cultures demonstrate differences in format.

1307. Kohut, Gary F., and Albert H. Segars. "The President's Letter to Stockholders: An Examination of Corporate Communication Strategy." *JBC* 29 (Winter 1992): 7–21.

Examines the content of the president's letters in various firms to discover communication strategies. Finds that financial performance influences reports.

1308. Maier, Paula. "Politeness Strategies in Business Letters by Native and Nonnative English Speakers." *ESP* 11 (1992): 189–205.

Studies how nonnative speakers utilize politeness strategies in business writing; argues that appropriate politeness strategies are recognized by the NNS but often not used correctly.

1309. Martella, Maureen. "The Rhetoric and Realities of Contingent Work: The Case of Women in Clerical Temporary Work." *DAI* 53 (December 1992): 2122A.

Adds to the debate about causes and consequences of contingent work from the perspective of women clerical temporary workers.

1310. Martin, Jeanette S., and Lillian H. Chaney. "Determination of Content for a Collegiate Course in Intercultural Business Communication by Three Delphi Panels." *JBC* 29 (1992): 267–81.

> The authors present the outcome of a study in which three Delphi panels yielded ten major topics and 87 subtopics for courses in intercultural business communication: 22 subtopics were "essential," 65 were "important."

1311. McCord, Elizabeth A. "Multiple Drafts and Legal Liability: A Hazard for Professional Writers." *IEEE* 35 (September 1992): 138–42.

> Points out that rough drafts of documents may be used against writers and their companies in litigation.

1312. McDonald, Daniel. "Achieving the Unreadable Memo." *ETC* 49 (Fall 1992): 279–84.

> Discusses memo-writing including humorous samples to illustrate the problems that ineffective memos cause for readers.

1313. Motes, William H, Chadwick B. Hilton, and John S. Fielden. "Reactions to Lexical, Syntactical, and Text Layout Variations of Print Advertisement." *JBTC* 6 (April 1992): 200–223.

> The study tests the extent to which language and text layout elements affect readers' perceptions of advertisements.

1314. Pomerenke, Paula J. "Writers at Work: Seventeen Writers at a Major Insurance Corporation." *JBTC* 6 (April 1992): 172–86.

> Presents findings from a survey on professional writers that explain habits regarding collaboration, standards, and document approval.

1315. Randels, James, Wendy Carse, and Judy E. Lease. "Peer-Tutor Training: A Model for Business Schools." *JBTC* 6 (July 1992): 337–53.

> Describes a training program for peer tutors working in writing labs.

1316. Rentz, Kathryn C. "The Value of Narrative in Business Writing." *JBTC* 6 (July 1992): 293–315.

> Analyzes narrative discourse and argues for the power of narrative in business writing.

1317. Roy, Sandra, and Emil Roy. "Direct-Mail Letters: A Computerized Linkage between Style and Success." *JBTC* 6 (April 1992): 224–34.

> The study of a computerized style checker outlines methods for correlating stylistic traits with sales success.

1318. Shaw, Gary. "Using Literature to Teach Ethics in the Business Curriculum." *JBTC* 6 (April 1992): 187–99.

> Argues that literature is an effective tool for teaching ethics to MBA and business communications students.

1319. Sims, Brenda R., and Stephen Guice. "Differences between Business Letters from Native and Nonnative Speakers of English." *JBC* 29 (Winter 1992): 23–39.

> The authors compare 214 letters of inquiry written by native and nonnative speakers. Their findings indicate that native speakers wrote more conventional letters.

1320. Stevens, Kevin T., Kathleen C. Stevens, and William P. Stevens. "Measuring the Readability of Business Writing: The Cloze Procedure Versus Readability Formulas." *JBC* 29 (1992): 367–82.

> Surveys arguments and evidence showing inaccuracy of easily used readability tests; proposes the use of cloze tests instead.

1321. Tebeaux, Elizabeth. "Renaissance Epistolography and the Origins of Business Correspondence, 1568–1640: Implications for

Modern Pedagogy." *JBTC* 6 (January 1992): 75–98.

> Locates the process (rhetorical) approach in the Renaissance tradition and supports the current emphasis on the methods of this tradition.

4.2.5 SCIENTIFIC AND TECHNICAL COMMUNICATION

1322. Allen, Jo. "Bridge Over Troubled Waters? Connecting Research and Pedagogy in Composition and Business/Technical Communication." *TCQ* 1 (Fall 1992): 5–26.

> Argues for a continuity between composition and professional communication studies in both pedagogy and research. Concludes with questions and avenues for further research.

1323. Allen, Nancy Jane. "Collaborative Voices: Rhetorical and Textual Features of Collaboratively Written Reports." *DAI* 53 (July 1992): 135A.

> Finds that collaboratively and individually written texts differ in the relationships established between writer and reader and in the definition of the rhetorical problem.

1324. Alred, Gerald J., Walter E. Oliu, and Charles T. Brusaw. *The Professional Writer: A Guide for Advanced Technical Writing*. New York: St. Martin's Press, 1992. 426 pages

> Combines theory with professional practice, and includes a case history of the production of an in-house publication. Among topics covered are managing collaborative work, computer graphics, layout and typography, review and evaluation process, document standards, and online documentation.

1325. Barnett, George A. "The Acoustical Presentation of Technical Information." *JTWC* 22 (1992): 39–52.

> Advocates listening to technical information in order to gain a greater and longer-term understanding of the relations among variables; specifies other potential benefits.

1326. Beard, John D., and David L. Williams. "A Survey of Practitioners' Attitudes toward Research in Technical Communication." *TC* 39 (November 1992): 571–81.

> Surveys professional technical writers: 751 responded that they value such research, use it to solve business problems, but seldom read the major journals.

1327. Bernhardt, Stephen A. "The Design of Sexism: The Case of an Army Maintenance Manual." *IEEE* 35 (December 1992): 217–21.

> Compares manuals from 1970 and 1990. Argues that a rhetoric of visual attractiveness will continue to exploit gender.

1328. Blyler, Nancy Roundy. "Narration and Knowledge in Direct Solicitations." *TCQ* 1 (Summer 1992): 59–72.

> Examines the role of narration in direct solicitations and how it socially justifies belief.

1329. Blyler, Nancy Roundy. "Shared Meaning and Public Relations Writing." *JTWC* 22 (1992): 301–18.

> Uses rhetorical theory to examine exophoric and intertextual references, metaphors, and narratives in generating a shared meaning in two different samples of public relations writing.

1330. Bosley, Deborah S. "Broadening the Base of a Technical Communication Program: An Industrial/Academic Alliance." *TCQ* 1 (Winter 1992): 41–56.

> Argues that technical communication programs should develop a "symbiotic relationship" with industry through advisory boards. Describes UNCCs two-year process of developing its technical communication program.

1331. Bosley, Deborah S. "Gender and Visual Communication: Toward a Feminist Theory of Design." *IEEE* 35 (December 1992): 222–29.

> Posits a feminist theory of design that is contextual, nonhierarchical, and social.

1332. Brown, Vincent Jay. "Audience Factors in the Collaborative Writing, Cycling, and Revision of a Technical Report at a Contract Research and Development Laboratory." *DAI* 53 (November 1992): 1499A.

This qualitative study examines how a team of nonacademic authors conceived of multiple audiences as they prepared a report of an outside client; discusses the effects of this factor on their composition process. Shows that the audience factor influenced many important composing and revising decisions.

1333. Bryan, John. "Down the Slippery Slope: Ethics and the Technical Writer as Marketer." *TCQ* 1 (Winter 1992): 73–88.

Examines ethical choices that technical writers must make in writing marketing materials. Focuses on engineering organizations.

1334. Burnett, Rebecca E. "Review of *Collaborative Writing in Industry: Investigations in Theory and Practice* and *Cooperative Learning Theory and Research*." *TCQ* 1 (Spring 1992): 97–102.

Examines the increased academic and industrial interest in collaboration.

1335. Burton, Barry W. "Dealing with Non-English Alphabets in Mathematics." *TC* 39 (May 1992): 219–25.

Presents a survey of alphabets (Greek, Germanic, and Hebrew) for technical communicators who must use these symbols in communicating mathematical concepts.

1336. Caernarven-Smith, Patricia. "An 8-Hour to 16-Hour Curriculum in Computer Hardware for Technical Writing Programs, with Reading List." *TC* 39 (May 1992): 175–81.

Lists eight topics to be covered in the course; includes topics such as bits and bytes, memory, buses, power, and logical structures.

1337. Campbell, Charles C. "Engineering Style: Striving for Efficiency." *IEEE* 35 (September 1992): 130–37.

Argues that improvements in efficiency come from aligning word-order with readers' expectations.

1338. Ceccio, Joseph. "Review of *Writing and Speaking in Business*; *Communication for Management and Business;* and *Business Communication Today*." *TCQ* 1 (Summer 1992): 102–4.

Surveys three landmarks in the development of business communication.

1339. Charney, Davida H. "Review of *The Development of Scientific Thinking Skills* and *Understanding the Representational Mind*." *TCQ* 1 (Summer 1992): 87–95.

Examines the role of developmental psychological research on metacognition in teaching technical writing students to assess evidence and argue effectively to avoid communication failures.

1340. Cilengir, Erika N. "Controlling Technology through Communication: Redefining the Role of the Technical Communicator." *TC* 39 (May 1992): 166–74.

Discusses ethical dimensions of the technical communicator's role as "Public Advocate" and "User Advocate" when discussing technology.

1341. Cole, Marian. "Guiding the Reader: Proposals and Persuasion." *TC* 39 (February 1992): 53–56.

Describes how readers employ headings. Shows six research subjects who read the same paragraph but with two different headings. Concludes that headings are important in persuasive writing.

1342. Colletta, W. John. "The Ideologically Biased Use of Language in Scientific and Technical Writing." *TCQ* 1 (Winter 1992): 59–70.

Examines how teachers might incorporate ideological inquiry into technical writing classes. Provides examples from biology, engineering, and physics.

1343. Coney, Mary B. "Technical Readers and Their Rhetorical Roles." *IEEE* 35 (June 1992): 58–63.

Presents a taxonomy of roles that readers play within technical documents: reader as receiver, user, decoder, colleague, and maker of meaning.

1344. Coney, Mary B. "Terministic Screens: A Burkean Reading of the Experimental Article." *JTWC* 22 (1992): 149–58.

Tests the value of Burke's methodology by exploring the scientific article reporting experimental results through three terministic screens—the sermon, the playscript, and the blueprint.

1345. Couture, Barbara. "Categorizing Professional Discourse: Engineering, Administrative, and Technical/Professional Writing." *JBTC* 6 (January 1992): 5–37.

Posits three categories of professional writing designed to explain how discourse is interpreted in organizational settings.

1346. Couture, Barbara. "A Response to Mohan Limaye [*JBTC* 6 (October 1992)]." *JBTC* 6 (October 1992): 491–92.

Clarifies her position on linguistic classification and categories of professional communication.

1347. Crew, Louie. "Importing Vocabularies to Describe Literary Structure." *JTWC* 22 (1992): 77–93.

Proposes that engineering, computer science, and business students can understand and analyze literature if encouraged to use the vocabularies of their own disciplines.

1348. Crook, Bernard. "Technical Communication and Theory: A Hermeneutic Approach." *DAI* 53 (October 1992): 1141A.

Discusses the obstacles confronting the field of technical communication and its attempts at full professionalism.

1349. Curry, Jerome M. "Technical Instruction and Definition Assignments: A Realistic Approach." *JBTC* 6 (January 1992): 116–22.

Argues for realistic writing assignments and outlines two such assignments.

1350. Day, Robert A. *Scientific English: A Guide for Scientists and Other Professionals*. Phoenix, AZ: Oryx, 1992. 125 pages

Provides grammatical, stylistic, and mechanical advice for writers in scientific and technical disciplines.

1351. Dennet, Joann Temple. "World Language Status Does Not Ensure World Class Usage." *IEEE* 35 (March 1992): 13.

Argues that since many use English as a foreign language, native speakers need to view English in its appropriate international context.

1352. Doheny-Farina, Stephen. *Rhetoric, Innovation, Technology: Case Studies of Technical Communication in Technology Transfers*. Cambridge, MA: MIT Press, 1992. 279 pages

Explores how a product is perceived by those transferring it from the laboratory to the marketplace. Discusses the role of technical writers in the emergency redesigning of a large-scale software product.

1353. Dolan, Catherine Rae. "Beliefs, Opinions and Attitudes from the Aerospace Engineering Field about Technical Communication Instruction." *DAI* 52 (June 1992): 4247A.

Develops a base for future investigations of the role and nature of communication instruction in the workplace and its relationship to discourse communities.

1354. Dombrowski, Paul M. "*Challenger* and the Social Contingency of Meaning: Two Lessons for the Technical Communication Classroom." *TCQ* 1 (Summer 1992): 73–86.

Describes a classroom exercise focusing on *Challenger* which strives to teach students how positivism can limit their understanding of the "social contingency of meaning."

1355. Dombrowski, Paul M. "A Comment on 'The Construction of Knowledge in Organizations: Asking the Right Questions about the

Challenger' [response to Winsor, *JBTC* 4 (September 1990)]." *JBTC* 6 (January 1992): 123–27.

> Questions assumptions about discourse ambiguity in Winsor's analysis of O-ring erosion in the *Challenger* disaster.

1356. Dragga, Sam. "Evaluating Pictorial Illustrations" *TCQ* 1 (Spring 1992): 47–62.

> Offers a 12-question heuristic based on Elizabeth Goldsmith's theory of illustration to help direct teachers and technical writers to compose and evaluate pictorial images.

1357. Eisenberg, Anne. "Metaphors in the Language of Science." *ScAm* 266 (May 1992): 144.

> Examines the increased use of metaphors and other rhetorical devices in current scientific and technical writing.

1358. Epstein, Julia. "Historiography, Diagnosis, and Poetics." *L&M* 11 (Spring 1992): 23–44.

> Analyzes the issues involved in understanding the "conventional structures of case-history writing" and the displacement of authority from writer to text.

1359. Gearhart, Kyle Anne. "A Collaborative Writing Project in a Technical Communication Course." *TC* 39 (August 1992): 360–66.

> Surveys research on skills needed in the industry and describes a course involving assignments correlating with these skills.

1360. Gilbert, Frederick. "The Technical Presentation." *TC* 39 (May 1992): 200–201.

> Offers general information on how to give a technical talk.

1361. Gitelman, Lisa Louise. "The World Recounted: Science and Narrative in Early Nineteenth-Century Exploration Accounts." *DAI* 52 (February 1992): 2931A.

> Examines the role of narrative in scientific writing of the first half of the nineteenth century.

1362. Goubil-Gabrell, Patricia. "A Practitioner's Guide to Research Methods." *TC* 39 (November 1992): 582–91.

> Shows that the two main methodologies are quantitative (e.g., empirical studies) and qualitative (scholarly inquiry and practitioner inquiry). Identifies when the use of each is appropriate.

1363. Greenwood, Claudia M. "Searching the Silence to Find a Voice." *JBTC* 6 (April 1992): 235–42.

> Argues that methodological and institutional norms can exclude alternative voices, including some gendered perspectives.

1364. Gribbons, William M. "Organization by Design: Some Implications for Structuring Information." *JTWC* 22 (1992): 57–75.

> Proposes a system for document organization based on cueing and page formatting techniques that result in increased reading speeds, ease of access, and comprehension.

1365. Hager, Peter J. "Teaching Students the Verticality of Technical Documentation." *TC* 39 (May 1992): 182–88.

> Prefers "vertical" teaching assignments—such as manuals for campus organizations—to "horizontal" assignments which introduce different types of formats.

1366. Harmon, Joseph H. "An Analysis of Fifty Citation Superstars from the Scientific Literature." *JTWC* 22 (1992): 17–37.

> Summarizes results of structural and stylistic analyses of 50 scientific papers from the top 100 most-cited in the Science Citation Index for 1945–88.

1367. Harris, R. A. "Commentary: A Response to K. Scott Ferguson and Frank Parker's 'Grammar and Technical Writing' [*JTWC* 18 (1988)]." *JTWC* 22 (1992): 53–56.

> Argues that Ferguson and Parker completely distort Harris's "Linguistics, Technical Writing, and Generalized Phrase Structure Grammar."

1368. Helyar, Pamela S. "Products Liability: Meeting Legal Standards for Adequate Instructions." *JTWC* 22 (1992): 125–47.

Defines legally adequate instructions and warnings as complete, accurate, and tested directions that meet government, industry, and company standards.

1369. Holliday, William G. "Helping College Science Students Read and Write: Practical, Research-Based Suggestions." *JCST* 22 (September 1992): 58–60.

Presents practical, research-based suggestions for both students and teachers to improve reading and writing skills in the context of content-based courses.

1370. Jansen, Carel, and Michael Steehouder. "Forms as a Source of Communication Problems." *JTWC* 22 (1992): 179–94.

Describes a study examining the problems encountered by people when filling in forms and describes a revision of forms that reduced errors by half.

1371. Johns, Frances A. "Word Processing and Technical Writing Textbooks: A Fledgling Alliance." *CACJ* 6 (Winter 1992): 24–28.

Argues that textbooks in technical writing should emphasize the importance, implications, and applications of word processing in the technical writing field.

1372. Katrathanos, Patricia, and M. Diane Pettypool. "A Network Approach to Formulating Communication Strategy." *JTWC* 22 (1992): 95–103.

Proposes that an examination and analysis of a company's overall communication network may provide some significant guidelines for increasing the organization's communication effectiveness.

1373. Keith, William, and Kenneth Zagachi. "Rhetoric and Paradox in Scientific Revolutions." *SCJ* 57 (Spring 1992): 165–77.

Examines the nature of rhetorical constraints on scientists and discusses available resolutions.

1374. Killingsworth, M. Jimmie, and Michael K. Gilbertson. *Signs, Genres, and Communities in Technical Communication*. Baywood Technical Communication Series, edited by Jay R. Gould. Amityville, NY: Baywood, 1992. 272 pages

The authors analyze the components of technical communication according to the general theory of signs and interpret technical genres in terms of their social impact on discourse communities. They provide teachers with a framework for organizing courses in technical communication and offer empirical researchers hypotheses to be tested in the field.

1375. Kirkman, John. "Which English Should We Teach for International Technical Communication?" *JTWC* 22 (1992): 5–16.

Suggests that for the international exchange of information, writers and editors find vocabulary, grammar, and usage common to both British and American versions of English.

1376. Ladd, Maria de Armas, and Marion Tangum. "What Difference Does Inherited Difference Make? Exploring Culture and Gender in Scientific and Technical Professions." *IEEE* 35 (September 1992): 183–90.

Presents a model for the integration of intercultural and gender issues in the technical communication classroom.

1377. Lemaye, Mohan. "Conceptual and Methodological Issues in Organizational Communication Research: A Comment on 'Categorizing Professional Discourse' [response to Couture, *JBTC* 6 (January 1992)]." *JBTC* 6 (October 1992): 488–90.

Offers alternatives for conceptualizing and studying categories of discourse in the workplace.

1378. MacNealy, Mary Sue. "Research in Technical Communication: A View from the Past and a Challenge for the Future." *TC* 39 (November 1992): 533–51.

Presents a survey of the International Technical Communication Conference proceedings; analyzes quantity, quality, and coherence in empirical research.

1379. McDaniel, Ellen, Robert E. Young, and Johann Vesterager. "Document-Driven Management of Knowledge and Technology: Denmark's CIM/GEMS Project in Computer-Integrated Manufacturing—Part 2." *IEEE* 35 (June 1992): 71–83.

Describes using system documentation to drive and manage technical development in technology-transfer projects.

1380. McDowell, Earl E. "A Survey of Employment Interviewing Practices for Technical Writing Positions." *JTWC* 22 (1992): 273–79.

Focuses on recruiters' perceptions of what information should be included in cover letters and résumés and on the roles of interviewees and interviewers in employment interviews.

1381. Mirel, Barbara. "Analyzing Audiences for Software Manuals: A Survey of Instructional Needs for 'Real World Tasks.' " *TCQ* 1 (Winter 1992): 13–38.

Presents a survey of 25 database users. Recommends that software documentation developers examine social and organizational factors which influence instructional needs.

1382. Monroe, William Frank, Warren Lee Holleman, and Marsha Cline Holleman. "Is There a Person in This Case?" *L&M* 11 (Spring 1992): 45–63.

Suggests a performance paradigm to enrich and enliven the notions of textuality and narrative embodied in the case-report genre.

1383. Moore, Patrick. "Intimidation and Communication: A Case Study of the *Challenger* Accident." *JBTC* 6 (October 1992): 403–37.

Defines intimidation and analyzes its function in organizational communication and decision making.

1384. Moore, Patrick. "When Politeness Is Fatal: Technical Communication and the *Challenger* Disaster." *JBTC* 6 (July 1992): 269–92.

Argues that inappropriate politeness strategies contributed to the *Challenger* disaster.

1385. Neel, Jasper. "Dichotomy, Consubstantiality, Technical Writing, Literary Theory: The Double Orthodox Curse." *JAC* 12 (Fall 1992): 305–20.

Examines the conflict between literary and composition theorists by picturing their studies as opposite extremes on a continuum; proposes a Rogerian discussion between the camps.

1386. Neeley, Kathryn A. "Woman as Mediatrix: Women as Writers on Science and Technology in the Eighteenth and Nineteenth Centuries." *IEEE* 35 (December 1992): 196–207.

Argues that mediative (popular) writing about science is an unrecognized but important aspect of the activity of science.

1387. Nore, Gordon W. E. "Clear Lines: How to Compose and Design Clear Language Documents for the Workplace." Frontier College, Toronto, Canada, 1991. ERIC ED 335 478. 87 pages

Offers a guide about clear language in the workplace.

1388. Norman, Rose, and Daryl Grider. "Structured Document Processors: Implications for Technical Writing." *TCQ* 1 (Summer 1992): 5–21.

Examines the role of Structured Document Processors in the workplace and explores how they might change the teaching of technical writing.

1389. Ornatowski, Cezar M. "Between Efficiency and Politics: Rhetoric and Ethics in Technical Writing." *TCQ* 1 (Winter 1992): 91–103.

Argues that when teachers recognize that technical writing is always rhetorical, with potential conflicts, they can begin to introduce ethics into the technical writing classroom.

1390. Ornatowski, Cezar M. "Between Efficiency and Politics: Technical Communications and Rhetoric in an Aerospace Firm." *DAI* 52 (February 1992): 2757A.

Examines the generation, circulation and functions of written texts in the social context of an aerospace firm.

1391. Pagnucci, Gian, and Dawn Abt-Perkins. "The Never-Making-Sense Story: Reassessing the Value of Narrative." *EJ* 81 (December 1992): 54–58.

Describes a summer science institute conducted by university professors for high school students; concludes that "narrative deserves a more central place" in education.

1392. Panko, Raymond R. "Managerial Communication Patterns." *JOC* 2 (Winter 1992): 95–122.

Looks at the use of time data that provide a detailed picture of communication patterns in the workdays of managers and other knowledge workers.

1393. Parsons, Gerald M. "Review of *Editing: The Design of Rhetoric* and *Technical Editing*." *TCQ* 1 (Spring 1992): 107–10.

Examines the development of the field of technical editing.

1394. Pestel, Beverly C., and Eugene A. Engeldinger. "Library-Labs-for-Science Literacy Courses." *JCST* 22 (September 1992): 52–54.

Describes a series of writing/research assignments designed to improve science literacy and critical thinking skills in classes of nonscience majors.

1395. Pinelli, Thomas E., and Rebecca O. Barclay. "Research in Technical Communication:" *TC* 39 (November 1992): 526–32.

Describes the problems hindering technical communication from developing a coherent research foundation in theory and practice, such as the different motivations found in academe versus industry.

1396. Pixton, William H. "Technical Writing and Terminal Modification." *JTWC* 22 (1992): 159–78.

Explains that increased attention to terminal modifiers, described in the work of Francis Christensen, would increase the options for effective expression by technical writers.

1397. Plumb, Carolyn, and Jan H. Spyridakis. "Survey Research in Technical Communication: Designing and Administering Questionnaires." *TC* 39 (November 1992): 625–38.

Discusses the strengths and weaknesses of conducting research with surveys; describes methods, such as determining target population, defining objectives, and measuring reliability.

1398. *Proceedings of the 39th International Technical Communication Conference.* Arlington, VA: Society for Technical Communication, 1992. 858 pages

Presents a collection of papers presented in May 1992. Subjects include education, training and professional development, management, research and technology, and visual communications.

1399. Reynolds, John Frederick. "Classical Rhetoric and the Teaching of Technical Writing." *TCQ* 1 (Spring 1992): 63–76.

Argues that technical writing textbooks have largely ignored classical rhetoric. Offers a framework for incorporating it into technical communication classes.

1400. Sageev, Pneena. *Helping Researchers Write . . . So Managers Can Understand.* Columbus, OH: Battelle Memorial Institute, 1992. 168 pages

Identifies the main problems of researchers' business and technical writing skills, and suggests the steps both writers and their managers can take to overcome and avoid these problems.

1401. Sauer, Beverly A. "The Engineer as Rational Man: The Problem of Imminent Danger in a Nonrational Environment." *IEEE* 35 (December 1992): 242–49.

Contends that technical communicators must understand how knowledge is constructed by underlying assumptions of male rationality.

1402. Sauer, Beverly A. *Sense and Sensibility in Technical Documentation: How Feminist Interpretation Strategies Can Save Lives in the Nation's Mines*. Cincinnati, OH: CCCC, March 1992. ERIC ED 347 534. 31 pages

Analyzes post-accident investigation reports from a feminist perspective, showing how a feminist interpretation can change how technical writers look at expertise and evidence.

1403. Schaible, Robert, and Gale Rhodes. "Metaphor in Science and Literature: Creating an Environment for Active Interdisciplinary Learning." *JCST* 22 (November 1992): 100–105.

Describes a course in which students actively seek and articulate relationships between science and literature. Describes class methodology and writing assignments.

1404. Schwager, Edith. *Medical English Usage and Abusage*. Phoenix, AZ: Oryx, 1991. 217 pages

Provides advice on usage and medical terminology for writers in scientific and technical disciplines.

1405. Schwartz, Helen. "Review of *Hypermedia and Literary Studies*; *Writing Space: The Computer, Hypertext, and the History of Technical Writing*; and *Writing Space: A Hypertext*." *TCQ* 1 (Summer 1992): 99–102.

Asserts that technical communication must examine the advantages of electronic writing and hypermedia quickly and more fully.

1406. Simpson, Henry. "A User-Friendly Electronic Mail System to Support Correspondence Instruction." *EdTech* 32 (December 1992): 20–25.

Examines electronic mail communication as a means of upgrading correspondence courses in hard sciences.

1407. Skelton, T. M. "Testing the Usability of Usability Testing." *TC* 39 (August 1992): 343–59.

Recommends in-house testing of new products because traditional methods such as beta testing do not leave time for major modifications. Suggests methods for effective implementation.

1408. Smith, Frank R. "The Continuing Importance of Research in Technical Communication." *TC* 39 (November 1992): 521–23.

Argues that research serves four purposes: it helps achieve professional status, prevents reinventing the wheel, develops a body of literature, and prevents working by intuition.

1409. Smith, Robert E. "The Classroom as Community: Composition Pedagogy and the Rise of the Technical Writing Model." *DAI* 52 (January 1992): 2538A.

Examines the hypothesis that teaching technical writing is not only a question of enculturation but also a matter of acclimatization to the culture of technology.

1410. Speck, Bruce W. "The Professional Writing Teacher as Author's Editor." *TCQ* 1 (Summer 1992): 37–57.

Argues that teachers can use the author's editor model to reduce the conflict between the role of "enabler" and "gatekeeper."

1411. Spyridakis, Jan H. "Conducting Research in Technical Communication: The Application of True Experimental Designs." *TC* 39 (November 1992): 607–24.

Explains that identifying the problem, reviewing literature, and formulating hypotheses is necessary in experimental design.

1412. Spyridakis, Jan. H., and Michael J. Wenger. "Writing for Human Performance: Relating Reading Research to Document Design." *TC* 39 (May 1992): 202–15.

Surveys major theories in reading research and their relevance to document design.

1413. Steinke, Jocelyn Dawn. "The Science Writing Process and Science Writers' Audience Awareness: An Exploration of Writers Working under Contextual Constraints." *DAI* 53 (July 1992): 10A.

Finds that professional science writers initiate many of the same tasks other writers do, but the ways they carry out these tasks and the frequency with which they employ them differ.

1414. Stibravy, John, and John Muller. "Using Technical Writing to Enhance Self-Esteem." *TC* 39 (August 1992): 376–83.

Argues that communication skills empower the user and provide her with control over her life.

1415. Strobos, S. "Philosophical Origins of the Concept 'Technical Writing.'" *JTWC* 22 (1992): 247–57.

Traces differences between technical and creative writing back through Richards, Snow, Coleridge, and Plato; argues that the final cause (*telos*), not Aristotle's material causes, accounts for differences.

1416. Sullivan, Patricia, and Rachel Spilka. "Qualitative Research in Technical Communication: Issues of Value, Identity, and Use." *TC* 39 (November 1992): 592–606.

Discusses the value of qualitative research and what it does best; describes common types such as case, field, and ethnographic studies.

1417. Tebeaux, Elizabeth, and M. Jimmie Killingsworth. "Expanding and Redirecting Historical Research in Technical Writing: In Search of Our Past." *TCQ* 1 (Spring 1992): 5–32.

Calls for a history of technical writing, identifies potential problems, suggests research questions and premises, and examines English Renaissance technical writing.

1418. Thompson, Isabelle. "An Educational Philosophy of Technical Writing." *TCQ* 1 (Spring 1992): 33–46.

Applies John Dewey's transactional epistemology and Louise Rosenblatt's transactional view of reading and writing to teaching technical writing.

1419. Thralls, Charlotte. "Rites and Ceremonials: Corporate Video and the Construction of Social Realities in Modern Organizations." *JBTC* 6 (October 1992): 381–402.

Examines corporate video as cultural rites facilitating organizational socialization.

1420. Townsend, Jacqueline. "Tips for High-Tech Public Relations Writers." *TC* 39 (August 1992): 399–400.

Presents practical advice on generating comprehensible public relations materials on high tech topics.

1421. Valentino, Marilyn J. "Writing in the Workplace: A Descriptive Study of How Writers Perceive the Effects of Information and Structure." *DAI* 53 (December 1992): 1895A.

Compares expected and actual information types and structures in company reports; identifies influences on inclusion and exclusion of information.

1422. Walters, Mary James, and Charles E. Beck. "A Discourse Analysis of Software Documentation: Implications for the Profession." *IEEE* 35 (September 1992): 156–67.

Compares primary and secondary computer manuals. Finds that in trade books writers provide a richer context of theory and example.

1423. Wandersee, James H., and Catherine L. Cummins. "Using an Interdisciplinary Poster-Newsletter to Improve Communications between University Scientists and Science Educators." *JCST* 22 (November 1992): 115–18.

Describes the development of this project as a means of improving interdisciplinary communication among faculty, staff, and students at LSU and the faculty of the local public school.

1424. Weiss, Timothy. " 'Ourselves among Others': A New Metaphor for Business and Technical Writing." *TCQ* 1 (Summer 1992): 23–36.

Argues for replacing the metaphors of "selling" and "reader-centeredness" with one of "bridge building" to highlight growing interculturalism and internationalism in a global marketplace.

1425. Wieringa, Douglas, Christopher Moore, and Valerie Barnes. *Procedure Writing: Principles and Practices*. Columbus, OH: Battelle Press, 1992. 211 pages

Presents a process approach to procedure writing that covers the basics, format and organization, and complex steps in writing such documents. The book is based on a modified version of a manual prepared for the United States Department of Energy.

1426. Wilkins, Harriet Adamson. "Becoming a Writer at Work: The Transition Experiences of Novice Engineers." *DAI* 52 (March 1992): 3208A.

Examines the development of professional writing abilities in junior engineers.

1427. Wilkinson, A. M. "Jargon and the Passive Voice: Prescriptions and Proscriptions for Scientific Writing." *JTWC* 22 (1992): 319–25.

Argues that prescriptions and proscriptions about jargon and passive voice in scientific writing are based on the erroneous notion that scientists write for a general reader.

1428. Williams, Thomas R., and Earl C. Butterfield. "Advance Organizers: A Review of the Research—Part I." *JTWC* 22 (1992): 259–72.

The authors review research that shows advance organizers inspire significant increases in comprehension of expository text but questionable efficacy in facilitating the acquisition of subordinate text detail.

1429. Williams, Thomas R., and Earl C. Butterfield. "Effects of Advance Organizers and Reader's Purpose on the Level of Ideas Acquired from Expository Text—Part II." *JTWC* 22 (1992): 281–99.

The authors report on the results of two studies of the influence of background knowledge, advance organizers, and the importance and placement of ideas on the recall of factual information.

1430. Williams, Thomas R., and Jan H. Spyridakis. "Visual Discriminability of Headings in Text." *IEEE* 35 (June 1992): 64–70.

Studies readers' ability to relate the format of headings to importance of text. Finds that discrimination is easier when headings vary on few dimensions.

1431. Winsor, Dorothy A. "A Response to Paul M. Dombrowski [*JBTC* 6 (January 1992)]." *JBTC* 6 (January 1992): 128–29.

Regarding her analysis of ambiguity in the *Challenger* disaster, the author maintains that ambiguity is less a characteristic of evidence than an interpretation/perception of evidence.

1432. Winsor, Dorothy A. "What Counts as Writing? An Argument from Engineers' Practice." *JAC* 12 (Fall 1992): 337–48.

Argues that writing occurs in many, as of yet unacknowledged, areas.

1433. Woolbright, Meg. *Scientific Writing: Tales from the Dark Side?* Cincinnati, OH: CCCC, March 1992. ERIC ED 344 223. 7 pages

Describes a scientific writing course team-taught by a composition teacher and a biologist. Studies pedagogical and rhetorical differences between the two disciplines.

See also 375, 376, 443

4.2.6 WRITING IN LITERATURE COURSES

1434. Anaya, Rudolpho. "The Censorship of Neglect." *EJ* 81 (September 1992): 18–20.

Argues that educators "must infuse into the study of language and literature the stories of the many communities that compose our country."

1435. Arnett, David B. "(Teaching to Learn): Or How I Turned a Disastrous Midterm into a Paper on Macbeth." *UEJ* 20 (1992): 26–29.

Uses William Perry's scheme of cognitive and moral growth to teach students how to analyze literary characters.

1436. Bates, Robin. *The Anthologized Literature Classroom: A Community of Interpreters.* Cincinnati, OH: CCCC, March 1992. ERIC ED 346 507. 8 pages

Presents a literature course where student essays on literature are selected and collected in an anthology.

1437. Benedict, Susan, and Lenore Carlisle, eds. *Beyond Words: Picture Books for Older Readers and Writers.* Portsmouth, NH: Heinemann, 1992. 144 pages

Fourteen essays explore possible uses for picture books in literature and writing courses.
Essayists: Brazee, P. E.; Carlisle, L. R.; Councell, R. T.; Crockett, T.; Heard, G.; Hickman, J.; Jenks, C. K.; LeTord, B.; Ludlam, D.; Newkirk, T.; Rief, L.; Rynerson, B. B.; Sims-Bishop, R.; Weidhass, S.

1438. Bowman, Michael S., and Cindy J. Kistenberg. "*Textual Power* and the Subject of Oral Interpretation: An Alternate Approach to Performing Literature." *CEd* 41 (July 1992): 287–99.

Describes how to use Scholes' semiotics model—reading, interpretation, and criticism—in the classroom.

1439. Britton, James. *Literature in Its Place.* Portsmouth, NH: Boynton/Cook, 1992. 136 pages

Explores the role literature can play in nurturing the human imagination.

1440. Brown, Carl R. V. "Contemporary Poetry about Painting." *EJ* 81 (January 1992): 41–45.

Recommends the inclusion of ekphrastic poetry, namely "poetry written in response to, or interpreting, paintings or other works of art," in contemporary literature classes.

1441. Cooper, Charles R. *Comparison-Group Studies: One Way of Learning about Writing-to-Learn.* Cincinnati, OH: CCCC, March 1992. ERIC ED 346 450. 6 pages

Reports on a study that uses comparison-group methods to examine the effectiveness of dialogic journal writing in a Chinese literature course.

1442. Danis, M. Francine. *Sitting Swimmers and Stuffed Armadillos in Sundresses: Reader-Response and Classroom Creativity.* San Antonio, TX: College English Association, April 18–20, 1991. ERIC ED 340 034. 13 pages

Uses convergence of reader response and writing across the curriculum to help writers understand other voices and to fashion their own voices for an audience.

1443. Degan, James N. *"Utopia, Limited": Narratives from a Writer's Workshop.* Cincinnati, OH: CCCC, March 1992. ERIC ED 344 238. 10 pages

Discusses an honors program course in literature and composition focused on utopian and dystopian texts.

1444. Duke, Charles R., and Sally A. Jacobsen, eds. *Poets' Perspectives: Reading, Writing, and Teaching Poetry.* Portsmouth, NH: Boynton/Cook, 1992. 256 pages

Includes essays in which poets discuss their methods of writing poetry, suggesting ways of encouraging students to engage with poetry.
Essayists: Barth, R.; Bell, Marvin; Billings, Philip; Bizzaro, Patrick; Cohen, Michael; Duke, Charles R.; Eimers, Nancy;

Gallager, Tess; Heynen, Jim; Jacobsen, Sally A.; Kennedy, X. J.; Liner, Tom; Marcus, Stephen; McElroy, Colleen J.; Miller, Danny L.; Mullican, James S.; Nelson, Marie Wilson; Olsen, William; Piercy, Marge; Raynor, Deirdre; Stensland, Anna Lee; Wakoski, Diane; Wendt, Ingrid; Wolfe, Denny, Jr.

1445. Gardner, Peter. "Makers and Users of Knowledge: Literary Recreation in the Classroom." *JTW* 11 (Spring/Summer 1992): 19–33.

Argues that film adaptations of literary works support students' learning of "structural, creative, and aesthetic qualities of two narrative media." Considers them a motivating addition to critical analysis.

1446. George, Diana. "When Politics Become Apolitical, It's Time to Think Again: Considering a Course on Literature from the Vietnam War." *JTW* 11 (Spring/Summer 1992): 129–36.

Reviews Barry Kroll's *Teaching Hearts and Minds* (1992); praises the described course for teaching critical inquiry but critiques Kroll's inattention to protesters against the Vietnam war.

1447. Harste, Jerome C. *Literature Guilds*. [Videotape]. Portsmouth, NH: Heinemann, 1992.

Part of the series on whole language classrooms, this tape shows the uses of talk in a classroom by recording students' initial discussions of a piece of literature.

1448. Harwayne, Shelley. *Lasting Impressions: Weaving Literature into the Writing Workshop*. Portsmouth, NH: Heinemann, 1992. 368 pages

Explains how writing workshop methods can "make life-long readers and writers."

1449. Klein, Diane. "Coming of Age in Novels by Rudolpho Anaya and Sandra Ciscernos." *EJ* 81 (September 1992): 21–26.

Emphasizes Chicano/a people's need "to find identities that are true to themselves as individuals and artists" and "that do not betray their culture and their people."

1450. Kroll, Barry M. *Teaching Hearts and Minds: College Students Reflect on the Vietnam War*. Carbondale, IL: Southern Illinois University Press, 1992. 215 pages

Describes students' processes of reflection in four domains of inquiry—"connected" or emotional/personal, literary, critical, and ethical—as demonstrated in a course on Vietnam War literature developed and taught by the author. Argues for a largely subjective/interpretive exploration of students' responses to the material and the course.

1451. Messina, Susan, and Diane White. *Classroom Research: Writing Assessment in Paired and Separate History and English Courses*. San Francisco, CA: College Reading and Learning Association Conference, April 1992. ERIC ED 343 636. 43 pages

The results, which are based on essay exams and final grades, indicate improved student learning in both writing and history in an integrated class.

1452. Schneiderman, Beth Kline. "Designing a New Writing Assignment for a Literature Course." *TETYC* 19 (October 1992): 210–14.

Presents a course in which students assemble their own short story anthology, writing introductions, headnotes, and bibliographies.

1453. Taylor, Louise Todd. "Students Write Back: Letters in American Literature." *TETYC* 19 (October 1992): 201–5.

Looks at a course in which students in an American literature class write letters about the readings; uses five letters to replace one essay assignment.

1454. Xu, George Q. "Cumulative Reading Notes." *ExEx* 38 (Fall 1992): 8–9.

Describes a collaborative exercise in which students, in groups of four, build on each other's written responses to a literary work.

4.2.7 COMMUNICATION IN OTHER DISCIPLINES

1455. Bekken, John Everett. "Working-Class Newspapers, Community and Consciousness in Chicago, 1880–1930." *DAI* 53 (July 1992): 6A.

Focuses on Chicago working-class and labor newspapers published between 1880 and 1930. Argues that the working-class press encouraged workers to participate in shaping and producing their own media.

1456. Blyer, Nancy R., and Charlotte Thralls, eds. *Professional Communication: The Social Perspective*. Newbury Park, CA: Sage, 1992. 292 pages

Sixteen essays explore developments in professional communciation research and examine the problems inherent in viewing traditional rhetorical concepts in a social context.
Essayists: Barton, B.; Blyer, N. R.; Berkenkotter, C.; Burnett, R. E.; Comprone, J.; Freed, R. C.; Herzberg, B.; Huckin, T. N.; Kent, T.; Kostelnick, C.; Lauer, J. M.; Lay, M. M.; Morgan, M.; Porter, J. E.; Rymer, J.; Thralls, C.

1457. Bradford, Linda Burrell Henderson. "Writing across the Curriculum: A Study of Faculty Practices at a Southern University." *DAI* 52 (January 1992): 2385A.

Concludes that the emphasis in WAC courses appeared to be on the quantity of writing, and that few faculty members used process writing.

1458. Brent, Rebecca, and Richard M. Felder. "Writing Assignments—Pathways to Connections, Clarity, Creativity." *CollT* 40 (Spring 1992): 43–47.

Recommends a variety of writing tasks for any subject, based on asssumptions and categories of cognitive theorists.

1459. Carson, Jay. *Recognizing and Using Context as a Survival Tool for WAC*. Cincinnati, OH: CCCC, March 1992. ERIC ED 346 497. 16 pages

Posits that the only way WAC programs can survive is to attach themselves to their own contexts.

1460. Fassinger, Polly A., Nancy Gilliland, and Linda L. Johnson. "Benefits of a Faculty Writing Circle—Better Teaching." *CollT* 40 (Spring 1992): 53–56.

Sociology faculty discuss benefits of their writing group and applications in their classes, emphasizing feminist goals and practices.

1461. Favre, Betty Atkinson. *From Plato to Wall Street: A Rhetoric Program for MBAs*. Ypsilanti, MI: Annual Conference on Languages and Communication for World Business and the Professions, April 1991. ERIC ED 335 684. 20 pages

Points out that the program objectives are to enhance students' abilities to think, write, make ideas visual, and to speak effectively.

1462. Fellows, Nancy Jane. "A Window into Thinking: Using Student Writing to Understand Knowledge Restructuring and Conceptual Change." *DAI* 52 (May 1992): 3861A.

Finds that student writing serves as a "window" for observing knowledge restructuring of science concepts during the course of a learning unit.

1463. Fink, Conrad C. *Introduction to Professional Newswriting: Reporting for the Modern Media*. White Plains, NY: Longman, 1992. 476 pages

Defines news and explains its uses; discusses style and organization as well as ethics and legal matters; gives examples of good and bad news articles; suggests ways in which beginning writers can gain experience in newswriting on their campuses; discusses writing for broadcasts and for public relations; and includes exercises to measure comprehension.

1464. Greenia, George D. "Computers and Teaching Composition in a Foreign Language." *FLA* 25 (February 1992): 33–46.

Presents a model for using a word-processing program in upper level foreign language composition classes with suggestions for use at all levels.

1465. Hoff, Katharine T. *WAC Politics: Winning Friends and Influencing People*. Cincinnati, OH: CCCC, March 1992. ERIC ED 344 234. 11 pages

Describes how Rider College institutionalized a WAC program.

1466. Huot, Brian. "Finding Out What They Are Writing: A Method, Rationale, and Sample for WAC Research." *WPA* 15 (Spring 1992): 31–40.

Proposes a systematic means for talking to faculty and administrators across campus about what their students are writing.

1467. Johannessen, Larry R., and Elizabeth A. Kahn. *Writing across the Curriculum*. Summit, IL: Teachers' Institute, January 1991. ERIC ED 336 726. 25 pages

Describes successful methods and activities for teaching students complex thinking skills involved in making and supporting generalizations, producing arguments in composition, and creating extended definitions.

1468. Jones, Joan, and Ronald Jackson. "English Language Skills and Their Effect on U.S. History Course Success at Oxnard College (Oxnard Research Report 91–03)." Oxnard College, Claremont, CA, 1991. ERIC ED 337 235. 14 pages

Studies the relationship between English language/writing skills and academic performance in a college level U. S. History course.

1469. Kinney, Marjory Ann. "Writing in the Disciplines: The Use of Writing in the Undergraduate Sociology Curriculum at Bowling Green State University." *DAI* 52 (May 1992): 3901A.

An empirical study of the Sociology Department suggests that it lacks an informed and coherent undergraduate writing pedagogy.

1470. Kipling, Kim J., and Richard Murphy, Jr. *Symbiosis: Writing and an Academic Culture*. Portsmouth, NH: Boynton/Cook, 1992. 140 pages

Details the success of one university's implementation of a writing across the curriculum program.

1471. Lofty, John Sylvester. *Time to Write: The Influence of Time and Culture on Learning to Write*. SUNY Series, Literacy, Culture, and Learning: Theory and Practice. Albany, NY: State University of New York Press, 1992. 276 pages

Studies students whose resistance to writing was grounded in the tension between community/cultural representations of time and school/clock representations of time. Shows how practices of literacy in school can differ from those of the community, and thus how school can put some children at a loss.

1472. McLeod, Susan H., and Margot Soven, eds. *Writing across the Curriculum: A Guide to Developing Programs*. Newbury Park: Sage, 1992. 304 pages

Chapters include how to run WAC workshops, what role administrators can play, and how WAC can be integrated into the university curriculum.
Essayists: Farris, Christine; Graham, Joan; Haring-Smith, Tori; Harris, Muriel; Kuriloff, Peshe C.; Magnotto, Joyce Neff; McLeod, Susan H.; Peterson, Linda H.; Sandler, Karen Wiley; Smith, Raymond; Soven, Margot; Stout, Barbara R.; Thaiss, Christopher; Walvoord, Barbara E.

1473. Miller, L. Diane. "Begin Mathematics Class with Writing." *MT* 85 (May 1992): 354–55.

Suggests using writing as a way to make the first few minutes of class a productive transitional time.

1474. Murdick, William. "Writing to Learn in College Art Classes." *DAI* 52 (May 1992): 3847A.

　　Examines the effectiveness of writing-to-learn activities in college art history and art studio courses.

1475. Savage, Gerald. *Beyond Evangelism: Ideology and Social Responsibility in WAC.* Cincinnati, OH: CCCC, March 1992. ERIC ED 346 478. 10 pages

　　Argues that writing instructors should fulfill the ideological task of promoting an understanding of the ways knowledge is formulated through social discourse.

1476. Schlumberger, Ann Lewis. "The Effects of Elaboration on Community College Students' Execution of a Reading-Writing Task." *DAI* 52 (May 1992): 3875A.

　　Finds that training in elaboration helps students to articulate unifying concepts and organizational plans in their essays and heightens their interest to write from sources.

1477. Sheese, Judy. " 'When Ain't Isn't, and What Is?' The Grammar Gestapo Is after You." *IndE* 16 (Winter1992): 22–25.

　　Supports teaching standard English but accepts different dialects in appropriate settings.

1478. Shibli, Abdullah. "Increasing Learning with Writing in Quantitative and Computer Courses." *CollT* 40 (Fall 1992): 123–27.

　　Discusses applications and provides examples of writing assignments in statistics and programming courses.

1479. Sommers, Jonita. "Statistics in the Classroom: Written Projects Portraying Real-World Situations." *MT* 85 (April 1992): 310–12.

　　Describes projects designed to relate math to real life situations and to integrate writing with math study.

1480. Stewart, Margaret E., and Ronald A. Palcie. *Writing to Learn Mathematics: The Writer-Audience Relationship.* Cincinnati, OH: CCCC, March 1992. ERIC ED 347 549. 12 pages

　　Reports on a survey study that examined the role of audience in the writing experiences of preservice mathematics education students.

1481. Weiser, Michael S. *Building on Common Ground: Overcoming Resistance to WAC in the Technical College.* Cincinnati, OH: CCCC, March 1992. ERIC ED 346 493. 11 pages

　　Explains principles that WAC administrators should follow when working with technical college faculty.

1482. Whittis, Judith. "A Regional Survey of Writing in Six Subject Areas in Colleges and Universities Accredited by the North Central Association of Colleges and Schools." *DAI* 52 (May 1992): 3819A.

　　Investigates the nature and frequency of writing tasks in six subject areas in accredited colleges and universities.

4.3　ADULT AND GRADUATE EDUCATION

1483. *Adult Education. The Quality of Life.* ASPBAE. Courier Number 52: South Pacific Bureau of Adult Education, October 1991. ERIC ED 338 900. 65 pages

　　Six articles examine the quality of life as it can be improved by adult—especially women's—education, in Asia, Africa, and South Pacific.
　　Essayists: Mayor, Federico; Walters, Shirley; Farooq, Nishat; Sedere, Mohottige U.; Mingchuan, Dong; David, Vincent A.

1484. Aronson, Anne Louise. "Literacy and Identity: The Writing Histories of Undergraduate Reentry Women." *DAI* 52 (February 1992): 2903A.

　　Examines how gender, race, class and other identities shape women's histories as writers.

1485. Benton, Lauren, and Thierry Noyelle. "Adult Literacy and Economic Performance." Organisation for Economic Cooperation and Development, Centre for Educational Research and Innovation, Paris, France, 1992. ERIC ED 340 922. 87 pages

Surveys industrialized nations of the Organisation for Economic Cooperation and Development; finds that high levels of functional illiteracy affect economic performance.

1486. Cherem, Barbara F. Brown. "A Connected Classroom in an Adult B. A. Degree-Completion Program: Perceived Effects on Three Women's Development." *DAI* 53 (October 1992): 1022A.

Presents a case study of three female students in a "connected classroom" which shows how this environment enhances women's learning.

1487. Dugan, Penelope. *Blurring Genres, Crossing Boundaries, and Calling the Question: The Dissertation at SUNY-Albany*. Boston, MA: CCCC, March 1991. ERIC ED 336 675. 8 pages

Presents the experiences of a graduate student writing a dissertation at the University of New York (SUNY) Albany.

1488. Fayne, Francis Augustine, Jr. "An Ethnographic Approach to the Development of New Curriculum Guides and Materials for Adult Illiterates: Kingston, Jamaica—A Case Study." *DAI* 52 (January 1992): 2388A.

Argues for the development of new teaching materials and methods of instruction that recognize curriculum and student-identified goals and needs.

1489. Imel, Susan. "Adult Literacy: Trends and Issues Alerts." ERIC Clearinghouse on Adult, Career, and Vocational Education, Columbus, OH, 1991. ERIC ED 340 944. 3 pages

Describes trends and issues in adult literacy education, and provides a brief, annotated list of resources.

1490. Loberger, Gordon J. *The Composition Instructor and the Inmate-Student: Utilizing Prisoner's Attitude*. Cincinnati, OH: CCCC, March 1992. ERIC ED 346 488. 10 pages

Claims the prisoner's attitude and point of view can be exploited to great advantage in the teaching of composition.

1491. McGivney, Veronica, and Frances Murray. "Adult Education in Development, Methods and Approaches from Changing Societies." National Institute of Adult Continuing Education, Leicester, England, 1991. ERIC ED 338 906. 105 pages

Case studies provide examples of initiatives illustrating the role of adult education in developing countries. Subjects include health education, literacy, rural development, and the role of women.

1492. Monroe, Margaret E., and Kathleen M. Heim. *Partners for Lifelong Learning: Public Libraries and Adult Education*. Washington, DC: U.S. Government Printing Office, 1991. ERIC ED 341 393. 63 pages

Presents two commissioned papers on the role of libraries in adult literacy education. Includes a brief bibliography.

1493. Mowery, Carl D., Jr. *Teaching Composition in Prisons: Methods and Materials*. Cincinnati, OH: CCCC, March 1992. ERIC ED 346 460. 13 pages

Reports on a pilot survey of materials and methods used in teaching composition in prisons in Tennessee, Kentucky, Illinois, and Missouri.

1494. Phillips, Connie Ruth. "The Function of Discourse Events in a Graduate Seminar: Reading, Writing, and Talk as Symbolic Action." *DAI* 53 (December 1992): 1893A.

Points out that an analysis of doctoral students' writing as symbolic action revealed that case study writers deliberately violated conventions to demonstrate tensions between the writer's multiple identities.

1495. Popp, Robert. "A Guide to Funding Sources for Family Literacy." National Center for Family Literacy, Louisville, KY, 1991. ERIC ED 340 875. 46 pages

> Provides help in locating and securing funds for family literacy programs, offering examples of successful program implementation.

1496. Prete, Barbara, and Gary E. Strong, eds. *Literate America Emerging: Seventeen New Readers Speak Out*. Portsmouth, NH: Heinemann, 1992. 144 pages

> Seventeen new readers, identified by their first names, describe the problem that illiteracy caused them, their efforts to become literate, and the joys that they experienced when they did learn to read and write.

1497. Reed-Jones, Susan. *Faith in the Reality of Belonging: The Story of Alonso A.* Cincinnati, OH: CCCC, March 1992. ERIC ED 346 481. 15 pages

> Reports on a case study that illustrates the danger of a monocultural approach to education and the impact of marginalization and alienation on persons of color.

1498. Reif, Margaret Rossini. "In Their Own Voices: Adult Learners on Writing. A Study of Nontraditional Graduate Students' Stories about Writing." *DAI* 52 (March 1992): 3156A.

> Catalogues target groups' stories about writing; describes their struggles, strategies, and success.

1499. Showler, Janice Reckeweg. "On and under the Desk: Sanctioned and Unsanctioned Adolescent Writing in a Catholic School Community." *DAI* 53 (December 1992): 1829A.

> Investigates the writing behaviors of Catholic college preparatory school boys in their construction of their world in the word and with the word.

1500. Stoffel, Judith. *So, You're a Woman, 38, Back in School, and Writing "Research Papers"?* Cincinnati, OH: CCCC, March 1992. ERIC ED 345 267. 15 pages

> Studies 25 adult women returning to college, drawing conclusions about adult education.

1501. Wittman, Eugene. "Situational Factors Influencing Writing Apprehension in the Community College Composition Classroom." *DAI* 52 (June 1992): 4250A.

> Focuses on the causes of writing apprehension for adults in the community college system.

4.4 ENGLISH AS A SECOND LANGUAGE

1502. Adipattaranum, Nitida. "An Examination of the Variables of the Writing Process of ESL/EFL Students in a Process-Oriented Freshman Composition Course." *DAI* 53 (December 1992): 1826A.

> The study suggests that how ESL/EFL students write and revise depends on how students are taught, the quality of peer partners, their commitment to success, and their language difficulties.

1503. Alderson, J. Charles, and Alan Beretta, eds. *Evaluating Second-Language Education*. The Cambridge Applied Linguistics Series, edited by Michael H. Long and Jack C. Richards. New York: Cambridge University Press, 1992. 374 pages

> The contributors discuss the evaluation of programs, bilingual primary education, and classroom interaction. They also provide guidelines for the evaluation of language education.
> *Essayists:* Alderson, J. Charles; Beretta, Alan; Coleman, Hywel; Lynch, Brian; Mitchell, Rosamond; Palmer, Adrian; Ross, Steven; Scott, Mike; Slimani, Assia.

1504. An, Jung-Hee. *Effects of the Text Structure-Based Reading Strategy on the Comprehension of EFL Classroom Text*. European University Studies: Anglo-Saxon Language and Literature, vol. 253. New York: Peter Lang, 1992. 228 pages

Presents the results of an empirical investigation of the effectiveness of schemata-based reading instruction, using a pretest-posttest design, for EFL students in a Korean high school. Argues that teaching text structures improved the comprehension of expository texts.

1505. Arndt, Valerie. *First and Foreign Language Composing: A Protocol-Based Study*. Reading, England: The British Association for Applied Linguistics, September 1992. ERIC ED 346 744. 17 pages

Reports on a comparative study of the first (Chinese) and foreign (English) language writing processes of six postgraduate EFL students.

1506. Ashworth, Mary. *The First Step on the Longer Path: Becoming an ESL Teacher*. Pippin Teacher's Library. Portsmouth, NH: Heinemann, 1992. 128 pages

Introduces issues and problems particular to ESL instruction.

1507. Bardovi-Harlig, Kathleen. "A Second Look at T-Unit Analysis: Reconsidering the Sentence." *TESOLQ* 26 (Summer 1992): 390–95.

Analyzes 86 compositions written by ESL adult learners at seven proficiency levels; indicates that sentence analysis is superior to T-unit analysis.

1508. Britton, James, Robert E. Shafer, and Ken Watson, eds. *Teaching and Learning English Worldwide*. Bristol, PA: Taylor and Francis Group, 1990. 358 pages

The book contains historical studies of the teaching of English in 13 different countries where English is a first language or a significant second language. Describes how the teaching of English exists in the social and political context of that society. *Essayists:* Aitken, Russell; Alisjahbana, S. Takdir; Britton, James; Burgess, Tony; Catherwood, Vince; Das, S.K.; Davis, Diana; Drayton, Kathleen; Gambell, Trevor; Gonzalez, Andrew B.; Hong, Chua Seok; Janks, Hilary; Johnson, Nan; Killeen, John; Martin, Nancy; Mullins, Tom; Northcroft, David; Paton, Jonathan; Rathgen, Elody; Robinson, Sam; Shadiow, Linda K.; Shafer, Robert E.; Sibayan, Bonificio P.; Simmons, John S.; Walker, Laurence; Watson, Ken.

1509. Brogger, Fredrik Chr. *Culture, Language, Text: Culture Studies within the Study of English as a Foreign Language*. New York: Oxford University Press, 1992. 168 pages

Focuses on the anthropological concept of culture as belief systems; argues that culture studies should be primarily concerned with the analysis of the interplay between language and ideology.

1510. California State Department of Education. "Nonliterate Adult ESL Students: An Introduction for Teachers." California State Department of Education, and the Adult Alternative and Continuation Division, Sacramento, CA, 1981. ERIC ED 337 058. 34 pages

Provides a teaching guide for teachers of adult students from Vietnam, Cambodia, Laos, China, and Spanish speaking countries.

1511. Carson, Joan G. "Becoming Biliterate: First Language Influences." *JSLW* 1 (January 1992): 37–60.

Discusses reasons for literacy levels; looks at ways of teaching and learning reading and writing in Japan and China. Presents implications for ESL classrooms.

1512. Celce-Murcia, Marianne. "Teaching Issues: Formal Grammar Instruction—An Educator Comments." *TESOLQ* 26 (Summer 1992): 406–9.

Argues for teaching contextualized formal grammar to adult L2 learners; points out that without it such learners will not develop full communicative competence.

1513. Chen, Chien-ping. "Language Proficiency and Academic Achievement: An Ethnographic Investigation of Language Demands and Problems Confronted by Chinese

Graduate Students Functioning in University Classrooms." *DAI* 53 (November 1992): 1413A.

Discusses sociolinguistic factors that influenced or interfered with Chinese science or humanities graduate students' learning. Finds that proficiency in language is less demanding for science students.

1514. Chevillet, François. "Received Pronunciation and Standard English as Systems of Reference." *EnT* 8 (January 1992): 27–32.

Argues for the retention of RP and the standard language as models for foreign learners.

1515. Collignon, Francine Filipek. "ESL/Literacy for Adult Nonnative Speakers of English. A Handbook for Practitioners." International Institute of Rhode Island, Providence, RI, 1991. ERIC ED 339 252. 171 pages

Describes a learner-centered program for improving access to literacy for ESL students in Rhode Island. Provides a review of literature and descriptions of specific practices.

1516. Connor, Ulla. "A Reader Reacts [response to Raimes, *TESOLQ* 24 (Autumn 1990)]." *TESOLQ* 26 (Spring 1992): 177–79.

Refutes Raimes' claim that ETS does not conduct enough research on TWE and does not permit its data to be used by researchers.

1517. Cumming, Alister, and Jaswinder Gill. *Learning Literacy and Language among Indo-Canadian Women*. Chicago, IL: American Educational Research Association, April 1991. ERIC ED 337 050. 31 pages

Presents findings of a Canadian study of a part-time literacy instruction program for Punjabi-speaking female immigrants.

1518. Diaz-Rico, Lynne T. "Error Correction Simulation for Instructors of English as a Second Language." *JEdM&H* 1 (Fall 1992): 471–79.

Underscores the importance for the user to review the results of performance to advance self-management ability and metacognitive awareness.

1519. El-Shiyab, Said. "The Structure of Argumentation in Arabic: Editorials as a Case Study." *DAI* 52 (March 1992): 3261A.

Examines argumentative structures found in editorials, noting linguistic and semantic characteristics and problems for English readers.

1520. Engber, Cheryl Ann. "A Study of Lexis and the Relationship to Quality in Written Texts of Second Language Learners of English." *DAI* 53 (December 1992): 1888A.

Analyzes skills with which second language writers use lexical resources to produce meaningful discourse.

1521. Farghal, Mohammed. "Naturalness and the Notion of Cohesion in EFL Writing Classes." *International Review of Applied Linguistics in Language Teaching*. 30 (February 1992): 45–50.

Maintains that cohesion needs to be taught as a tool for achieving coherence in a text. Argues that exercises in cohesion separated from meaningful contexts produce poor results.

1522. Flowerdew, John. "Salience in the Performance of One Speech Act: The Case of Definitions." *DPr* 15 (April–June 1992): 165–81.

Considers ways in which university lecturers use stress, paralanguage, and other cues to highlight key parts of definitions. The audience for this study consisted of nonnative speakers of English.

1523. Fortune, Alan. "Self-Study Grammar Practice: Learners' Views and Preferences." *ELTJ* 46 (April 1992): 160–71.

Points out that action research shows that students' preference for inductive exercises increases with language level. Argues that exercises with linguistic context were more popular than uncontextualized sentences.

1524. Freeman, Yvonne S., and David E. Freeman. *Whole Language for Second Language Learners*. Portsmouth, NH: Heinemann, 1992. 272 pages

> The authors advise teachers on ways to employ the whole language approach to teaching ESL students, contrasting traditional assumptions about ESL education with whole language alternatives.

1525. Freudenstein, Reinhold. "Communication Peace." *EnT* 8 (July 1992): 3–8.

> Proposes peace education as the regimental in the teaching of English as a foreign language in the twenty-first century.

1526. Gosden, Hugh. "Research Writing and NNSs: From the Editors." *JSLW* 1 (1992): 123–39.

> Surveys professional research journal editors regarding NNSs' writing; implies that the teaching of research writing to NNSs needs to be changed.

1527. Halimah, Ahmad Mustafa. "EST Writing: Rhetorically Processed and Produced. A Case Study of Kuwaiti Learners." *DAI* 53 (August 1992): 481A.

> Investigates expository writing skills in an attempt to identify the major problems faced by the learners.

1528. Heath, Shirley Brice, and Linda Mangiola. "Children of Promise: Literate Activity in Linguistically and Culturally Diverse Classrooms (NEA School Restructuring Series)." American Educational Research Association, Washington, DC, 1991. ERIC ED 335 944. 66 pages

> Offers suggestions for ESL instruction; provides a model for university/school collaboration.

1529. Hill, Elizabeth F. "A Comparative Study of the Cultural, Narrative and Language Content of Selected Folktales Told in Burma, Canada and Yorubaland." *DAI* 52 (May 1992): 4042A.

> Presents a method of reading folktales which helps assess their potential for use in ESL classrooms.

1530. Hinkel, Eli. "L2 Tense and Time Reference." *TESOLQ* 26 (Autumn 1992): 557–72.

> Surveys 130 ESL learners on English tenses and time concepts; indicates that NNS concepts of time differ from those of NS, affecting NNS English tense usage.

1531. Hwang, Hae Jin. "The Development of English Writing Proficiency among Korean Students from Ninth-Grade to College Juniors." *DAI* 52 (May 1992): 3814A.

> Finds a clear development pattern of writing ability among grades in terms of general writing proficiency and patterns of syntactic and semantic errors.

1532. Jewell, Cora Mae. "Gender Roles and Second Language Acquisition in Hmong Acculturation." *DAI* 53 (October 1992): 1083A.

> Using ethnographic methodology, Jewell explores the relationship between gender roles and second language acquisition of the Hmong refugees in the United States.

1533. Johnson, Donna M. *Approaches to Research in Second Language Learning*. White Plains, NY: Longman, 1992. 261 pages

> Discusses six approaches to conducting research in the learning of second languages: correlational, case study, survey, ethnographic, experimental, and multimethod (multisite, large-scale).

1534. Johnson, Karen E. "Cognitive Strategies and Second Language Writers: A Reevaluation of Sentence Combining." *JSLW* 1 (January 1992): 61–75.

> Using data from think-aloud protocols of nine advanced ESL learners, Johnson's study supports the value of sentence-combining in ESL composition classes.

1535. Kleifgen, Jo Anne, and Muriel Saville-Roike. "Achieving Coherence in Multilingual Interaction." *DPr* 15 (April–June 1992): 183–206.

Examines interactions between nonnative and native-speaker school children and teachers. Argues that top-down strategies predominate in speakers' efforts to achieve comprehension.

1536. Kobayashi, Junko. "Helping Japanese Students Write Good Paragraphs." *The Language Teacher* 16 (June 1992): 21–22.

Suggests techniques for helping Japanese students solve five problems they have in writing English paragraphs.

1537. Kobayashi, Toshihika. "Native and Nonnative Reactions to ESL Compositions." *TESOLQ* 26 (Spring 1992): 81–112.

Compares responses of 269 evaluators (Japanese or English native speakers with various academic statuses) to Japanese ESL learners' compositions. Advocates process-oriented pedagogy for Japanese ESL teachers.

1538. Kokkino, Eleni Katsarou. "Home Culture and School Ethos: Four Students' Second Language Literacy and Academic Achievement." *DAI* 53 (October 1992): 1009A.

Discusses the aspects of the sociocultural environment that contributed towards the literacy development and academic achievement of four second language students.

1539. Krashen, Stephen D. "Teaching Issues: Formal Grammar Instruction—Another Educator Comments." *TESOLQ* 26 (Summer 1992): 409–11.

Argues against teaching formal grammar to L2 learners and maintains that "the best way of increasing grammatical accuracy is comprehensible input" through reading.

1540. Kulick, Katherine. "Principles of Adult Learning: Implications for Second Language Instruction of Returning Students." *DAI* 52 (June 1992): 4320A.

Presents classroom strategies for second language instruction for returning adult students.

1541. Lam, Clara Yin Ping. "Revision Process of College ESL Students: How Teacher Comments, Discourse Types, and Writing Tools Shape Revision." *DAI* 52 (June 1992): 4248A.

Argues that most students did not revise differently in response to a change in discourse type. Points out that computers enabled writers to make more changes during writing the first drafts.

1542. Lay, Nancy Duke S. "Learning from Natural Language Labs." *JBW* 11 (Fall 1992): 74–81.

Examines distinctions between "natural language labs" and "artificial language labs." Discusses greater benefits of former for ESL students.

1543. Leeds, Bruce. "Fact and Judgment in the ESL Writing Class." *IndE* 16 (Winter 1992): 14–17.

Argues that ESL students need help distinguishing between near copying and paraphrasing, fact and judgment, and report and inference or judgment. Points out that connotations unapparent to ESL students can hinder their understanding of academic discourse.

1544. Leki, Ilona. *Understanding ESL Writers: A Guide for Teachers*. Portsmouth, NH: Boynton-Cook, 1992. 168 pages

Discusses the background of ESL instruction; analyzes ESL students concerns, expectations, errors, and methods of learning a second language; suggests ways of responding to their writing.

1545. Lewitt, Philip Jay. "Sincerest Form: Writing Poetry in Another Language." *LT* 16 (July 1992): 9–11.

Suggests that Japanese students study English verse forms and write poems based on models.

1546. Liebman, JoAnne D. "Toward a New Contrastive Rhetoric: Differences between Arabic and Japanese Rhetorical Instruction." *JSLW* 1 (May 1992): 141–65.

Reviews and critiques previous research on contrastive rhetoric. Based on data from a survey of 89 students, the study maintains that Japanese stress expressive writing, whereas Arabs stress transactional.

1547. Macdonald, Andrew, and Gina Macdonald. "Variations on a Theme: Film and ESL." *ExEx* 37 (Spring 1992): 15–19.

Offers suggestions for developing a successful film course which introduces ESL students "to both language and culture, to writing and speaking."

1548. Mangelsdorf, Kate. "Peer Reviews in the ESL Composition Classroom: What Do the Students Think?" *ELTJ* 46 (July 1992): 274–84.

A study of 40 advanced ESL writers indicates that peer response helps during drafting when the response task is carefully structured. Suggests response strategies.

1549. Mangelsdorf, Kate, and Ann Schlumberger. "ESL Student Response Stances in a Peer-Review Task." *JSLW* 1 (1992): 235–54.

Presents a study of how ESL students respond to student papers in a peer-review task; discusses pedagogical implications.

1550. Matta, William Bruce. "University Writing and the Nonnative Speaker of English: A Preliminary Case Study of Selected United States High School Graduates." *DAI* 53 (October 1992): 1084A.

Examines the writing abilities of four foreign-born university graduate students who were raised in non-English-speaking environments, immigrated to the United States, and graduated from United States high schools.

1551. Moragné Silva, Michele Lowe. "Cognitive, Affective, Social, and Cultural Aspects of Composing in a First- and Second Language: A Case Study of One Adult Writer." *DAI* 52 (June 1992): 4249A.

Examines evidence of the cognitive processes in writing as well as cultural and social influences using the texts generated by one adult writer writing in Portuguese.

1552. Mumford, David John. "The Contextual Language Class: A Comparative Case Study of the Teaching and Learning of English and Spanish at Columbia University." *DAI* 52 (January 1992): 2538A.

Examines the advantages and disadvantages of contextual language teaching methods as it is applied to two distinct groups of university language learners.

1553. Mustapha, Sali Zahlia. "Reading and Writing in a Specific Environment: The Malaysian Experience." *DAI* 52 (March 1992): 3233A.

Describes how Malaysian college students read, process, and retain information supplied by academic texts.

1554. Office of Vocational and Adult Education. "Teaching Adults with Limited English Skills: Progress and Challenges." Department of Education, Office of Vocational and Adult Education, Division of Adult Education and Literacy, Washington, DC, 1991. ERIC ED 341 296. 81 pages

Summarizes current demographic trends, best practices, and federal initiatives in literacy programs for adults with limited English skills.

1555. Ostergren, Joan Caryl. "Relationship among English Performance, Self-Efficacy, Anxiety, and Depression for Hmong Refugees." *DAI* 52 (February 1992): 4455B.

Shows that students who do well in ESL programs are more literate and educated and less depressed. Argues that women and older people do less well.

1556. Paddock, Mark. "Tutors' Column." *WLN* 16 (April 1993): 9–10.

Shows that cultural differences inhibit an ESL student's "understanding of Western methods of writing." Points out that the student's writing can be improved through patience and determination.

1557. Patthey-Chavez, Genevieve G., and Constance A. Gergen. "Culture as an Instructional Resource in the Multiethnic Composition Classroom." *JBW* 11 (Spring 1992): 75–96.

Outlines strategies for drawing on contrasting beliefs and practices held by teachers and students regarding academic prose and approaches to literacy.

1558. Paulston, Christina Bratt. *Linguistics and Communicative Competence: Topics in ESL*. Bristol, PA: Taylor and Francis Group, 1992. 160 pages

Emphasizes practical concerns of classroom procedures and the cross-cultural aspects of teaching English around the world. Discusses linguistic interaction, intercultural communication, and communicative language teaching.

1559. Petrella, Barbara A. "Literature or What? Thoughts on the Reading/Writing Connection in ESL College Composition." *Leaflet* 91 (Fall 1992): 26–33.

Explores choices in writing courses for a diverse ESL population and concludes that literature-based composition courses are a promising approach.

1560. Quinn, David Hugh. "International Issues as Perceived by Students of English as a Second Language at the American Language Program, Columbia University." *DAI* 52 (January 1992): 2445A.

Examines how a group of high-level ESL students apply a critical thinking paradigm to international issues.

1561. Railey, Kevin, Joanne Devine, and Phil Boshoff. *The Implications of Cognitive Models in L1 and L2*. Cincinnati, OH: CCCC, March 1992. ERIC ED 346 455. 14 pages

Reports on a survey and text-analysis study that investigated one dimension of metacognition in first and second language writing.

1562. Raimes, Ann. "The Author Responds to Connor [*TESOLQ* 26 (Spring 1992)]." *TESOLQ* 26 (Spring 1992): 179–80.

Acknowledges Connor's research experience with ETS but points to other researchers who have had less cooperation with ETS regarding TWE.

1563. Raimes, Ann. "The Author Responds to Traugott, Dunkel, and Carrell [*TESOLQ* 26 (Spring 1992)]." *TESOLQ* 26 (Spring 1992): 186–90.

Points out that Core Readers and research referred to by Traugott, Dunkel, and Carrell are funded by ETS. Calls for independent scrutiny of TWE.

1564. Reid, Joy. "A Computer Text Analysis of Four Cohesion Devices in English Discourse by Native and Nonnative Writers." *JSLW* 1 (May 1992): 79–107.

Uses Writer's Workbench to analyze 768 English essays written by NSs of English, Arabic, Chinese, and Spanish. Codes frequency of pronouns, coordinators, paragraphs, and prepositions.

1565. Rodby, Judith. *Appropriating Literacy: Writing and Reading English as a Second Language*. Portsmouth, NH: Boynton-Cook, 1992. 164 pages

Examines the various meanings of ESL literacy by synthesizing ideas from linguistics, anthropology, composition, literary criticism, and literacy studies; discusses methods of teaching ESL in universities and adult schools; suggests ways teachers can respond effectively to ESL students' writing.

1566. Rodriguez, Yvonne Enid Gonzalez. "The Effects of Bilingualism on Cognitive Development." *DAI* 53 (October 1992): 1104A.

Investigates the effects of bilingualism on the verbal and nonverbal cognitive development and linguistic performance of children at various ages.

1567. Rosenthal, Judith W. "The Limited English Proficient Student in the College Science Classroom." *JCST* 22 (December 1992/January 1993): 182–85.

Offers strategies for modifying teaching methods, student-faculty interactions, and written assignments and tests to improve communication in the classroom.

1568. Rousos, Linda. "Report on MPAEPA Innovative Grant Project: Individualized ESL Literacy Instruction for Refugees." Prime County Adult Education, Tucson, AZ, 1991. ERIC ED 337 054. 3 pages

Describes an ESL literacy project with participants from Vietnam, Ethiopia, Nicaragua, and Laos, including creative writing, grammar, and computer and survival skills.

1569. Santos, Terry. "Ideology in Composition: L1 and ESL." *JSLW* 1 (January 1992): 1–15.

Discusses reasons for ideological differences between L1 and L2 composition. Points out that L2 composition has a scientific basis, practical aims, and an international scope.

1570. Saravia-Shore, Marietta, and Steven P. Arviz. *Cross-Cultural Literacy*. Studies in Education and Culture, vol. 3. Hamden, CT: Garland, 1992. 566 pages

Presents an anthropological approach to teaching and learning in multiethnic classrooms which includes ethnographic case studies of such classrooms in the United States.

1571. Saumweber, Judy. "ESL Workplace Literacy Curriculum for a JTPA/Family English Literacy Demonstration Project." Department of Education, and Department of Labor, Washington, DC, 1991. ERIC ED 339 248. 90 pages

Describes a workplace literacy program for Hmong refugees involving four levels of ESL instruction including simulations and job applications.

1572. Subbiah, Mahalingam. "Adding a New Dimension to the Teaching of Audience Awareness." *IEEE* 35 (March 1992): 14–17.

Argues that native English speakers need to be sensitive to cultural differences when they communicate with nonnative speakers of English.

1573. Traugott, Elizabeth Closs, Patricia Dunkel, and Patricia L. Carrell. "An Acknowledgement of Concern and Concern for Lack of Acknowledgement [a response to Raimes, *TESOLQ* 24 (Autumn 1990)]." *TESOLQ* 26 (Spring 1992): 180–85.

Points out inaccuracies in Raimes' argument by listing TWE research studies currently being conducted.

1574. Wadden, Paul. "Teaching the Argumentative Essay." *LT* 16 (September 1992): 19, 21.

Describes a teacher's presentation, peer conferences, revision stages, and curriculum for teaching Japanese students to write argumentative essays in English.

1575. Winer, Lise. " 'Spinach to Chocolate': Changing Awareness and Attitudes in ESL Writing Teachers." *TESOLQ* 26 (Spring 1992): 57–80.

Presents a change from negative to positive attitudes toward writing by using data from trainees' practicum journals. Advocates merging teacher training and development through "learning by doing."

1576. Zamel, Vivian. "Writing One's Way into Reading." *TESOLQ* 26 (Autumn 1992): 463–85.

Discusses writing and reading as similar, interdependent processes, which enable an increase of knowledge. Provides instructional activities using writing to improve reading.

4.5 RESEARCH AND STUDY SKILLS

1577. Breivik, Patricia Senn. "Information Literacy: An Agenda for Lifelong Learning." *AAHE* 44 (March 1992): 6–9.

Advocates integration of research instruction and assignments into a wider spectrum of college courses in order to develop students' ability to find information.

1578. Clery, Carolsue, and Gayle A. Pikrone. *Reading Autobiographies Written by Speech Admission College Freshmen*. Crystal City, VA: College Reading Association, November 1992. ERIC ED 341 029. 22 pages

Analyzes narratives of reading experiences written by students in college reading and study strategies courses at a midwestern university.

1579. Davis, Kevin. "Student Cheating: A Defensive Essay." *EJ* 81 (October 1992): 72–74.

Recommends encouraging students to collaborate in solving procedural tests.

1580. Hatch, Gary Layne. *The Crime of Plagiarism: A Critique of Literary Property Law*. Cincinnati, OH: CCCC, March 1992. ERIC ED 346 477. 14 pages

Traces the history of plagiarism and suggests that plagiarism be redefined as fraud, introducing the intention of the criminal into the handling of plagiarism cases.

1581. Roen, Duane H., and Geraldine McNenny. *Collaboration as Plagiarism—Cheating Is in the Eye of the Beholder*. Cincinnati, OH: CCCC, March 1992. ERIC ED 347 548. 26 pages

Argues that since consciousness and language are social constructs, individual utterance is never entirely original. Recommends a sense of true collaboration where ideas are shared by everyone.

5
Testing, Measurement, and Evaluation

5.1 EVALUATION OF STUDENTS

1582. Allen, Michael S. "Assessment and Invention: Roundtable Report." ERIC/RCS, 1992. ERIC ED 346 457. 11 pages

Reports on a pilot project in portfolio assessment at Northwest Missouri University.

1583. Baker, Nancy Westrich. "The Effect of Portfolio-Based Instruction on Composition Students' Final Examination Scores, Course Grades, and Attitudes toward Writing." *DAI* 53 (August 1992): 385A.

Indicates that portfolio-based and traditional process approaches to composition yield similar results.

1584. Barrow, Dorian A. "The Use of Portfolios to Assess Student Learning." *JCST* 22 (December 1992/January 1993): 148–53.

Argues that the use of portfolios in chemistry classes allowed students to organize and structure their learning. Discusses advantages, drawbacks, and assignment design.

1585. Betz, Renee. "Using Portfolios to Help Students Self-Assess." *Portfolio Newsletter* 1 (Spring 1992): 3–6.

Argues that asking developmental students to write a self-assessing reflective essay introducing their portfolios allows teachers and students to see improvement in their writing.

1586. Birken, Marcia. *Writing Assessment in the Department of Mathematics at Rochester Institute of Technology.* Cincinnati, OH: CCCC, March 1992. ERIC ED 346 487. 7 pages

Describes writing assessment procedures with the objective of assuring that students can communicate about mathematics in a manner appropriate to their future careers.

1587. Bochner, Joseph, John Albertini, Vincent Samar, and Dale Evans Metz. "External and Diagnostic Validity of the NTID Writing Test: An Investigation Using Direct Magnitude Estimation and Principal Components Analysis." *RTE* 26 (October 1992): 299–314.

The authors found that for impromptu essays written by deaf students, professional and nonprofessional readers agreed on overall quality but not on component-diagnostic scores for four factors.

1588. Brand, Alice G. "Portfolio and Test Essay: The Best of Both Writing Assessment Worlds at SUNY Brockport (Eric Digest)." ERIC/RCS, Bloomington, IN, 1992. ERIC ED 347 572. 3 pages

Discusses writing assessment at the State University of New York at Brockport; describes a method which alternates the single-test essay and portfolio.

1589. Brand, Alice G. "Writing Assessment at the College Level (ERIC Digest)." ERIC/RCS, Bloomington, IN, 1992. ERIC ED 345 281. 3 pages

Provides an overview of writing assessment at selected colleges and universities.

1590. Conway, Martin A., Gillian Cohen, and Nicola Stanhope. "Why Is It That University Grades Do Not Predict Very-Long-Term Retention?" *JEPG* 121 (September 1992): 382–84.

A research study shows that test/examination scores may not reliably predict long-term retention of information, while course grades do.

1591. Cosgrove, Cornelius. *Text against Text: Counterbalancing the Hegemony of Assessment*. Cincinnati, OH: CCCC, March 1992. ERIC ED 343 156. 13 pages

Examines fourteen assessment tests and concludes that many assessors are less definite and assertive about the process of writing than originally assumed.

1592. Despain, LaRene, and Thomas L. Hilgers. "Readers' Responses to the Rating of Nonuniform Portfolios: Are There Limits on Portfolios' Utility?" *WPA* 16 (Fall/Winter 1992): 24–37.

Reports the findings of a study that suggests potential problems with reader reliability when assessing nonuniform portfolios.

1593. Drummond-Thompson, Phil, and James Wisdom. *Assessment at Kingston University*. Kingston upon Thames, Surrey: Kingston University, 1992. 44 pages

Organizes multi-disciplinary and multi-purpose postsecondary assessment into nine "methods"—self assessment, self/peer assessment, peer assessment, group/self assessment, group/peer assessment, group assessment, group/individual assessment, individual assessment, and computer-based assessment—that are classroom situated; includes an annotated bibliography.

1594. Fremer, John. *Changing Large Scale Testing Programs: Learning from the Experience of Others*. Breckenridge, CO: Conference on Assessment of the Education Commission of the States/Colorado Department of Education, June 1991. ERIC ED 341 708. 35 pages

Describes the changes that will be implemented in the Scholastic Aptitude Test (SAT) in 1994. Includes more emphasis on critical reading.

1595. Gibson, Michelle. "Alone and Loving It." *JTW* 11 (Spring/Summer 1992): 119–28.

Presents eight key elements in managing portfolios for instruction in a single classroom. Argues that portfolios enhance students' creativity, collaboration, and investment in their writing.

1596. Gould, Christopher. *Assessment in a Social Context: Grading as an Interpretive Community*. Cincinnati, OH: CCCC, March 1992. ERIC ED 345 228. 13 pages

Reports on the outcome of an experiment in which students negotiated their own final examination topic.

1597. Greenburg, Karen L. "Validity and Reliability Issues in the Direct Assessment of Writing." *WPA* 16 (Fall/Winter 1992): 7–22.

Discusses issues in direct assessment and reemphasizes the need for "naturalistic, context-rich, qualitative" approaches to the evaluation of student writing.

1598. Hamp-Lyons, Liz, ed. *Assessing Second Language Writing in Academic Contexts.* Norwood, NJ: Ablex, 1991. 347 pages

Contains 21 essays that examine issues in assessing second language writing. Discusses the contexts in which assessment occurs, aspects of decision-making and design in a writing assessment program, evaluating the assessment program, public reporting, and prospects for the future.
Essayists: Allaei, Sara Kurtz; Ballard, Brigid; Basham, Charlotte S.; Carlisle, Robert; Carlson, Sybil B.; Clanchy, John; Connor, Ulla; Davidson, Fred; Henning, Grant; Horowitz, Daniel; Johns, Ann; Kwachka, Patricia E.; Lorenz, Frederick O.; McKenna, Eleanor; Meyer, Daisy M.; Vann, Roberta J.; Vaughan, Caroline.

1599. Hannah, Charles Austin. "The Effects of Holistic Scoring and Peer-Evaluation on the Narrative and Expository Writing of 10th-Graders." *DAI* 52 (March 1992): 3167A.

Results indicate positive effects on the evaluation of written drafts and expository writing performance.

1600. Haswell, Richard H., and Janis E. Tedesco. *Gender and the Evaluation of Writing.* Seattle, WA: NCTE, November 1991. ERIC ED 343 141. 14 pages

Studies 32 teachers and 32 first-year composition students; finds that a culturally determined way of looking at gender affects writing evaluation.

1601. Haviland, Carol Peterson, and J. Milton Clark. "What Can Our Students Tell Us about Essay Examination Designs and Practices?" *JBW* 11 (Fall 1992): 47–60.

The preferences of 336 students in phrasing, number, and content of essay questions lead faculty to rethink the appropriateness of impromptu essays to course goals.

1602. Holladay, Sylvia A. "The Impact of Writing Assessment on Curriculum and Instruction in the Two-Year College." *TETYC* 19 (October 1992): 177–84.

Examines controversies regarding the influence of wide-scale writing assessments on composition classrooms and discusses the limits of existing research to inform any opinion.

1603. Janopoulos, Michael. "University Faculty Tolerance of NS and NNS Writing Errors: A Comparison." *JSLW* 1 (1992): 109–21.

Presents a study of faculty tolerance of writing errors from NS and NNS students and discusses possible differing standards and expectations for the two groups.

1604. Janopoulos, Michael. "Using Written Recall Protocols to Measure Aspects of Holistic Assessment of Second Language Writing Proficiency: The Effect of Task Awareness." ERIC/RCS, Bloomington, IN, 1991. ERIC ED 335 869. 57 pages

Uses written recall protocols to investigate the relationship between how much holistic scorers comprehend of a text and how high they rate text quality.

1605. Keithley, Zoe. " 'My Own Voice': Students Say It Unlocks the Writing Process." *JBW* 11 (Fall 1992): 82–102.

Presents the results of a questionnaire which asked students to distinguish the most helpful instructional factors and activities aiding their writing progress in a Story Workshop.

1606. Kiefer, Kate. "Real Evaluation: Portfolios as an Effective Alternative to Standardized Testing." *ELQ* 13 (February 1992): 2–4.

Outlines the benefits of portfolio assessment for students, for teachers, and for the larger community of parents, administrators, and employers.

1607. Leahy, Richard. "Competency Testing and the Writing Center." *WPA* 15 (Spring 1992): 41–56.

Explains how the Writing Center at Boise State University participated effectively in competency testing.

1608. Leggo, Carl. "A Poet's Pensées: Writing and Schooling." *EQ* 23.3–4 (1992): 4–10.

Records the experiences of a poet who broke through the constraints imposed by the models and evaluation procedures of his school.

1609. Lindner, Richard, and Bruce Harris. "Self-Regulated Learning: Its Assessment and Instructional Implications." *ERQ* 16 (December 1992): 29–37.

The authors present a study in which they developed and administered a self-reporting instrument measuring the effect of "self-regulated" (meta-cognitive) learning. They conclude that it can be so measured and that its importance is positively correlated to GPAs.

1610. Lovitt, Carl R. *Assessment as a Team Effort: The Pearce Center Assessment Research Team*. Cincinnati, OH: CCCC, March 1992. ERIC ED 345 259. 22 pages

Describes Clemson University's WAC program, including a team assessment of its effectiveness.

1611. Mayo, Wendell. *Initial Gestures: Point of View and Context in Responding to Student Writing*. Cincinnati, OH: CCCC, March 1992. ERIC ED 343 121. 10 pages

Discusses the different roles and points of views that a teacher assumes when evaluating student writing.

1612. McKendy, Thomas. "Locally Developed Writing Tests and the Validity of Holistic Scoring." *RTE* 26 (May 1992): 149–67.

Argues against teacher grades as a valid criterion for predictive validity; argues that better criteria include multiple samples and teacher ratings of "writing ability," a construct which he considers suspect in itself.

1613. Mitchell, Felicia. *Is There a Text in This Grade?* Cincinnati, OH: CCCC, March 1992. ERIC ED 346 475. 14 pages

Urges awareness of the signals being sent to students in written comments on compositions because they influence students' perceptions of their texts as well as their attitudes toward writing.

1614. Mitchell, Ruth. "Measuring Up: Student Assessment and Systematic Change." *EdTech* 32 (November 1992): 37–40.

Outlines portfolio assessment features of transformed self-directed education systems.

1615. Moffett, James. *Detecting Growth in Language*. Portsmouth, NH: Boynton/Cook, 1992. 88 pages

Offers alternative ways of evaluating "growth sequences" in language usage, from vocabulary to the ability to manage different discourse types.

1616. Morton, Johnnye L. "What Teachers Want to Know about Portfolio Assessment." ERIC/RCS, Bloomington, IN, 1991. ERIC ED 336 728. 8 pages

Provides brief answers to eight of the most frequently asked questions about portfolio assessment.

1617. Moxley, Joseph M. "Teacher's Goals and Methods of Responding to Student Writing." *CS/FEN* 20 (Fall 1992): 17–33.

Analyzes responses of 419 teachers to a survey about responses to student writing. Finds that teachers are trying alternatives to traditional written responses but that they also experience time constraints.

1618. Murphy, Sandra, and Mary Ann Smith. *Writing Portfolios: A Bridge from Teaching to Assessment*. Pippin Teacher's Library. Portsmouth, NH: Heinemann, 1992. 96 pages

The authors provide a practical introduction to the uses of the portfolio in assessment and teaching writing as a process.

1619. "New Studies Yield Surprising Results about Student Performance on Essay Questions." *ETS* 38 (Fall 1992): 5.

Finds that hand-written essays composed by college writers received higher scores than word-processed essays, and that advance disclosure of essay topics did not improve scores.

1620. Perrin, Robert. "The Rhetorical Stance of Assessment." *ELQ* 13 (February 1992): 10–12.

Argues that Wayne Booth's rhetorical context of role, reader, and purpose is applicable to the "writing situation" constituted when teachers evaluate student writing.

1621. Plumb, Carolyn Sue. "An Investigation of the Levels of Knowledge and Strategies Used when Revising." *DAI* 52 (February 1992): 2866A.

Reports the results of three studies that investigated the roles of topic knowledge, linguistic knowledge, and conscious strategy use during the revising process.

1622. Purves, Alan C. "Reflections on Research and Assessment in Written Composition." *RTE* 26 (February 1992): 108–22.

Argues that measuring writing adequately requires several samples, that products (not processes) still are the item assessed, and that no assessment is free of observer bias.

1623. Rhodes, Lynn K., ed. *Literacy Assessment: A Handbook of Instruments*. Portsmouth, NH: Heinemann, 1992. 152 pages

Provides literacy assessment instruments that may be photocopied and used by teachers; includes comprehension checklists, attitude surveys, self-assessment guides, reading and writing evaluations, and an observation checklist and guide. Provides interviews with students and parents.

1624. Rouscalp, Edwin E., and Gerald H. Maring. "Portfolios for a Community of Learners." *JR* 35 (February 1992): 378–85.

Describes how the language arts supports learning across the curriculum. Reviews research and the theoretical perspective on how portfolios contribute to community development and instruction.

1625. Shiffman, Betty Garrison. "Reading Our Students/Ourselves: Toward a Feminist Theory of Evaluation." *TETYC* 19 (February 1992): 24–31.

Argues that feminist pedagogy combined with composition theory produces a more humane evaluation; includes protocols of teachers engaging in the grading process.

1626. Shohamy, Elana, Claire M. Gordon, and Roberta Kraemer. "The Effect of Raters' Background and Training on the Reliability of Direct Writing Tests." *Language Journal* 76 (Spring 1992): 26–33.

Finds that procedural training but not background (professional versus lay) affects the reliability of raters evaluating EFL writing samples.

1627. Stanley, Jan. "Coaching Student Writers to Be Effective Peer Evaluators." *JSLW* 1 (1992): 217–33.

Shows how extensive coaching of students can help to increase the effectiveness of peer evaluators in composition classes.

1628. Stern, Caroline. *Writing Portfolios: A Resource for Reading and Assessment*. Boston, MA: CCCC, March 1991. ERIC ED 336 757. 14 pages

Discusses the merits of writing portfolios and offers suggestions for using them.

1629. Valentino, Marilyn J. *Examining the Constraints of Response: What Are We Modeling When We Respond to Student Writing?* Cincinnati, OH: CCCC, March 1992. ERIC ED 345 232. 10 pages

Studies teachers' written responses to student texts; finds that while an emphasis on communication and ideas is most effective, most comments emphasized grammar and mechanics.

1630. VanLeirsburg, Peggy, and Jerry L. Johns. "Assessment Literacy: Perceptions of Preservice and Inservice Teachers Regarding Ethical Considerations of Standardized Testing Procedures (Literacy Research Report Number 12)." Northern Illinois University,

Curriculum and Instruction Reading Clinic, Dekalb, IL, 1991. ERIC ED 341 666. 24 pages

> Surveys preservice and inservice teachers regarding knowledge of assessment procedures; suggests that more training would be useful.

1631. Werchan, James E. "An Empirical Study of the Use of Holistic Evaluation as a Classroom Activity." *DAI* 53 (September 1992): 746A.

> Finds that holistic evaluation over the course of the semester did not make a significant difference in students' writing; argues that peer work provides a similar function to holistic activity.

1632. White, Edward M. *Assessing Higher Order Thinking and Communication Skills in College Graduates through Writing*. Washington, DC: Assessing Higher Order Thinking and Communication Skills in College Graduates (National Center for Education Statistics), November 17–19, 1991. ERIC ED 340 767. 44 pages

> Reviews multiple-choice tests, essay examinations, and portfolios as a means of assessing higher order skills of communication. Recommends portfolio assessment for any national writing assessment.

1633. Willey, Robert John. "The Effects of Attention to Audience at Different Times during Composing on the Quality of Freshmen's Essays." *DAI* 52 (April 1992): 3592A.

> Points out that because of low inter-rater reliability, holistically scored essays of randomly placed students provided no significant results for "attention" (during composing) to possible essay audiences.

1634. Yancey, Kathleen Blake, ed. *Portfolios in the Writing Classroom: An Introduction*. Urbana, IL: NCTE, 1992. 128 pages

> Advocates the use of writing portfolios to learn new ways to think about the teaching of writing and to understand ourselves in new ways as teachers and learners. Discusses ways to use portfolios from middle school to college-level writing classes. Includes an annotated bibliography.
> *Essayists:* Camp, Roberta; D'Aoust, Catherine; Ewing, Sheila C.; Gold, Sue Ellen; Kneeshaw, David; Lucas, Catherine; Murphy, Sandra; Newkirk, James E.; Smith, Mary Ann; Weiser, Irwin.

5.2 EVALUATION OF TEACHERS

1635. "Classroom Performance Assessments: Creating a Portrait of the Beginning Teacher." *ETS* 38 (Fall 1992): 2–4.

> Describes the intent, history, and domains of the Praxis III classroom-teaching component of the Praxis teacher-certification series; outlines the training provided to assessors.

1636. Cumming, Alister. "Instructional Routines in ESL Composition Teaching: A Case Study of Three Teachers." *JSLW* 1 (1992): 17–35.

> Presents a study of six consistent teaching routines used by three different ESL composition instructors; gives implications for curriculum changes.

1637. Cunningham, Mary Elizabeth. "Implications of Connected Epistemology for the Development of Teaching Styles." *DAI* 52 (February 1992): 2787A.

> Based on Mary Belenky et al.'s work, this examination concludes that a causal relationship was not established between epistemological orientations and preference of teaching style.

1638. Elbow, Peter. "Making Better Use of Student Evaluations of Teachers." *Profession* 92 (1992): 42–48.

> Suggests ways "to dignify student evaluations of teachers and to make the process thoughtful and reflective rather than mechanical."

1639. Gordon, Randall A., and Uwe Stuecher. "The Effect of Anonymity and Increased Accountability on the Linguistic Complexity of Teaching Evaluations." *JPsy* 126 (November 1992): 639–49.

The authors examine the effects of anonymity and accountability on teaching evaluations; they confirm most previous studies and suggest that increased accountability encourages linguistic complexity.

1640. Gould, Christopher. "Assessing Teaching Effectiveness in English: Procedures, Issues, Strategies." *ADE Bulletin* 102 (Fall 1992): 44–52.

Surveys instructional evaluation, explaining the role of students, peers, and self; includes forms for peer review of dossier and class observation as well as self-evaluation.

1641. "New Teacher Assessments Build on a Holistic View of Teaching." *ETS* 37 (Summer 1992): 6–7.

Describes the Praxis Series that will replace the NTE, including Praxis I, an academic skills test; Praxis II, subject matter and curriculum-design tests; and Praxis III, a classroom-based performance test.

1642. Swain, Margaret. "A Direct Intervention." *EQ* 24.1 (1992): 23–24.

Discusses the conditions under which a principal should intervene directly in a teacher's methodology.

5.3 EVALUATION OF PROGRAMS

1643. Carliner, Saul. "What You Should Get from a Professionally Oriented Master's Degree in Technical Communication." *TC* 39 (May 1992): 189–99.

Presents a Master's program from the perspective of a nonacademic. Recommends sections in theory, professional skills, technical proficiency, and internship.

1644. Carter, Dundan, and Ben McClelland. "WPAs Assess the CCCCs 'Statement of Principles and Standards.' " *WPA* 16 (Fall/Winter 1992): 71–87.

Discusses ten questions raised by WPAs at the 1990 Portland Conference that focused on CCCC "Statement of Principles and Standards."

1645. Dunn, Patricia. *First Steps: New Faculty, New Writing across the Curriculum Program*. Cincinnati, OH: CCCC, March 1992. ERIC ED 343 163. 8 pages

Discusses the difficulties of a newly formed committee on writing and the problems faced by WAC programs.

1646. Farmer, Vernon. "Developing a Perspective on Assessment of Effectiveness in Developmental Education." *ERQ* 16 (September 1992): 25–33.

Argues that developmental programs are assessed according to varying criteria and that a unified perspective would provide coherence to multiple assessments and research findings.

1647. Hilgers, Thomas L., and Joy Marsella. *Making Your Writing Program Work*. Newbury Park, CA: Sage, 1992. 328 pages

Offers faculty and administrators of writing programs curricular alternatives, assessment methods, and budgeting and hiring procedures; includes examples from composition, writing across the curriculum, technical, and creative writing programs.

1648. Hult, Christine and the Portland Resolution Committee. "The Portland Resolution." *WPA* 16 (Fall/Winter 1992): 88–94.

Presents the conditions and guidelines drawn up at the 1990 CCCC conference intended to help WPAs and others "develop quality writing programs in their institutions."

1649. Larson, Richard L. "Classes of Discourse, Acts of Discourse, Writers and Readers." *EJ* 81 (December 1992): 32–36.

Presents the outcome of a study on composition curricula of 240 colleges and universities. Explains why traditional categorizations of discourse "misteach and mislead" students; provides alternative conceptualizations.

1650. McLeod, Susan H. "Evaluating Writing Programs: Paradigms, Problems, Possibilities." *JAC* 12 (Fall 1992): 373–82.

Examines quantitative and qualitative methods of program evaluation; argues that one key to success with either is the recognition of the paradigm out of which it grows.

1651. Rainey, Kenneth T., and Rebecca S. Kelly. "Doctoral Research in Technical Communication: 1965–1990." *TC* 39 (November 1992): 552–70.

Presents two survey results. The first looks at United States schools awarding doctorates in technical communication; the second discusses the categories of dissertations.

1652. Swinwood, Linda. "Making a Difference." *EQ* 24 (July 21, 1992): 6–9.

Presents internal monologues of a teacher, a student, and a parent as background for the teacher's decision to pilot a Language Arts Programme Assessment.

1653. Talley, Ronald Keith. "An Evaluation of the Impact of the Illinois Writing Assessment Program on English Language Arts Classrooms." *DAI* 53 (December 1992): 1784A.

Asserts that written composition is at the forefront of the field of teaching English and examines the effect of this emphasis.

5.4 OTHER

1654. Graves, Donald H., and Bonnie S. Sunstein, eds. *Portfolio Portraits*. Portsmouth, NH: Heinemann, 1992. 212 pages

The essayists examine writing portfolios composed by students K–graduate school; they discuss how portfolios shape the way writing and development are viewed and how portfolios could improve large scale assessment; and they profile four portfolio composers (a school superintendent, a college writer, and two second-graders).
Essayists: Chiseri-Strater, E.; Fu, D. L.; Graves, D. H.; Hansen, J.; Matthews, C.; Milliken, M.; Rief, L.; Romano, T.; Seger, F. D.; Simmons, J.; Sunstein, B. S.; Voss, M. M.

1655. Greenberg, Karen. "Validity and Reliability Issues in the Direct Assessment of Writing." *WPA* 16 (Fall/Winter 1992): 7–22.

Historicizes the development of writing assessments that have replaced indirect measures ("objective" tests) with direct measures, attributing changes to more sophisticated conceptualizations of writing as a construct.

1656. Ory, John C. "Meta-Assessment: Evaluating Assessment Activities." *RHE* 33 (August 1992): 467–82.

Identifies 30 standards which were proposed by a multi-disciplinary group of assessment experts to evaluate assessment activities; divides them into four categories: utility, feasibility, propriety, and technical accuracy.

Subject Index
Name Index

Subject Index

Numbers in the right-hand column refer to sections and subsections (see Contents). For example, entries containing information on achievement tests appear in Section 5, Subsection 5.1 (Evaluation of Students). When the right-hand column contains only a section number, information on the subject appears in several subsections. Entries addressing assignments in the classroom, for example, appear in several subsections of Section 4, depending on the kind of course for which the assignments are appropriate.

Academic Aptitude, 2.10
Academic Aptitude Tests, 5.1
Academic Freedom, 3.0
Academic Records, 3.2
Accountability, 3.4
Accountability Measures, 5.0
Accreditation, Institutional, 5.3
Accreditation of Teachers, 3.1
Achievement Tests, 5.1
Activities, Classroom, 4.0
Administration, 3.2
Admissions Tests, 5.1
Adolescent Development, 2.10
Adult Education Courses, 4.3
Adult Learning, 2.10
Advanced Composition Instruction, 4.2.3
Advanced Placement Tests, 5.1
Advertising in Instruction, 4.0
Advertising Research, 2.5
Affirmative Action, 3.2
Age/Grade Placement Policies, 3.2
Age/Grade Placement Tests, 5.1
Alphabets, 2.8
Ambiguity, 2.0
Anthropological Linguistics, 2.8
Anxiety Research, 2.9
Applied Linguistics, 2.8

Apprenticeships for Students, 4.3
Apprenticeships for Teachers, 3.1
Aptitude Tests, 5.1
Argumentative Discourse, 2.1
Argumentative Writing Instruction, 4.0
Arrangement in Discourse, Rhetorical, 2.1
Arrangement Instruction, Rhetorical, 4.0
Assignments, Classroom, 4.0
Assignments, Testing, 5.0
Attendance Policies, 3.2
Audience in Discourse, 2.0
Audience Instruction, 4.0
Autobiographical Writing Instruction, 4.0

Basic Skills Instruction, 4.0
Basic Writers, 2.0
Basic Writing Courses, 4.21
Behavior Theories, 2.9
Benefits, Employee, 3.2
Bibliographies, 1.0
Bilingual Instruction, 4.4
Bilingualism, 2.8
Boards, Governing, 3.2
Body Language, 2.15
Brain Research, 2.9
Budgets, 3.2

Business Communication Instruction, 4.2.4
Business Communication Theories, 2.5

Censorship, 3.4
Certification of Teachers, 3.1
Cheating, 4.5
Checklists, 1.0
Child Development, 2.10
Child Language, 2.8
Citizen Participation, 3.4
Classroom Communication, 4.0
Classroom Observation Techniques, 5.2
Class Size, 3.2
Cloze Procedure Measures, 5.0
Cloze Procedure Research, 2.7
Code Switching Instruction, Language, 4.0
Code Switching Research, Language, 2.8
Cognition, 2.9
Cognitive Development, 2.9
Cognitive Measurement, 5.1
Coherence, Teaching Techniques, 4.0
Coherence in Discourse, 2.1
Collaboration, Schools/Colleges, 3.4
Collaborative Learning, Teaching Techniques, 4.0
Collaborative Learning Research, 2.0
Collective Bargaining, 3.2
College Curriculum, 4.2
Community Relations, 3.4
Competency-Based Education, 4.0
Competency Tests, 5.1
Composing Processes, 2.1
Composition Instruction, 4.0
Composition Research, 2.1
Comprehension, 2.7
Comprehension Instruction, 4.0
Computer-Assisted Instruction, 4.0
Computer Literacy, 2.4
Computer-Managed Instruction, 4.0
Concept Formation, 2.9
Conferences, Professional, 3.3
Conferences, Student/Teacher, 4.0
Consulting as Professionals, 3.4
Consulting with Professionals, 3.4
Continuing Education Courses, 4.3
Continuing Education for Teachers, 3.1
Contract Grading, 5.1
Contracts, Teacher, 3.2
Contrastive Linguistics, 2.8
Core Curriculum, 4.0
Correctional Education, Prisons, 4.3
Correspondence Courses, 4.0
Course Descriptions, 4.0
Course Evaluation, 5.3

Courses, 4.0
Creative Writing Courses, 4.2.7
Creativity Research, 2.9
Creativity Tests, 5.1
Credentials, Teacher, 3.1
Critical Theory, 2.6
Critical Thinking, 2.9
Critical Thinking Instruction, 4.0
Cross-Curricular Writing Courses, 4.2.7
Cross-Disciplinary Research, 2.14
Cultural Literacy, 2.4
Cumulative Sentence Writing, 4.0
Curriculum, 4.0
Curriculum Evaluation, 5.3
Curriculum Research, 2.10

Day Care, Employee Benefits, 3.2
Deconstruction, 2.6
Degree Programs for Teachers, 3.1
Degree Programs in Writing, 4.0
Descriptive Discourse, 2.0
Descriptive Writing Discourse, 4.0
Development, Individual, 2.9
Developmental Studies Programs, 4.2.1
Diachronic Linguistics, 2.8
Diagnostic Tests, 5.1
Dialect Instruction, 4.0
Dialect Studies, 2.8
Dictionary Skills Instruction, 4.5
Discourse Theories, 2.1
Discussion, Teaching Techniques, 4.0
Doublespeak, 2.8
Doublespeak Instruction, 4.0
Drama, Teaching Techniques, 4.0
Drama as Literature, 2.6

Editing, Teaching Techniques, 4.0
Editing in Publishing, 2.11
Educational Administration, 3.2
Educational Assessment, 5.0
Educational Research, 2.10
Educational Programs for Teachers, 3.1
Educational Strategies, 4.0
Educational Television, 3.3
Educational Testing, 5.0
Emotional Development, 2.9
Employer/Employee Relationships, 3.2
Engineering Education, 4.2.7
English, Instruction, Second Language, 4.4
English, Research, Second Language, 2.8
English Coalition Conference, 3.4
English Language Instruction, 4.0
English Language Theories, 2.8

SUBJECT INDEX

English Literary Criticism, 2.6
English Literature Instruction, 4.0
English-Only Legislation, 2.4
English Teacher Education, 3.1
Error, Theories of, 2.1
Error Evaluation, 5.1
Essay Test Instruction, 4.0
Essay Tests, 5.1
Essay Writing, 4.0
Ethnic Studies, 4.0
Ethnography, 2.0
Evaluation, 5.0
Experimental Curriculum, 4.0
Expository Discourse, 2.1
Expository Writing Instruction, 4.0

Faculty Development, 3.1
Faculty Evaluation, 5.2
Federal Legislation, 3.4
Figurative Language, 2.0
Figurative Language Instruction, 4.0
Film Courses, 4.0
Film Criticism, 2.6
First-Year Composition Courses, 4.2.2
Folk Culture Instruction, 4.0
Folklore Research, 2.14
Forced Choice Tests, 5.1

General Semantics, 2.8
Generative Rhetoric, 2.1
Generative Rhetoric Instruction, 4.0
Governing Boards, Institutional, 3.2
Grading, 5.1
Graduate Study for Teachers, 3.1
Graduate Teaching Assistants, 3.0
Graduate Writing Courses, 4.3
Grammar Instruction, 4.0
Grammatical Theories, 2.8
Grants, 3.3
Grievance Procedures, 3.2
Group Activities, 4.0
Group Discussion, 4.0
Grouping Through Assessment, 5.1
Group Instruction, 4.0
Guidance Centers, 3.3

Handwriting, 2.15
Higher Education Curriculum, 4.2
History of Rhetoric, 2.2
Homework, 4.0
Honors Curriculum, 4.0
Humanities Instruction, 4.0

Illiteracy Studies, 2.4
Imagination, 2.9
Imitation, Teaching Techniques, 4.0
Individual Development, 2.9
Individualized Instruction, 4.0
Industrial Education, 4.0
In-Service Teacher Education, 3.1
Instructional Techniques, 4.0
Intellectual Development, 2.9
Intelligence Tests, 5.1
Interdisciplinary Course, 4.2.7
Interdisciplinary Research, 2.14
Interpretive Skills, 2.7
Interpretive Skills Instruction, 4.0
Invention Instruction, Rhetorical, 4.0
Invention Research, Rhetorical, 2.1

Journalism Education, 4.2.7
Journalism Research 2.11
Journals, Teaching Techniques, 4.0
Judicial Rhetoric, 2.3

Laboratories, 3.3
Language Acquisition, 2.8
Language Disorders, 2.13
Language Instruction, Native, 4.0
Language Instruction, Second, 4.4
Language Planning, 2.4
Language Research, 2.8
Language Tests, 5.1
Language Theories, 2.8
Laws, 3.4
Learning Disabilities, 2.10
Learning Disabled, Programs for, 4.6
Learning Resources Centers, 3.3
Learning Theories, 2.10
Legal Rhetoric, 2.3
Legal Writing Instruction, 4.2.7
Levels of Abstraction in Discourse, 2.1
Levels of Abstraction Instruction, 4.0
Libraries, 3.3
Library Skills Instruction, 4.5
Linguistic Theories, 2.8
Listening Instruction, 4.0
Listening Research, 2.4
Literacy, 2.4
Literacy Instruction, 4.0
Literary Criticism, 2.6
Literature Courses, 4.2.6
Logic, 2.12

Mass Media Instruction, 4.0
Measurement, 5.0

Media Centers, 3.3
Medical Writing, 2.13
Medical Writing Instruction, 4.2.7
Memory Research, 2.9
Methods of Teaching, 4.0
Minimum Competency Testing, 5.1
Minority Cultures in Instruction, 4.2.7
Minority Teachers, 3.2
Miscue Analysis in Instruction, 4.0
Miscue Analysis Research, 2.7
Moral Development, 2.9
Morphology, Language, 2.8
Motivational Techniques, 4.0
Multicultural Instruction, 4.0
Multicultural Research, 2.14
Multimedia Instruction, 4.0
Multiple Choice Tests, 5.0

Narrative Discourse, 2.1
Narrative Writing Instruction, 4.0
Native Language Instruction, 4.0
Neurolinguistics, 2.8
Neurological Research, 2.9
Nonstandard Dialects in Instruction, 4.0
Nonstandard Dialect Studies, 2.8
Nonverbal Communication, 2.15
Note Taking Instruction, 4.5

Objectives, Educational, 4.0
Objective Tests, 5.1
Oral Language Instruction, 4.0
Oral Language Research, 2.4
Organization, Teaching Techniques, 4.0
Organization in Discourse, 2.1
Organizations, Professional, 3.3
Orientation Programs, 3.3

Paragraphs, Teaching Techniques, 4.0
Paragraphs in Discourse, 2.1
Parent/Teacher Conferences, 3.4
Parts of Speech, 2.8
Parts of Speech Instruction, 4.0
Part-Time Employment, 3.2
Peer Evaluation, 5.0
Peer Teaching, 4.0
Perception, 2.9
Personality Theories, 2.9
Personnel Evaluations, 5.2
Personnel Policies, 3.2
Persuasive Discourse, 2.0
Persuasive Writing Instruction, 4.0
Philosophy of Language, 2.12
Phonemics, 2.8
Phonology, 2.8

Placement Procedures, 5.1
Placement Tests, 5.1
Plagiarism, 4.5
Play Writing, 4.0
Poetry Instruction, 4.0
Police Education, 4.3
Political Rhetoric, 2.3
Popular Culture Instruction, 4.0
Positional Statements, Professional, 3.2
Position Statements, Instructional, 4.1
Position Statements, Public Policies, 3.4
Practicums for Teachers, 3.1
Preaching (Religious Rhetoric), 2.3
Pre-Service Teacher Education, 3.1
Pretests/Posttests, 5.1
Prewriting Instruction, 4.0
Prewriting Research, 2.1
Priming Effects, 2.7, 2.9
Prison Programs, 4.3
Problem-Solving Instruction, 4.0
Problem-Solving Research, 2.1
Professional Development, 3.1
Professional Organizations, 3.3
Program Administration, 3.2
Program Descriptions, 4.0
Program Evaluation, 5.3
Promotion, Occupational, 3.2
Propaganda, Political, 2.3
Propaganda in Advertising, 2.5
Propaganda Instruction, 4.0
Proposal Writing Instruction, 4.0
Prose Instruction, 4.0
Prose Theories, 2.0
Psycholinguistics, 2.8
Psychological Services, 3.3
Psychology, 2.9
Public Relations, School/Community, 3.4
Public Relations Research, 2.5
Public Television, 3.3
Publishing Industry, 2.11
Punctuation, 2.8
Punctuation, Teaching Techniques, 4.0
Purpose, Teaching Techniques, 4.0
Purpose in Discourse, 2.1

Questioning Techniques, 4.0
Questionnaires, 5.0

Radio, 3.3
Rating Scales, 5.0
Readability Research, 2.7
Reader-Response Criticism, 2.6
Reading Centers, 3.3
Reading Instruction, 4.0

SUBJECT INDEX

Reading Research, 2.7
Reading Tests, 5.1
Religious Rhetoric, 2.3
Remedial Instruction, 4.0
Report Writing Instruction, 4.0
Research Methodology, 2.0
Research Needs, 2.0
Research Skills Instruction, 4.5
Resource Centers, 3.3
Revision Instruction, 4.0
Revision Research, 2.1
Rhetorical History, 2.2
Rhetorical Instruction, 4.0
Rhetorical Theories, 2.1
Roleplaying, 4.0

Salaries, 3.2
School/Community Relationships, 3.4
Schools/Colleges, Collaboration, 3.4
Scientific Communication Theories, 2.13
Scientific Writing Instruction, 4.2.5
Second Language Instruction, 4.4
Self-Evaluation, 5.0
Semantics, 2.8
Semiotics, 2.8
Sentence-Combining Instruction, 4.0
Sentence-Combining Research, 2.8
Sentences, Teaching Techniques, 4.0
Sentences in Discourse, 2.1
Sociolinguistics, 2.8
Speech Act Theories, 2.1
Speech Communication Research, 2.0
Speech Instruction, 4.0
Spelling Instruction, 4.0
Staff Development, 3.1
Standardized Tests, 5.0
State Departments of Education, 3.2
State Legislation, 3.4
Storytelling, 4.0
Structural Linguistics, 2.8
Student Evaluation by Teacher, 5.1
Student Evaluation of Courses, 5.3
Student Evaluation of Teachers, 5.2
Student Placement, 5.1
Student/Teacher Conferences, 4.0
Study Skills Instruction, 4.5
Stylistic Instruction, 4.0
Stylistics, 2.1
Substitute Teachers, 3.2
Summer Programs for Students, 4.0
Summer Teachers' Institutes, 3.1
Syntax, 2.8
Syntax Instruction, 4.0
Systemic Linguistics, 2.8

Tagmemics, Teaching Techniques, 4.0
Tagmemic Theory, 2.8
Teacher Centers, 3.3
Teacher Education, 3.1
Teacher Evaluation, 5.2
Teacher/Parent Conferences, 3.4
Teacher Researchers, Training, 3.1
Teacher/Student Conferences, 4.0
Teacher Welfare, 3.2
Teaching Assistants, Training, 3.1
Teaching Load, 3.2
Technical Communication Theories, 2.13
Technical Writing Instruction, 4.2.5
Television, 3.3
Television Viewing Instruction, 4.0
Temporary Employment, 3.2
Tenure, 3.2
Testing Programs, 5.0
Test Taking Instruction, 4.5
Textbook Selection, 3.2
Thinking Instruction, Critical, 4.0
Thinking Research, 2.9
Traditional Grammar, 2.8
Traditional Grammar Instruction, 4.0
Transformational Grammar, 2.8
Translation in Publishing, 2.11
Tutoring, Peer, 4.0
Tutoring Programs, 3.3
Two-Year College Curriculum, 4.2

Unemployment, 3.2
Usage Instruction, 4.0
Usage Studies, 2.8

Verbal Development, 2.8
Verbally Gifted Students, 2.10
Verbally Gifted Students, Programs for, 4.0
Visual Literacy Instruction, 4.0
Visual Literacy Research, 2.4
Vocabulary Instruction, 4.5
Vocational Education, 4.0

Women's Studies, 4.0
Word Study Skills Instruction, 4.0
Work Load, Faculty, 3.2
Writing About Literature Instruction, 4.0
Writing Across the Curriculum Courses, 4.2.7
Writing Across the Curriculum Research, 2.0
Writing Centers, 3.3
Writing Exercises, Classroom, 4.0
Writing Exercises, Testing, 5.0
Writing Program Administrators, 3.2
Writing Program Evaluation, 5.3

Name Index

This index lists authors of anthologized essays as well as authors and editors of main entries.

Abbott, Michael M., 1152
Abbott, Susan, 1120
Aber, John, 821
Abt-Perkins, Dawn, 1177, 1391
Adams, John, 670
Adams, Maurianne, 826
Ademan, Deborah, 1212
Adipattaranum, Nitida, 1502
Adler, Jonathan E., 1121
Adnan, Etel, 618
Afflerbach, Peter, 391
Agatucci, Cora, 1122
Agmon, Ora, 541
Agnew, Eleanor, 822, 1178, 1179
Ahmad, Aijaz, 8
Ahn, Dong-Keun, 531
Aitchison, Jean, 655
Aitken, Avril, 780
Aitken, Russell, 1508
Alasti, Ahmad, 565
Albano, Theresa Ann, 636
Albertini, John, 1587
Alcoff, Linda, 9
Alderson, J. Charles, 1503
Alexander, David, 524
Algeo, John, 720
Alisjahbana, S. Takdir, 1508

Allaei, Sara Kurtz, 1598
Allen, C., 414
Allen, Jo, 1322
Allen, Michael S., 1582
Allen, Nancy Jane, 1323
Allen, Paula Gunn, 1145
Allen, S., 1129
Allister, Jan, 1213
Allsopp, Jeannette, 656
Almasi, Janice, 391
Alpern, Sara, 965
Alred, Gerald J., 1324
Altschuler, Glenn C., 877
Alvarado, Manuel, 567
Alway, Joan, 10
Amato, Joe, 375, 376
Amato, Katya, 1050
Amdahl, Mark, 377
An, Jung-Hee, 1504
Anaya, Rudolpho, 1434
Andas, Ann, 782
Anderson, Amanda, 921
Anderson, Benedict, 567
Anderson, Claire, 542
Anderson, Ellen, 596
Anderson, James A, 826
Anderson, Kristi S., 11

Anderson, Warwick, 823
Andresen, Julie Tetel, 657
Andrews, Deborah Brunson, 1123
Andrews, William L., 181
Angrosino, Michael V., 1003
Angus, Ian, 922
Annas, Camille, 378
Anson, Chris M., 1012
Anthony, Mary Anne, 1124
Antler, Joyce, 965
Antonovsky, Aaron, 984
Applbaum, Ronald L., 1041
Apple, Michael, 836
Appleby, Bruce C., 1111
Arac, Jonathan, 592
Archer, Nuala, 618
Arcuri, Luciano, 760
Arends, Richard I., 1013
Aristar-Dry, Helen, 658
Armstrong, Isobel, 13
Armstrong, Lilian, 895
Arndt, Valerie, 1505
Arnett, David B, 1435
Arnold, Jack David, 379
Arnold, Rick, 1004
Aronowitz, Stanley, 306, 534
Aronson, Anne Louise, 1484
Artz, Sibylle, 1031
Arviz, Steven P., 1570
Ashburn, Elizabeth A., 1013
Ashworth, Mary, 1506
Ashworth, Thomas Edward, 944
Astuto, Terry, 1110
Athanases, Steven Z., 966
Atkins, J. D. C., 670
Atkinson, N., 414
Atwell, N., 1129
Atwill, Janet Marie, 14
Au, Terry Kit-fong, 760
Audoin-Rouzeau, Stephane, 878
Auer, J. Jeffrey, 372
Augustine, Catherine, 15
Austing, Patricia J., 1012
Auten, Janet Beghart, 16
Axtell, James, 967
Ayim, Maryann, 17
Ayres, Lioness, 961
Azuike, Macpherson Nkem, 18

Baber, Chris, 521
Badran, Margot, 181
Bagley, Carole, 380
Bailey, Francis W., 968

Bailey, Richard W., 659
Baily, Mary, 781
Baird, John R., 1031
Baird, Scott, 1135
Baker, Anna Belle, 566
Baker, Isabel MacDonald, 1180
Baker, James Wesley, 19
Baker, Melinda E., 1005
Baker, Nancy Westrich, 1583
Baldasty, Gerald J., 879
Baldwin, Dolly Langela Serreno, 1006
Ball, Arnetha Fay, 1125
Ballard, Brigid, 1598
Ballaster, Ros, 13
Ballaster, Rosalind, 224
Ballenger, Bruce, 1214
Bamberg, Betty, 1215
Bammer, Angelika, 176
Bammesberger, Alfred, 702
Barbour, Dennis H., 1301
Barclay, Rebecca O., 1395
Bardovi-Harlig, Kathleen, 86, 1507
Barker, Randolph T., 1302
Barker, Thomas T., 7
Barnes, Douglas, 1031, 1126
Barnes, Valerie, 1425
Barnett, George A., 1325
Baron, Dennis, 670, 1145
Barone, Thomas E., 836
Barrow, Dorian A., 1584
Barry, Peter, 329
Bartelt, Pearl W., 1152
Barth, R., 1444
Bartine, David, 637
Barton, B., 1456
Bartonsenki, Mary, 1051
Bartter, Martha, 660
Basham, Charlotte S., 1598
Bass, Jeff D., 372
Bates, Robin, 1436
Bathrick, David, 1145
Bator, Paul G., 195
Batschelet, Margaret, 1181
Batten, M. A., 873
Bauernschmidt, Mary Catherine, 1182
Bauman, J. F., 89
Baumlin, James S., 195
Baumlin, Tita French, 195
Bayani, Ruby, 1056
Bazerman, Charles, 56, 218, 1152
Beach, R., 89
Beach, Richard, 115, 968
Beale, Marjorie, 543

NAME INDEX

Beard, John D., 1326
Beck, Charles E., 1422
Beck, Christine, 138
Becker, Howard S., 836
Beckum, Leonard C., 1013
Beddoes, Julie A., 20
Begelow, W., 513
Begg, Ian Maynard, 782
Beichner, R. J., 1134
Bekken, John Everett, 1455
Belanger, Joe, 1007
Belanger, Kelly, 1303
Bell, Debbie, 1108
Bell, Jean, 1127
Bell, Marvin, 1444
Bellamy, Mary Louise, 1031
Belsey, Catherine, 567
Belz, Herman, 307
Bender, John, 80
Benedict, Helen, 880
Benedict, Susan, 1437
Benjamin, Andrew, 202
Bennett, Carla, 1041
Bennett, Tony, 567
Bennett, William J., 670
Benson, Beverly, 1183
Bentley, Roy, 1185
Benton, Lauren, 1485
Bereiter, Carl, 790
Beretta, Alan, 1503
Berger, Arthur Asa, 897
Berger, Eva, 824
Bergman, David, 570
Berkenkotter, C., 1456
Berkman, Dave, 881
Berkowitz, Leonard J., 1184
Berlin, James A., 21, 56, 218, 825
Bernhardt, Stephen A., 1327
Berry, Sarah, 913
Best, Felton, 568
Betz, Renee, 1585
Beverley, John, 181
Beynon, John, 382
Bhabha, Homi K., 80
Biber, Douglas, 22
Biesecker, Barbara A., 23
Bietila, S., 513
Billings, Philip, 1444
Bilmes, J., 210
Bird, Gloria Frances, 783
Bird, Tom, 1008
Birken, M., 34
Birken, Marcia, 1586

Birkerts, Sven, 1156
Bishop, J. L., 513
Bishop, Wendy, 24, 1009, 1038
Bizzaro, Patrick, 1444
Bizzell, Patricia, 222, 1128
Bjelic, D., 210
Black, Edwin, 25
Blake, N. F., 703
Blakesley, D., 1111
Blanchard, Margaret A., 308
Blankenship, Jane, 372
Blattner, Meera M., 381
Blau, Sheridan, 195
Blitz, Michael, 1108
Blomeyer, Robert L., Jr., 382
Bloo, David E., 670
Bloom, Lynn Z., 234
Bloome, David, 513, 968
Blyer, Nancy R., 1456
Blyler, Nancy Roundy, 1328, 1329
Boardman, Kathleen A., 1010
Bochard, Terrance H., 661
Bochner, Joseph, 1587
Boddy, Janice, 984
Bodroghkozy, Aniko, 913
Bogdan, Deanne, 569
Bolin, Anne, 1003
Bolter, Jay David, 383, 534
Bonfield, E. H., 551
Bonge, Dennis R., 784
Boninger, David Samuel, 785
Boon, James A., 176
Booth, Alan, 329
Border, Laura L. B., 826
Borgmann, Albert, 384
Boser, Judith A., 26
Boshoff, Phil, 1561
Bosley, Deborah S., 1330, 1331
Bosmajian, Haig A., 309
Boswell, John, 189
Boulding, Elise, 969
Bourgeois, Susan, 828
Bové, Paul, 592
Bowen, B. A., 1129
Bowlby, Rachel, 13
Bowles, George, 27
Bowman, C., 1111
Bowman, Michael S., 1438
Bown, Lalage, 385, 524
Boyd, Todd Edward, 223
Boyle, Craig, 386
Bracewell, R. J., 89
Braddock, R., 89

Braden, Gordon, 252
Bradford, Linda Burrell Henderson, 1457
Brand, Alice G., 1588, 1589
Brand, Dana, 567
Branham, Robert J., 372
Brannon, Lil, 1109
Branscombe, N. Amanda, 1129
Brant, Clare, 224
Brasefield, Marleen JoAnn, 310
Brashers, Dale, 138
Brathwaite, Richard, 985
Braun, L. A., 64
Brauner, Daniel J., 961
Brazee, P. E., 1437
Breivik, Patricia Senn, 1577
Brent, Doug, 638
Brent, Rebecca, 1458
Bretzer, Joanne, 670
Brewer, William, 157
Brezin, M. K., 89
Brickman, Bette, 1267
Bridwell-Bowles, Lillian, 28
Brinkman, Carolyn Ruth, 29
Brinton, Alan, 225
Briscoe, P. Annette, 311
Bristow, Joseph, 570
Britain, David, 662
Britton, James, 1129, 1152, 1439, 1508
Brock, Mark N., 494
Brockmann, John, 387
Brodersen, Lynn, 1052
Brodkey, Linda, 30, 218, 513, 968
Brogger, Fredrik Chr., 1509
Bromwich, David, 827
Brooke-Rose, Christine, 928
Brooks, Anne M., 226
Brose, Roselore, 768
Brossard, Nicole, 618
Broumas, Olga, 618
Brown, Andrew, 31
Brown, Carl R. V., 1440
Brown, Carlton E., 1013
Brown, Cynthia, 895
Brown, Joan, 970
Brown, JoAnne, 786
Brown, Judith K., 984
Brown, Julia, 1216
Brown, Juliet, 1217
Brown, Lady Falls, 388
Brown, R. A., 389
Brown, Richard, 329
Brown, Robert, 1216
Brown, Stuart C., 32, 56

Brown, Vincent Jay, 1332
Brunner, D. D., 1134
Brusaw, Charles T., 1324
Bryan, John, 1333
Bryant, Coralie, 571
Brydon, Steven R., 894
Brynes, Deborah A., 787
Buckley, Cozetta W., 1013
Buckley, William K., 828
Buckrop, Jacquelyn Jo, 312
Bullough, Robert V., 1011
Bunge, Robert, 670
Burchfield, Robert, 663
Burgchardt, Carl R., 313
Burgess, Tony, 1508
Burke, Bev, 1004
Burke, C. J., 794
Burleson, Brant R., 33
Burnett, R. E., 1456
Burnett, Rebecca E., 1334
Burnham, Christopher C., 56, 1130
Burnier, DeLysa, 372
Burnley, David, 703
Burns, Hugh, 425, 428
Burns, Teresa, 572
Burris, James F., 945
Burtis, P. J., 790
Burton, Barry W., 1335
Busemeyer, Jerome R., 788
Bushman, Donald E., 227
Buss, Helen M., 596
Butler, Sydney J., 1185
Butterfield, Earl C., 1428, 1429
Bynum, Joyce, 664

Caernarven-Smith, Patricia, 1336
Cain, Mary Ann, 1053
Cairns, Francis, 617
Calderón, José, 670
Caldwell, Larry W., 1105
Calero-Breckeimer, Ayxa, 640
Cameron, Deborah, 665, 666, 778
Cameron, S. M., 513
Camille, Michael, 895
Camp, Roberta, 1634
Campbell, Charles C., 1337
Campbell, Elizabeth Humphreys, 1218
Campbell, J. Louis, III, 314
Campbell, JoAnn, 228, 1131
Campoy, Renee, 829
Capossela, Toni-Lee, 34, 1132
Cárdenas, José, A., 670
Carey, Linda, 218

NAME INDEX

Carino, Peter, 1054
Carlberg, Judith, 1048
Carliner, Saul, 1643
Carlisle, Lenore R., 1437
Carlisle, Robert, 1598
Carlson, Sybil B., 1598
Carlton, Susan Brown, 35
Carpenter, Bob, 711
Carpenter, Thomas W., 1186
Carrell, Patricia L., 1573
Carroll, Jeffrey, 52, 1106
Carruthers, Peter H., 923
Carse, Wendy, 1315
Carson, Jay, 1459
Carson, Joan G., 1511
Carter, Dundan, 1644
Carter, Kathy, 1031
Carter, Nancy Carson, 573
Carter, Robin, 372
Carver, Craig M., 720
Casari, Laura E., 7
Casbergue, Reneé, 1012
Casey, Kenneth Stewart, 229
Casmir, Fred L., 897
Castellano, Mariso, 1194
Castellanos, Diego, 670
Castillo, Debra A., 181
Castillo-Velez, Clara Maria, 789
Castle, Terry, 570
Castro, Max, 670
Catherwood, Vince, 1508
Caucci, Frank, 828
Cavazza, Marc, 1055
Cazden, C., 1129
Cazden, Courtney B., 390
Ceccio, Joseph, 1338
Celce-Murcia, Marianne, 1512
Center, Candy, 138
Cercy, Steven P., 813
Cervetti, Nancy, 315
Cervi, David, 775
Chadwick, Carol Susan, 1219
Chaffee, Steven H., 897
Chakraborty, Goutam, 544
Chalmers, Hero, 224
Chamberlain, Lori, 202
Chan, Carol K. K., 790
Chaney, Lillian H., 1310
Chapman, David W., 1133
Chapman, Iris Thompson, 1187
Chapman, Simon, 916
Charney, Davida H., 1304, 1339
Charon, Rita, 946

Chase, Dorothy Rhea, 1220
Cheema, Indra, 810
Chen, Chien-ping, 1513
Chen, Edward M., 670
Cherem, Barbara F. Brown, 1486
Cherry, Roger D., 218
Cheshire, Jenny, 667
Chester, Suzanne, 181
Chetin, Sara, 574
Cheung, Anthony, 494
Chevillet, François, 1514
Chi, Wei-Jan, 575
Chiaro, Delia, 882
Child, Abigail, 618
Child, Paul William, 947
Chin, Elaine, 883
Chin, Philip C., 1013
Chiseri-Strater, E., 1654
Chisholm, William, 668
Chism, Nancy Van Note, 826
Chismar, Connie, 1242
Chizzone, Nick, 1101
Choi, Jung Min, 727
Chong, Siat-May, 1149
Chow, Mayling, 830
Christiano, David, 966
Christy, Daniel Merton, 669
Chrysostom, Dio, 230
Church, Kenneth, 711
Church, S. M., 513
Cilengir, Erika N., 1340
Cincik, Elena, 144
Cirkesena, M. Kathryn, 36
Civikly, Jean M., 831
Cixous, Hélène, 576
Claggett, Fran, 970
Clairborne, Gay Don, 37
Clanchy, John, 1598
Clancy, Patricia, 832
Clandinin, D. Jean, 1031
Clare, Janet, 329
Clark, Anne, 391
Clark, Cecily, 702, 703
Clark, Christopher M., 836
Clark, David, 1110
Clark, J. Milton, 1601
Clark, Kate, 772
Clark, Lorraine, 828
Clark, Timothy, 924
Clay, Diskin, 231
Clemson, Shelley, 1013
Clery, Carolsue, 1578
Clewell, Suzanne, 391

Clifford, J., 64
Clyde, J. A., 873
Cochran, Cynthia, 89
Cochran-Smith, Marilyn, 1129, 1012
Cohen, Akiba A., 897
Cohen, Elizabeth, 596
Cohen, Gillian 1590
Cohen, Judith Beth, 1156
Cohen, Judith, 1211
Cohen, L. Jonathan, 925
Cohen, Michael, 1444
Cohen, Thomas V., 596
Cohen, Walter, 80
Cohn, Marilyn, 1110
Cohn, Victor, 948
Cole, Marian, 1341
Cole, Sally, 596
Cole, Thomas, 231
Coleman, Hywel, 1503
Coleman, I., 1129
Coles, E. K. Townsend, 524
Coles, William E., Jr., 38
Collecott, Diana, 570
Collett, Jonathan, 826
Colletta, W. John, 1342
Collignon, Francine Filipek, 1515
Collins, James L., 1134
Collins, Marian, 1135
Combs, James E., 353
Combs, Mary Carol, 670
Comley, Nancy R., 91, 1111
Comprone, Joseph J., 175, 1221, 1456
Condon, M. W. F., 873
Condon, William, 392
Condravy, Joan C., 39
Coney, Mary B., 1343, 1344
Conley, Tom, 202
Connet, Caroline, 378
Connor, Ulla, 1516, 1598
Connors, Robert J., 115, 218
Constantino, Roselyn, 971
Constas, Mark A., 833
Conte, Gian Biagia, 231
Conway, Martin A., 1590
Cook, L., 513
Cook, Linda Anne McFerrin, 232
Cook, William W., 577
Cook-Gumperz, Jenny, 968
Cook-McEachern, Kelly, 1095
Cooke, Nathalie, 596
Coon, A. C., 34
Cooper, Charles R., 1152, 1441
Cooper, Thomas W., 897

Coppinger, Stanley K., 1188
Corbett, Edward P. J., 428, 1039
Corder, J. W., 56
Corrada, Baltasar, 670
Corson, Gail Shanley, 1222
Cortazzi, Martin, 972
Cosgrove, Cornelius, 1591
Couch, Lezlie Laws, 1292
Coulliard, Ted V., 393
Councell, R. T., 1437
Counts, Dorothy Ayers, 984
Courtright, Jeffrey Lee, 316
Couture, Barbara, 1345, 1346
Covington, Martin V., 834
Covino, William A., 233
Cox, Earnest, 1056
Cox, Gary N., 394
Crain, Stephen, 711
Crane, Gwen Ellen, 578
Crawford, Emily, 545
Crawford, James, 670
Crew, Louie, 1347
Crigler, Ann N., 903
Crisp, Sally, 1056
Crockett, T., 1437
Croft, Mary, 1057
Cronin, John Joseph, 546
Crook, Bernard, 1348
Crossland, Donna, 1056
Crosswhite, James, 40
Crow, Gary M., 973
Crow, Nedra A., 1011
Crowder, Robert G., 639
Crowe, Chris, 1012
Crowley, Tony, 671, 778
Crump, Eric, 1058, 1059, 1060
Crusius, Timothy W., 218, 926
Cullen, Roxanne, 1061
Culler, Johnathan, 928, 1145
Culley, Margo, 234
Cumming, Alister, 1517, 1636
Cummins, Catherine L., 1423
Cunningham, Mary Elizabeth, 1637
Curry, Jerome M., 1349
Curtis, Marcia, 395, 428
Czapla, Pamela, 884

D'Acci, Julie, 913
D'Ammassa, Algernon, 672
D'Angelo, Frank, 41, 42
D'Aoust, Catherine, 1634
D'Souza, Patricia Veasey, 399
Dahl, Karin L., 1012

NAME INDEX

Dahl, Veronica, 711
Damasio, Antonio R., 791
Damasio, Hanna, 791
Daniell, Beth, 43
Danis, M. Francine, 1442
Dansereau, Donald F., 89, 847
Darling, George J., 1223
Darling-Hammond, Linda, 1110
Das, S. K., 1508
Dasenbrock, R. W., 56
Dasenbrock, Reed Way, 91
Datan, Nancy, 984
Daughton, Suzanne Marie, 44.
Davenport, Doris, 1108
David, D. L., 1134
David, Vincent A., 1483
Davidson, Arnold, 189
Davidson, Fred, 1598
Davies, Carole Boyce, 181
Davis, Alan J., 673
Davis, Charles, 252
Davis, Diana, 1508
Davis, Dona Lee, 1003
Davis, Hayley G., 778
Davis, Judith Rae, 1224
Davis, Kevin, 1062, 1579
Davis, Robert Con, 45, 91
Davy, George Alan, 46
Dawkins, John, 674
Day, Robert A., 1350
Dayan, Daniel, 885
de Asua, Miguel J. C., 235
de Romilly, Jacqueline, 236
Dean, Sharon L., 579
Deetz, Stanley A., 547, 1041
Degan, James N., 1443
Deitrich, Margaret A., 1012
Delamaramo, Mark James, 396
Delamont, Sara, 974
DelFattore, Joan, 317
Delgado-Gaitan, Concha, 835
Demarest, Jack, 548
Deming, Mary, 1183
Deming, Robert H., 913
Dempsey, John V., 460
Dennet, Joann Temple, 1351
Denzer, Debra, 1183
Denzin, Norman K., 975
Descutner, David, 372
Deshpande, Shekhar A., 580
Despain, LaRene, 1592
Devet, Bonnie, 1063
Devine, Joanne, 1561

Devitt, Amy J., 1136
Diamond, Arlyn, 234
Diamondstone, J., 1129
Dias, Patrick, 1137
Diaz-Rico, Lynne T., 1518
DiCamilla, Frederick Joseph, 47
Dickstein, Morris, 48
Didacus, Jules, 524
Diederich, P., 873
Dienst, Richard Welton, 581
Dilena, M., 414
Dillard, Jill, 1012
Dillon, George L., 218, 772
Dilworth, Mary E., 1013
Dinkler, Pamela Diane, 1225
DiPardo, Anne Louise, 1064, 1189
DiPiero, Thomas, 176
Dixon, Kathleen Grace, 49
Dobie, Ann B., 1201
Dobson, Lee, 830
Doe, J., 873
Doheny-Farina, Stephen, 218, 1352
Dolan, Catherine Rae, 1353
Dolinsky, Kaaren, 1226
Dollimore, Jonathan, 570
Dombrowski, Paul M., 1354, 1355
Donelson, Ken, 1012
Donmoyer, Robert, 836
Donougho, Martin, 176
Donovan, Brian R., 237
Dorczah, Anita, 582
Dorner, Jane, 397
Dornsife, Robert Stewart, Jr., 1227
Dorwick, Keith, 398
Doughty, Catherine, 494
Dow, Bonnie J., 886
Dragga, Sam, 1356
Drain, Susan, 1107
Draper, Jamie B., 670
Draper, Virginia, 976
Drayton, Kathleen, 1508
Dreher, Mariam Jean, 391
Dresher, B. Elan, 711
Drexler, Susan, 966
Drummond-Thompson, Phil, 1593
Du Bosc, Jacques, 985
Ducey, Mary K., 927
Dufficy, P., 414
Dugan, Penelope Ann, 50
Dugan, Penelope, 1487
Duin, Ann Hill, 400
Duke, Charles R., 1444
Dulek, Ronald E., 1305

Dunkel, Patricia, 494, 1573
Dunlap, Louise, 1152
Dunn, Francis M., 231
Dunn, Patricia Ann, 1190
Dunn, Patricia, 1645
Durst, Russel K., 1012
Dynes, Wayne R., 189
Dyson, Anne Haas, 401

Earl, Elizabeth Noel, 318
Echevarriarza, Maria Paz, 999
Eco, Umberto, 928
Ede, Lisa, 51, 115
Edelsky, Carole, 402
Edelstein, Arnold, 52
Ediger, Marlow, 1138, 1139
Edlund, John R., 53
Edmond, White Eugene, 54
Edmunds, Sheila, 895
Edwards, Derek, 792
Edwards, Viv, 667
Ehrlich, Susan, 678
Eichhorn, Jill, 55
Eidelberg, Paul, 793
Eiler, Mary Ann, 403
Eimers, Nancy, 1444
Eisenberg, Anne, 319, 949, 1357
Eisenhart, Margaret A., 94, 1003
Eisner, Eliot W., 836
El-Shiyab, Said, 1519
Elbow, Peter, 1638
Eldred, J. Carey, 428
Ellis, John, 567
Ellsworth, Elizabeth, 124
Elman, Sandra E., 1040
Elmes-Crahall, Jane Matilda, 320
Enders, Jody, 238, 239
Endicott, Phyllis Stevens, 1065
Engber, Cheryl Ann, 1520
Engel, B. S., 1129
Engeldinger, Eugene A., 1394
Englert, Carol Sue, 1191
Enos, Richard Leo, 56, 218, 240
Enos, Theresa, 56
Enright, Louisa, 1228
Enstein, Dan, 913
Enzenberger, Hans M., 404
Epps, Garrett, 321
Epstein, Julia, 1358
Epstein, Noel, 670
Epstein, Steven, 189
Eribon, Didier, 57
Erickson, G., 1031

Esch, Deborah, 80
Esling, John H., 494
Estes, W. K., 794
Evans, Richard Allen, 405
Ewell, Barbara C., 91
Ewen, Stuart, 887
Ewing, Sheila C., 1634

Faerm, Elizabeth, 1066
Fagan, William T., 406
Fairclough, Norman, 679
Farghal, Mohammed, 1521
Farinacci, Suzanne, 782
Farmer, Frank Marion, 58
Farmer, Vernon, 1646
Farnan, Nancy, 1140
Farnham, Mary L., 420
Farooq, Nishat, 1483
Farrell, Eileen, 1156
Farrell, Pam, 1067
Farris, Christine, 1472
Farris, Sara, 55
Farrow, Steve, 778
Fassinger, Polly A., 1460
Faust, Mark A., 583, 654
Favre, Betty Atkinson, 1461
Fayne, Francis Augustine, Jr., 1488
Feathers, Karen M., 1012
Fecho, R., 1129
Feeney, D. C., 617
Feenstra, Robert, 252
Fehlman, Richard E., 888
Felder, Richard M., 1458
Feldman, Ann Matsuhashi, 968
Feldman, Tony, 407
Fellows, Nancy Jane, 1462
Fennick, Ruth McLennan, 59
Ferguson, Frances, 80
Ferrara, Kathleen, 60
Ferreira, Leonardo, 897
Ferreira-Buckley, Linda, 1304
Ferry, Christopher Joseph, 61
Fiedler, Klaus, 760
Fielden, John S., 1313
Figg, Kristen, 1229
Figueroa, John, 770
Files, J., 873
Fillmore, Lily Wong, 670
Finders, Margaret, 1141
Fine, Leslie Marie, 549
Finegan, Edward, 720, 1145
Fingeret, Hanna Arlene, 408
Fink, Conrad C., 1463

NAME INDEX

Fink, Steven, 241
Fiorella, Claudia, 362
Firbas, Jan, 680
Fischel, Anne Beth, 584
Fischer, Claude S., 242
Fischer, Gerhard, 409
Fischer, Olga, 703
Fisher, Philip, 80
Fishman, Joshua A., 670, 681
Fishman, Stephen M., 1152
Fishman, Steve, 1014
Fisk, Mary Lou, 1306
Fitz, Chad, 1056
Five, Cora Lee, 1012
Flammia, Madelyn, 410
Fleckenstein, Kristie S., 1293
Fletcher, John, 570
Fletcher, Ralph, 1142
Flexo, Scott W., 322
Flitterman-Lewis, Sandy, 913
Flood, David H., 950
Flood, James, 1140
Floriak, M., 89
Flower, Linda, 56, 218
Flowerdew, John, 1522
Flynn, Elizabeth A., 91
Flynn, Thomas Richard, 62
Fodor, Janet Dean, 711
Fontaine, Sheryl I., 63
Forbes, Ella, 323
Forman, Janis, 64
Forston, Maureen Tyson, 795
Fortune, Alan, 1523
Fortune, Ron, 411, 428
Foster, David, 65
Foster, Gavin, 191
Foto, Sandra Sims, 682
Foucault, Michel, 189
Fowler, Judy, 7
Fox, Thomas, 412
Frager, Alan M., 1012
Frances, Christie, 683
Francis, Gill, 772
Franklin, Benjamin, 670
Fraser, Kay Losey, 1194
Fraser, Rebecca Jean, 1143
Frazer, Elizabeth, 666
Freed, R. C., 1456
Freedenberg, Philip, 514
Freedman, Sarah Warshauer, 89, 401
Freeman, David E., 1524
Freeman, Yvonne S., 1524
Freidus, Helen, 1015

Fremer, John, 1594
French, Martha Stone, 413
Freudenstein, Reinhold, 1525
Frick, Jane, 1068
Friedman, Rachelle Elaine, 324
Fries, Peter, 684
Fritsch, Kilian Joseph, 796
Frost, Richard, 897
Fu, D. L., 1654
Fukuchi, Isamu, 66
Fulkerson, R., 56
Fulwiler, L., 873
Fulwiler, Toby, 1144, 1152, 1294
Funk, J. L., 89
Furniss, Elaine, 414
Furrow, Melissa, 685

Gaarder, A. Bruce, 670
Gadamer, Hans-Georg, 67
Gadbow, Kate, 1069
Gaillet, Lynee Lewis, 243
Gale, Frederic Gordon, 325
Gall, Sharon Nelson-Le, 847
Gallager, Tess, 1444
Gallego, Margaret A., 433
Gallegos, Bernardo P., 837
Gambell, Trevor, 1508
Gamber, Cayo, 585, 1048
Gannett, Cinthia, 68
Garbowsky, Maryanne, 1070
Gardiner, Michael Edward, 69
Gardner, Peter, 1445
Garfield, E., 1129
Garfinkel, H., 210
Garfinkle, Robert J., 504
Garibaldi, Antoine M., 1013
Garner, Jeanette, 548
Garrison, Dee, 965
Garrison, James W., 1017
Gaskins, Jake, 1071
Gates, Henry Louis, Jr., 80, 1145
Gawron, Mark, 711
Gearhart, Kyle Anne, 1359
Gearhart, Suzanne, 592
Gee, J. P., 513
Geisler, Cheryl, 70
Geisler-Brenstein, Elke, 813
Gelb, Richard G., 415
Geok-lin Lim, Shirley, 234
Geonetta, Sam, 7
George, Diana, 1446
George-Castagna, Susan, 686
Gerbner, George, 889

Gere, A. R., 64
Gergen, Constance A., 1557
Gergits, Julia M., 1230
Gervasi, Anne, 71
Gessey, Patricia A., 72
Getman, Julius, 1117
Ghosh, Sanjukta Tultul, 586
Gibaldi, Joseph, 1145
Gibbons, Pamela A., 760
Gibson, Carolyn M., 416
Gibson, Michelle, 1595
Gibson, Walker, 326
Gilbert, David, 1231
Gilbert, Frederick, 1360
Gilbert, Michael A., 73
Gilbert, Ron, 687
Gilbertson, Michael K., 111, 1374
Gilder, Eric, 74
Gill, Jaswinder, 1517
Gillam, Alice M., 75
Gilles, Roger Wayne, 891
Gillespie, Patti Peete, 1041
Gillett, Grant, 929
Gilliland, Nancy, 1460
Gillmor, Donald M., 327
Gilmore, L., 513
Ginzberg, Carlo, 567
Giovanini, Maureen J., 1003
Giroux, Henry A., 76, 513, 838, 839, 840, 1108
Gitelman, Lisa Louise, 1361
Givon, Talmy, 688
Glaim, Marilyn, 587
Glushko, Robert J., 417
Godden, Malcolm R., 702
Goetz, Ernest T., 640
Goggin, M. Daly, 56
Gold, Alex, 1156
Gold, Barbara K., 231
Gold, Sue Ellen, 1634
Golden, Joanne M., 968
Golding, Sue, 930
Goldstein, Robert J., 329
Gollnick, Donna M., 1013
Gonzales, Félix Rodriguez, 689
Gonzalez, Andrew B., 1508
Gonzalez, Norma, 690
Goodell, Elizabeth, 77
Goodman, Marcia Renee, 1146
Goodnight, G. Thomas, 372
Goodwin, David, 244
Goold, G. P., 617
Goozé, Marjanne E., 892
Gorak, Kathleen S., 400

Gordon, Ann D., 234
Gordon, Barbara Elizabeth, 78
Gordon, Christie Marie, 1016
Gordon, Claire M., 1626
Gordon, Randall A., 1639
Gordon, Sallie, 418
Gore, Jennifer, 124
Gorrell, Nancy, 1012
Gosden, Hugh, 1526
Goswami, Dixie, 1129
Goubil-Gabrell, Patricia, 1362
Goul, Michael, 496
Gould, Christopher, 1596, 1640
Gould, Janice, 181
Gowen, Sheryl Greenwood, 419
Gozzi, Raymond, Jr., 691, 692, 693, 897
Grabowski, Barbara L., 519
Graesser, Arthur C., 968
Graff, Gerald, 80, 828, 1145
Grafton, A. T., 252
Graham, Joan, 1472
Graham, Kathryn, 1232
Graham, Keith, 931
Graham, Robert Joe, 588
Grandgenett, Neal, 420
Grant, Damian, 329
Grant-Davie, Keith, 115
Graumann, Carl F., 760
Graves, Darlene Richards, 589
Graves, Donald H., 1654
Graves, Roger Charles W., 1147
Gray, Nancy, 79
Green, Judith L., 968
Green, Pamela, 414
Green, Stuart, 641
Greenberg, Bradley S., 897
Greenberg, James D., 826
Greenberg, Joseph H., 694
Greenberg, Karen, 1655
Greenberger, R., 1129
Greenblatt, Stephen, 80
Greenburg, Karen L., 1597
Greene, Brenda, 1192
Greene, Maxine, 124
Greenhalgh, Anne M., 81
Greenia, George D., 1464
Greenwald, Marilyn Sue, 245
Greenwood, Claudia M., 1111, 1363
Greer, Jane, 1303
Greetham, D. C., 1145
Gregg, Noel, 1201
Greig, Flora Estella Ramírez, 695
Grenier, Gilles, 670

NAME INDEX

Greve, Janis, 234
Gribbons, William M., 1364
Grider, Daryl, 1388
Griffin, Jasper, 252
Griffith, Kevin, 1233, 1295
Griggs, Kenneth A., 421
Grimm, Nancy, 1072
Grossman, Pamela, 1110
Grossvogel, David I., 877
Grudin, Johntan, 409
Grumet, Madeline R., 836
Guba, Egon, 836
Guderian, Gregory Joseph, 246
Guest, Harriet, 13
Gugino, Vincent F., 247
Guice, Stephen, 1319
Guignon, Charles, 176
Guista, Michael, 1234
Gummer, P., 414
Gumperz, John J., 968
Gundlach, Robert, 968
Gunn, Giles, 80, 932, 1145
Gunn, Janet Varner, 181
Gunn, John, 720
Gurak, Laura J., 422
Gurman, Ernest B., 797
Gustafson, Thomas, 248
Gutmann, David, 984
Guy, Gregory, 670

Haas, Christina, 89, 218
Haas, Lynda, 841
Habinek, Thomas N., 231
Hachten, Harva, 893
Hachten, William A., 893
Hackett, Helen, 224
Hacking, Ian, 189
Hadaway, Nancy L., 977
Haefner, Joel, 82, 590
Hager, Peter J., 1365
Hain, Bonnie A., 828
Hairston, Maxine, 1235
Hajduk, Thomas, 89
Hak, T., 210
Hakuta, Kenji, 670
Halasek, Kay, 195
Hale, S., 873
Haley, Darryl, 1056
Halimah, Ahmad Mustafa, 1527
Halio, Marcia Peoples, 423
Hall, Jacquelyn Dowd, 965
Hallin, Annika, 249
Halloran, S. M., 56

Halsey, A. H., 842
Hamalainen, Matti, 1148
Hamant, Sharon, 1193
Hamburger, Henry, 711
Hamilton, David L., 760
Hamilton-Wieler, Sharon, 1236
Hammersley, Martyn, 978
Hammett, R. F., 513
Hamp-Lyons, Liz, 1598
Hampton, Sally, 218
Handa, C., 1134
Handel, Ruth D., 424
Haney, Steve, 425
Hannah, Charles Austin, 1599
Hannah, Matthew Gordon, 83
Hansen, Edmund, 1149
Hansen, J., 1654
Hanus, Karen, 391
Haralovich, Mary Beth, 913
Harding, Wendy, 250
Haring-Smith, Tori, 1472
Harkin, Patricia, 426
Harlin, Rebecca, 84
Harmon, Joseph H., 1366
Haro, Paz, 999
Harper, Yolanda Y., 784
Harrington, Helen L., 1017
Harrington, Hugh J., 847
Harris, Bruce, 1609
Harris, Elizabeth Ann, 427
Harris, Joseph, 642, 1237
Harris, Muriel, 85, 1472
Harris, Neil, 567
Harris, R. A., 1367
Harris, Roy, 778
Harrison, Colin, 494
Harrison, Viola May, 979
Harry, Beth, 843
Harryman, Carla, 618
Harste, Jerome C., 643, 844, 845, 846, 980, 1447
Hart, Ellen Louise, 1108
Hartford, Beverly, 86
Hartley, James, 798
Hartling-Clarck, J., 513
Hartman, Sandee L., 951
Harvey, Penelope, 666
Harwayne, Shelley, 1448
Hashim, Safaa, 1148
Hastert, Marie Paule, 772
Haswell, Richard H., 1600
Hatch, Gary Layne, 87, 1580
Haugen, Einar, 670
Haviland, Carol Peterson, 1065, 1601

Hawcroft, Michael, 591
Hawisher, Gail E., 425, 428
Hawryluk, Paul, 88
Hayakawa, S. I., 670
Hayes, John R., 89, 218, 968
Hayes, Karen, 55
Haynes-Burton, Cynthia, 1073
Hays, Michael, 592
Healy, Dave, 1150
Healy, Mary K., 1012, 1129
Heap, James L., 210, 968
Heard, G., 1437
Heath, Christian, 1151
Heath, Shirley Brice, 89, 513, 670, 1129, 1528
Heath, Stephen, 567
Heck, Jim, 514
Hedden, Chet, 429
Heeter, Carrie, 897
Hegler, Barbara Finley, 593
Heilker, Paul, 90
Heim, Kathleen M., 1492
Heinlen, Michael, 895
Hejinian, Lyn, 618
Helgerson, Richard, 328
Hellinga, Lotte, 895
Hellweg, Susan A., 894
Helyar, Pamela S., 1368
Henderson, Sarah A., 1238
Henke, Linda, 873
Henkelman, James, 1013
Hennesy, C. Margot, 234
Henning, Grant, 1598
Henricksen, Bruce, 91
Henry, David, 361
Henry, Jim, 218
Hensel, William A., 952
Henton, Caroline, 778
Hepler, Molly, 425, 430
Hernandez, Adriana, 55
Herrington, Anne J., 218, 1152
Hertz-Lazarowitz, Rachel, 847
Herwitt, Richard M., 696
Herzberg, B., 1456
Hesford, Wendy S., 981
Hess, John David, 594
Hesse, Doug, 92, 431
Hester, S., 210
Heynen, Jim, 1444
Hickman, J., 1437
Hicks, Deborah, 697
Hickson, Mark, 1041
Higham, John, 670
Hikins, James W., 922

Hilgers, Thomas L., 1152 , 1592, 1647
Hill, Charles, 1239
Hill, D. E., 617
Hill, Elizabeth F., 1529
Hillocks, George, Jr., 89, 968
Hilton, Chadwick B., 1313
Hindman, Jane E., 1240
Hindman, Sandra, 895
Hinkel, Eli, 1530
Hinz, Evelyn J., 596
Hirst, Graeme, 493
Hitchens, Christopher, 698
Hobbes, Renne, 897
Hobson, Eric H., 1074, 1075
Hockey, Susan, 432
Hoff, Katharine T., 1465
Hoff, Lee Ann, 1003
Hoffman, Amy, 1241
Hoffman, Gregg, 699, 700, 701
Hoffman, Regina M., 93
Hogg, Richard M., 702, 703
Hoh, Pau-san, 704
Holcomb, Phillip J., 802
Holian, Gail C., 1242
Holladay, Sylvia A., 1602
Holland, Dorothy C., 94, 1003
Holleman, Marsha Cline, 1382
Holleman, Warren Lee, 1382
Holliday, William G., 1369
Hollingsworth, Sarah, 433
Hollis, Karyn L., 1018
Holmes, Janet, 95
Holsapple, Clyde W., 1148
Holt, Elizabeth Jane, 705
Holt, Mara, 96, 175
Holub, Robert C., 97
Holubec, Edythe Johnson, 1108
Holyoak, Keith J., 819
Holzer, Jenny, 618
Hon, David, 434
Honda, Charlotte, 1152
Honey, Margaret, 474
Hong, Chua Seok, 1508
Hopper, Robert, 706
Horko, Hilda, 1031
Horn, Susanna, 1076
Horner, Bruce, 98, 99
Horner, Winifred Bryan, 251
Horowitz, Daniel, 1598
Horton, John, 670
Horton, M. S., 64
Hovey, Kenneth Alan, 828
Howe, Kenneth R., 848

NAME INDEX

Howell, Charles, 100
Hoy, Pat C., II., 1156
Huagh, Jane, 391
Hubbard, Philip, 494
Huberman, A. Michael, 836
Huckin, Thomas N., 115, 1456
Huddleston, Walter, 670
Hudson-Ross, S., 1134
Hudspeth, LeLayne, 435
Huenecke, Dorothy, 436
Hughes, Jannese, 644
Hull, Glynda, 437, 1194
Hult, Christine, 1019, 1648
Hunsaker, Linda, 1020
Hunt, James M., 551
Hunt, R. A., 89
Hunt, Russell, 968
Hunter, Barbara, 380
Hunter, John O., 438
Hunter, Kathryn Montgomery, 953
Hunter, Susan, 645
Huot, Brian, 1466
Hur, Young, 439
Hurlbert, C. Mark, 1108
Hurst, Marietta, 830
Hutchings, Pat, 1021
Hutson, Lorna, 13, 224
Hutton, Christopher, 778
Hwang, Hae Jin, 1531
Hyde, Michael J., 922
Hyland, Fiona, 1153
Hyland, Ken, 1153
Hyland, Paul, 329
Hynds, Susan, 968
Hytheker, V. I., 89

Iaumsupanimit, Somchit, 101
Iddings, James Henry, 595
Ide, Richard S., 1243
Ihle, Elizabeth L., 849
Iltis, Robert S., 330
Imel, Susan, 1489
Imperia, Giovanna, 542
Inch, Edward Spencer, 331
Inglehart, Ronald F., 670
Ingram, David, 175
Inkster, Robert P., 1244
Irizarry, Estelle, 440, 441
Irvine, Jacqueline Jordan, 1013
Irving, Katrina Mary, 102
Isaacs, Harold R., 670

Jablonski, John Jesse, 103
Jackson, Alan, 1245

Jackson, Philip W., 836
Jackson, Ronald, 1468
Jackson, Rosemary F., 1197
Jacobsen, Cheryl, 104
Jacobsen, Pauline, 711
Jacobsen, Sally A., 1444
Jacobson, Karen Hallinan, 1195
Jacquemond, Richard, 202
Jaffe, Gloria, 653
James, Carl, 1004
James, Paige, 1056
Jamieson, Kathleen Hall, 332
Jandt, Fred E., 1041
Janks, Hilary, 1508
Janopoulos, Michael, 1603, 1604
Jansen, Carel, 1370
Jansen, Louise, 494
Jarratt, Susan C., 55
Jasinski, James, 372
Jefferson, Debrah J., 826
Jenks, C. K., 1437
Jenkyns, Richard, 252
Jensen, George H., 175, 176
Jensen, Marilyn D., 1246
Jensen, Richard J., 333
Jenseth, R., 34
Jewell, Cora Mae, 1532
Jhappan, Carol Radha, 334
Jiménez, Martha, 670
Johannessen, Larry R., 1467
Johns, Ann, 1598
Johns, Frances A., 1371
Johns, Jerry L., 1630
Johnson, Alex, 1156
Johnson, David W., 847, 1108
Johnson, Deborah K., 372
Johnson, Donna M., 105, 1533
Johnson, Eric, 442
Johnson, Iris W., 1302
Johnson, Karen E., 1534
Johnson, Linda L., 1460
Johnson, M. K., 253
Johnson, Nan, 1508
Johnson, Robert Ralph, 443
Johnson, Roger T., 847, 1108
Johnson, Victoria Rae, 896
Johnson, Wendell, 106
Johnson, Yvonne, 982
Johnson-Eilola, Johndan, 444
Johnston, John, 176, 202
Johnston, Marilyn, 1020
Johnston, Mark D., 254
Johnston, P., 1129

Jolliffe, David A., 218
Jolliffe, Lee, 707
Jones, Daniel R., 7
Jones, Joan, 1468
Jones, Kevin T., 335
Jones, L., 34
Jones, Margaret C., 828
Jordan, Elaine, 13
Joseph, R., 799
Jowett, Garth S., 552
Joyce, Michael, 445
Joyrich, Lynne, 913
Juhasz, Alexandra Jeanne, 954
Junge, Maxine Borowshy, 800
Just, Marion R., 903

Kable, June, 1041
Kachru, Braj B., 720
Kadar, Marlene, 596
Kahn, Elizabeth A. 1467
Kahn, Russell L., 446
Kaid, Lynda Lee, 553
Kale, J., 414
Kamil, Michael L., 968
Kanevsky, Rhoda, 697
Kanneh, Kadiatu, 13
Kantor, Victor, 1156
Kaplan, Andrew, 255
Kaplan, Caren, 181
Karls, Elaine, 871
Karolides, Nicholas J., 597
Karseno, Arief, 554
Kassebaum, Karen, 1052
Kastovsky, Dieter, 702
Katrathanos, Patricia, 1372
Katz, Elihu, 885
Katz, Yaacov J., 447
Kaufer, D. S., 428
Kaufert, Patricia A., 984
Kaufman, John A., 1041
Kay, Carol, 592
Kazmierczak, J., 1129
Kean, Mary-Louise, 711
Keane, Ellen, 1077
Keith, William, 1373
Keithley, Zoe, 1196, 1605
Kelb, Barbara Jeanne, 107
Kellner, Douglas, 555
Kellner, Hans, 175
Kellogg, Ronald T., 801
Kelly, Kathleen Ann, 1154
Kelly, Rebecca S., 1651
Kemp, Fred, 448

Kemp, Leroy, 1022
Kenkel, James M., 708
Kennedy, George A., 252
Kennedy, X. J., 1444
Kent, Thomas, 933, 1456
Kenway, Jane, 124
Kern, Richard G., 983
Kernan, Jerome B., 551
Kerns, Virginia, 984
Keroes, Jo, 1155
Kerr, Nancy H., 1247
Kerr, Paul, 567
Kerridge, Richard, 329
Kerrigan, William, 80
Keyes, Cheryl, 108
Keyes, D. E., 1129
Kibler, Thelma, 1012
Kiefer, Kate, 449, 1606
Kiger, Gary, 787
Kilbourn, Brent, 1031
Killeen, John, 1508
Killingsworth, M. Jimmie, 109, 110, 111, 112, 1374, 1417
Kim, Tong-Sik, 934
Kincaid, J. Peter, 653
King, Barbara J., 984
King, Estelle, 862
King, Nancy M. P., 955
King, Nathalia, 256
King, Ruth, 678
Kingston, Maxine Hong, 598
Kinney, Marjory Ann, 1469
Kintgen, Eugene R., 772
Kipling, Kim J., 1470
Kirby, John R., 113
Kirby, John T., 114
Kirch, Ann, 1248
Kirk, David, 450
Kirkman, John, 1375
Kirkus, Valerie Benveniste, 847
Kirsch, Gesa, 115
Kirscht, Judith, 991
Kistenberg, Cindy J. 1438
Kleifgen, Jo Anne, 1535
Klein, Diane, 1449
Klein, Joan Larsen, 985
Kleine, Michael, 175
Klem, E., 428
Kliebard, Herbert M., 850
Kline, Nancy, 1156
Klonoski, Edward, 451
Knechel, Sharon, 847
Kneeshaw, David, 1634

NAME INDEX

Knoblauch, C. H., 176, 851, 1109
Knopp, Sherron E., 570
Knotts, Lester William, 452
Knowles, J. Gary, 1011
Knudsen, Jennifer, 1110
Kobayashi, Junko, 1536
Kobayashi, Toshihika, 1537
Kohut, Gary F., 1307
Kokkino, Eleni Katsarou, 1538
Koneck, Jeff, 420
Konig, Eberhard, 895
Konstant, Shoshana Beth, 1078
Korhanis, Dimitri, 425
Korzenny, Felipe, 897
Koskinen, Patricia, 391
Kostelnick, C., 1456
Kounios, John, 802
Kovar, Susan K., 1041
Kraemer, Don J., Jr., 116
Kraemer, Roberta, 1626
Kramer, Michael P., 257
Kramer-Dahl, Anneliese, 772
Kramsch, Claire J., 1145
Krashen, Stephen D., 670, 1539
Krause, Katherine C., 956
Krause, P., 873
Krauss, Kenneth Gohfried, 599
Kroll, Barry M., 1450
Krome, Frederic, 600
Ku, Linlin, 897
Kuehner, Alison, 1249
Kuhn, Annette, 567
Kulick, Katherine, 1540
Kulkarni, Diane, 1079
Kuriloff, Peshe C., 1472
Kusterer, Faith, 391
Kutzer, M. Daphne, 1108
Kwachka, Patricia E., 1598
Kynell, Teresa, 1157

Labio, Catherine, 258
Ladd, Maria de Armas, 1376
LaFarge, Catherine, 13
Lafferty, William, 913
LaFollette, Marcel Chotkowski, 898
Laliker, William B., 1118
Lam, Clara Yin Ping, 1541
Lamazares, Ivonne Mercedes, 453
Lambek, Michael, 984
Lambiotte, J. G., 89
Lampert, D. A., 89
Lancaster, Jane B., 984
Lance, Donald M., 714

Land, Betty Lou, 1205
Landow, George P., 91, 454, 534
Lane, Barry, 1250
Lang, Berel, 336
Langer, Judith A., 601, 1152
Langsdorf, Lenore, 922
Lanham, Richard, 534
Lanigan, Richard L., 922
Lankewish, Vincent A., 1108
Lapp, Diane, 1140
Larking, Mamie, 1080
Larsen, Elizabeth, 259
Larson, Becky, 420
Larson, C. O., 89
Larson, Marion Hogan, 117
Larson, Richard L., 1649
La Russo, Dominic A., 336
Lasch, Christopher, 828
Lashley, Leroy L., 907
Laskowski, Briget, 1056
Lass, Roger, 703
Latchaw, Joan S., 118
Lather, Patti, 124
Latiolais, Christopher, 119
Latta, John N., 455
Lattin, Ferrol, 1056
Lau, Tuen-yu, 897
Lauer, Janice M., 56, 120, 218, 1456
Laughlin, James S., 1296
Laurence, David, 1042
Lawrence, S. M., 34
Lawrence, Sandra, 766
Lay, M. M., 64, 1456
Lay, Mary, 291
Lay, Nancy Duke S., 1542
Lazaraton, Anne, 709
Lazere, Donald, 121
Le M. Duquesnay, Ian M., 617
Lea, Luanne C., 710
Lea, Martin, 456
Leader, Zachary, 803
Leahy, Richard, 1081, 1082, 1607
Leaker, J., 414
Lease, Judy E. 1315
LeBlanc, Paul, 425, 428, 457
Lee, Christopher M., 1197
Lee, Linda, 571
Lee, Louise Leyi, 556
Lee, Richard B., 984
Leech, Geoffrey, 772
Leeds, Bruce, 1543
Leeman, Richard, 260
Lefkovitz, Lori H., 91

Leggo, Carl, 1608
Leibman, Nina, 913
Leibowicz, Joseph, 670
Leigh, David, 1251
Leigh, Dorothy, 985
Leighton, Angela, 13
Leighton, Gordon, 1048
Leki, Ilona, 1544
Leland, Chris M., 553
Lemaye, Mohan, 1377
Lemco, Jonathan, 670
Lemke, Andreas, 409
Lemon, Hallie S., 1158
Lenig, Stuart, 1252
Lennard, John, 602
Leonard, Marcellus J., 1198
Lester, Valerie, 1048
LeTord, B., 1437
Levine, D., 513
Levine, George, 80
Levine, Linda, 122, 973
Levine, Robert, 711
Levine, Suzanne Jill, 202
Levy, Elena, 123
Lewis, Magda, 124
Lewis, Michael, 458
Lewis, Vicki, 418
Lewitt, Philip Jay, 1545
Li, Hairong, 897
Lian, Andrew, 494
Lichtenstein, Gary, 1110
Lidh, Todd, 1083
Lieberman, Ann, 1110
Liebman, JoAnne D., 1546
Lim, Shirley Geok-lin, 181
Lincoln, Yvonna S., 836
Lindner, Richard, 1609
Liner, Tom, 1444
Linkon, Sherry Lee, 1253
Linton, David, 459
Lionnet, Françoise, 181
Lipa, Sara, 84
Lippert, Paul, 712
Lipsitz, George, 913
Litchfield, Brenda C., 460
Little, Jeannie, 1149
Little, Warren, 1110
Livdahl, Barbara Smith, 1023
Lloyd, Michael, 261
Lloyd-Jones, Richard, 262, 1159
Loberger, Gordon J., 1490
Lock, Margaret, 984
Locke, David Millard, 957

Locker, K. O., 64
Lockett, H., 1129
Lofty, John Sylvester, 1471
Logue, Cal M., 338
LoNano, Mari, 461
Lonberger, Rosemary, 84
Long, Elenore, 1254
Long, Keith, 797
Longley, Kateryna Olijnyk, 181
Lorenz, Frederick O., 1598
Lovas, John C., 1255
Love, Nigel, 778
Lovejoy, Kim Brian, 713, 714
Lovitt, Carl R., 339, 1610
Lowe, Gail, 263
Lowe, K., 414
Lowrey, Burling, 340
Lowry, Kerri, 1056
Lowry, Pei, 1156
Lu, Min-Zhan, 1256
Lu, Xing, 264
Luboff, Gerald F., 1257
Lucas, Catherine, 1634
Lucas, Ceil, 670
Lucchetti, Anne E., 33
Lucy, John Arthur, 715
Ludlam, D., 1437
Luff, Paul, 1151
Luke, A., 414
Luke, Allan, 462, 716
Luke, Carmen, 124
Lundberg, Patricia Lorimer, 828
Lunengeld, Marvin, 341
Lunsford, Andrea A., 125, 1145
Lutz, William, 326, 717, 718, 719
Lynch, Brian, 1503
Lynch, M., 210
Lyon, Arabella, 126
Lyons, Greg, 1084
Lyons, James J., 670
Lytle, Susan L., 1012, 1129

Maass, Anne, 760
Mabrito, Mark, 463
Macdonald, Gina, 464, 1547
MacDonald, Martin, 127
MacDonald, Susan Peck, 1152
Macdonald, Andrew, 1547
Machan, Tim Williams, 720
Mack, Nancy, 873, 1108
MacKenzie, Nancy, 1258
Macleod, Norman, 772
MacNealy, Mary Sue, 1378

NAME INDEX

Macrorie, K., 1129
Maddalena, Nicholas Charles, 986
Madden, Kate, 897
Maddux, Clebourne D., 465
Madigan, Chris, 195
Magliano, Joseph P., 968
Magnotto, Joyce Neff, 1472
Maher, Frances, 826
Mahiri, Jabari, 852
Maier, Paula, 1308
Makaryk, Irene, 128
Malinowitz, H., 1134
Maltese, John Anthony, 342
Manfred, Madge, 1279
Mangelsdorf, Kate, 1199, 1548, 1549
Mangiola, Linda, 1528
Mann, Denise, 913
Mann, Mary, 899
Manning, JoAnn B., 1013
Manning, Robert T. 960
Mannix, Patrick, 603
Manzoor, Ahmed, 524
Mao, LuMing, 721
Maoz, Benjamin, 984
Marbeck, Richard, 1259
Marchant, Fred, 1156
Marcus, Laura, 13
Marcus, Leah S., 80
Marcus, Stephen, 1444
Maring, Gerald H., 1624
Marius, Richard, 80, 1156, 1160
Marlatt, Daphne, 618
Marquez, Candida Colon, 466
Marrs, Robert, 1052
Marsden, James D., 467
Marsella, Joy, 1152, 1647
Marshall, Donald G., 1145
Martella, Maureen, 1309
Martin, A., 1129
Martin, C. Dianne, 382
Martin, D'Arcy, 1004
Martin, James E., 722
Martin, Jeanette S., 1310
Martin, Judy L., 1200
Martin, Nancy J., 1129, 1152, 1508
Martindale, Charles, 252
Maruyama, Geoffrey M., 847
Masiello, Lea, 1085
Mason, Jimmie, 1108
Mason, Mary G., 234
Matalene, Carolyn, 129
Matchett, Michele L., 89
Matta, William Bruce, 1550

Mattelart, Armand, 900
Matthews, C., 1654
Matz, Louie John, 935
Maule, R. William, 468
Mauro, James, 812
Mayer, Kenneth R., 469
Mayfield, Leroy, 1056
Mayher, John S., 1086
Maylath, Bruce, 1012
Mayo, Wendell, 1611
Mayor, Federico, 1483
McAfee, Christine O'Leary, 470
McAlexander, Patricia J., 1201
McArthur, Colin, 567
McArthur, Tom, 265
McBroom, Geraldine L., 1024
McCaffrey, Juliet, 524
McCaffrey, Maggie 89
McCall, Raymond, 409
McCarthey, Sarah J., 847
McCarthy, Lucille, 987
McCartney, Sarah T., 130
McClelland, Ben, 1644
McClelland, Susan Mary, 1025
McCloskey, Michael, 503
McClure, Laura Kathleen, 604, 1111
McClure, Michael F., 1260
McClure, Robert M., 1110
McComiskey, Bruce, 266
McCord, Elizabeth A., 1311
McCorduck, Pamela, 534
McCormick, Kathleen, 605
McCormick, Washington J., 670
McCracken, Nancy Mellin, 1111
McCroskey, James C., 1041
McDaniel, Ellen, 1379
McDermott, Peter, 1026
McDonagh, Josephine, 13
McDonald, Daniel, 1312
McDonald, James C., 1087, 1202
McDonald, Robert L., 131
McDowell, Earl E., 1380
McElroy, Colleen J., 1444
McEnteer, James, 901
McGee, Lea M., 1012
McGhee, W. P. T., 471
McGinley, William, 646
McGivney, Veronica, 1491
McGlone, Edward L., 1041
McGowan, Kate, 132
McGregory, Jerrilyn, 133
McGuire, Claire V., 760
McGuire, William J., 760

McHale, Brian, 772
McIntosh, Mary, 189
McIntyre, G. G., 1129
McKaegue, Patricia M., 1088
McKendy, Thomas, 1612
McKenna, Eleanor, 1598
McKerrow, Raymie E., 922
McKinnon, Catharine A., 1003
McKoon, Gail, 647
McLaren, Clemence, 1152
McLaren, Peter, 853, 968
McLaughlin, Daniel, 382, 472
McLaughlin, Milbrey W., 1110
McLaughlin, T. F., 471
McLeod, Poppy L., 473
McLeod, Susan H., 1043, 1472, 1472, 1650
McLeod-Porter, Delma, 723
McLoughlin, Maryann, 134
McMahon, Susan, 847
McMillan, Katie, 474
McNeill, David, 123, 724
McNenny, Geraldine, 135, 1581
McPhail, Mark Lawrence, 136
McQuade, Donald, 80, 137
McQuillan, Jodi, 420
McVicar, Ken E., 343
McVitty, John Dwight, 267
Medress, Tammy, 1089
Meek, Margaret, 475
Mehlman, Jeffrey, 202
Mehrez, Samia, 202
Melnick, Jane, 268
Merriman, N., 1129
Messina, Susan, 1451
Metz, Dale Evans, 1587
Metzger, Dwayne, 269
Meyer, Charles F., 725
Meyer, Daisy M., 1598
Meyers, C., 1129
Meyers, Renée A., 138
Middendorf, Marilyn, 1203
Middleton, Anne, 80
Middleton, Timothy Andrew, 139
Milanés, Cecilia Rodríguez, 1108
Miles, Matthew B., 836
Miles, Suzanne Laura, 140
Miller, Alan, 804
Miller, C. R., 56
Miller, Carolyn, 218
Miller, Danny L., 1444
Miller, David James, 922
Miller, Gregory Robert, 141
Miller, J. L., 1111

Miller, Jane, 618
Miller, L. Diane, 1473
Miller, Lynne, 1110
Miller, Norman, 847
Miller, Richard E., 1261
Miller, Susan, 115, 142
Milliken, M., 1654
Mills, H., 873
Mills, Johnnie Ruth, 1013
Mills, Sara, 772
Milroy, James, 703
Milz, Vera E., 1012
Mineo, Paul James, 805
Mingchuan, Dong, 1483
Minh-ha, Trinh T., 618
Minns, Garold O. 960
Mirel, Barbara, 476, 1381
Mirtz, Ruth Marie, 806, 1262
Mitch, David Franklin, 477
Mitchell, Claudia, 144
Mitchell, Felicia, 1161, 1613
Mitchell, Jean, 1013
Mitchell, Rosamond, 1503
Mitchell, Ruth, 1614
Mittan, Robert K., 115
Modleski, Tania, 567
Modra, Helen, 124
Moerman, M., 210
Moffett, James, 1129, 1162, 1615
Mohan, Bernard, 494
Mohan, Rajeswari, 143
Mohanty, Satya P., 592
Moll, Luis C., 968
Mondak, Jeffery J., 344
Monfasani, John, 270
Mongnobove, Lisa, 1056
Monroe, Margaret E., 1492
Monroe, Rick, 1012
Monroe, William Frank, 1382
Monson, R. J., 873
Montaner, Carlos Alberto, 670
Montgomery, Michael Vincent, 606
Montrose, Louis, 80
Moody, L., 513
Mooney, M., 414
Moonilal-Masur, Patricia, 144
Moore, Christopher, 1425
Moore, E., 873
Moore, James Duff, 607
Moore, Jane, 13
Moore, Kathleen, 807
Moore, Michael, 726
Moore, Patrick, 1383, 1384

NAME INDEX

Moragné Silva, Michele Lowe, 1551
Moran, Aidan, 808
Moran, Charles, 395, 428, 1152
Moran, Michael O., 145
Morello, John T., 345
Moretti, Franco, 567
Morgan, Michael, 897, 1456
Morgan, Oliver John, 809
Morgan, Sharon, 1049
Morgan, Thaïs E., 91
Morissey, Sharon, 478
Morley, David, 567
Morowitz, Harold J., 958
Morreale, Susan E., 1090
Morris, Marshall, 778
Morrison, James L., 479
Morrison, Minion KC, 826
Morse, Philip S., 146
Mortensen, Peter L., 115, 480
Morton, Johnnye L., 1616
Moshenberg, Daniel, 147
Moss, Beverly J., 115
Motes, William H, 1313
Mountford, Roxanne Denise, 346
Mowery, Carl D., Jr., 1493
Moxley, Joseph M., 1617
Moyer, Albert E., 959
Muhlhausler, Peter, 778
Muir, Jannette Kenner, 372
Mukhapadyaya, Moitraye, 524
Mullen, Faith Elizabeth, 347
Muller, John, 1414
Mullican, James S., 1444
Mullins, Tom, 1508
Mulvey, Laura, 567
Mulvihill, Peggy, 481
Mumford, David John, 1552
Munby, Hugh, 1031
Mundy, JaNae, 977
Munslow, Alan, 271
Murdick, William, 1474
Murphy, Gregory, 148
Murphy, John M., 348, 349
Murphy, John W., 727
Murphy, Kathleen V., 1263
Murphy, Peter F., 149
Murphy, R. J., 1129
Murphy, Richard, Jr., 1470
Murphy, Sandra, 1618, 1634
Murray, Frances, 1491
Mustapha, Sali Zahlia, 1553
Mutnick, D., 1134
Myung, In Jae, 788

Nagarkatte, Umesh P., 482
Nagarkatte, Shailaja U., 482
Nagasaka, Akemi, 648
Nager, Nancy, 973
Nair, Rukmini Bhaya, 772
Nakadate, Neil, 218
Nash, J. G., 89
Nash, Walter, 150, 728
Nathanson, Tenney, 608
Natriello, Gary, 1110
Nead, Lynda, 13
Nealon, Jeffrey T., 936
Neel, Jasper, 1385
Neeley, Kathryn A., 1386
Nellhaus, Tobin, 895
Nelms, Ben F., 1012
Nelson, Carol Jean, 151
Nelson, J., 89
Nelson, Linda, 729
Nelson, Marc S., 951
Nelson, Marie Wilson, 1444
Nelson, Sandra J., 469
Nelson, Ted, 534
Nelson, Wayne A., 484
Nelson-Barber, Sharon S., 1013
Nettles, Evelyn Elaine, 272
Neuleib, Janice, 152
Neuman, Shirley, 596
Neumann, Anne Waldron, 772
Neumann, W. Russell, 902, 903
Neuwirth, C. M., 428
Newkirk, James E., 1634
Newkirk, Thomas, 115, 1012, 1437
Newsome, Alice, 1204
Ng, Joseph S., 1264
Nicasio, Lino Evora, 351
Nichols, M. Celeste, 352
Nicolau, Siobhan, 670
Nida, Eugene N., 730
Nieto, S., 513
Nietzsche, Friedrich, 731
Nimmo, Dan D., 353
Nisbet, R. G. M., 617
Noble, Douglas D., 854
Nordman, Leo, 752
Nore, Gordon W. E., 1387
Norman, Rose, 1388
North, Stephen M., 153
Northcroft, David, 1508
Norton, Camille, 618
Norton, Priscilla, 485, 486, 487
Norton, Terry, 1205
Novek, Eleanor M., 488

Noyelle, Thierry, 1485
Nucich, Joy, 830
Nummikoski, Ritva M., 855
Nunan, David, 732, 856
Nunberg, Geoffrey, 670
Nussbaum, Jon F., 1027
Nuttall, A. D., 609
Nyberg, Adells M., 1163
Nydahl, J., 34

Oakley, Francis, 857
O'Banion, John D., 273
Obbink, Laura Apol, 154
Ochs, Elinor, 155
Odell, Lee, 218, 1152
O'Donnell, Angela M., 89, 847
O'Donnell, Victoria, 552
O'Donoghue, Rosemary, 489
Oerhle, Richard T., 711
Offen-Brown, Gail, 1164
Ohanian, S., 1134
O'Hara, Daniel T., 592
Ohtsuka, Keisuke, 156
Okigbo, Charles, 354
Olalquiaga, Celeste, 937
Olendzenski, Michael Felix, 1265
Oliu, Walter E., 1324
Olivarez, Arturo, Jr., 640
Olsen, William, 1444
Olshtain, Elite, 1211
Olson, C. B., 34
Olson, Gary A., 157, 859
Olson, Richard K., 649
O'Meara, Anne, 1258
O'Neal, Barbara Jean, 1044
O'Neal, Betty, 490
O'Neill, John, 610
Oram, Andrew, 491
O'Regan, Daphne Elizabeth, 611
Orescovich, Robert, 557
Orlans, Harold, 1045
Ornatowski, Cezar M., 1389, 1390
Orner, Mimi, 124
O'Rourke, Sean Patrick, 274
Orr, Bridget, 224
Ory, John C., 1656
O'Shea, Carol Sue, 154
O'Shea, Cynthia, 1110
Ostergren, Joan Caryl, 1555
Ostrom, Hans, 1266
Ostwald, Jonathan, 409
Oswal, Sushi K., 159
Otte, George, 160

Pace, Barbara G., 612
Pacheco, Anne-Louise, 1267
Paddison, John, 1268, 1269
Paddock, Mark, 1556
Padgug, Robert, 189
Pagnucci, Gian, 1391
Pahl, M. M., 873
Palcie, Ronald A. 1480
Palczewski, Catherine Hellen, 372
Palen, John, 904
Palmer, Adrian, 1503
Palmer, Jacqueline S., 112
Palmquist, M., 89
Palumbo, David B., 484
Panko, Raymond R., 1392
Pao, Miranda Lee, 988
Papin, Liliane, 161
Paré, Anthony, 1270
Parks, Leland H., 960
Parmeter, Sarah-Hope, 1108
Parsons, Gerald M., 1393
Parsons, Priscilla Kay, 1028
Paterson, K., 513
Paton, Jonathan, 1508
Patterson, Annabel, 329, 1145
Patterson, Cheryl, 1056
Patthey, Ghislaine G., 492
Patthey-Chavez, Genevieve G., 1557
Patton, Cynthia Kay, 355
Paul, S. Pamela, 826
Paulston, Christina Bratt, 1558
Paxton, Nancy L., 181
Payette, Julie, 493
Payne, David, 613
Payne, Doris, 733
Peacock, John, 828
Pearce, C. Glenn, 1302
Pearce, W. Barnett, 372
Pearson, P. David, 968
Pease, Donald, 592
Peckham, Irvin Wherry, 162
Pedrick, Victoria, 231
Pedwell, Denise, 113
Pelliccia, Hayden, 231
Peluso, Robert, 275
Pemberton, Michael A., 1091, 1297
Pennington, Martha C., 494
Penrose, Ann, 163
Perdue, Virginia, 1271
Peréz-Bustillo, Camilo, 670
Perkins, William, 985
Perloff, Marjorie, 80
Perrin, Robert, 1620

NAME INDEX

Perry, Devern J., 558
Perry, Elisabeth Israels, 965
Persak, Christine Anne, 276
Peshkin, Alan, 836
Pestel, Beverly C., 1394
Petersen, Debra Lynn, 356
Petersen, Renee, 847
Peterson, Linda H., 1472
Peterson, Nancy Jean, 989
Peterson, Ralph, 860
Petrella, Barbara A., 1559
Petrie, Duncan, 614
Petrovic, Otto, 495
Pettypool, M. Diane, 1372
Pfau, Michael, 894
Pfeifer, Mark P., 1092
Phelps, L. Wetherbee, 56
Phelps, Louise Wetherbee, 1046
Philipsen, Gerry, 734
Phillippakis, Andrew, 496
Phillips, Betty Jean, 615
Phillips, Connie Ruth, 1494
Phillips, D. C., 836
Phillips, Theodore Hart, 497
Phinney, M. Y., 873
Piatt, Bill, 670
Piazza, Stephen, 1165
Picciotto, Madeleine, 1166, 1247
Pienemann, Manfred, 494
Pierce, B. N., 513
Pierce, John C., 357
Piercy, Marge, 1444
Pikrone, Gayle A., 1578
Pinchen, Jennifer E., 616
Pinelli, Thomas E., 1395
Pippen, Carol Lawson, 1298
Pirkle, James, 391
Pixton, William H., 1396
Place, Janey, 567
Plumb, Carolyn Sue, 1621
Plumb, Carolyn, 1397
Pocheptsov, Oleg G., 735
Pohland, Paul A., 382
Poirier, Suzanne, 961
Pollington, Mary, 1112
Pomerenke, Paula J., 1314
Popken, Randall, 164
Popp, Robert, 1495
Porter, Dennis, 567
Porter, J. E., 56, 1456
Porter, James, 165, 524
Porth, Helen Louise, 277
Posey, Evelyn, 498

Posner, Rebecca, 252
Potter, Jonathan, 792
Poulton, M., 414
Pounds, Wayne, 195
Powell, Johnathan, 617
Powell-Hart, Betty Leona, 499
Powers-Stubbs, Karen, 55
Pradl, G. M., 1129
Prater, Doris L., 1012
Pratt, Mary Louise, 166
Pregler, Diane, 1052
Prete, Barbara, 1496
Pringle, Ian, 736
Proudfoot, Gail, 500
Provenzo, Eugene, 534
Pryor, John B., 760
Psathas, G., 210
Puette, William J., 905
Pula, Robert P., 739, 740, 741
Purcell, Nicholas, 252
Purkiss, Diane, 224
Purves, Alan C., 1622
Purvis, Teresa M., 1272
Pytlik, B., 34

Quinby, Lee, 181
Quinn, David Hugh, 1560

Rabin, Karen M., 501
Race, William H., 231
Rack, John P., 649
Railey, Kevin, 1561
Raimes, Ann, 1562, 1563
Rainey, Kenneth T., 1651
Rains, Charleen, 167
Raitt, Suzanne, 13
Rajan, Gita, 181
Rakow, Lana F., 278, 559
Ramanathan, Srinivas, 502
Rampton, M. B. H., 666
Ramus, Peter, 279
Randels, James, 1315
Rangan, P. Venkat, 502
Ranieri, Paul W., 1167
Rank, Hugh, 743
Rankin, Elizabeth, 1047
Ransdell, Sarah, 503
Rasco, Teresa L., 952
Raskin, Victor, 534
Ratcliff, Roger, 647
Rathgen, Elody, 1508
Ratliff, Kelly, 386
Ray, Ruth, 115

Raybeck, Douglas, 984
Rayman, Jack, 1304
Raynaud, Claudine, 181, 990
Raynor, Deirdre, 1444
Read, Donald, 906
Recchio, Thomas E., 1029
Reed, Joel, 280
Reed-Jones, Susan, 1497
Reeder, Glenn D., 760
Reese, Carol McMichael, 358
Reeves, Brent, 409
Reeves, Carol, 962
Reid, Barbara V., 1003
Reid, Joy, 1564
Reif, Margaret Rossini, 1498
Reiff, John, 991
Reigeluth, Charles M., 504
Reinharz, Shulamit, 992
Reinking, David, 505
Reis, Elizabeth, 1088
Rennie, John, 650
Rentz, Kathryn C., 1316
Resis, Humphrey A., 907
Reuter, Dennis, 746
Reyhner, Jon, 670
Reynolds, John Frederick, 1399
Reynolds, Nedra, 281
Rhedding-Jones, J., 414
Rhodes, Gale, 1403
Rhodes, Lynn K., 1623
Rice, Donald E., 359
Rice, William Craig, 861
Richardson, Ingrid, 747
Richardson, John T., 862
Richardson, Kay, 666
Richardson, Kim, 425
Richmond, Virginia P., 1041
Riding, Richard, 810
Ridpath, Sandra, 1093
Rief, L., 1437, 1654
Riffe, Daniel, 908
Riggs, Douglas Lee, 360
Rist, Ray, 382
Ritchie, Joy S., 651
Ritter, Kurt K. W., 361
Robbins, Bruce, 80
Roberts, Ian F., 1094
Roberts, M. J. D., 329
Robinson, Lou, 618
Robinson, Sam, 1508
Roche, Mark W., 828
Rocklin, T., 89
Rodburg, Maxine, 1156

Rodby, Judith, 720, 1565
Rodriguez, Yvonne Enid Gonzalez, 1566
Rodríguez, Richard, 670
Roeh, Itzhak, 897
Roen, Duane H., 105, 115, 135, 1111, 1581
Rogers, Alan, 524
Rogers, Carl R., 195
Rogers, P. S., 64
Rojas, Gomez, 362
Rolley, Katrina, 329
Rolph, Daniel, 168
Romaine, Suzanne, 720
Roman, Leslie, 836
Romano, T., 1654
Romano, Thom, 1012
Roob, Andy, 169
Roop, L. J., 64
Roosevelt, Theodore, 670
Roper, Donna G., 506
Rorty, Richard, 928
Rose, Jacqueline, 567
Rose, Mark, 909
Rose, Mike, 1194
Roselin, Eucharius, 985
Rosenblum, Lorie, 961
Rosenmeyer, Thomas G., 231
Rosenthal, Anne Marie, 993
Rosenthal, Judith W., 1567
Ross, Philip E., 748
Ross, Steven, 1503
Ross, Susan, 363
Rosteck, Thomas, 364, 910
Roth, Jeffrey, 863
Roth, John K., 828
Roth, Michael S., 176
Rothbart, Myron, 760
Rothenberg, Julia, 1026
Rothschild, Joyce M., 7
Rouscalp, Edwin E., 1624
Rouse, R. H., 252
Rouse, Joy, 282
Roush, Rick, 507
Rousos, Linda, 1568
Rowan, David, 749
Rowe, John Carlos, 80
Roy, Emil, 508, 1317
Roy, Sandra, 1317
Royster, Jacqueline Jones, 1152
Rubal-Lopez, Alma, 750
Rubin, L., 34
Rubin, Lois, 1206
Rudd, Niall, 617
Rude, Carolyn, 509

NAME INDEX

Rude-Parkins, Carolyn, 1030
Rudinow, Joel, 170
Rudnick, Lois, 965
Rudolph, Dina, 156
Ruhlen, Merritt, 694
Rule, Rebecca, 1168
Rury, John L., 864
Rushing, Janice Hocker, 171
Russ, David Allen, 811
Russell, David R., 1152
Russell, Tom, 1031
Rutter, Russell, 7, 283
Ryback, David, 195
Rymer, J., 1456
Rynerson, B. B., 1437

Sabor, Peter, 329
Sachs, Jacqueline, 77
Sacks, Karen Brodkin, 984
Sadker, David, 826
Sadker, Myra, 826
Sadoski, Mark, 640, 938
Saenger, Paul, 895
Sageev, Pneena, 1400
Salazar, Rubén, 670
Saleemi, Anjum P., 751
Saling, Joseph, 1095
Salisbury, David F., 865
Samar, Vincent, 1587
Sammells, Neil, 329
Sampson, Geoffrey, 494
Samter, Wendy, 33
Sanborn, J., 1111
Sandberg, K., 34
Sanders, Linda, 1031
Sanders, Ted, 752
Sanders, Wayne, 911
Sandler, Karen Wiley, 1472
Sands, Kathleen Mullen, 234
Sanger, Kerran L., 284
Santos, Terry, 1569
Saraswathi, L. S., 524
Saravia-Shore, Marietta, 1570
Sarris, Greg, 181
Sartre, Jean-Paul, 939
Sassoon, John, 753
Sauer, Beverly A., 1401, 1402
Sauerbrey, Judith L., 285
Saumweber, Judy, 1571
Saunders, David, 329
Savage, Gerald, 1475
Savas, Diana Natalie, 1273
Saville-Roike, Muriel, 1535

Sawin, Gregory, 754, 755
Scanlon, Matthew, 812
Scarbrough, V., 1129
Scardamalia, Marlene, 790
Schaafsma, D., 1129, 1134
Schaafsma, David, 871
Schaible, Robert, 1403
Scheie, Timothy Jon, 619
Schell, Eileen E., 1113
Schenkenber, Mary Martin, 510
Schiff, Elizabeth, 897
Schilb, John, 64, 994
Schleifer, Ronald, 45
Schleppergrell, Mary, 756
Schlumberger, Ann Lewis, 1476
Schlumberger, Ann, 1549
Schmandt-Besserat, Denise, 757, 758
Schmeck, Ronald R., 813
Schmeltzer, Dennis K., 511
Schmid, Carol, 670
Schmitz, Betty, 826
Schneiderman, Beth Kline, 1452
Schneirov, Mathew, 912
Schofield, Janet Ward, 836
Scholes, Robert, 91, 1145
Schor, Naomi, 1145
Schrag, Calvin O., 922
Schriver, Karen A., 115, 218
Schrum, Lynne, 512
Schuhmann, Ana Marie, 1013
Schuldt, W. John, 784
Schultz, Jean Marie, 983, 1164
Schultz, Kara L., 995
Schwager, Edith, 1404
Schwartz, E., 1129
Schwartz, Helen, 534, 1405
Schwartz, Jeffrey, 1129
Schwarz, Norbert, 760
Schwichtenberg, Cathy, 172
Sciachitano, Marian M., 55
Scobie, Ingrid Winther, 965
Scott, B. T., 89
Scott, Charles T., 720
Scott, Gail, 618
Scott, Mike, 1503
Scott, R. L., 56
Scott, Randall K., 1041
Scott, Robert Ian, 759
Seashore, Louis, 1110
Sebberson, David, 173
Sedere, Mohottige U., 1483
Sedgewick, Eve Kosofsky, 80
Segal, Charles, 231

Segall, Mary T., 1274
Segars, Albert H., 1307
Seger, F. D., 1654
Seiler, Robert M., 210
Selfe, Cynthia L., 64, 425, 428
Selfe, R. J., 428
Semin, Gün R., 760
Serra, J. K., 89
Serrano, Basilio, 826
Severino, Carol, 174, 1207
Shadiow, Linda K., 1508
Shafer, Gregory Robert, 1169
Shafer, Robert E., 1508
Shalaby, Nadia Abdelgalil, 620
Shanahan, James, 897
Shanahan, Timothy, 968
Shange, Ntozake, 618
Shank, Michael H., 175
Shannon, Patrick, 513
Shannon-Morla, Crystal Elaine, 761
Shapiro, Alan, 1108
Shapiro, Arthur, 514
Shapiro, Joseph P., 762
Shapiro, Lewis P., 711
Shapiro, Michael J., 365
Shapiro, Nancy, 1114
Sharf, Barbara F., 961
Shaw, Gary, 1318
Shearer, Brenda A., 1170
Shearer, Christine, 1288
Sheese, Judy, 1477
Sheridan, Paraic, 763
Sherman, Jeffrey, 760
Sherwood, Steve, 1096
Shibli, Abdullah, 1478
Shiffman, Betty Garrison, 1625
Shilling, Wynne A., 515
Shipman, Frank, 409
Shoaf, R. A., 91
Shohamy, Elana, 1626
Shor, Ira, 866
Short, Bryan Collier, 621
Short, Doug, 425
Showler, Janice Reckeweg, 1499
Shull, Ellen, 622
Shulman, Judith H., 1032
Shumacher, G., 89
Shumway, Norman, 670
Shuy, Roger, 670
Sibayan, Bonificio P., 1508
Sides, Charles H., 560
Siedlecki, Peter, 828
Siefert, Diana, 764

Siegel, Marjorie, 968
Sills, Caryl Klein, 1299
Sills, Chip, 175, 176
Silverman, Barry G., 516
Silverman, Kaja, 623
Silvers, Sally, 618
Simmons, Jay, 1012, 1654
Simmons, John S., 1508
Simon, Linda., 1156
Simon, R. I., 513
Simon, Sherry, 202
Simonian, Margaret Ann, 1097
Simons, Jennifer Allen, 177
Simpson, Henry, 1406
Simpson, Paule, 772
Sims, Brenda R., 1319
Sims-Bishop, R., 1437
Sinclair, Karen P., 984
Sinfield, Alan, 570
Sitko, Barbara M., 1208
Siu-Runyan, Y., 873
Skagestad, Peter, 175
Skelton, T. M., 1407
Skerpan, Elizabeth Penley, 286
Sklar, Kathryn Kish, 965
Skura, Meredith, 80
Slater, Niall W., 231
Slatin, John M., 517
Slavin, Robert E., 847
Slimani, Assia, 1503
Sloane, Sarah Jane, 518
Sloat, Elizabeth, 1209
Smagorinsky, Peter, 815, 1134
Small, Ruth V., 519
Smart, Graham, 178
Smeaton, Alan F., 763
Smit, David W., 1275
Smith, Adrian, 329
Smith, Craig R., 922
Smith, Edward, 652
Smith, Elizabeth, 509
Smith, Eric E., 520
Smith, Frank R., 1408
Smith, Jeanne Jacoby, 179
Smith, Jeremy J., 720
Smith, Lindsay, 13
Smith, Louis M, 382, 836
Smith, M., 1134
Smith, Maggy, 1276
Smith, Mark Edward, 1277
Smith, Mary Ann, 1618, 1634
Smith, Michael W., 815
Smith, Michael, 765

NAME INDEX

Smith, Philip E., II, 1171
Smith, Ralph Handy, 180
Smith, Raymond, 1472
Smith, Ripley L., 897
Smith, Robert E., 1409
Smith, Robert M., 1041
Smith, Ruth, 156
Smith, Sidonie, 181, 234
Smith, W. L., 89
Smock, Sue Marx, 1040
Smyth, John, 867
Snarrenberg, Robert, 996
Snodgrass, Gwendolyn L., 1092
Snow, Catherine E., 670
Snowling, Margaret J., 649
Snyder, Jon, 1110
Sohn, David, 816
Solarz, Stephen J., 670
Soltis, Jonas F., 836
Solway, Jacqueline S., 984
Sommers, E., 428
Sommers, Elizabeth, 766
Sommers, Jonita, 1479
Sommers, Nancy, 182
Soricelli, Rhonda L., 950
Sosnoski, James, 426
Sotiriou, Peter Elias, 183
Soven, Margot, 1472
Spaeth, Catherine Therese Christians, 287
Spanier, Bonnie B., 1152
Spanos, William, 868
Spears, Russell, 456
Speck, Bruce W., 1410
Speer, Tom, 1172
Spellmeyer, Kurt, 869
Sperling, Melanie, 184
Spicer, Christopher H., 1041
Spigel, Lynn, 913
Spilka, Rachel, 1416
Spivak, Gayatri Chakravorty, 997
Spivey, N. N., 89
Spooren, Wilbert, 752
Sprague, Jo, 1033
Springer, Craig Michael, 914
Sprott, Richard, 185
Spyridakis, Jan H., 1397, 1411, 1412, 1430
Stabler, Edward P., Jr., 711
Stacey, David Edward, 186
Stacks, Don W., 908, 1041
Staiger, Mary Elizabeth, 378
Stake, Bernadine Evans, 382
Stanford, Ann Folwell, 955, 961
Stanhope, Nicola 1590

Stanley, Jan, 1627
Stano, Michael, 1041
Stanton, N. A., 522
Stanton, Neville, 521
Staton, Ann Q., 1041
Stay, Byron L., 1098
Stearney, Lynn M., 187
Steckline, Timothy Jerome, 188
Steehouder, Michael, 1370
Stees, Yvette, 653
Stein, Edward, 189
Stein, S. E., 89
Steinberger, Jillian, 913
Steinke, Jocelyn Dawn, 1413
Stensland, Anna Lee, 1444
Stephens, Charlotte Stringer, 561
Stephens, David, 524
Stephens, Diane, 968
Stephens, Rebecca, 195
Stern, Caroline, 1628
Stern, Milton R., 828
Stevens, Kathleen C., 1320
Stevens, Kevin T., 1320
Stevens, Vance, 494
Stevens, William P., 1320
Steward, Joseph L., 767
Stewart, Donald C., 288, 289
Stewart, Larry R., 963
Stewart, Margaret E., 1480
Stibravy, John, 1414
Stimpson, Catherine R., 80
Stimpson, Catherine T., 234
Stocking, George W., Jr., 998
Stoffel, Judith, 1500
Stolarek, Elizabeth A., 190, 1278
Stopford, Charles, 523
Storer, John H., 1003
Storia, Steven R., 1034
Stotsky, Sandra, 1108
Stout, Barbara R., 1472
Stover, L., 1111
Strachan, W., 1129
Strack, Fritz, 760
Strasma, Kip, 191
Stratman, John, 870
Stratton, Marcia, 192
Straubhaar, Joseph D., 897
Street, Brian, 524
Strenski, Ellen, 1035, 1279
Strickland, James, 525
Strobos, S., 1415
Stroessner, Steven J., 760
Strohner, Hans, 768

Strom, Sharon Hartman, 290
Strong, Gary E., 1496
Stroop, J. Ridley, 817
Strudler, Neal, 382
Struening, Karen, 366
Stubbes, Philip, 985
Stuckey, J. E., 1129
Stuecher, Uwe, 1639
Stumbo, Carol, 1108, 1129
Sturk, A., 513
Subbiah, Mahalingam, 1572
Suh, Yongmoo, 1148
Suhor, Charles, 1165
Suleiman, Susan Rubin, 624
Sulentic, Margaret Mary, 391
Sullivan, J. P., 252
Sullivan, Patricia A., 115, 526, 1416
Sunstein, B. S., 1654
Sure, Kembo, 769
Sutcliffe, David, 770
Sutton, Jane, 193
Swain, Katheleen M., 234
Swain, Margaret, 1642
Swearingen, C. Jan, 218
Swilky, Jody, 1036
Swinger, Alice K., 1012
Swinney, David, 652
Swinwood, Linda, 1652
Swope, John Wilson, 1280
Szymaniski, S., 1134

Talley, Ronald Keith, 1653
Tangum, Marion, 1376
Tankha, Vijay, 940
Tarbox, James Jeffrey, 367
Tassoni, John, 1108
Taves, Ann, 234
Tayko, Gail, 1108
Taylor, Angela L., 527
Taylor, Anita, 1041
Taylor, Carolyn, 156
Taylor, Charles, 194
Taylor, J. B., 1129
Taylor, Louise Todd, 1453
Taylor, Marjorie, 760
Taylor, P., 428
Taylor, Paul, 528
Taylor, Philip M., 915
Taylor, P. V., 529
Taylor, R. G., 522
Taylor, Talbot J., 778
Tchudi, Stephen, 871
Teale, William H., 1012

Tebeaux, Elizabeth, 291, 1321, 1417
Tebo, Mike, 1281
Tedeschi, Martha, 895
Tedesco, Janis E., 1600
Teich, Nathaniel, 195
Templeton, Alice, 625
Tenorio, R., 513
Tetreault, Mary Kay Thompson, 826
Thaiss, Christopher, 1472
Tharp, Marty, 530
Thelin, William, 1282
Thernstrom, Abigail, 872
Thickstun, William, 828
Thomas, Andrew Lambert, 771
Thomas, Anne Cameron, 626
Thomas, Barb, 1004
Thomas, Brook, 91
Thomas, C., 89, 1129
Thomas, David, 196
Thomas, Douglas Edward, 941
Thomas, Margaret, 653
Thomas, Rosalind, 292
Thomas, S., 1134
Thomassen, Niels, 942
Thompsen, Philip A., 531
Thompson, Isabelle, 1418
Thomson, Elizabeth Lee, 368
Thralls, Charlotte, 64, 1419, 1456
Tichi, Cecelia, 80
Tidwell, Paula M., 968
Tiefer, Leonore, 189
Tingle, Nick, 197
Tingley, Stephanie A., 1283
Ting-Toomey, Stella, 897
Tinkler, John F., 293
Tolan, S. S., 513
Tomlinson, Sophie, 224
Tompkins, Gail E., 198, 1012
Toolan, Michael, 772, 778
Toomey, D., 414
Toon, Thomas E., 702, 720
Toth, Csaba, 294
Totten, Nancy, 1149
Totten, Samuel, 1108
Townsend, Jacqueline, 1420
Townsend-Fuller, C., 513
Trachsel, Mary, 532
Trasvina, John, 670
Traugott, Elizabeth Closs, 702, 773, 1573
Trautman, Karl, 369
Travis, Molly Abel, 627
Treadaway, Glenda, 563
Trefil, James S., 958

Tribby, Jay, 295
Trimbur, John, 64, 513, 175, 1099
Trimmer, Joseph, 628
Tulloch, John, 567, 916
Tuman, Myron C., 533, 534
Turbin, Carole, 296
Turner, Graeme, 567
Tusser, Thomas, 985
Tway, Eileen, 1012
Tweedie, L. A., 522
Twitchett, Denis Crispin, 370
Ty, Eleanor, 596
Tyler, Lisa, 199
Tyndall, Belle, 774

Uchida, Aki, 200
Udall, Ida Hunt, 629
Ulmer, Greg, 534
Ulmer, Gregory L., 91
Unrau, Norman J., 1173
Upton, James, 1100

Valdés, Guadalupe, 999
Valdes, Mario J., 630
Valdivieso, Rafael, 670
Valentino, Marilyn J., 1421, 1629
Valeri-Gold, Maria, 1183
Vampola, David, 175
Vande Kopple, William J., 218
Vandenberg, Peter, 201, 1300
VanLeirsburg, Peggy, 1630
Vann, Roberta J., 1598
Van Ryder, Betty, 1012
Van Wart, Alice, 596
Varg, Paul A., 371
Varnum, Robin, 297
Vasile, Kathy, 1101
Vatalaro, Paul, 1284
Vatuk, Sylvia, 984
Vaughan, Caroline, 1598
Venuti, Laurence, 202
Verdun, Christl, 596
Vesterager, Johann, 1379
Vin, Harrick M., 502
Vine, Harold A., Jr., 654
Vinz, R., 1134
Vipond, Douglas, 818, 968
Vives, Juan Luis, 985
Vivian, Barbara G., 203
Vogt, Randall, 913
vom Saal, Diane R., 826
Vonnegut, Kristin Sawin, 298

Voss, M. M., 1654
Vyborney, Wende Michelle, 536

Wadden, Paul, 1574
Wagner, Julia, 1174
Wagner, Richard K., 639
Wajnryb, Ruth, 775
Wakoski, Diane, 1444
Waldman, Anne, 618
Waldmann, Michael R., 819
Walker, Carolyn, 1285
Walker, Charlesena, 1056
Walker, Laurence, 1508
Walker, Nancy, 234
Walkerdine, Valerie, 124
Wallace, D. L., 89
Wallace, M. Elizabeth, 204
Walsh, P. G., 617
Walsh, Steve, 1175
Walters, Amy R., 205
Walters, J., 414
Walters, Margaret Bennett, 206
Walters, Mary James, 1422
Walters, Shirley, 1483
Walton, Douglas N., 207, 208
Walvoord, Barbara E., 1472
Wandersee, James H., 1423
Wang, Chaobo, 209
Ware, Susan, 965
Warland, Betsy, 618
Warner, Sterling, 1119
Warnke, Georgia, 176
Washington, Gene, 1176
Wasley, Patricia, 1110
Watkin, David, 252
Watkins, Patsy Guenzel, 917
Watson, Graham, 210
Watson, Julia, 181
Watson, Ken, 1508
Watson, R., 210
Watts, Carol, 13
Waugh, Patricia, 943
Waywell, Geoffrey, 252
Weaver, Constance, 873
Webb, Christopher Lee, 537
Webb, Kenneth, 631
Webb, Noreen M., 847
Weber, Jean Jacques, 772
Weber, Robert J., 820
Webster, Noah, 670
Weidhass, S., 1437
Weiler, Kathleen, 1108
Weiler, Michael, 372

Weinrich, James, 189
Weinstein, Edith K., 1286
Weiser, Irwin, 211, 1634
Weiser, Michael S., 1481
Weisman, Leslie Kanes, 1002
Weiss, Timothy, 1424
Weitzel, Al R., 373
Welch, Kathleen A., 299
Welforce, Win, 562
Weller, Rebecca, 1102
Wendler, L., 89
Wendt, Ingrid, 1444
Wenger, Michael J., 1412
Werchan, James E., 1631
Wert-Gray, Stacia, 138
Weshsler, Stephen Mark, 776
West, James Thomas, 212
West, M., 1134
West, Richard Lee, 874
Westhoff, Guy M., 520
Weston, Joan Ellard, 538
Wexler, Alice, 965
Whalen, Elizabeth, 918
Whatling, Clare, 570
Wheeler, Susan, 1168
Whichard, Nancy Wingardner, 1048
Whinston, Andrew B., 1148
Whitaker, William, 1048
White, Barbara, 329
White, Chris, 570
White, Diane, 1451
White, E., 1129
White, Edward M., 1632
White, Eugene E., 213
White, Fred D., 1287
Whitehead, Tony L., 1003
Whiting, Beatrice Blyth, 984
Whitney, Susan, 553
Whittenberger-Keith, Kari, 214
Whittis, Judith, 1482
Wicks, Robert H., 897
Wieder, L., 210
Wiener, Harvey S., 1210
Wieringa, Douglas, 1425
Wierzbicka, Anna, 777
Wikoff, Katherine Hennessey, 300
Wiley, Mark, 215
Wilhoit, Stephen, 1288
Wilkins, Harriet Adamson, 1426
Wilkinson, A. M., 1427
Willey, Robert John, 1289, 1633
Williams, David E., 563
Williams, David L., 1326

Williams, Gordon, 617
Williams, Joseph M., 720
Williams, Linda R., 13
Williams, Raymond, 567
Williams, Thomas R., 1428, 1429, 1430
Williams, William F., 539
Williamson, Janice, 596
Willis, Sharon, 202
Wills, P., 873
Wilson, Anna Marslen, 632
Wilson, D., 1129
Wilson, Ronald Bruce, 216
Wilsox, Earl J., 1115
Winer, Lise, 1575
Winfield, Linda F., 1013
Winkelmann, Carol L., 301
Winograd, Peter, 391
Winsor, Dorothy A., 1431, 1432
Winterowd, W. Ross, 217
Winters, Rod, 1012
Wintersole, Margaret Marian, 633
Winton, Calhoun, 329
Wisdom, James, 1593
Wiseman, Sue, 13
Wiseman, T. P., 617
Witek, Catherine A., 302
Witte, Kim, 897
Witte, Stephen P., 218
Wittman, Eugene, 1501
Witton, Nic, 494
Wojciszke, Bogdan, 760
Wolcott, Harry F., 836
Wolf, George, 778
Wolfe, Denny, Jr., 1444
Wolin, Ross, 303
Wong, Gay Yuen, 1013
Wood, Elizabeth Springston, 219
Woodman, Tony, 617
Woodson, Linda, 1181
Woodward, Margaret, 670
Woolbright, Meg, 1103, 1433
Woollacott, Janet, 567
Wresch, William, 540
Wright, Guy, 670
Wright, W. W., 428
Wright, Will, 964
Wright, William, 1108
Wright, William W., 1290
Wyatt-Brown, Anne, 304

Xiao, Xiaosui, 305
Xu, George Q., 779, 1454

NAME INDEX

Yahya, Zawiah, 1000
Yancey, Kathleen Blake, 1634
Yang, Xiao-Ming, 220
Yarborough, Ralph, 670
Ybarra, Raul, 1291
Yerkes, Diane, 1049
Yorke, Liz, 570, 634
Young, Art, 1104
Young, Ida Delores, 221
Young, Marilyn J., 372
Young, R., 56
Young, Richard E., 89, 195
Young, Robert E., 1379
Yu, Xiao-Ming, 876

Zack, Michael H., 564
Zagacki, Kenneth S., 374, 922, 1373
Zagnoli, Lucinda J., 1003

Zaller, John R., 919
Zamel, Vivian, 1576
Zappen, James P., 195
Zawilinski, Kenneth, 920
Zebroski, James Thomas, 1108
Zeiger, W., 34
Zellermayer, Michal, 1211
Ziebarth, Ray, 420
Zimmerman, D. H., 210
Zimpher, Nancy L., 1013
Zins, Daniel, 828, 1108
Zizek, Slavoj, 635
Zoukis, E., 1129
Zuidervaart, Lambert, 175
Zumwalt, Karen K., 1110
Zumwalt, Rosemary Lévy, 1001
Zweigenbaum, Pierre, 1055
Zwicky, Arnold M., 711